FIFTH EDITION

Working Through Conflict

Strategies for Relationships, Groups, and Organizations

Joseph P. Folger

Temple University

Marshall Scott Poole

Texas A&M University

Randall K. Stutman

Temple University

PEARSON

and

Boston ▪ New York ▪ San Francisco
Mexico City ▪ Montreal ▪ Toronto ▪ London ▪ Madrid ▪ Munich ▪ Paris
Hong Kong ▪ Singapore ▪ Tokyo ▪ Cape Town ▪ Sydney

Executive Editor: *Karen Bowers*
Series Editor: *Brian Wheel*
Series Editorial Assistant: *Jennifer Trebby*
Marketing Manager: *Mandee Eckersley*
Editorial-Production Administrator: *Anna Socrates*
Editorial-Production Service: *Omegatype Typography, Inc.*
Manufacturing Buyer: *JoAnne Sweeney*
Composition and Prepress Buyer: *Linda Cox*
Cover Administrator: *Joel Gendron*
Electronic Composition: *Omegatype Typography, Inc.*

For related titles and support materials, visit our online catalog at www.ablongman.com.

Between the time Website information is gathered and then published, it is not unusual for some sites to have closed. Also, the transcription of URLs can result in unintended typographical errors. The publisher would appreciate notification where these errors occur so that they may be corrected in subsequent editions.

Library of Congress Cataloging-in-Publication Data

CIP data not available at time of publication.

ISBN: 0-205-41490-7

Printed in the United States of America

10   9   8   7   6   5   4   3   2   1   09   08   07   06   05   04

Credits: pp. 272–273; Excerpt from Wallace Shawn and André Gregory, *My Dinner with André.* Copyright 1981. Reprinted by permission of Grove/Atlantic, p. 282, Excerpt from M. H. Bazerman and M. A. Neale, "Heuristics in Negotiation: Limitations to Dispute Resolution Effectiveness," In *Negotiating in Organizations*, M. H. Bazerman and R. Lewicki, eds. Copyright 1983 by Sage Publications. Reprinted by permission of Sage Publications.

CONTENTS

7 Doing Conflict: Strategies, Styles, and Tactics   213

8 Changing Conflict Dynamics   272

LIST OF CASES

PREFACE

The Study of Conflict

The fifth edition of *Working Through Conflict* has the same essential goals of prior editions. Its main objective is to provide a summary and synthesis of social science research and theory on conflict. It offers students of conflict a review of the core concepts and theoretical frameworks that enhance an understanding of human behavior in a wide range of conflict situations. The research and theory covered in this book reflect the many social science disciplines that have contributed to the study of conflict.

Although it takes an interdisciplinary view of conflict, this book emphasizes understanding conflict as a communication phenomenon. It assumes that conflict is something that people create and shape as they interact with each other. Sometimes conflict interaction is immediate and face-to-face. In other instances, it is played out in a series of moves, actions, and responses that occur over time and in different places. This book highlights the interactive nature of conflict, no matter what form it takes. This focus on communication means that readers can gain an appreciation for how mutual influence occurs, how language and message choices shape conflict, and how patterns of behavior and the structure of human discourse create important dimensions of any unfolding conflict.

In addition, *Working Through Conflict* offers a road map for how theory and research can be used to understand and influence conflict dynamics in everyday life. The field of conflict management is supported by a long history of useful research and theory that form a basis for a wide variety of conflict management work. This book demonstrates how conflicts across settings can be understood by seeing them through a range of theoretical lenses. It illustrates how students of conflict can begin thinking and acting in ways that can have profound effects on the dynamics of difficult conflicts.

Developing Theory-Based Intuition

It is often said that people who are good at their work have excellent intuition. Usually this means that they instinctively make good decisions and employ effective strategies to create change or accomplish productive objectives. Intuition is often assumed to be innate—it is seen as a gift that some people have. But in most cases effective professional intuition comes from a broad background of knowledge developed, study done, and experience gained over time. *Working Through Conflict* is written for those who want to develop good intuition about how to react, interact, and intervene in conflict situations. Conflict is usually complex—it is often multilayered, steeped in a history of events, and shaped by diverse perspectives and understandings. As a result, having good intuition about conflict starts by mastering a broad repertoire of ideas—ideas that create different possible explanations for why conflict interaction moves in destructive or constructive directions.

Working Through Conflict covers a wide range of essential concepts and theories that clarify the practical implications for managing conflicts in relationships, groups, teams, and organizations. It is a primer for those who might want to pursue professional work in the conflict management field as mediators, ombudspersons, facilitators, or conciliators. It can also help build a strong intuition in those who deal with conflict daily in work and professional settings and in those who want to have an impact on conflicts in their personal lives within families, romantic relationships, marriages, and friendships.

Key Features of Fifth Edition

The essential structure of *Working Through Conflict* has not been altered in this fifth edition; although, several changes have been made to help strengthen the book and to incorporate helpful suggestions from those who have read prior editions. One change is that the core definition of conflict we offer in the Introduction has been broadened. The emphasis of the new definition is on perceived incompatibility of any kind, regardless of whether people have similar or different goals. This change was needed to reflect the increasing awareness that conflict often emerges because of communication style differences and other perceptual factors that create a sense of incompatibility, independent of differences in the instrumental goals people may hold.

In addition, some material in the book has been reorganized to streamline chapters and to supplement the specific objectives of several chapters. For example, we have combined coverage of culture and climate in presenting the core properties of conflict and communication in Chapter 1. The sections on trained incapacities and working habits have been moved to Chapter 8 where their applied implications are more easily emphasized. We have also moved coverage of reciprocity theory to Chapter 7 because it is so closely tied to the use of conflict tactics. These changes have helped in achieving a better balance in the amount of material covered across the chapters.

We have updated references to research and theory throughout this book to capture the most current thinking about the topics covered. In many instances, we retain older references because they point to core work in the field that has served as a foundation for more recent studies. Current developments are important, but we believe that students should also be aware of the field's conceptual roots as represented in classic conflict literature.

Case studies continue to play a key role in this edition of *Working Through Conflict.* Not only do the cases help to illustrate the various theories covered in the book, but they also demonstrate the complexity and nuances of real-life conflict. We have found that case studies stimulate thoughtful discussion of strategies and ethics, as well as intervention possibilities. They also serve as excellent models for students who want or need to write their own case analyses. Inevitably, readers will notice how almost all theories covered here have specific case illustrations.

This allows students to see how they might analyze conflicts they have observed or experienced themselves and to see the utility of providing contrasting theoretical understandings of the same conflict events.

This book is designed to develop students' understandings of how various theories of conflict differ. It describes key differences between cognitive and interactional theories of conflict. This distinction will help students appreciate the underlying assumptions of social science theories, in general, and to see what any particular theory can and cannot offer to our understanding of human behavior. This feature of the book is meant to supplement students' understandings of the nature of theory development, as well provide insight about the goals and boundaries of various theoretical frameworks.

Like previous editions, this one gives equal weight to conflicts occurring in a wide range of arenas, from intimate relationships and friendships to group, intergroup, organizational, and negotiation settings. This added breadth makes the book suitable as a primary text for courses in conflict and conflict management, as well as a useful supplement to courses that devote substantial attention to conflict or third-party work.

The title of this book is an intentional double entendre. Because its major emphasis is on communication patterns people use when attempting to manage conflict, we hope that the book will help people successfully *work through* difficult conflicts. The book is also built on the assumption that people can complete successful work *through the emergence of conflict*. It is our hope that this book will encourage and assist people to confront their conflicts and to work through them creatively rather than suppressing or superficially "resolving" conflicts.

Acknowledgments

Thanks are still due to those who helped make the first edition possible. We owe our greatest debt to our colleagues at the Center for Conflict Resolution in Madison, Wisconsin. We are very grateful to Lonnie Weiss for her insight and help with our analyses. We also thank Syd Bernard, Jim Carrilon, Jay Herman, Jan Shubert, Rick Sloan, Dennis Smith, and Kathy Zoppi for reacting to parts or all of the manuscript. In addition, we turned to Betsy Densmore, Robert Everett, and Tommy Vines for an evaluation of the manuscript from a managerial perspective. For extremely helpful manuscript reviews of the first edition, we thank Wayne Beach, Robert J. Doolittle, Dennis Gouran, Thomas Harris, Linda Putnam, Gale Richards, Michael Sunnafrank, and Paul Yelsma. We also thank Linda Klug, Jean Kebis, and Wayne Beach for supplying the transcript of interaction in Chapter 6.

We are particularly grateful to Elizabeth Vegso for helping to revise the case study format and generate discussion questions for the third edition. Once again, this fifth edition is the product of many valuable comments and contributions from students and instructors. We are grateful to the students in our classes who became enthusiastic about documenting and analyzing real-life conflicts. Over the years, they contributed several detailed cases to the book. We appreciate the feedback reviewers provided for this edition: Laura L. Jansma, University of California–Santa Barbara, and Tracy Routsong, Winona State University. Kevin Real and Misti Freeman of Texas A&M University reviewed the manuscript and did research for the fourth edition. We are indebted to those who provided feedback and suggestions for the fourth edition, including Lori Carrell, University of Wisconsin at Oshkosh; Alice Crume, State University of New York–Brockport; Susan Rice, California State University at Long Beach; Shirley Van Hoeven, Western Michigan University. Useful and insightful suggestions for the third edition were provided by Steven Colmbs, Loyola Marymount University; Gary Hartzell, University of Nebraska at Omaha; Keven E. McCleary, Southern Illinois University at Edwardsville; Susan Rice, California State University at Long Beach; and Dale L. Shannon, Western Michigan University. We are also thankful to those who provided suggestions for the second edition, including Tom Biesecker, University of Kansas; Bruce Gronbeck, University of Iowa; David A. Frank, University of Oregon; Dale Hample, Western Illinois University; Sara E. Newell, West Chester University; Stella Ting-Toomey, Arizona State University; and Hal R. Witteman, The Pennsylvania State University; and to Charles R. Conrad, Texas A&M University; Tricia Jones, Temple University; Cynthia Stohl, Purdue University; and Shirley A. Van Hoeven, Western Michigan University, who offered insightful commentary on earlier drafts of the second edition. The excellent editorial and production staff at Allyn & Bacon including Brian Wheel, Karon Bowers, Jennifer Trebby, and Anna Socrates have assisted greatly with the production of this volume. Thanks also to Shannon Foreman at Omegatype for production assistance and to Randy Duque for the development of the index.

Joseph P. Folger
Marshall Scott Poole
Randall K. Stutman

INTRODUCTION

Conflict Interaction

As do most things in life, conflict offers a mixture of the good, the bad, and the uncertain. On the positive side, conflicts allow us to air important issues; they produce new and creative ideas; they release built-up tensions. Handled properly, conflicts can strengthen relationships; they can help groups and organizations to reevaluate and clarify goals and missions; and they can also initiate social change to eliminate inequities and injustice. These advantages suggest that conflict is normal and healthy, and they underscore the importance of understanding and handling conflict properly.

But, perhaps more familiar is the negative side of conflict. Heated exchanges spiral out of control, resulting in frustration, tension, hard feelings, and, ultimately, more conflict. Low-grade family conflicts, perpetuated through criticism, arguments, nagging, and verbal abuse, not only distance parents from children and husbands from wives, but also lower self-esteem and create problems that can follow people throughout their entire lives. Additionally, conflicts are sometimes violent, not only between strangers, but also in the workplace and within the family. Sometimes *not being able* to start a conflict is the source of frustration. If one friend persistently denies that a problem exists or changes the subject when it comes up, the other cannot discuss the things that are bothering her, and the friendship suffers. The various negative experiences we all have with conflict are reinforced in the media, where it often seems that the only effective way to solve problems is to shoot somebody.

Conflicts also bring uncertainty. As we will see, the great "unpredictables" in life often center around how interactions occur. Conversations, meetings, conflicts all have in common the fact that they may suddenly turn in unexpected directions. Indeed, as Chapter 2 discusses, the uncertainties that arise during conflicts often cause them to turn in negative directions.

The twists and turns of the following specific case—in this instance a conflict in a small office—offer a good illustration of the positive, negative, and uncertain sides of conflict.

The conflict at the women's hotline initially exhibits several negative features and might easily turn in a destructive direction. First, the situation is tense and threatening. This was an extremely difficult time for the workers. Even for "old hands" at negotiation, conflicts are often unpleasant and frightening. Second, the participants are experiencing a great deal of uncertainty. They are unable to understand what is going on and how their behavior affects the conflict. Conflicts are confusing; actions can have consequences quite different from those

1

CASE **I.1A**

The Women's Hotline Case

Imagine yourself as a staff member in this organiza-tion: How would you react as this conflict unfolded? What is it about this particular conflict that makes it seem difficult to face—let alone solve?

Women's Hotline is a rape and domestic crisis center in a medium-sized city. The center em-ploys seven full- and part-time workers. The workers, all women, formed a cohesive unit and made all important decisions as a group. There were no formal supervisors. The hotline started as a voluntary organization and had grown by capturing local and federal funds. The group remained proud of its roots in a democratic, feminist tradition.

The atmosphere at the hotline was rather informal. The staff members saw each other as friends, but there was an implicit understand-ing that people should not have to take respon-sibility for each other's cases. Because the hotline's work was draining, having to handle each other's worries could create an unbear-able strain. This norm encouraged workers to work on their own and keep problems to themselves.

The conflict arose when Diane, a new counselor who had only six months of experi-ence, was involved in a very disturbing inci-dent. One of her clients was killed by a man who had previously raped her. Diane had trou-ble dealing with this incident. She felt guilty about it; she questioned her own ability and asked herself whether she might have been able to prevent this tragedy. In the months fol-lowing, Diane had increasing difficulty in cop-ing with her feelings and began to feel that her co-workers were not giving her the support she needed. Diane had no supervisor to turn to, and, although her friends outside the hotline were helpful, she did not believe they could understand the pressure as well as her co-workers could.

Since the murder, Diane had not been able to work to full capacity, and she began to

notice some resentment from the other coun-selors. She felt the other staff members were more concerned about whether she was adding to their work loads than whether she was recovering from the traumatic incident. Although Diane did not realize it at the time, most of the staff members felt she had been slow to take on responsibilities even before her client was killed. They thought Diane had gen-erally asked for more help than other staff members and that these requests were adding to their own responsibilities. No one was will-ing to tell Diane about these feelings after the incident, because they realized she was very disturbed. After six months, Diane believed she could no longer continue to work effec-tively. She felt pressure from the others at the center, and she was still shaken by the tragedy. She requested two weeks off with pay to get away from the work situation for a while, to reduce the stress she felt, and to come back with renewed energy. The staff, feeling that Diane was slacking off, denied this request. They responded by outlining, in writing, what they saw as the responsibilities of a full-time staff worker. Diane was angry when she real-ized her request had been denied, and she decided to file a formal work grievance.

Diane and the staff felt bad about having to resort to such a formal, adversarial proce-dure. No staff member had ever filed a work grievance, and the group was embarrassed by its inability to deal with the problem on a more informal basis. These feelings created addi-tional tension between Diane and the staff.

Discussion Questions

- *Can you foresee any benefits to this conflict?*
- *Is it possible to foresee whether a conflict will move in a constructive or destructive direction?*
- *What clues would lead you to believe that this conflict is going to be productive?*

intended because the situation is more complicated than had been assumed. Diane did not know her co-workers thought she was slacking even before the tragedy. When she asked for time off, she was surprised at their refusal, and her angry reaction nearly started a major battle. Third, the situation is extremely fragile. A conflict may evolve in very different ways depending on the behavior of just a single worker. If, for example, the staff chooses to fire Diane, the conflict may be squelched, or it may fester and undermine relationships among the remaining staff. If, on the other hand, Diane wins allies, the others might split over the issue

CASE I.1B
The Women's Hotline Case (Continued)

Imagine yourself in the midst of this conflict: What would you recommend this group do to promote a constructive outcome to this conflict?

The committee who received Diane's grievance suggested that they could handle the problem in a less formal way if both Diane and the staff agreed to accept a neutral third-party mediator. Everyone agreed that this suggestion had promise, and a third party was invited to a meeting where the entire staff would address the issue.

At this meeting, the group faced a difficult task. Each member offered reactions they had been unwilling to express previously. The staff made several pointed criticisms of Diane's overall performance. Diane expressed doubts about the staff's willingness to help new workers or to give support when it was requested. Although this discussion was often tense, it was well-directed. At the outset of the meeting, Diane withdrew her formal complaint. This action changed the definition of the problem from the immediate work grievance to the question of what levels of support were required for various people to work effectively in this difficult and emotionally draining setting. Staff members shared doubts and fears about their own inadequacies as counselors and agreed that something less than perfection was acceptable. The group recognized that a collective inertia had developed and that they had consistently avoided giving others the support needed to deal with difficult rape cases. They acknowledged, however, the constraints on each woman's time; each worker could handle only a limited amount of stress. The group recognized that some level of mutual support was essential and felt they had fallen below that level over the past year and a half. One member suggested that any staff person should be able to ask for a "debriefing contract" whenever he or she felt in need of help or support. These contracts would allow someone to ask for ten minutes of another person's time to hear about a particularly disturbing issue or case.

The group adopted this suggestion because they saw that it could allow members to seek help without overburdening each other. The person who was asked to listen could assist and give needed support without feeling that she had to "fix" another worker's problem. Diane continued to work at the center and found that her abilities and confidence increased as the group provided the support she needed.

Discussion Questions
- *In what ways did the parties in this conflict show "good faith"?*
- *Is "good faith" participation a necessary prerequisite to constructive conflict resolution?*

and ultimately dissolve the hotline. As the case continues, observe staff members' behavior and their method of dealing with this tense and unfamiliar situation.

This is a "textbook" case in effective conflict management because it resulted in a solution that all parties accepted. The members of this group walked a tightrope throughout the conflict, yet they managed to avoid a fall. The tension, unpleasantness, uncertainty, and fragility of conflict situations make them hard to face. Because these problems make it difficult to deal with issues constructively and creatively, conflicts are often terminated by force, by uncomfortable suppression of issues, or by exhaustion after a prolonged fight—all outcomes that leave at least one party dissatisfied. Entering a conflict is often like making a bet against the odds: You can win big if it turns out well, but so many things can go wrong that many people are unwilling to chance it.

The key to working through conflict is not to minimize its disadvantages, or even to emphasize its positive functions, but to accept both and to try to understand how conflicts move in destructive or productive directions. This calls for a careful analysis of both the specific behaviors and the interaction patterns involved in conflict and the forces that influence these patterns.

This chapter introduces you to conflict as an interaction system. We first define conflict and then introduce the three arenas for interpersonal conflict that this book explores. Following this, we discuss an important reference point—the distinction between productive and destructive conflict interaction—and the behavioral cycles that move conflict in positive and negative directions. Finally, we lay out the plan of this book, which is written to examine the key dynamics of conflict interaction and the forces that influence them.

Conflict Defined

Conflict is the interaction of interdependent people who perceive incompatibility and the possibility of interference from others as a result of this incompatibility. Several key features of this definition should be considered.

The most important feature of conflict is that it is based in interaction. Conflicts are constituted and sustained by the behaviors of the parties involved and their reactions to one another, particularly verbal and nonverbal communication. Conflict interaction takes many forms, and each form presents special problems and requires special handling. The most familiar type of conflict interaction is marked by shouting matches or open competition in which each party tries to defeat the other. But conflicts also can be more subtle. People may react to conflict by suppressing it. A husband and wife may communicate in ways that allow them to avoid confrontation, either because they are afraid the conflict may damage a fragile relationship or because they convince themselves that the issue "isn't worth fighting over." This response is as much a part of the conflict process as fights and shouting matches. This book deals with the whole range of responses to conflict and how those responses affect the development of conflicts.

People in conflict perceive that there is some existing incompatibility with others and that this incompatibility may prompt others to interfere with their own desires, goals, personal comforts, or communication preferences. The key word here is *perceive.* Regardless of whether incompatibility actually exists, if the parties believe incompatibility exists, then conditions are ripe for conflict. Whether one employee really stands in the way of a co-worker's promotion, if the co-worker interprets the employee's behavior as interfering with his promotion, then a conflict is likely to ensue. Communication is important because it is the key to shaping and maintaining the perceptions that guide conflict behavior.

Communication *problems* can be an important source of incompatibility among people. Conflict can result from misunderstandings that occur when people have different communication styles (Tannen 1986; Grimshaw 1990). For example, Tannen argues that men and women have different approaches to interpersonal communication: Whereas men are mostly task-oriented and concerned with establishing their position relative to others in conversations, women use conversations to build relationships and establish connections with others. As a result, men and women may interpret the same act in very different ways. When a man makes a demand during a conflict, he might mean to signal that he is strong and has a definite position; a woman hearing a demand is likely to focus more on its implications for the relationship, perhaps interpreting it as a signal that it will be very difficult to deal with this man. As a result, the woman may become more competitive toward her male partner than she would have had she interpreted his demand in the man's terms. According to Tannen, stylistic differences of this sort create communication barriers that make misunderstanding—and the conflict that results from it—inevitable in male–female relationships. Similar communication problems can occur across almost any social divide, such as those between people of different cultures, ages, educational backgrounds, and socioeconomic classes.

Conflict interaction is colored by the interdependence of the parties. Interdependence determines parties' incentives in the conflict. There is an incentive to cooperate when parties perceive that gains by one will promote gains by the other or losses for one party will result in corresponding losses for the other. There is an incentive to compete when parties believe that one's gain will be the other's loss. Resentment to Diane built up among the other workers at the hotline because they felt that if she got what she needed—time off—it would result in more work and pressure for them. This set up a competitive situation that resulted in conflict escalation. However, purely competitive (or cooperative) situations rarely occur. In most real situations there is a mixture of incentives to cooperate and to compete. The other staff members at the hotline wanted to maintain a cordial atmosphere, and several liked Diane. This compensated to some degree for their resentment of Diane and set the stage for a successful third-party intervention.

The greater the interdependence among people, the more significant the consequences of their behaviors are for each other. The conflict at the hotline would not have occurred if Diane's behavior had not irritated the other workers and if their response had not threatened Diane's position. Furthermore, any action taken in response to a conflict affects both sides. The decision to institute a "debriefing contract" required considerable change by everyone. If Diane had been fired, that, too, would have affected the other workers; they would have had to "cover" Diane's cases and come to terms with themselves as co-workers who could be accused of being unresponsive or insensitive.

There is one final wrinkle to interdependence: When parties are interdependent, they can potentially aid or interfere with each other. Parties know about their respective abilities to cooperate or to compete, and their interpretations of each others' communication and actions shape how the conflict develops. In some instances, one party may believe that having his or her point accepted is more important, at least for the moment, than proposing a mutually beneficial outcome. When Diane asked for two weeks off, she was probably thinking not of the group's best interest, but of her own needs. In other cases, someone may advance a proposal designed to benefit everyone, as when the staff member suggested the debriefing contract. In still other instances, a comment may be offered with cooperative intent, but others may interpret it as one that advances an individual interest. Regardless of whether the competitive motive is intended by the speaker or assigned by others, the interaction unfolds from that point under the assumption that the speaker is competitive. As we will see, subsequent interaction is colored by this negative interpretation, and people's experiences may further undermine their willingness to cooperate in a self-reinforcing cycle. The same cyclical process also can occur with cooperation, creating a positive momentum.

Arenas for Conflict

This book examines a broad range of conflicts in three general settings. One important conflict arena is the *interpersonal relationship*. Interpersonal conflicts include those between husbands and wives, siblings, friends, and roommates. But interpersonal relationships are broader than this, encompassing those among co-workers, supervisors and employees, landlords and tenants, and neighbors. Interpersonal conflicts tell us a great deal about styles of conflict interaction, emotional and irrational impulses, and the diversity of resources people exchange in close or long-term relationships.

A second important genre of conflicts are those that occur in *groups or teams*. This arena includes families, work teams, small businesses, classes, clubs, juries, and even therapy or consciousness-raising groups. Because much work is done in groups, this arena has been studied extensively and offers a wide range of conflict situations for analysis. Conflicts in this arena offer insights about group cohesion; the influence of climates, coalitions, and working habits; and the distribution of power.

Finally, the book examines conflicts that occur in *intergroup* settings. In this case, the focus is on individuals as representatives of social groups rather than as unique and special individuals. This arena includes conflicts among people who represent different gender, ethnic, or cultural groups. Intergroup conflicts also can arise among parties who are viewed as representatives of different teams, organizations, or political action groups. In these conflicts, the individual's identity is supplanted by issues of group identity. Prejudice, stereotyping, and ideologies often come into play (Putnam and Poole 1987).

The three arenas differ in several respects. One obvious difference is in the number of people typically involved in a conflict. Interpersonal conflicts are characterized by face-to-face exchanges among a small number of people. The parties may belong to a larger group or organization (for example, siblings are part of the same family), but the divisive issues are those that the parties view as centrally their own. The conflict is played out between them and not in the group as a whole. Group conflicts involve a number of people who are members of some larger unit. The parties know each other, have interacted with each other in meetings or work settings, and attempt to reach decisions as a group. The divisive issues in these conflicts are central to the group as a whole. Intergroup conflicts involve parties representing two or more large groups such as organizations, cultural groups, or genders. Issues in intergroup disputes are often carried over from long-standing grievances and conflicts between the "parent" units.

As the number of people involved in a conflict increases, important features of the interaction change as well. For example, in interpersonal conflicts, people usually speak for themselves. In group or intergroup conflicts, spokespersons, representatives, or various counselors, such as attorneys, union representatives, or presidents of organizations, are more likely to speak for the collective. In addition, the group, team, or organizational climate becomes important as the number of people in a conflict increases.

These arenas of conflict also differ in the type of interdependence that typically exists among the parties. The resources available to parties shift across these contexts. In interpersonal relationships, parties depend on each other for a wide range of emotional, psychological, and material resources (Levinger 1979; Roloff 1981; Cahn 1990a). Among the resources exchanged in interpersonal relationships are: emotional support; images one holds of oneself as a talented, generous, loving, sensuous, or loyal person; financial security; and the ability to meet physical needs. These resources are at stake when conflicts emerge in interpersonal relationships. In group and intergroup conflicts, the range of interdependence is generally narrower. In task-oriented units, people are dependent on each other for achieving the goals the group has set for itself, for financial security (if the group provides income for members), and for a person's professional or public identity (for example, images parties hold of themselves as competent, fair-minded, or cooperative). In intergroup relationships, individuals are dependent on each other for the advancement and continuation of the group vis-à-vis other groups (for example, many Serbs in Yugoslavia worked to achieve "Greater Serbia" by attacking other groups such as the Kosovars), and also for their identities as members of a well-defined social unit (for example, the sense of self one has as a human being, a Christian, a Hispanic American, a Republican). The different types of interdependence in each arena make the use of power different in each of them.

Although these arenas differ in important ways, they are similar in one important sense: in all of them *interaction is central* to conflict (Roloff 1987a). Regardless of the number of parties involved or the type of interdependence among them, conflict unfolds as a series of moves and countermoves premised on people's perceptions, expectations, and strategies. Because of this fundamental similarity, many of the principles of conflict examined apply across the arenas. As Putnam and Folger (1988, p. 350) put it:

> Theoretical principles apply across (conflict) contexts because interaction processes form the foundation of conflict management. Fundamental to all conflicts are the series of actions and reactions, moves and countermoves, planning of communication strategies, perceptions, and interpretations of messages that directly affect substantive outcomes.

Because interaction is the key feature of conflict across all three arenas, they share a number of common characteristics as well. For example, violent exchanges can occur in interpersonal, intragroup, or intergroup conflicts. So too, can parties engage in negotiation in any of these settings. Because labor-management or political negotiations are the most commonly reported examples in the media, people often think of negotiation or bargaining as a separate arena. However, husbands and wives can negotiate divorce agreements, a professor and student can negotiate a grade, environmental groups can negotiate a land-use policy, or neighborhood groups can negotiate historical preservation standards. Another aspect of conflict common to all three arenas is power, because power is integral to all forms of interdependence. These and other commonalities are explored throughout this book.

Productive and Destructive Conflict Interaction

As previously noted, people often associate conflict with negative outcomes. However, there are times when conflicts must be addressed regardless of the apprehension they create. When differences exist and the issues are important, suppressing conflict is often more dangerous than facing it. The psychologist Irving Janis points to a number of famous political disasters, such as the Bay of Pigs invasion and the failure to anticipate the Japanese attack on Pearl Harbor, where poor decisions can be traced to the repression of conflict by key decision-making groups (Janis 1972). The critical question is: What forms of conflict interaction will yield obvious benefits without tearing a relationship, a group, a team, or an organization apart?

The sociologist Lewis Coser (1956) distinguished realistic from nonrealistic conflicts. *Realistic* conflicts are based in disagreements over the means to an end or over the ends themselves. In realistic conflicts, the interaction focuses on the substantive issues the participants must address to resolve their underlying incompatibilities. *Nonrealistic* conflicts are expressions of aggression in which the sole end is to defeat or hurt the other. Participants in nonrealistic conflicts serve their own interests by undercutting those of the other party involved. Coser argues that because nonrealistic conflicts are oriented toward the expression of aggression, force and coercion are the means for resolving these disputes. Realistic conflicts, on the other hand, foster a wide range of resolution techniques—force, negotiation, persuasion, even voting—because they are oriented toward the resolution of some substantive problem. Although Coser's analysis is somewhat oversimplified, it is insightful and suggests important contrasts between productive and destructive conflict interaction (Deutsch 1973).

What criteria could be used to evaluate whether a conflict is productive? In large part, productive conflict interaction depends on *flexibility.* In constructive conflicts, members engage in a wide variety of behaviors ranging from coercion and threat to negotiation, joking, and relaxation to reach an acceptable solution. In contrast, parties in destructive conflicts are likely to be much less flexible because their goal is more narrowly defined: They are trying to defeat each other. Destructive conflict interaction is likely to result in uncontrolled escalation or prolonged attempts to avoid issues. In productive conflict, on the other hand, the interaction changes direction often. Short cycles of escalation, deescalation, avoidance, and constructive work on an issue are likely to occur as participants attempt to manage conflict.

Consider the hotline case. The workers exhibited a wide range of interaction styles, from the threat of a grievance to the cooperative attempt to reach a mutually satisfactory solution. Even though Diane and others engaged in hostile or threatening interactions, they did not persist in this mode, and when the conflict threatened to escalate, they called in a third party. The conflict showed all of the hallmarks of productive interaction. In a destructive conflict, the members might have responded to Diane's grievance by suspending her, and Diane might have retaliated by suing or by attempting to discredit the center in the local newspaper. Her retaliation would have hardened others' positions, and they might have fired her, leading to further retaliation.

In an alternative scenario, the hotline conflict might have ended in destructive avoidance. Diane might have hidden her problem, and the other workers might have consciously or unconsciously abetted her by changing the subject when the murder came up or by avoiding talking to her at all. Diane's problem would probably have grown worse, and she might have had to quit. The center then would have reverted back to "normal" until the same problem surfaced again. Although the damage done by destructive avoidance is much less serious in this case than that done by destructive escalation, it is still considerable: the hotline loses a good worker, and the seeds for future losses remain. In both cases, it is not the behaviors themselves that are destructive—neither avoidance nor hostile arguments are harmful in themselves—but rather the inflexibility of the parties that locks them into escalation or avoidance cycles.

In *productive conflicts, everyone believes that all sides can attain important goals* (Deutsch 1973). Productive conflict interaction exhibits a sustained effort to bridge the apparent incompatibility of positions. This is in marked contrast to destructive conflicts, where the interaction is premised on participants' belief that one side must win and the other must lose. *Productive conflict interaction results in a solution satisfactory to all* and produces a general feeling that the parties have gained something (for example, a new idea, greater clarity of others' positions, or a stronger sense of solidarity). In some cases, the win–lose orientation of destructive conflict stems from the fear of losing. People attempt to defeat alternative proposals because they believe that if their positions are not accepted they will lose resources, self-esteem, or the respect of others. In other cases, win–lose interaction is sparked, not by competitive motives, but by the parties' fear of working through a difficult conflict. Groups that rely on voting to reach decisions often call for a vote when discussion becomes heated and the members do not see any other immediate way out of a hostile and threatening situation. Any further attempt to discuss the alternatives or to pursue the reasons behind people's positions seems risky. A vote can put a quick end to threatening interaction, but it also induces a win–lose orientation that can easily trigger destructive cycles. Group members whose proposals are rejected must resist a natural tendency to be less committed to the chosen solutions and avoid trying to "even the score" in future conflicts.

Productive conflict interaction is sometimes competitive. Both parties must stand up for their own positions and strive for perceived understanding if a representative outcome is to be attained (Cahn 1990b). This may result in tension and hostility, but they should be regarded as paths to a higher goal. Although parties in productive conflicts hold strongly to their positions, they are also open to movement when convinced that such movement will result in the best decision. The need to preserve power, save face, or make the opponent look bad does not stand in the way of change. In contrast, during destructive conflicts parties may become polarized, and the defense of a "noble," nonnegotiable position often becomes more important than working out a viable solution.

Of course, this description of productive and destructive conflict interaction is an idealization. It is rare that a conflict exhibits all the constructive or destructive qualities just mentioned. Most conflicts exhibit both productive and destructive interactions. However, better conflict management will result if parties can sustain productive conflict interaction patterns, and it is to this end that this book is dedicated.

Judgments About Conflict Outcomes

To this point we have focused on assessing conflict interaction. This approach has been taken because we believe it is important to know where a conflict is heading while we are in the midst of it. But the *outcomes of conflicts are also important.* Parties must live with the outcomes, and whether they accept and are satisfied with them determines whether the conflict is resolved or continues to smolder, waiting for some future spark to set it off again.

The most obvious and most desirable outcome *measure* would give an objective account of the *gains and losses* that result for each party. If these can be assessed in an objective manner for each party, they can then be compared to determine things such as who won, how fair the outcome of the conflict was, and whether a better outcome was possible. We can determine relative gains and losses in more or less objective terms if the outcome can be stated in numerical terms. Some numerical measures use values that correspond to real things (for example, money or the number of hours in a day someone agrees to work), whereas others simply measure value on an arbitrary scale such as the "utility" of an outcome to a party.

As desirable as it is, determining gains and losses is more difficult for outcomes that cannot be reduced to numerical terms. For example, the outcome of a conflict between a brother and sister over who gets the corner bedroom is difficult to quantify, though a winner and loser can be identified immediately afterward—who got the bedroom? However, over the longer term, the "winner" may discover that he or she finds the room too hot because of the sun beating through the windows and too noisy because it is right over the game room. Outcomes, such as bedrooms, are complicated to measure, and although there might be gains on some dimensions, there may be losses on other dimensions. Whether there is an overall gain or loss may depend as much on what aspects parties choose to emphasize as on "real" values of the items. If the winner chooses to regard the sun as cheerful (but hot!) and instead focuses on the nice furniture in the room, outcomes are more favorable than if heat is the main focus. Moreover, as our example illustrates, outcomes can change over time. What appears to be a fine outcome right after the conflict is settled may turn out to be negative over the long run, and vice versa.

A second way to evaluate conflicts is in terms of the *level of satisfaction* people feel about the resolution. One definition of an integrative resolution is the solution that all parties are most satisfied with. This criterion gets around some of the limitations of objective outcome measures because we can always determine parties' perceptions and evaluations, even when there is no direct measure of outcomes. The satisfaction criterion also enables us to compare outcomes—at least in relative terms—because parties may be more or less satisfied.

A third judgment that can be made about conflict outcomes concerns their fairness. Two types of *fairness, or social justice,* have a bearing on evaluation of conflict outcomes. *Distributive* justice refers to the fair allocation of resources among two or more recipients. *Procedural* justice is concerned with the fairness of the process by which decisions are made to resolve the conflict.

The answer to the key question regarding distributive justice—Have outcomes been allocated fairly?—depends on the value system we apply. Thompson (1998, p. 194) distinguished three value systems: (a) "The *equality rule,* or blind justice, prescribes equal shares for all." The U.S. legal system is an example of this value system. (b) "The *equity rule, or proportionality of contributions principle,* prescribes that distribution should be proportional to a person's contribution." A case in which it was decided that workers who put in more hours on a project should get a greater share of the bonus earned than should those who put in relatively little effort would be following the equity rule. (c) "The *needs-based rule, or welfare-based allocation,* states that benefits should be proportional to need." Universities give out much of their financial aid based on this principle. Exactly what is regarded as a just outcome will differ depending on which of these three systems applies.

Judgments about procedural justice depend on how outcomes are determined rather than the specific outcomes themselves. In many cases, procedural justice is more important than the actual distribution of outcomes. Parties will sometimes accept great disparities in outcomes if they believe that the allocation was fairly made.

In evaluating the outcomes of conflict, it is important not to emphasize one of these four criteria so much that we forget about the others. Each of the outcomes can cloud the others. For example, an objectively good outcome for both parties may also be perceived as unfair because the proper procedures were not followed. And an outcome that satisfies both parties may be grossly unfair from the viewpoint of distributive justice. Ideally all four criteria will be considered in evaluating the outcomes of a conflict.

More on Conflict Interaction

Conflict is, by nature, interactive; it is never wholly under one person's control. Suppose Robert criticizes Susan, an employee under his supervision, for her decreasing productivity. Susan may accept the criticism and explain why her production is down, thus reducing the conflict and moving toward a solution. Susan may also shout back and sulk, inviting escalation, or she may choose to say nothing and avoid the conflict, resulting in no improvement in the situation. Once Robert has spoken to Susan and she has responded, the situation is no longer totally under Robert's control: His next behavior will be a response to Susan's reaction. Robert's behavior, and its subsequent meaning to Susan, is dependent on the interchange between them.

A behavioral cycle of initiation–response–counterresponse results from the *conflict interchange.* This cycle cannot be understood by breaking it into its parts, into the individual behaviors of Robert and Susan. It is more complex than the individual behaviors and, in a real sense, has a "life" of its own. The cycle can be self-reinforcing, if, for example, Susan shouts back at Robert, Robert tries to discipline her, Susan becomes more recalcitrant, and so on, in an escalating spiral. The cycle could also limit itself if Robert responds to Susan's shouting with an attempt to calm her and listen to her side of the story. Conflict interaction cycles acquire a momentum of their own. They tend to take a definite direction—toward escalation, toward avoidance and suppression, or toward productive work on resolving the conflict.

The complexity of conflict interaction becomes even more apparent when we remember that Robert formulated his criticism on the basis of his previous experience with Susan. That is, Robert's move is based on his perception of Susan's likely response. In the same way, Susan's response is based not only on Robert's criticism, but on her estimate of Robert's likely reaction to her response. Usually such estimations are "intuitive"—that is, they are not conscious—but sometimes parties do plot them out ("If I shout at Robert, he'll back down, and maybe I won't have to deal with this"). They are always based on the parties' perceptions of each other, on whatever theories or beliefs each holds about the other's reactions. Because these estimates are only intuitive predictions, they may be wrong to some extent. The estimates will be revised as the conflict unfolds, and this revision will largely determine what direction the conflict takes.

The most striking thing about this predictive process is the extraordinary difficulties it poses for attempts to understand the parties' thinking. When Susan responds to Robert on the basis of her prediction of Robert's answer, from the outside we see Susan making an estimate of Robert's estimate of what she means by her response. If Robert reflects on Susan's intention before answering, we observe Robert's estimate of Susan's estimate of his estimate of what Susan meant. This string of estimates can increase without bounds if one tries to pin down the originating point, and after a while the prospect is just as dizzying as a hall of mirrors.

Several studies of different phenomena, such as arms races (Richardson 1960; North, Brody, and Holsti 1963), marital relations (Watzlawick, Beavin, and Jackson 1967; Rubin 1983; Scarf 1987), and employee–supervisor interactions (Brown 1983), have shown how this *spiral of predictions* poses a critical problem in conflicts. If the parties do not take this spiral into account, they run the risk of miscalculation. However, it is impossible to calculate all of the possibilities. At best, people have extremely limited knowledge of the implications their actions may hold for others, and their ability to manage conflicts is therefore severely curtailed. Not only are parties' behaviors inherently interwoven in conflicts, but their thinking and anticipations are as well.

Plan of the Book

The key question this book addresses is: How does conflict interaction develop destructive patterns—radical escalation, prolonged or inappropriate avoidance of conflict issues, inflexibility—rather than constructive patterns leading to productive conflict management? A good way to understand conflict interaction is to think of parties in a conflict as poised on a precipice. The crest represents productive conflict management, and the chasm below the downward spiral into destructive conflict. Maintaining a productive approach to a conflict requires diligence and the ability to strike a careful balance among all of the forces that influence interpersonal conflict interaction. Managed properly, these forces can be used to maintain a proper balance and to keep the conflict on a constructive path. However, lack of attention to powerful dynamics surrounding conflicts can propel them into developing a momentum that pushes the parties over the edge in an accelerating plunge.

This book considers several major forces that direct conflicts and examines the problems people encounter in trying to control these forces to regulate their own conflict interactions. To sort out the most influential forces in moving conflicts in destructive or constructive directions, the major theoretical perspectives on communication and conflict are examined. Chapter 1 offers an introduction to communication in conflict centered on four properties of conflict interaction, each of which highlights key influences on conflict. Chapter 2 focuses on the inner experience of conflict—psychological dynamics that influence conflict interaction.

Chapter 3 then moves into the arenas of conflict and reviews a number of perspectives that characterize conflict as interaction.

Building on this theoretical foundation, we devote the next four chapters to understanding important forces that influence conflict interaction—power, face-saving, climate, and conflict strategies and tactics—and how to work with each of them to encourage productive conflict management. Chapter 9 turns to third-party intervention in conflicts, and how third-parties can facilitate constructive conflict interaction.

Summary and Review

What is conflict?

Conflict is interaction among parties who are interdependent and perceive incompatibility with another. It is important to recognize that conflicts can be driven by perceptions, not merely by the objective situation. Interdependence plays a critical role in conflict because it sets up tendencies to compete or cooperate that drive conflict interaction.

What are important arenas for interpersonal conflict?

Interpersonal conflicts occur in interpersonal relationships, small groups, and intergroup settings. Each of these arenas differs in terms of the number of people potentially involved in the conflict and in the type of interdependence among parties. They have in common the fact that conflict in all three arenas is first and foremost a type of interaction.

What is the role of interaction in conflict?

Conflicts are constituted by interaction among parties in that conflicts only exist in the moves and countermoves of parties. Conflicts unfold as parties act them out. This means that conflict is never wholly under the control of any single party; all parties involved have at least some degree of control over how the conflict is to be pursued over time. One particularly strong force in conflict interaction is the tendency of behavioral cycles to be self-reinforcing such that competitive behavior begets competition in response, and cooperative behavior prompts cooperative responses, and so on, in a repeating spiral.

Can different types of conflict be distinguished?

Scholars have distinguished productive from destructive modes of conflict. In productive conflicts, parties take flexible approaches and believe a mutually acceptable solution can be developed. Destructive conflicts are characterized by inflexible behavior and attempts to defeat the other party. In destructive conflicts, parties' goals often shift from achieving an acceptable outcome to defeating the other party, regardless of other considerations. It is worth noting, however, that destructiveness and competitiveness are not synonyms. Competition can occur in constructive conflicts; it just never leads parties to excesses.

What are the standards by which conflict outcomes can be evaluated?

We can distinguish four different criteria that can be used to evaluate conflict outcomes—objective gains/losses, participant satisfaction, distributive justice, and procedural justice. Because most conflicts are complex, it is desirable to use more than one of these criteria to judge the quality of outcomes for participants.

What are the major factors influencing conflict interaction?

As we will see in the remainder of this book, particularly important factors are power, face-saving concerns, climate, and strategies/tactics. Several other psychological and social dynamics also play a role in conflicts, and we will consider them as well. One moral of this book is that *conflict is a complex phenomenon,* and that no single factor is the key to effective conflict management. Like all communication skills, conflict management requires us to be aware of the forces that influence conflict and to be capable of working with those forces to channel conflicts in productive directions.

1 Communication and Conflict

We have developed the idea that conflicts are best understood if we view them as a form of interaction. But interaction is an extraordinarily complicated phenomenon. How can we get a grasp on what happens in conflicts and how can we use that knowledge to turn conflict interaction in productive directions?

This chapter provides an introduction to conflict interaction. First, we describe a normative model of conflict interaction as a "balancing act." The model proposes that in order to manage a conflict effectively, parties must first define and understand the differences in their positions and interests. Once this has been done, they can then move toward a mutually acceptable, integrative solution. However, this is a precarious process, fraught with difficulties. If parties make the wrong moves, their differentiation may spiral off into uncontrollable escalation or, alternatively, to rigid suppression and avoidance of a conflict that they feel they should be able to face and manage. Walking the tightrope to productive conflict management requires insight into the forces that push conflict in negative directions and the appropriate actions required to control them.

The second part of this chapter presents four basic conflict interaction properties, which suggest a number of factors that are important in conflicts. These factors, discussed in subsequent chapters, can move conflict in productive and destructive directions and suggest various levers parties can use to manage conflict effectively.

A Model of Effective Conflict Management

At the outset it is a good idea to consider effective conflict management, the type of interaction that will lead to productive conflict. In his book *Interpersonal Peacemaking*, Walton (1969) describes a simple yet powerful model of conflict behavior that reflects insights on conflict management echoed by a number of other influential writers (Deutsch 1973; Fisher and Ury 1981; Pruitt and Carnevale 1993; Thomas 1975). The model views conflict in terms of two broad phases: a differentiation phase followed by an integration phase. In *differentiation*, parties raise the conflict issues and spend sufficient time and energy clarifying positions, pursuing the reasons behind those positions, and acknowledging the severity of their differences. At the point where further escalation seems fruitless, an *integration* phase begins.

Parties begin to acknowledge common ground, explore possible options, and move toward some solution—sometimes one that meets everyone's needs, but sometimes simply one they can live with. If integration is not completely successful, the conflict may cycle back through a new differentiation phase.

Although this two-phase model of conflict is elementary in one sense, it is highly suggestive because it indicates what parties must do to move through a conflict successfully. How or whether conflict interaction moves from differentiation through integration is complicated. We will consider in further detail some of the dynamics of this two-phase analysis of conflict.

Moving Through Differentiation and Integration

The differentiation phase of conflicts is often difficult because of the seemingly unbridgeable differences that emerge and the intense negative feelings that often accompany them. The combination of hostility and irreconcilable positions may lead to behavior that spurs uncontrolled, hostile escalation into a destructive conflict. In a different overreaction, parties fearful of escalation and loss of control may "sit on" and suppress the conflict, which festers and undermines their relationship. But it is important to navigate differentiation successfully to get to integration, during which "parties appreciate their similarities, acknowledge their common goals, own up to positive aspects of their ambivalence, express warmth and respect, and/or engage in other positive actions to manage their conflict" (Walton 1969, p. 105). The simultaneous need for and fear of differentiation poses a difficult dilemma for parties who want to work through important conflicts. A closer examination of this dilemma reveals how it becomes the basis for people's inability to redirect their destructive interactions.

Adequate differentiation is necessary for constructive conflict resolution. Without a clear statement of each party's position, finding a problem-solving solution— one in which "the participants all are satisfied with their outcomes and feel they have gained as a result of the conflict"—is a hit-or-miss venture (Deutsch 1973, p. 17). Unless parties honestly acknowledge their differences and realize that they must tackle the conflict and work it out, they may not be sufficiently motivated to deal with the problem.

Differentiation initially personalizes the conflict as individuals clarify their stands and people are identified with positions. However, it is not until these positions are articulated that the conflict can finally be depersonalized. Once individual positions have been clarified, the groundwork has been laid for members to realize that the conflict lies in the incompatibility of positions and not in the arbitrary needs or sentiments of one person or faction. Through differentiation people can gain a depersonalized view of the conflict that sets it apart from any one party. If people can clarify the issues and air diverse positions without losing control (a difficult problem in its own right), they can recast the conflict as an external obstacle that all must overcome together. Once achieved, this depersonalized view provides a basis for commonality. It often marks the beginning of an integrative phase, but by no means signifies the end of the conflict process. The parties must still generate ideas and choose a solution that, as Simmel (1955, p. 14) puts it, "resolves the tension between contrasts" in the group or social relationship. From this point of view, people can build on the accomplishments of differentiation.

Differentiation and Escalation.   Although differentiation is necessary for constructive conflict resolution, it can also nourish destructive tendencies. Differentiation surfaces disagreements that parties previously feared or were not motivated to deal with. The stakes seem higher because an unsuccessful attempt to resolve an issue means that members must live with a keener awareness of differences and a more vivid understanding of the negative consequences of leaving the issue unresolved.

In some cases, the process of differentiation can spiral out of control into "malevolent cycling"—highly personalized or hostile conflict that is not directed toward issues (Walton 1969). Baxter, Wilmot, Simmons, and Swartz (1993) conducted open-ended interviews with students that suggested that spiraling escalation is common in interpersonal conflicts. One commonly occurring type of conflict in their interviews they labeled "Escalatory Conflict" because it involved increasing emotional intensity and multiple stages in which the scope and intensity of the conflict increased over time. One female respondent provided this example from a romantic relationship: "I might bring up a topic. Then he will get mad that I brought up this particular topic. Then I will lose my patience and get frustrated. He, in turn, will get more mad" (Baxter et al., 1993, p. 98). This type of escalation also occurs in workplace conflicts, conflicts between groups, and international conflicts (North, Brody, and Holsti 1963; Walton 1969).

Research from several areas points to dynamics that can create and sustain spiraling escalation:

1. Research on *balance theory* (Swensen 1973) suggests that relationships will become strained when group members disagree over important issues. Balance theory assumes people attempt to maintain consistency among their beliefs and feelings; for example, people tend to like those they agree with and dislike the ones with whom they do not agree. When a person finds out that someone he or she likes disagrees on an important issue, the inconsistency creates an uncomfortable cognitive strain. Balance theorists argue that this strain is usually resolved either by a change in the person's beliefs about the issue or by a change in the person's liking for the other. These changes are assumed to follow the path of least resistance: Feelings about whichever is less important—the issue or the person—will change the most. Hence, the longer two people who like each other hold to opposing positions, and the more crucial these positions seem to them, the greater pressure they are under to feel hostility and lose respect for each other.

2. Leary's (1957) classic research on *interpersonal reflexes* also points to likely sources of emotional escalation during this process. If a comment is made that is perceived as hostile, Leary's analysis predicts that it is likely to elicit further hostile responses. Similarly, Gibb's (1961) analysis of defensiveness indicates that evaluative comments (such as, "I don't think that proposal is any good because . . . ") can easily elicit defensive responses because they seem threatening to the listener. Because differentiation calls for evaluation, defensiveness is likely to develop.

3. Research on the nature of *commitment* (Kiesler 1971; Janis and Mann 1977) suggests that making a position public or restating it several times can increase one's commitment to the position or behavior. When commitment to a position is high and that position is called into question by new information or arguments, people often intensify their stands in an effort to preserve their "good name" and self-image. Comments that attack others' positions run the risk of increasing polarization even further because parties may respond by taking more extreme stands than they originally held. Apfelbaum (1974) summarizes a number of experimental studies that indicate that once one side in a conflict openly signals commitment to a position, and thus indicates competitiveness rather than cooperation, the other side becomes more inflexible as well. Thus, the positions people take and their styles of interaction can become rigidified when members commit themselves to some position in front of the group. Because differentiation calls for statements of positions, the risk of escalation is higher during this phase of the conflict process.

Taken together, balance theory, interpersonal reflexes, and commitment generate potent forces toward destructive cycling. To break this cycling, some means of counteracting these effects must be found.

Differentiation and Avoidance.   Although parties sometimes fall prey to the dangers of differentiation, they can also fall victim to an overly zealous attempt to avoid these dangers. When parties try hard to avoid divisive issues, they may never realize their own potential for finding creative solutions to important problems (Pruitt and Lewis 1977). Indeed, early acceptance of a solution about which most parties feel lukewarm and dissatisfied often signals a group's retreat from the pressures of differentiation. The Guetzkow and Gyr (1954) study of seventy-two decision-making conferences illustrates this.

Guetzkow and Gyr compared interaction in groups with high levels of *substantive* conflict (conflict focused on the issues and on disagreements about possible solutions) to interaction in groups with high levels of *affective* conflict (interpersonal conflict characterized by extreme frustration, according to an outsider's observations). They were interested in the difference between substantive and affective conflicts because affective conflicts are more likely to exhibit spiraling escalation. Affective conflict is highly correlated with how critical and punishing members are to each other and how unpleasant the emotional atmosphere is. In essence, affective conflict is a sign of differentiation gone awry. The objective of Guetzkow and Gyr was to determine what conditions allowed each type of group to reach consensus about the issue they were attempting to resolve.

These researchers found very different behaviors contributing to each group's ability to reach consensus. Groups that were high in substantive conflict and were able to reach consensus sought three times as much factual information and relied on that information more heavily in reaching a decision than did groups that were not able to reach consensus. In other words, substantive conflict was resolved by a determined pursuit of the issue.

In contrast, groups high in affective conflict engaged mostly in flight or avoidance to reach consensus. Members withdrew from the problem by addressing simpler and less controversial agenda items, showed less interest in the discussion overall, and talked to only a few others in the group. When consensus was achieved in the affective conflict groups, it was most often the result of ignoring the critical problem at hand and finding an issue on which members could comfortably reach agreement. If the group's or organization's goal is to reduce tension and discomfort at any cost, then flight behaviors will serve it well. When people cannot easily ignore an issue, however, destructive tension can result from their inability to pursue the conflict. Baxter et al. (1993) also found this type of avoidance in their study of interpersonal conflict. One of the interviewees in their study called this type of conflict "don't talk about it" conflict. When confronting particularly serious issues, friends reported that they would change the subject and avoid the conflict because they did not want to threaten their relationship.

Differentiation and Rigidity.   Avoidance is one possible outcome of an unsuccessful attempt to deal with the demands of differentiation. Spiraling, hostile escalation is another possible outcome of an inability to differentiate. The anxiety-producing nature of differentiation gives rise to a set of possible intermediary behaviors, which can lead to either avoidance or radical escalation. The most direct link between the stress of differentiation and either avoidance or escalation is the tendency for people to cling inflexibly to patterns of interaction that occur during differentiation.

Figure 1.1 expresses the relationship among differentiation, inflexibility, and possible conflict resolution outcomes. One source of inflexibility can be found in the psychodynamic theories discussed in the next chapter. These developmental theories of maladaptive, repetitive behavior—behavior that persists despite its destructive outcomes—trace the origin of the behaviors to a threatening or anxiety-inducing environment (Volkan 1994). The psychoanalyst Alfred Adler, for example, maintains that running through a normal person's life is a consistent pattern of responses, a way of reacting to the world. This orientation gives rise to the person's character and

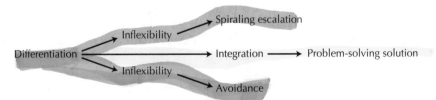

FIGURE 1.1   Possible Responses to the Demands of Differentiation in Conflict Situations

a set of guiding principles used to make decisions; to deal with people; and, in general, to give meaning to the events of one's life. There are points in life, however, when a person's orientations clash with events in the world, when a guiding principle appears false. Adler offers an explanation for why, in some cases, individuals fasten onto their orientations despite severe clashes with reality (cited in Luchins and Luchins 1959, p. 19):

> The relatively normal person, when he [*sic*] realizes that his scheme is seriously in conflict with reality, is adaptable and modifies his orientation, abandoning what is patently false. But there are certain situations which work against flexibility and adaptability and favor rigid adherence to the guiding fictions. These are conditions in which the individual experiences exaggerated feelings of inferiority and psychological uncertainty, conditions that spell anxiety to him since anxiety is the sensation accompanying a strong uncompensated inferiority feeling. Under such conditions even a normal person may cling to his guiding fictions despite their conflict with reality. There are some individuals who live quite constantly under such anxiety-inducing conditions; and so rigidly do they adhere to their guiding fictions that these become accentuated and create a rigid, hardened lifestyle or character, an orientation out of tune with reality but nonetheless dogmatically maintained.

In much the same way, parties in conflict are faced with anxiety-inducing conditions that work against flexibility and adaptability. These conditions are the result of the inherent demands of differentiation. The conditions that produce anxiety for people are those pressures that work toward radical escalation: (1) an initial personalization of the conflict, (2) the stress of acknowledging opposing stands, (3) hostile and emotional statements, (4) uncertainty about the outcomes of the conflict, and (5) heightened awareness of the consequences of not reaching a resolution (Holsti 1971; Smart and Vertinsky 1977).

Failure to differentiate and search for an acceptable resolution can rigidify relationships as well. The Baxter et al. (1993) interviews indicated that relational conflicts sometimes exhibit predictable repetitions, and they label these *déjà vu conflicts*. In these cases, the parties enact the same conflict over and over again. In one case, an interviewee indicated that "she and her partner 'know in advance' that they will (a) enact a conflict on a certain topic or issue, (b) know how the conflict will play itself out, and (c) know that the enactment will never end in genuine resolution" (p. 97). This sort of frustrating "broken-record" interaction is fed by rigidity and can be overcome if parties engage and explore their differences directly.

Differentiation is a necessary but anxiety-provoking process that people face during any conflict. If parties pursue issues and work through the demands of differentiation without rigidly adhering to counterproductive interaction patterns, there is a clear promise of innovation and of finding an integrative solution to the conflict (Alberts 1990). The pressures toward escalation are formidable, however, and the anxiety of differentiation can promote rigidity of behavior, resulting in either spiraling conflict or flight from the issue.

Taking the Middle Path: Moving Toward Integration

The key to effective conflict management is to achieve the benefits of differentiation—clear understanding of differences, acceptance of others' positions as legitimate (but not necessarily agreement with them), and motivation to work on the conflict—and to make a clean transition to integration, which sets the conflict on an entirely different course. Making the transition from differentiation to integration is not always easy. It requires parties to make a fundamental change in the direction of the conflict, turning it from a focus on differences—often accompanied by intense emotions and a desire to defeat each other—to negotiation and cooperative work. Several measures can facilitate this transition.

First, it is important to ensure that differences have surfaced as completely as possible. If parties feel that they have not stated their issues completely, they are likely to return to make them later on, moving what had been constructive work back into differentiation. There is less temptation to do this if parties attain a thorough understanding of each others' positions, even if they do not agree with each other. A second condition that promotes a transition to integration is when parties realize that others will not give into them or be pushed into an inferior settlement. It is an old adage that armies go to the negotiating table when they reach a "standoff." Chapter 4 discusses how the balance of power affects conflicts and how parties can attain a workable balance.

Pruitt, Rubin, and Kim (1994) recommend that parties be encouraged to set ambitious goals for themselves in negotiation. If parties "aim high" and strive for outcomes that are truly meaningful to them, rather than settling for subpar results, they are more likely to stand their ground and act decisively. This, in turn, is likely to convince others that they will not be intimidated or easily moved, and those others are likely to recognize the need to deal with the party on terms other than competition.

Experiencing the negative consequences of differentiation can also motivate parties to work on the conflict. Sometimes parties must inflict serious practical or emotional damage on each other before they realize that it is not appropriate or workable to compete, but that some other route must be taken to resolve the situation. For example, many married couples seek counseling only after repeated damaging fights. This is unfortunate, but a case can be made that these couples seek counseling only because they finally realize the dire consequences of continuing in their present, miserable patterns. This last point reemphasizes the paradox of the positive results that can emerge from enduring the often negative and unpleasant experience of differentiation.

It is important for parties to synchronize their transition to the integrative phase (Walton 1969). If one party is ready to work on the problem, but the other still wants to fight, the first might give up on cooperation and restart escalating conflict. The burden of synchronizing often falls to the one who first develops cooperative intentions. This party must endure the other's "slings and arrows" and attempt to promote cooperation and a shift to problem solving. The transition to integration will be hastened to the extent that the other feels that his or her position has been heard. Active listening—in which the party draws out the other's issues and grievances and responds in a respectful manner—encourages concilia- tion. This enables both parties to build "positive face," as explained in Chapter 5. Chapter 7 discusses strategies and tactics that promote integration. One such strat- egy is "reformed sinner"—after an initial period of competition, the party offers cooperation and signs of goodwill in response to the other's behavior; if the other continues to compete, the party responds with competition and then returns to cooperation. This indicates that the party could compete if he or she wanted to, but instead prefers cooperation. A final condition that promotes integration is a coop- erative climate—the general situation surrounding the conflict is not threatening or defensive. The ways in which climates are created and sustained are discussed in Chapter 6.

In many cases, a third party can be a significant help in making the transition from differentiation to integration. People sometimes become so involved in the conflict that they have neither the motivation nor the insight to take the necessary actions. A third party has a more objective stance and can often determine what must be done to move the conflict into integration. In addition, individuals often trust the third party and will follow advice that they would not accept from each other. A discussion of third parties and their role in sharpening conflicts and induc- ing integration can be found in Chapter 9.

One key to moving through differentiation and integration is the ability to recognize destructive and productive patterns, which we turn to now.

Recognizing Destructive Cycles

It is often difficult to determine when conflict interaction has turned in a destruc- tive direction. Conflict can develop tendencies in gradual and subtle steps, and sometimes it is difficult to assess the consequences of gradual changes. Conflicts can also be difficult to understand due to conscious efforts by some parties to keep the conflict "hidden"—out of the more public forums in a group or organization (Kolb and Bartunek 1992). Unsuspecting parties may suddenly find themselves caught in an escalating spiral or active avoidance. Once in these destructive cycles, the rigidity that sets in may prevent parties from pulling out. It is important to be constantly on the alert for signs of destructive patterns and to act quickly to alter them. Developing the ability to recognize protracted, destructive spirals is a key conflict management skill because such insight is the first step in taking some con- trol over the conflict. People in conflict must be aware of concrete symptoms that signal the possible onset of escalation or avoidance.

Table 1.1 summarizes several symptoms of when a conflict is heading toward destructive escalation or avoidance. The mere appearance of any symp- tom should not be an automatic cause for concern. Productive conflict interaction can pass through periods of escalation, avoidance, constructive work, and relax- ation. Cycles only become threatening when they are repetitive and preempt other responses.

TABLE 1.1   Interaction Symptoms of Escalation or Avoidance Cycles

Symptoms of Avoidance	Symptoms of Escalation
Marked decrease in the parties' commitment to solving the problem ("Why would we care?")	An issue takes much longer to deal with than was anticipated
Quick acceptance of a suggested solution	Parties repeatedly offer the same argument in support of a position
Parties stop themselves from raising controversial aspects of an issue	Parties overinflate the consequences of not reaching agreement
People "tune out" of the interaction	Threats are used to win arguments
Unresolved issues keep emerging in the same or different form	Mounting tension is felt
Discussion centers on a safe aspect of a broader and more explosive issue	The parties get nowhere but seem to be working feverishly
Little sharing of information	Name-calling and personal arguments are used
Outspoken people are notably quiet	Immediate polarization on issues or the emergence of coalitions
No plans are made to implement a chosen solution	Hostile eye gaze or less-direct eye contact between parties
No evaluation is made of evidence that is offered in support of claims	Sarcastic laughter or humor used as a form of tension release
	Heated disagreements seem pointless or are about trivial issues

Once a destructive cycle has been recognized, parties (or third parties) can intervene to break the cycle. The previous section mentioned some measures, and we will explore these and other interventions throughout the remainder of this book. Countermeasures against destructive cycles need not be formal or particularly systematic. Simply making a surprising comment can jolt a conflict out of destructive cycles. We recall a group member who recognized a fight developing and suddenly said, "Are we having fun yet?" This cliché got others to laugh at themselves, defusing the situation.

Tacking Against the Wind

Effective conflict management is much like tacking a sailboat to move upstream against an unfavorable wind. A sailor wishing to move her boat against the wind can do so by directing the boat at an angle, back and forth across the water, taking advantage of the fact that the sails can capture some force from the opposing wind if they are set at an angle to it, as illustrated in Figure 1.2. In the same way, the tensions introduced by the danger points of escalation and avoidance may provide useful forces to move the conflict in productive directions, because they "jar loose"

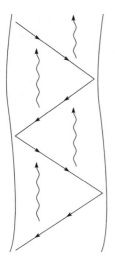

FIGURE 1.2   Tacking Against the Wind

parties' assumptions that things are going well and encourage them to realize that others may have opinions/needs that differ from their own. Even though tacking a sailboat takes time and does not seem as direct as moving straight to one's destination, it is in fact the only choice we have when we want to steer our ship in a productive direction. There is no way to get a sailboat to go against the wind without tacking, and there is no way to work through a conflict without braving the balance between rampant escalation and stubborn avoidance.

In performing this balancing act, it is important to manage conflict interaction effectively. This is no easy task because, as noted in the introduction, interaction often seems to have a "mind of its own." It seems to be driven by forces beyond our control, and sometimes may even seem incoherent and uncontrollable. This encourages people to ignore the give-and-take of interaction and rely instead on generalizations or rules of thumb. For instance, there is a temptation to say "she is just a difficult person to get along with" as a way of explaining why discussions with Joelle always seem to end in conflicts. Of course, this ignores the fact that Joelle might be reacting to our rather aggressive presentation of our position. Alternatively, we might assume that "the best way to win our position is to never disclose it, but rather to find out the others' position and try to exploit any weaknesses." This rule of thumb eliminates the need to make sense of an evolving situation because we have decided to do the same thing no matter what the other party does. However, this inflexible approach may discourage a cooperative party and lead her to adopt a competitive stance in the face of manipulation. It is important to avoid these easy paths and to recognize that the key to conflict management is understanding conflict interaction and taking appropriate measures to redirect it in positive directions.

It is easy to say this, but now how do we go about doing it? There is no simple answer to this challenge. However, starting about fifty years ago scholars in sociology, social psychology, communication, conflict studies, labor relations, and other fields began to untangle the puzzle that is human interaction. Our knowledge has grown rapidly, increasingly so over the past thirty years, to the point where we can understand some of the general contours and also specific dynamics of human interaction. We are not yet at a point where we can predict it with any certainty, and it may be impossible to get to such a point. Additionally, many aspects of interaction remain uncharted territory—unknown, unmapped, unstudied. But some general principles have emerged, and we center this book on them.

Properties of Conflict Interaction

Four properties of conflict interaction offer keys to understanding the development and consequences of conflicts:

1. Conflict is constituted and sustained by moves and countermoves during interaction.
2. Patterns of behavior in conflict tend to perpetuate themselves.
3. Conflict interaction is shaped by the culture and climate of the situation.
4. Conflict interaction is influenced by and in turn affects relationships.

If we "unpack" these simple statements, we discover a number of important points about conflict.

We introduced the idea of conflict as interaction at the beginning of this book, and Property 1 expands this idea by distinguishing moves and countermoves as the basic features of interaction. This suggests that it will be useful to explore the range of tactics that can be used to enact conflicts. Property 1 also highlights the importance of power in conflict, because moves and countermoves depend on power. As we will see, power is often regarded as a possession or personal characteristic; for example, it is common to use phrases like "he or she is powerful." In Chapter 4, however, we explain that power is created and sustained during interaction. So moves and countermoves play an important role in determining a person's power in a given situation.

Property 2 expands on the previous section to focus on the momentum that conflicts develop. Sometimes momentum contributes to destructive cycles of avoidance or escalation, but in other cases momentum for productive conflict management develops. Momentum depends on psychological and behavioral dynamics that parties are often unaware of. We will cover several in discussions of psychodynamic theory, trained incapacities, attributions, game theory, and framing. With so many factors, no wonder conflicts sometimes escape our control!

The third property addresses how the cultural backgrounds of people and the immediate character of the situation shape conflict interaction. Both of these factors create the general character of the conflict overall. Cultural orientation is a well-known influence on how people act and respond during conflict. Several broad cultural patterns are discussed under this property. The unfolding situation also has a character—generally known as climate—that gives rise to patterns of conflict interaction. Climate refers to the general interpretations that parties attach to a situation, such as whether it is competitive or threatening. In Chapter 6, we discuss how these interpretations develop and their consequences for conflicts. Important aspects of the situation that contribute to climate are the incentives it provides for cooperation and competition (also discussed under game theory) and the stereotypes parties hold about one another. We will focus on how these channel the interaction that creates and sustains climate.

Property 4 directs our attention to relationships. The prior history of the relationships among parties has a powerful influence on conflict. *Face,* which refers to the side of themselves that people try to present in public, is particularly important in conflict. Interactions go differently for those perceived to be honorable, competent, or intelligent than it does for those perceived to be untrustworthy, incompetent, or simple-minded. During conflicts people often challenge face and the drive to maintain or restore it can dominate all other concerns. In Chapter 5, we explore how face and other relational concerns influence conflicts. Other relational aspects of conflict will be discussed in terms of their consequences for conflict.

The four properties of conflict interaction suggest points at which conflicts can be influenced by judicious interventions. Many of these interventions can be undertaken by the parties themselves. In some cases, it may be more effective for third-parties—facilitators, mediators, arbitrators, even therapists and lawyers—to intervene. We will discuss interventions throughout this book. Chapters 4 through 7 have special sections on intervention, and Chapter 8 focuses on methods for managing conflict. Chapter 9 considers how third-parties can help manage conflicts.

Now let us turn to each of the four properties, with special emphasis on the role of communication.

Property 1: Conflict is constituted and sustained by moves and countermoves during interaction.

Conflicts emerge as a series of actions and reactions. The "He did X and then she said Y and then he said Z and then . . ." formula is often used to explain a quarrel. When incompatibilities arise, people try to cope with them, and the way in which their actions mesh plays an important role in the direction the conflict takes. Moves and countermoves depend on participants' ability and willingness to exert power. *Power* can be defined as the capacity to act effectively. Power sometimes takes the form of outward strength, status, money, or allies, but these are only the most obvious sources of power. There are many other sources, such as time, attractiveness, and persuasive ability that operate in a much more subtle fashion.

In the Women's Hotline (Case I.1), for example, Diane might have used the other workers' guilt to try to get her way, and the workers did use their seniority and familiarity with their jobs to pass judgment on her by drafting a list of worker responsibilities. In both cases, power operates much more subtly and indirectly than is commonly assumed. More generally, a person is powerful when he or she has the resources to act and to influence others and the skills to do this effectively (Deutsch 1973). The third party in the hotline case provides a good example of the effective use of power: She had certain resources to influence the group—experience with other conflicts and knowledge about how to work with groups—and made skillful use of them to move both sides toward a solution.

Participants' attempts to mobilize and apply power can drastically shift the direction conflict takes. As possible solutions to the conflict are considered, the parties learn how much power each is willing to use to encourage or to prevent the adoption of various alternatives. This is critical in the definition of conflict issues and solutions because it signals how important the issue is.

The balance of power often tips the scale in a productive or destructive direction. If a party perceives that he or she can dominate others, there is little incentive to compromise. A dominant party can get whatever he or she wants, at least in the short run, and negotiation only invites others to cut into the party's solution. In the same vein, feeling powerless can sap parties' resolve and cause them to appease more powerful individuals. Of course, this method often encourages powerful people to be more demanding. Only when all participants have at least some power is the conflict likely to move in a productive direction. At the Women's Hotline, the third party was called in only after both sides, Diane and the workers, had played their first "trumps"—the workers by informing Diane of her responsibilities, and Diane by filing a grievance. The use of power could have prompted additional moves and countermoves: Rather than calling in a third party, both sides could have continued to try to force each other to yield, and the conflict could have continued escalating. In this case, however, the two sides perceived each other's power and, because they wanted the hotline to survive, backed off. As risky as this process of balancing power is, many social scientists have come to the conclusion that it is a necessary condition for constructive conflict resolution (Deutsch 1973; Folberg and Taylor 1984; Pruitt and Rubin 1986).

Power often begets power. Those who have resources and the skills to use them wisely can use them in such a way that their power increases and reinforces itself. Those with little power find it difficult to assert themselves and to build a stronger base for the future. Yet, for conflicts to maintain a constructive direction, there should be a balance of power. This requires members to reverse the usual flow: The weaker parties must build their power; the stronger ones must share theirs, or at least not use it to force or dominate the weaker ones. As shown in Chapter 4, managing this reversal is both tricky and risky. It is tricky because power is difficult to identify, and sharing power may run up against members' natural inclinations. It is risky because the process of increasing some parties' power and decreasing or suspending others' is a sensitive operation and can precipitate even sharper conflicts.

Regardless of how unpleasant or risky it may be to deal with power, power is a fact of life in conflicts (Berger 1994). Ignoring it or pretending power differences do not exist is a sure formula for failure because power is operating and will direct the moves and countermoves in the conflict. Power is one of the strongest influences on conflict. Power as a force that influences conflict moves and conflict interactions is discussed in detail in Chapters 4 and 7.

Property 2: Patterns of behavior in conflicts tend to perpetuate themselves.

Almost inevitably, conflict interaction gains a momentum or life of its own. It tends toward repetitive cycles. This tendency is present in all types of human interaction. Any message is based on some, perhaps only barely conscious, assumption about how it will be received. Each assumption or prediction about the reaction is based on an estimate, a best guess, about the other person or social unit as a whole. The choice of message anticipates and reflects the response it seeks, and thus promotes the reaction included in its construction. A predictable sequence of act–response–counterresponse gets established quickly in conflict interaction because each message in the sequence helps to elicit the response it receives.

This tendency toward self-perpetuation is encouraged and reinforced by its own utility. People in conflict find it useful to "know what to expect." Any basis of predictability is more assuring than not knowing what the group will do next. One can prepare counterresponses and strategies during a conflict if one can predict reactions to one's own statements. For this reason, people are often willing to make assumptions about the way others will act before any move is made (Kriesberg 1973; Sillars 1980b). They therefore run the risk of eliciting the response they assume will occur. As discussed earlier, anticipating that someone will react with a certain style, like a tough battler, can encourage a battling response. It becomes the appropriate response, given the previous comment. Because all parties can find this predictability useful in preparing their own responses, the cycle feeds on itself. In some cases, a cycle may be helpful: Cycles can be productive if they include a periodic check for possible inflexibility or if they lead to success on "easy" issues, which then carries over to more difficult disputes (Karrass 1970). In many other cases, however, the cycles become the basis for inflexibility and lead to uncontrolled destructive interaction.

Diverse context research suggests that conflict interaction is self-perpetuating. Studies comparing distressed and nondistressed intimate couples, for example, have found differences in how repetitive the communication patterns are for these couples (Gottman 1979; Ting-Toomey 1983). Couples in the more distressed conflict relationships tend to interact in highly structured ways—their interaction tends to be built on more repetitive cycles and exchanges. This repetition is symptomatic of self-perpetuating interaction in which one party's move elicits a highly predictable response that in turn produces a predictable counterresponse. In addition, these studies reveal the nature of these repetitive cycles. In distressed intimate couples, parties tend to exchange hostile and confrontive remarks so that common exchanges include one person complaining or confronting while the other defends (Ting-Toomey 1983; Gaelick, Bodenhausen, and Wyer 1985). In family conflict, there is a tendency for opposition statements to continue across speakers in successive turns at talking (Vuchinich 1984, 1986). Studies of children's conflicts suggest that an opposition move made by one child is likely to elicit a sequence of oppositional moves (Eisenberg and Garvey 1981; Goodwin 1982). These repetitive cycles of hostile or negative actions and responses have also been found to characterize labor-management negotiations (Putnam and Jones 1982b; Pruitt and Carnevale 1993).

In both intimate and labor-management contexts, cycles of positive responses, such as supportive statements and agreements, have also been found to occur, usually when the conflict has taken a fundamental turn toward a constructive direction (Donohue, Diez, and Hamilton 1984; Gaelick et al. 1985).

The self-perpetuating nature of conflict suggests that when conflict interaction is examined closely, on a turn-by-turn basis, it is often not resolved in any real sense (Vuchinich 1984). Conflict often unfolds in waves of somewhat repetitive interaction sequences and moves that start and stop in a variety of ways. Repetitive sequences can end, for example, with topic switches, withdrawals, or standoffs, and may resurface later and end differently the next time the repetitive sequence occurs (Vuchinich 1990).

The self-perpetuating nature of conflict interaction makes conflict highly sensitive to any force that prevents parties from stopping or reversing a conflict cycle. For this reason, the working habits that people adopt can be influential in moving conflict interaction in either destructive or constructive directions. These working habits can blind parties to what is happening in a conflict when they emerge as trained incapacities, as we will discuss in Chapter 8.

Property 3: Conflict interaction is shaped by the culture and climate of the situation.

Although shouting matches or heated discussions are often the first images that come to mind when we think of conflict, our conception argues for a more broadly based understanding of conflict interaction. Active suppression of issues, an exchange over who is an authority on some issue, a round of comments explaining positions to a third party, a discussion of the decision-making procedures that the group should adopt, or a series of comments that back the group away from a stand so that one member is allowed to "win" a point are all forms of conflict interaction as well. Conflict interaction is *any exchange* of messages that represents an attempt by participants to address some incompatibility.

Although conflicts can emerge and be played out in many forms, they are not chaotic or anarchic. As confused and irrational as the conflict situation may seem to participants and observers, nearly every conflict exhibits definite themes that lend coherence to the exchanges and make certain forms of interaction more likely to emerge than others (Kolb and Bartunek 1992). Even in a brutal, cutting free-for-all, a competitive coherence can be discerned. These themes, and the general character of the conflict, are created by the culture and climate of the situation. *Culture* is the more global influence on people's conflict behaviors while *climate* emerges from the more immediate situation itself.

Culture is an important influence on how people think across situations; we are not born knowing how to think. Patterns of thinking and reasoning are learned as we mature, and the culture we are born into, which favors certain ways of thinking over others, is the primary source of these patterns (Hofstede 1991). Glen (1981) distinguished different cultures based on their typical thought patterns and these cultural differences have been linked to different ways of responding to conflicts. Table 1.2 briefly describes the main types of cultures Glen identified.

Kozan (1997) has identified three different conflict models that stem from the different ways of thinking in diverse cultures. His framework suggests that people with different cultural backgrounds will react differently to conflict: They will have different attitudes toward conflict, different expectations about appropriate conflict behavior, as well as different approaches to managing conflict. Kozan's three cultural models—the harmony model, the confrontational model, and the regulative model—are summarized in Table 1.3. The harmony model tends to emerge in associative cultures, while the confrontational and regulative models tend to emerge in abstractive cultures (Table 1.2). These culturally based models of conflict have a significant impact on how conflict interaction unfolds. Differences in conflict styles across cultures have been found in a variety of cross-cultural settings (Zupnik 2000; Tingley 2001; Ellis and Maoz 2002).

Although culture is more global, climate emerges from the enduring and momentary pursuits of people in relationships. It is a generalized composite of properties that arise from and guide people's interactions (Lewin 1951; Tagiuri 1968). The climate provides important information to the parties about how conflict

TABLE 1.2   Types of Cultures

Associative Culture

- Reliance on a particular way of thinking—requires close reading of immediate and past contexts
- People are keenly aware of obligations to others
- People value the group over the individual (collectivist)
- People are highly dependent on others in the immediate situation
- Communication is not always open and explicit
- Meanings have to be inferred from contextual cues

Abstractive Culture

- Reliance on a universal way of thinking—knowledge can be shared across large groups
- People value assertion of self over group commitment (individualism)
- Communication is precise and explicit
- Meanings are assumed to be stated openly and interpretations rely less on contextual cues

TABLE 1.3   Cultural Models of Conflict and Their Characteristics

Harmony Model

- Emphasizes maintaining smooth relationships
- Tendency to prevent or avoid open expression of conflict
- Reliance on cooperativeness and connection
- Lack of self-assertion
- Restriction on negative emotional displays
- Emphasis on use of third parties who are from the community
- Preservation of honor, pride, and face
- Strives for long-term, stable outcomes to a conflict

Confrontational Model

- Emphasizes the aggressive pursuit of individual goals
- Conflicts are valued because they can address the needs of individuals
- Less emphasis on relationship or group preservation
- Tendency to open up conflict and to engage in negotiations
- Emotions are experienced intensely and expressed openly
- Use of third parties to help facilitate the negotiation between parties
- Interventions strive for short-term gains

Regulative Model

- Emphasizes settling conflict through application of principles
- Reliance on codes, rules, and laws to address differences or issues
- Personal aspects of the conflicts tend to be underplayed or ignored
- Emotions are underplayed and are seen as less relevant to the conflict resolution process
- Third parties are usually people in ascribed roles who have the power to apply rules to specific conflict situations
- Procedural justice is an important element of conflict resolution process
- Short-term resolutions are valued over long-term concerns

is likely to be handled; more specifically, it sets expectations about what participants can safely say, establishes the emotional tenor of the interaction, influences how much tolerance for disagreement seems possible, and determines whether the emergence of any conflict will be an immediate threat to personal relationships. A change in climate most often means a noticeable difference in the way parties interact. Consider the illustration of a shift in climate and its influence on interaction (Case 1.1).

CASE **1.1**

The Columnist's Brown Bag

Imagine yourself as a student attending this seminar: How would you have recognized the change in climate?

An editorial columnist from the *New York Times* was asked to participate in one of a series of brown-bag discussions that a university's department of journalism hosted over the course of a semester. Faculty, students, and journalists from the community attended these noon-hour seminars. Although some speakers in this series of talks gave formal presentations and then left a few minutes for questions afterward, this columnist said, at the outset of his talk, that although he had prepared comments on a number of different topics he would rather spend the entire hour responding to questions.

Within a few minutes after the session began, a climate of open interaction was established in this group of twelve people. The speaker responded to a wide range of questions. People asked about national economic policy, press coverage of news events, politically based indictments of the press, and the use and misuse of the term "the media." Despite the potentially controversial nature of many of these issues, there was an expectation set in the group that the questions would seek information or opinions from the columnist, who had more than thirty years of experience on the prestigious newspaper. In his first answers, the speaker told amusing anecdotes, gave background information about recent news events, and offered unmuted commentary on key issues. The atmosphere was relaxed, almost reverent, and the speaker himself continued to eat his brown-bag lunch as he spoke.

During the last ten minutes of the question-and-answer discussion, there was a sudden shift in climate that brought about a remarkable change in the interaction. A student sitting in the back of the room sat up and leaned forward in his chair. Speaking more loudly than anyone else during the previous forty-five minutes, he said he had a question about editorial responsibility. He said that the *Times* ran a story about atrocities in an African tribe but the paper made no editorial comment on the killings until three years after they had occurred. He wanted to know if the paper had an editorial responsibility to comment on this event at the time it happened. It soon became clear that both the student asking the question and the columnist knew, as the question was asked, that American arms had been used in the killings. The student did not, however, explicitly mention this when he asked the question.

Almost immediately, a journalism professor, who had introduced the speaker and was instrumental in getting him to visit the campus, defended the paper's policy before the guest speaker had a chance to respond. Neither this professor nor anyone else in the group had previously interrupted the question–answer–question format that the group had adopted; no one had previously made a comment in response to any other person's question. The professor was visibly upset by the student's question, said he had worked on the paper himself at the time the story broke, and contended that the editorial decision was justified because insufficient information was available about the incident for quite some time. The student responded with a pointed declaration of mistrust in the paper. The columnist then took the floor and commented that, although the paper had made several editorial blunders during the years he worked at the paper, he could not accept the accusation that editorial comments were withheld because U.S. arms were involved. There were, he said, too many editorials to the contrary in the paper.

As this exchange occurred, people sitting in the room indicated their discomfort. Some people turned to look back at the person who

(continued)

CASE **1.1**   Continued

was asking the questions, some side comments were made, and a few people smiled uncomfortably at each other. A second professor interrupted the columnist and said, in a somewhat self-conscious tone of voice, "we had better leave the seminar room because another class has to meet in it soon."

Discussion Questions

■ *In what ways did the shift in climate affect the interaction in this seminar?*

■ *Suppose the seminar had begun with a confrontational climate. What kind of event might cause the climate to shift toward a more relaxed direction?*

To understand how conflict interaction unfolds, it is necessary to explore how climates are created and changed and the effect this has on the direction of conflicts. The climate of the journalism seminar shifted in midstream, with profound effects on the interaction. With the student's question and the first response it received, the previously established climate in the group changed. The expectation that questions would be asked to seek information or a desired opinion from the speaker was overturned by the student's entry into the exchange. The student sought a defense of the paper's policy and assumed that the speaker would take a stand supporting the paper. The rest of the group may have resented the attempt to change the tone of the interaction, yet in some ways they facilitated the change by disrupting the seminar's format themselves. The shift in climate resulted in new ways of interacting for everyone in attendance. Climate as a force that influences conflict interaction is examined more closely in Chapter 6.

Property 4: Conflict interaction is influenced by and in turn affects relationships.

It is easy to focus mainly on the substantive issues in a conflict, on the problem and its proposed solutions. In fact, centering only on issues and ignoring the other, "emotional" aspects of a conflict has sometimes been recommended as the best way to deal with conflicts. However, focusing on the "bare facts" of the case can cause one to overlook the important effects. Conflicts are often emotionally laden and tense. This is in part because participants are concerned about getting (or not getting) what they want, but it also stems from the implications the conflict has for one party's present and future relationship to the other party.

The Women's Hotline situation (Case I.1) had the potential to drastically alter the relationships in the group. Until the staff openly challenged Diane for not living up to her responsibilities, she believed she was doing adequate work and was regarded as an equal by the other workers. The reprimand called her competence and responsibility into question, and she realized that others felt she was not on an equal footing. Her attitudes and assumptions about her relationship with the other workers were challenged, causing her a great deal of self-doubt and soul-searching, as well as stimulating her angry retaliation against the center. The workers' judgment of Diane also affected their attitudes and assumptions about her. Coming to the conclusion that Diane was slacking off generated distrust for her in the minds of the other staff members. It also made her an object of anger, and some admitted a tendency to want to "gunnysack"; that is, pile up a long list of problems with Diane and then attack her with it. Luckily, this never happened, and the third party was able to restore some trust and encourage a more open and understanding approach among the parties.

This case illustrates two levels operating in all communication: every message conveys not only substantive content but also information about the relationship of the speaker to the hearer (Bateson 1958; Watzlawick et al. 1967). If Diane angrily says, "I don't deserve this reprimand. I'm filing a grievance!" to her co-workers, her statements convey two levels of meaning. First, and most obvious, is the information that she is angry and is filing a grievance to challenge the reprimand, a countermove in the conflict. But second, Diane's message also carries the information that she believes her relationship with the workers has deteriorated to the point that she must file a formal grievance: It redefines the relationship between Diane and her co-workers. Even in formal negotiation contexts, verbal and nonverbal cues carry relational information that has significant impact on the relationship between negotiating parties (Donohue, Diez, and Stahle 1983).

This relational aspect of communication is critical because it affects both present and future interaction. It affects present interaction because people often respond to relational messages immediately and emotionally. If someone insults us, we may become angry and want to retaliate. If someone implies that our friendship is in jeopardy because of an argument, we may back down and become conciliatory. However, relational communication has its most profound effects through influencing future interaction. How people interact in conflicts is colored by their assessments of others—judgments about things such as others' trustworthiness, intentions (good or bad), and determination to win. These assessments bear directly on the relational aspects of communication and, because of this, people often try to project a certain image in order to shape others' assumptions about their relationship (Canary and Spitzberg 1989, 1990). For example, one person may act very defiant and angry to project an image of cold determination that tells the other, "Our relationship is not that important to me, as long as I get what I want." If this projection is successful, the second person may back down, believing the first person has no regard for him or her and will go to any lengths to win. Of course, this tactic could also backfire and make the second person resentful and defiant because the first seems cold and ruthless. Attempts at managing image and relationships prompt many moves and countermoves in conflict.

As important as relational management is in conflicts, it is not surprising that it plays a critical role in generating the direction conflicts take. *Face-saving,* people's attempts to protect or repair their images to others, has great potential to send conflicts into destructive spirals. One particularly dangerous form of face-saving stems from people's fear of losing ground in an exchange (Brown 1977). People in conflict often believe that if they move from a stated position or back away from a set of demands, they will appear weak or vulnerable in the eyes of the group. This concern for face—a concern for how one appears to others during the conflict interaction and the effects this will have on future relationships—can encourage people to keep arguing for a position even though they no longer believe in it or to back down because they recognize it is not contributing to a workable resolution to the conflict.

A second form of face-saving can prompt groups to continually ignore or avoid an important conflict issue. In relationships that have had a history of resolving conflicts in a friendly and cooperative manner, a concern for face may prevent parties from raising an issue that is far more threatening than any conflict the parties have previously addressed. People may believe that if they raise the issue, others will perceive it as an attempt to destroy the friendly relationships that have been cautiously protected and valued. This concern for face can prevent parties from calling in a third party when intervention is needed because they are reluctant to admit that they cannot resolve an issue on their own.

People's ability to define and maintain positive working relationships during conflict interaction depends heavily on how much concern they have for saving face as they approach the issue, take stands, and try to construct a resolution. For this reason, it is important to understand how people create pressures or incentives that heighten or lessen concern for saving face during conflict interaction (Cupach and Metts 1994). Face as a force in conflict interaction is examined in Chapter 5.

Summary and Review

What is effective conflict management?

Although there are a number of excellent models for conflict management, a particularly useful one distinguishes two phases in a well-managed conflict: a differentiation phase and an integration phase. When differentiation is handled effectively, parties are able to express their positions and emotions. At the end of effective differentiation, parties have come to understand others' positions (though they might not agree with them), to recognize the legitimacy of others, and to have the motivation to resolve the conflict. During effective integration, parties explore a range of solutions, develop a solution that meets the needs of all, and work out a means of implementing the resolution. In order to work through these two phases, parties have to prevent the uncontrolled avoidance and escalation cycles mentioned in the introduction. This requires them to perform a tricky balancing act in which they have to disagree, but cannot let the disagreements get too far out of control.

What are the dangers in differentiation?

Differentiation initially personalizes the conflict and often involves expression of intense and negative emotions. There is a danger that this can either infuriate parties, resulting in escalation, or terrify them, resulting in rigid avoidance. As long as parties can avoid rigid, inflexible, knee-jerk responses to differentiation, they have a good chance of navigating to an effective integration phase. As unpleasant as it may be, differentiation is important because it provides the basis for real solutions later on; if parties understand and respect their differences, they have the best chance of working toward a mutually beneficial solution.

What causes rigidity?

Anxieties about differences and emotions in conflicts, as well as the uncertainties about the outcome of the conflict, tend to produce rigid and inflexible behavior in conflicts.

How do parties manage the transition between differentiation and integration?

The transition is easier to make (a) if parties feel that they have been able to express their positions fully, (b) if they believe that they cannot get what they want by forcing the other or by avoiding conflict altogether, and (c) if they synchronize their cooperative initiatives. A third party is sometimes useful to help move the conflict from differentiation to integration.

How do we recognize when destructive cycles have set in?

Table 1.1 summarizes several symptoms or indicators of destructive conflict interaction. Signs of avoidance cycles include quick acceptance of proposals, low levels of involvement, and discussion of safe issues. Signs of escalation cycles include threats, difficulty in defining the issues, and sarcasm.

Are there some basic principles of interaction that can help in understanding conflict?

In this chapter, four basic properties of conflict interaction that highlight the role of communication in conflict are defined. Together these properties indicate a web of variables and processes that influence conflict.

What does it mean to say that conflict is constituted by moves and countermoves in interaction?

This property builds on the argument from the introduction. Conflicts exist not because of differences between parties, but because of the actions parties take in responding to their differences. These moves and countermoves create and define the conflict, and they sustain it insofar as parties continue to make more moves and countermoves. This underscores the importance of power in interpersonal conflicts because the types and effectiveness of moves depends on how skillfully parties use their power.

Why do patterns of behavior in conflicts perpetuate themselves?

Self-reinforcing cycles of conflict are fed by several processes and factors discussed in this chapter, including the desire to appear consistent to others, the interpersonal reflex, the escalation of commitment, predictions about others' responses, and behavior that elicits the expected response (creating self-fulfilling prophecies). These self-perpetuating patterns give conflicts a momentum of their own and may make it difficult to change the direction of conflicts.

How do cultural differences shape conflict interaction?

We distinguished two different cultural types and three different models of conflict based on these cultural differences. The harmony, confrontational, and regulative models of conflict entail different views of the purpose and nature of conflict, different behaviors appropriate to conflict, different conflict management styles, different uses for third parties, and different emphases on various conflict outcomes.

How does the situation influence conflict interaction?

Shared interpretations of the conflict situation have been termed the climate of conflict interaction. Climates are composed of generalized beliefs about the situation, including whether it calls for competition or cooperation and how safe it is on a psychological or emotional level. Climates are produced and sustained by interaction among the parties to the conflict and by other important actors in the situation.

What role do relationships play in conflict interaction?

Conflict obviously can have profound effects on relationships. How conflicts unfold also depends on prior relationships among the parties. A particularly important dimension of relationships in conflict is face—the image a person wants to present to others. Efforts to create and sustain positive face and to save face in response to perceived attacks can exert profound influence on conflicts.

Conclusion

This chapter focuses on four properties of conflict interaction. These properties draw a complex net of ideas, which will be explored in the remainder of this book. We will constantly return to the point that conflict interaction, deceptively simple on the surface, is actually quite complex and can only be understood by analyzing its flows and the forces that shape them. Conflict, like any other form of behavior, can only be understood at the level of concrete interaction where moves and countermoves take many forms and unfold in diverse episodes yet maintain some level of coherence, where interaction patterns tend to perpetuate themselves in destructive and constructive cycles, and where messages define and alter relationships among people.

The chapters of this book, of course, concern conflict, but they also concern change. Because conflicts are rooted in differences and incompatible interests, conflict always confronts participants with the possibility of change. Indeed, that differences arise at all is a flag indicating a need for adjustment in response to conflicts between members or a need to resolve an external problem. Once a conflict emerges, resolution of differences may require redefinition of policies or goals, reassignment of responsibilities, shifts in expectations for or of individuals, or even changes in the unit's power and status structures. Members' recognition of these possible changes guides the forms that conflict interaction takes.

The active suppression of issues, the positive or negative evaluation of possible solutions, and the clarification of differences are all forms of conflict interaction, which can be motivated and shaped by the participants' awareness of imminent change. In a very real sense, as a group manages its conflicts, so too does it deal with the need to change in response to its environment or people's needs. Some wise sage in the 1960s said that "not to change is to die." The same can almost be said for failure to work through conflict.

2 The Inner Experience of Conflict

Perspectivism and Conflict

A conflict can be viewed from many different angles, from many different perspectives. This book is guided by an idea commonly called perspectivism. *Perspectivism* posits that we can know no fact without interpretation, hold no claim of reality independent of belief. Perspectivism also holds that there are many ways of viewing a phenomenon, many angles that offer promise to the viewer. There is no best perspective, only a field of choices from which to select. A perspective colors one's world, guiding the search for answers, determining which questions are worth asking, evaluating what data are worth collecting.

Taking a perspective on conflict or any social phenomenon is much like adopting a style of painting. Through the years, painters have represented objects in very different styles of visual representation. Sometimes the same object—the Eiffel Tower, London Bridge, a garden, a bowl of fruit—has been painted in realistic, impressionistic, or cubist styles. Different styles reveal different features and aspects of these objects, much like perspectives reveal different aspects of the same social phenomenon.

Perspectivism maintains that one cannot view a phenomenon without relying on a catalog of assumptions that influence that view. Selecting a perspective, however, is not an irrevocable decision. Perspectivism also means believing in the value of multiple perspectives. After exhausting the potential of a particular perspective, it can be temporarily abandoned for another, allowing one to see dynamics and dimensions that were previously hidden. Although the choice of one's perspective is highly consequential, the standard of judgment is one of utility—of usefulness—not of right or wrong. A good perspective is one that enables the viewer to explain the product or process in question and act on that explanation. Perspectivism is best illustrated with an applied example.

Imagine that your interest in conflict processes was brought to the attention of a powerful friend who operates a midsized pharmaceutical company. After hearing you expostulate on the nature and dynamics of conflict processes, she requests that you assist with a problem in her organization that involves conflict. She explains that her company of 4,000 employees develops and markets drugs related to heart disease. The company has turned a profit for several years largely because of an aggressive promotions department and sales force. Until recently these two functions were housed in separate divisions, but last quarter promotions and sales were merged, creating a single unit. Since the integration of the divisions, conflict has been the order of the day. It seems every time she turns around she is asked to settle a dispute in the new "marketing" division. She characterizes the situation as involving open hostility and suspicion. This animosity is most apparent between managers but also occurs with frequency between managers and subordinates. She could understand the situation more easily if the split existed along former division lines, promotions versus sales, but in her view the conflict does not discriminate. Given your interest and expertise, she asks that you assess the conflict and offer recommendations as to how it should be managed or resolved.

Granted, this is a complex problem, one that requires more background and context for intelligent study. But for the purposes of our discussion, let us say you work with the facts at hand. Obviously, you cannot intervene until you can accurately assess the situation and understand the reasons for the conflict. In addition to determining the root causes of or contributors to the conflict, discerning the effects of the struggle is also paramount. After all, the conflict may be producing productive as well as destructive outcomes. So where do you start? Where do you search for reasons and outcomes? A series of choices is apparent.

Would you look to the history of the company as told by top managers for clues? Or would you interview workers in the division and collect their views and perceptions about the conflict? Would you examine interpersonal or group interaction between division workers? Or would you ask them to report about their feelings, thoughts, and emotions during such encounters? Would you collect recent communications, such as office memos, reports, letters? Or would you collect organizational culture artifacts such as employment contracts, bylaws, or policy statements? If you choose to talk to division employees, would you seek to uncover their values, beliefs, and attitudes? Or would their stories, myths, and metaphors be more attractive to you? The choices you make will reflect the premises you hold.

Making a reasonable assessment of a conflict is a rational task, one that requires a series of conscious decisions. The choice of which data are to be included in the analysis and which will be ignored or deemed impractical for study is called *punctuating the conflict*. Conflict is like a flowing river. One cannot enter or exit the river at more than a single location at any one time. What counts as the source of the river and its delta depends on the perspective and/or theory one uses. The only sure bet is that the punctuation decision of when to begin and end the assessment cannot be avoided. One must enter and exit the river—begin and end the analysis—to make an assessment. Because conclusions are drawn based on observation or learning, how a conflict is punctuated is highly consequential, shaping conclusions much more than one would readily admit. By making this choice an active and conscious decision, the observer can avoid missing relevant data or feeding the urge to continually collect more and more data before an assessment can be drawn. As noted, any assessment or explanation of conflict requires punctuation, and one's perspective guides this choice.

In sum, the assumptions you privilege and the premises you prefer form your perspective—form the lens through which you will view conflict. As the metaphor suggests, this lens colors your vision, framing what you will and will not see. Your perspective provides focus. It brings conflict processes into sharp relief, revealing what is relevant for study. All scholars and practitioners who study conflict processes must make similar choices. The substantive assumptions or premises from which one views conflict constitute that perspective.

The Role of Theories

If perspectives are the lenses through which we view conflict, then what are theories? Simply stated, a theory is an explanation of the relationship between elements or variables. Theories explain the workings of a phenomenon by operating within the confines of a perspective or common set of assumptions. Metaphorically speaking, a perspective is the larger and more general category—an umbrella of premises and assumptions under which a theory operates. Protected from the precipitation of competing viewpoints, a theory capitalizes on the clarity afforded by the perspective, further clarifying the social phenomenon of interest. By explaining the relationship between a particular set of elements, the perspective has been shown to be important; a theory enhances understanding.

For example, it is commonly asserted in the conflict styles literature that the nature of the relationship between parties in conflict influences the styles that those parties employ. In essence the claim is that people select conflict styles based on the nature of the relationship involved. In particular, researchers have found that subordinates in organizations use more nonconfrontational strategies and fewer competing styles than do superiors (Korabik, Baril, and Watson 1993; Putnam and Wilson 1982; Rahim 1983). So far, a relationship has been stated: one variable, conflict style, is influenced by a second variable, relationship type. The theoretical question that can be posed here is: why? One such explanation focuses on the subordinate in work relationships.

According to Musser's (1982) theory, subordinates actively select conflict styles based on the perceived likelihood that the style will invite reprisals from superiors. Subordinates consciously evaluate such risks and then select a style less likely to result in retribution. Although the ultimate reprisal is dismissal from the organization, other sanctions, such as being verbally abused or ignored by the boss, also weigh heavily in the decision. Musser suggests that subordinates will consider how protected they are from arbitrary actions by their superiors. Perceived congruence between the subordinates' and superiors' attitudes and beliefs strengthens this protection. When subordinates perceive little protection, they are expected to choose more accommodating styles, whereas more assertive strategies should be selected when the subordinate perceives high protection. The heart of the explanation rests on what it suggests about conflict styles. Conflict styles, as explained by the theory, are consciously and actively selected on the basis of perceptions regarding possible sanctions from the superior. Change the perceptions or the nature of the relationship and one can expect changes in conflict styles. Not surprisingly, several other theories have been offered to explain conflict styles used by subordinates.

As explanations, theories, like perspectives, are rarely right or wrong. Rather, they are best judged by their utility. Good theories are useful theories. They explain relationships so that we might describe them more fully, predict their recurring features, and control their dependent outcomes. Theories are the engine of inquiry and must stand the test of moving us forward, propelling us to see things we have not seen before. A common question that misses this point is: What is the best perspective or theory for examining conflict? This is analogous to a novice chess player asking a grand master, "What is the best chess move?" The grand master would shake her head and explain that it would depend entirely on the game. "Show me the board, my opponent's positions and style, and I will suggest a 'good' move." There is no best chess move, just as there is no best conflict perspective or theory. Instead, there are many options from which to choose, each of which has different uses, strengths, and weaknesses.

In this chapter and the next, we outline a number of perspectives that are helpful in understanding conflict interaction. This research has been conducted by communication scholars, psychologists, sociologists, political scientists, economists, and management scholars. All can illuminate conflict processes, though some are more squarely focused on interaction than others. This chapter reviews theories and bodies of research that focus on inner, mostly psychological, processes associated with conflict.

Here the focus is on psychological approaches to conflict, whereas the next chapter examines interactional approaches. Although the two approaches shade into each other—interaction, for instance, influences what people think and their internal reactions, whereas psychological processes shape how people act—they can be distinguished in terms of their goals and approach to explaining conflict.

By history and definition, psychology accentuates the workings of the mind and its influence on behavior. This perspective is not unconcerned with behavior and interaction but places a far greater emphasis on what goes on in the mind. This perspective privileges perceptions and the characteristics of people over the social construction of meanings and the features of messages in interaction.

According to the psychological perspective, humans are fundamentally goal-oriented beings whose behavior can best be explained by processes internal to the individual, such as perception, interpretation, reasoning, information processing, memory, and emotion. It also contends that because people are unique, they interpret and produce messages in unique ways. Therefore, the personal characteristics of communicators play a central role in understanding conflict.

The cognitive approach in psychology and related fields has received a great deal of attention in recent years, largely supplanting traditional theories such as psychodynamics. It relies on an analogy between human and computer, and uses mechanisms—encoding, decoding, planning, strategizing, remembering, and imagining—as the building blocks of theories. Cognitive constructs and representations, such as beliefs, schemata, attitudes, values, perceptions, and attributions, revealed by these mechanisms serve to cement the blocks.

Three research questions dominate the psychological perspective:

1. How do individuals and groups differ in their approach to conflict? For example, are males more aggressive than females? Do conservatives use more hardline bargaining tactics than do liberals? Are people high in dogmatism more likely to perceive incompatible goals than people low in dogmatism?
2. What traits best predict communication in conflict? The search for personality traits and enduring beliefs has produced a long list of predispositions to behave, including domineeringness, verbal aggressiveness, assertiveness, locus of control, dogmatism, authoritarianism, and many others.
3. How do cognitive processes influence communication in conflict? For example, what are deemed socially appropriate strategies for handling conflict? Which strategies are viewed as most effective? What perceptions escalate or mitigate conflict?

To show how the different theories account for conflict, they will be used to explain the same conflict case. As this chapter and the next unfold, attention will center on how theories within these perspectives may complement and inform each other or how they may compete, sometimes operating from contradictory assumptions or frameworks.

Classic and Contemporary Theories

In this chapter, we discuss five theories of the psychological dynamics in conflict. Some of these theories have been around a long time, while others are more recent developments. All describe important factors affecting how parties perceive, interpret, and react to conflicts. These processes are instrumental in generating conflict behavior and so provide one view of the causes and consequences of conflict interaction. Several of the theories discussed in this and the following chapters have spawned a great deal of research, and it would be impossible to summarize this comprehensively. Instead, the focus is on the basic assumptions of each of the views as they relate to conflict. In this book, we attempt to evoke the spirit of each position and present its key ideas on conflict. The basic ideas will be reevaluated throughout the book as the major forces that influence interaction in conflicts are examined.

After first discussing the nuts and bolts of each theory, we will then consider how the theory would explain Case 2.1, The Parking Lot Scuffle. The aim is to illustrate how each theory would punctuate the conflict. As we will see, various theories and perspectives require markedly different pictures of conflict, and each gives us a very different portrait of the central influences on conflict.

Before diving into the first theory, refer to Case 2.1, which reviews a conflict between two relative strangers as it was captured by an observer. This is the actual dialogue recorded between the parties; only phrases that some readers might find offensive have been changed.

CASE **2.1**

The Parking Lot Scuffle

Imagine yourself as Jay: What assumptions are you making about Tim as the conflict unfolds?

Jay drove to work alone every weekday. On this particular Monday morning, he arrived in his office parking lot a few minutes before nine o'clock. He had several thoughts on his mind and was not ready to see a small moped parked in his reserved spot. In fact, because the moped was set back deep in the spot and between cars, he could not see it until he made the turn into the space. Jay slammed on the brakes but failed to stop before hitting the scooter. The moped wobbled and then fell to the ground. Jay backed up his car and then placed the car in park. He got out and moved quickly to examine the results. He was surveying the damage done to his own bumper when a person, Tim, whom he recognized but could not name, approached him on the run. The following conversation ensued:

1 T: What's your problem? What the hell did you do to my Honda? I said, 'What did you do?'
2 J: I drove into my spot and didn't see your bike. What was it doing parked there?
3 T: Look, my tire's flat. I can't move the wheel. Crushed in and doesn't move.
4 J: I didn't see it until I was on top of it.
5 T: You are going to have to pay for this. I can't afford this.
6 J: What was it doing in a parking space?
7 T: What's your problem? It was parked. Look at the wheel. You came around pretty good.

8 J: Listen, this is my spot. I didn't see it, and it shouldn't have been there. You're lucky I stopped when I did. Look at my bumper. What was it doing there?
9 T: You ass. Who cares whose spot it is? Some jerk like you drives over my Honda and says, 'This is my spot.' I don't care who you are. You will fix my Honda!
10 J: You are the one with a problem. Do you work here?
11 T: What does that have to do with anything? Stop looking at your bumper; it looks fine. I want your driver's license and insurance.
12 J: Who in the hell do you think you are? *(Starts walking away.)*
13 T: You are not going anywhere. *(Grabs J's arm.)*
14 J: Let go of me. You are screwed. I'm calling the police. *(Turns to move toward the office.)*
15 *Tim slugs Jay from behind. The two scuffle for a few moments until others arrive to break them apart.*

Discussion Questions
- *Why did this conflict escalate to physical violence?*
- *What assumptions does your answer reveal?*
- *Consider the explanations that have been offered for well-known conflicts: the war in Iraq, the role of gay clergy in churches, the Ruby Ridge shootings, or others. What assumptions underlie these explanations?*

The Psychodynamic Perspective

Landmark advances in art and science often elicit as much criticism as praise. At the turn of the century, Freud's psychoanalytic theory altered people's vision of themselves as much as French impressionist art had altered people's view of the world. Yet both Freud and the Impressionists at different times became the target of significant criticism, and even ridicule. Freud and his followers (Freud 1900/1953, 1925, 1923/1947, 1949; Adler 1927; Sullivan 1953; Rapaport 1951; Erikson 1950) studied the dynamics of the human mind. They tried to explain how intrapersonal states and mental activities give rise to behavior in social contexts.

The psychodynamic perspective is as controversial as it is ambitious, and it has been attacked and ridiculed many times over the years. The crazy psychiatrist in movies and television is just one example of the harsh reception Freudian ideas have often received. It is certainly true that many psychoanalytic ideas defy common sense, and that many writers have used them in unjustifiable ways. However, at its core, the psychodynamic perspective provides important insights that have become part of our day-to-day thinking—concepts such as the unconscious, the ego, and the id, and processes such as repression and wish fulfillment. Several ideas from psychodynamics are fundamental to an understanding of conflict (Coser 1956).

Are Conflict Theories Just Common Sense?

A student conversing with his professor expressed his chagrin over an encounter he had with his employer. He approached his employer and explained the benefits of a particular conflict theory and how their broadcasting company might profit from it. However, his employer replied that such an approach was simply "common sense." Frustrated by this response, the student confronted his professor and asked how she would respond to this criticism. "After all," he said, "it is common sense, isn't it?" Rather than arguing that good theory has a duty to make sense once it is explained and that this parsimony is at the heart of science, the professor instead attempted an analogy between art and science. "Imagine the most beautiful painting you have ever seen," she instructed him. "Do you have one in your mind?" After a moment the student nodded and offered a painting by the French Impressionist Renoir, *Two Women Sitting*, as his choice. "What makes this painting so beautiful?" she asked probingly. The student gave an arresting answer.

"I'm not sure, really. The gentle colors. The expression and mood the artist captured. The lines and composition. Everything really. It's just beautiful."

The professor replied: "Now when you look at such a beautiful work, what do you think? In other words, why are you so astonished?"

The student thought long and hard and then looked up. "I think 'Of course.' Why couldn't I see this before the painting. All the lines and colors work perfectly, yet simply."

"Exactly!" cried the professor. "Renoir's painting, like any artistic endeavor that works, is common sense. Yet it took Renoir to show us. Even though less talented persons can copy this work, without Renoir and his painting that simplicity remains hidden, unarticulated. The same is true for theory. Good theory is deceptively beautiful theory. It seems simplicity itself once explained. The challenge for researchers is to create explanations that capture the complexity of human behavior while working from simple premises. Once articulated it is then the charge of the creative practitioner to extend this explanation to practice. Anyone can say 'Why, that's common sense,' just like anyone can trace a painting. But industrious minds either labor over better explanations or use existing theories to their own advantage."

The Hydraulic Model of Psychic Energy.   Freud and his followers portray the human mind as a reservoir of psychic energy that is channeled into various activities. This energy is the impulse behind all human activity and can be channeled into any number of different behaviors, ranging from positive pursuits such as work or raising family to destructive impulses such as vandalism or verbal attack. But, however it is channeled, it must be released. If it is not released through one channel, energy builds up pressure to be released through another—hence, the analogy to a system of hydraulic pipes in which turning off one outlet puts pressure on others.

The frustrations and uncertainties involved in conflict generate two powerful energy impulses—the *aggressive impulse* and *anxiety*—which the human mind must manage. The various ways in which these two forms of energy are channeled play a critical role in conflict interaction because they determine how people react to conflict. The psychodynamic perspective suggests that aggressive energy frequently arises from feelings of guilt, a lack of self-worth, or frustrations resulting from unfulfilled needs or thwarted desires. Often this aggression is directed at the actual source of the guilt or frustration, either back at oneself in the form of self-hate or in attacks on another person. However, self-hatred is very destructive and aggression toward others is discouraged either by moral codes or by the negative consequences that may occur. As a result, individuals find various conscious or unconscious ways to redirect their aggressive impulses.

One strategy is to attempt to suppress aggressive drives. Suppression is often done simply by not acknowledging the drives, but by undertaking a substitute activity. For example, an employee who is angry at his boss for denying him a promotion may simply suppress his anger and rechannel it into working even harder. The psychodynamic perspective stresses the benefits of suppression because it leads to less anxiety, guilt, or pain than attempting to fulfill a destructive or impossible need would. If drives are recognized explicitly, people must make some conscious response to them, and this can increase anxiety or frustration if they go unsatisfied. On the other hand, if a need is never acknowledged, it can be treated as if it were nonexistent, and the energy associated with the need can be diverted into other channels.

Despite its benefits, suppression can be a double-edged sword. Suppressing a need is frustrating, and if no acceptable substitute is found, frustration can fester and erupt more violently later on. Also, when goals are suppressed, people may still be driven by the need without realizing it. Actions may be guided by unconscious drives or needs, and these may direct behavior in destructive ways. Thus, the unpromoted employee might take out his anger unconsciously by missing the deadline for an important report his boss must give to her superiors. By making his boss look bad, he is getting back at her and assuaging his anger without admitting it. However, this action may have bad consequences for the employee too—he might lose his job if his boss believes him to be incompetent or vindictive. Facing up to anger directly may be unpleasant for both the employee and his boss, but in this case it would have been less unpleasant than the consequences of suppression.

A second strategy for dealing with aggression is to direct it toward more vulnerable or acceptable targets than the actual source of frustration. This process, *displacement,* is more likely when the true source of frustration is powerful or valued by the individual. Rather than suffering the consequences of an attack on the true source, people attribute their frustrations to other parties so that their impulses can be legitimized. They look for distinctions between themselves and others so that "enemy lines" can be drawn and targets for their aggressive urges can be made availiable. In his insightful book, *The Functions of Social Conflict,* Coser (1956) notes that the scapegoating of a few group members may be the result of displaced aggression. When members of a group face failure or a crisis, they are often reluctant to direct their anger toward the whole group because they fear rejection. To avoid losing the benefits of belonging to the group, they attack a weak member or an outsider. This process can be very destructive for the scapegoat, but it serves to keep the group together because it allows members to vent aggressive energy. Kenwyn Smith (1989) argues that organizational conflicts are often redirected to issues and people other than those who provoke the initial reaction.

Several conflict scholars suggest that patterns of cultural displacement are at the heart of some long-standing ethnic and international conflicts that have produced deep-seated hatred and violence. Volkan (1994) and Gaylin (2003) argue that long-standing ethnic conflicts that have spawned wars and genocide are sometimes the products of large groups of people dealing with the difficulties of their own demeaning existence. When perceived inadequacies and deficiencies weigh on the minds of large groups of individuals, cultures often find a means to displace the feelings of inadequacy by singling out others as enemies. Deep-seated ethnic hatred becomes a form of needed attachment to the defined enemies. Enemies need to be identified and opposed so that members of the deprived culture can externalize the source of the despair or misery they are experiencing. Certain leaders prey on this psychological tendency and create the possibility for an ethnic group to act on these forms of rationalized hatred. In this view of the emergence of ethnic conflict, the more "tangible" issues, such as territory, property, or others' resources, that emerge exacerbate conflicts and become a part of them, but the core cause of conflict is seen as psychological. Deep feelings of psychological insecurity produce and propel the need for constant definition of enemies—enemies that become targets of hatred and violence.

In addition to aggressive impulses, anxiety is also a by-product of conflicts. *Anxiety* is an internal state of tension that arises when someone perceives impending danger. It arises when people believe their drives or needs will be thwarted. Because people in conflicts anticipate interference from others, anxiety is likely to exist until there is some hope that all parties are trying to reach an agreement that meets each person's needs. If there is little reason for hope, or if members suspect that other parties do not see the needs as legitimate, then anxiety is likely to increase throughout the conflict.

The psychodynamic perspective also points to two other sources of anxiety. First, it suggests that anxiety may result from people's fears of their own impulses. As noted, many drives are self-destructive or counterproductive. When people suspect that they may be acting on one of these deep-rooted impulses, they become anxious. They may be unsure about the limits of their own behavior and try to determine those limits and prove themselves by testing how far they will go with risky or self-endangering behavior. For example, a receptionist in a law office inadvertently overheard an insulting remark one of the lawyers made about her. She was very angry and began to berate the lawyer with insulting jokes in retaliation. Despite the possibility that the lawyer might fire her, she continued joking for several days. When a friend in the office asked her why she took the chance, she commented that she *was* really afraid the lawyer would fire her; however, she had to prove to herself that she was not a "mouse," so she continued her counterattack. Persisting in and strengthening counterproductive responses is one way of reassuring oneself that they are permissible.

Anxiety also may result from the judgments people make about themselves. People have strong behavioral tendencies based on inner needs and impulses, but the superego gives them a capacity to make judgments about their behavior. Anxiety ensues when people are uncomfortable with their actions and realize that they would not ordinarily act this way. Even if they disapprove of their own behavior, people may continue with the actions because at the time there seems to be some legitimate or important reason. They may, for instance, be trying to save face or see themselves using a questionable means to achieve a worthwhile end. The anxiety people experience from engaging in disapproved behaviors may decrease the chances that they will stop these behaviors: Anxiety can cloud thinking and prevent people from understanding their own ambivalence.

Anxiety influences conflict interaction by causing members to be excessively rigid and inflexible. Hilgard and Bower (1966) draw on psychodynamic principles to help explain compulsive or repetitive tendencies that can take hold of people's actions, despite the fact that they carry destructive consequences. The mere repetition of unpleasant behaviors is often rewarding because it allows people to achieve a sense of mastery over some activity. Mastery in itself is rewarding, and, hence, behaviors continue even if they eventually prove to be destructive. Hilgard and Bower note that this sense of mastery, and the compulsive behaviors it promotes, may reduce anxiety. It allows people to cope with a trying situation and it leads to overlearned behaviors that are highly resistant to change. Although this account aims to explain neurotic forms of individual behavior, it can also explain the nature of interaction cycles. Counterproductive interaction patterns can persist because they provide a way to deal with the anxiety that conflict produces. As Chapter 1 showed, these cycles, fed by members' rigidity, can be very threatening.

The psychodynamic perspective has generated several important insights into conflict interaction. The most important achievement is its explanation of the role of impulses, particularly aggression and anxiety, in conflicts. The idea that impulses build up and can be redirected into other activities, including attacks on a third person, is crucial to most conflict theories. The psychodynamic perspective recognizes the importance of substitute activities, displacement, scapegoating, and inflexibility in conflicts, and it allows many subtle processes to be taken into account. The idea of unconscious or subconscious motivation is also important. People do not always understand what is driving their conflict behavior. Unconscious motivation underscores the importance of helping members gain insight into their behavior. Once members understand what is driving conflicts, they can begin to control them. As powerful and interesting as they are, psychodynamic notions by themselves offer only a partial picture of conflict interaction (see Case 2.2).

Verbal Aggressiveness

In an attempt to explain verbal attacks in interpersonal communication, Infante and colleagues (Infante and Wigley 1986; Infante 1987) have proposed a theory of verbal aggressiveness. The theory views aggression as a personality trait that represents a learned predisposition to act in response to certain cues that are reminiscent of the context in which the learning occurred. For example, the theory posits that a person who has seen family members aggressively confront, insult, and taunt each other during disagreements would learn this behavior as a response to disagreement. The person would be likely to engage in similar types of aggressive behavior when someone disagrees with him or her. The likelihood of this response

---

CASE **2.2**

Psychodynamic Theory and the Parking Lot Scuffle

The accident immediately creates an arousal in Jay and Tim. Both are frustrated and angry—Jay because of the damage to his car and Tim because his scooter is crushed. The energy from this frustration must be channeled, and it is directed against each other, the source of the frustration. At first, Jay attempts to keep the conflict in check by giving explanations ("I didn't see it") and invoking social norms ("What was it doing in a parking space?"). This represents the action of the superego, which tries to keep the expression of psychic energy within socially approved bounds. However, Tim's attacks make Jay angry, and he drops his efforts to resolve the conflict through "normal" channels. Escalation develops as the two exchange insults and aggressive energy feeds on itself, further escalating the conflict.

The conflict might have taken a different turn if the two had displaced the conflict by blaming the parking company for mislabeling the parking slots. This would have united them as they redirected their anger at a different target. Another way to manage the psychic energy in this conflict would have been to suppress it. For example, Jay might have toned down his anger and conversed calmly with Tim to help Tim temper his anger. Then the two might have worked out a mutually acceptable resolution. Another way to suppress the conflict would have been for Jay to walk off and find an attendant or police officer who could have taken down the details of the accident. The case would then be referred to their insurance companies. The two methods of suppressing the conflict would have had very different outcomes. The first approach dissipates the psychic energy associated with the dispute. The second, however, leaves this energy intact, and Tim would need to deal with it, either by displacing it or by finding some way to take it out on Jay, perhaps at a different time or place.

Discussion Question
- *How might anxiety have played a role in this conflict?*
- *What is a possible source of anxiety, according to psychodynamic theory?*

depends on (a) how similar the disagreement in question is to those the person experienced in his or her family, (b) how often the person was exposed to the aggressive response in his or her family, and (c) the degree to which rewarding or positive consequences were seen as a result of the aggressive behavior in the person's family.

The theory distinguishes between verbal attacks made against ideas or positions and verbal attacks made against self-concept. *Argument* involves presenting and defending positions on issues while attacking positions held by others. *Verbal aggression,* on the other hand, also includes attacks on another's self-concept. The aggressiveness trait is a predisposition to use personalized attacks in interpersonal communication.

For Infante, verbal aggressiveness is yoked to a trait he labels *argumentativeness.* The theory maintains that to understand aggression, the concept of argumentativeness must be understood. A person's level of argumentativeness is created by two competing motivational tendencies: the motivation to approach argumentative situations and the motivation to avoid such situations. Highly argumentative people perceive arguing as exciting and intellectually challenging, and they experience feelings of invigoration and satisfaction after engaging in arguments. People who are low in argumentativeness find arguments uncomfortable and unpleasant; they generally associate argument with personal suffering. Not surprisingly, these individuals attempt to avoid arguments or keep them from occurring. In the aftermath of arguments, they often feel anxious and unsettled.

As a result of approaching or avoiding argumentative situations, people develop or fail to develop the social skills needed to succeed so an argument is unavoidable. Highly argumentative people tend to be more skilled at stating controversies in propositional forms, determining the major issues of contention, discovering ways to support a position, and delivering arguments effectively. Among the many factors promoting aggressive behavior, it is skill proficiency that weds the traits of argumentativeness and verbal aggressiveness.

In a series of studies, Infante and colleagues demonstrated that people low in argumentativeness are more likely to resort to attacks against the self-concept of the other party. In other words, low argumentatives are high in verbal aggressiveness. In a manner of speaking, the two traits represent the opposite poles of a single skill continuum. Because individuals who avoid argumentative confrontations are often frustrated and lack the skills to succeed in such situations, they turn to verbal aggression.

Argumentative behavior is a positive trait that is distinct from verbally aggressive behavior. The advantages of argumentativeness are numerous. Research has shown that argumentative behavior is positively related to career satisfaction, career achievement, superior–subordinate relationship satisfaction, and other organizational outcomes (Infante and Gorden 1985).

Verbal aggressiveness is a negative trait that can produce a variety of effects in interpersonal communication, including conflict escalation, long-lasting damage to self-concepts, and deterioration of relationships. Infante believes that teaching people to value argument and providing them with the skills to succeed in argumentative situations will increase productivity in society and reduce the amount of verbally aggressive acts during interpersonal conflicts.

What do we do about verbal aggressiveness? Infante and colleagues propose using workshops and therapy sessions that would focus on making the person aware of his or her tendencies and on developing alternative behavior patterns through rehearsal and feedback. Such measures are time consuming and require the consent of the verbally aggressive person, so they may not be of much help when confronting such a person during a conflict. When in a conflict with a verbally aggressive person, it is important to maintain distance from the exchange and not be drawn into mudslinging and name-calling. This is difficult to do in the heat of the moment, but it is critical not to buy into the verbal aggressive's assumptions about what is appropriate behavior. Steadfast resistance to the attacks of the verbal aggression is also important, as it signals to him or her that the approach will not work in this case. It is also useful to bear in mind that, in a small proportion of cases, a frustrated aggressive person may resort to physical violence or other means of reprisal; we need to protect ourselves from this possibility (see Case 2.3).

Attribution Theory

In a number of studies, Sillars (1980a, 1980b, 1980c) and Sillars and Parry (1982) have applied attribution theory to the study of interpersonal conflict processes. Before describing how this theory has been applied in the conflict arena, the nature of attribution processes must be reviewed.

At the heart of attribution processes are two premises. First, people interpret behavior in terms of its causes. People naturally attribute characteristics, intentions, and attitudes to the people they encounter. Through this linking process, people attempt to organize and understand the world around them. Second, these causal explanations affect reactions to the judged behavior. Attributions enable actors to behave appropriately toward others in varying contexts.

When trying to make sense of others' behavior, we scrutinize environments, settings, and people's actions in search of reasons behind their actions. After discovering a plausible reason or cause, the other's behavior is attributed to one of two categories: (1) *dispositional factors* or (2) *situational factors*. For example, ability, mood, effort, and knowledge are dispositional causes arising from the individual, whereas task difficulty, interference, and luck are causes considered to be situational in nature stemming from external sources. In other words, all factors internal to the individual are considered dispositional, and all factors external to the individual are deemed situational. Two critical biases influence the attributions that actors make.

First, individuals commonly attribute others' behavior to dispositional factors and their own behavior to situational factors (Jones and Nisbett 1971; Ross 1977). This has been called the *fundamental attribution error,* and it is especially likely to occur when people believe others' behavior is intentional and goal-directed (Heider 1958). For example, when searching for reasons for our own behavior, such as nervousness in speaking situations, we commonly attribute our unease to the situation, but when confronted with a nervous speaker, we are more

CASE **2.3**

Verbal Aggressiveness Theory and the Parking Lot Scuffle

In light of Infante's work, Case 2.1 is a clear example of verbally aggressive behavior between two parties. What is at issue here is unclear. The parties jockey back and forth without clarifying the major issues of contention or making any arguments in support of a position. Instead, what transpires, from the view of verbal aggressiveness theory, is an exchange of highly personalized attacks—a volley of verbally aggressive remarks.

Tim initiates the conflict with an attack by immediately accusing Jay of aberrant behavior. Although the accusations are couched as questions, their intent is to point a finger at Jay and to put him on the defensive. Jay responds defensively but continues to walk a fine line between seeking information and making a counteraccusation. Finally, by line 10, after absorbing a nonstop barrage, Jay responds with a clearly aggressive remark. The result is an escalation of the conflict from verbal to physical aggression.

Although Tim is clearly more aggressive in this encounter, to be fair, both parties per-

sonalized the exchange throughout the conflict by using the imperative "you," which has the potential, according to the theory, to count as aggressive. Jay's line 14 comments cannot be taken as anything less than a personalized attack.

Presumably, this situation's factors, such as damage to the bike, possible status differences, and the workplace setting, prompted the aggressiveness trait in Tim, energizing his verbal behavior into attacks against Jay's self-concept. Given the number of aggressive remarks Tim makes, the theory would presuppose that he lacks the skills to argue. As a direct result of this deficiency and the unknown factors that serve as learning cues in the situation, Tim resorts to verbal aggression to resolve this dispute.

Discussion Question
- *Could verbal aggressiveness theory be used to explain "mudslinging" during election campaigns? Why or why not?*

---

apt to attribute his unease as a permanent feature of his character. The tendency for attributors to underestimate the influence of situational factors and overestimate dispositional factors in attributing others' behavior is remarkably strong. Research confirms that attributors infer attitudes from behaviors even when they know the behavior has been severely constrained (Snyder and Jones 1974; Miller 1976). This tendency even occurs when observers are told of this bias.

Second, to maintain and enhance self-esteem individuals often defensively attribute actions resulting in negative consequences to external forces and attribute positive consequences of the action to themselves (Bradley 1978; Zuckerman 1979; Snead and Ndede-Amadi 2002). This *self-serving bias* is especially likely to occur in situations involving success and failure. One educational study nicely illustrates this tendency: Based on test scores, math teachers either believed that a student improved or regressed in math skills (Beckman 1970). When asked to explain this difference, the teachers consistently attributed student improvement to their teaching prowess, but they attributed lower performance to factors related to the students. Predictably, students reached the opposite conclusion, attributing their success to internal factors and their failure to their teachers.

Attribution processes have important impacts on conflict interaction. In several studies, Sillars and his associates investigated three types of conflict management strategies that we have introduced and will continue to discuss throughout this book: integrative, avoidance, and distributive strategies. Sillars and his co-workers defined *integrative* strategies as messages designed to manage conflict openly through discussion while refraining from negative evaluations of the partner. These benevolent strategies place a premium on collaboration and joint problem solving. *Avoidance* strategies were defined as attempts to avoid direct discussion and management of the conflict. These strategies include statements that deny the presence of conflicts, shift the focus of conversations, and sidestep discussions about conflict through indirect or ambiguous talk. In moderation, avoidance can be a useful strategy (see Chapter 7); but taken to the extreme it can be destructive, as noted in Chapter 1. *Distributive* strategies include attempts to resolve the conflict in a zero-sum manner in which one party wins at the others' expense. Distributive messages often include negative evaluations of the partner, such as insults and direct criticism. Again, moderate use of distributive strategies can be productive, but excessive and rigid employment moves conflicts in negative directions, as we have seen in Chapter 1 and will develop further in Chapter 7.

Sillars has made a strong case that a party's attributions influence conflict interaction in at least three ways. First, due to the self-serving bias, people are more likely to attribute the negative effects of conflict to partners rather than to themselves. This tends to heighten resentment of others as the negative effects of conflict are felt, which in turn increases people's likelihood of responding distributively. Second, also due to the self-serving bias, people more often think that they use integrative strategies (which are perceived as socially desirable and positive) and others use distributive or avoidance tactics (Thomas and Pondy 1977). This can lead parties to mistakenly assume that they are doing more to resolve the conflict than others are.

Third, the fundamental attribution error heightens conflict by encouraging people to see others' behavior as planned and intentional and their own as driven by the situation. So when others act distributively, parties tend to view their actions as intentional aggression. On the other hand, if the party acts distributively toward others, there is a tendency for him or her to view this behavior as a natural response that is called for by the situation (such as the other's distributive behavior). The result is that parties see their own behavior as caused by others and others' behavior toward them as due to others' intentional plans. So they grow angry with others who are acting distributively or avoiding, but they rationalize their own aggression as a sensible response to others'. Clearly this sets up a vicious cycle whereby the party believes his or her distributive or avoidant behavior is justified by another's bad intentions.

One assumption underlying most attribution research is that the parties have common background knowledge. The fundamental attribution error and self-serving bias occur even in cases in which parties know each other quite well.

However, in situations where parties come from very different backgrounds or social groups, errors of attribution are much more likely to occur. Parties from different cultures, genders, or economic classes are particularly prone to misattributions and misinterpretations of one another. Because they have little common experience and no common set of beliefs and values, parties from different groups are prone to major misunderstandings that include, but go well beyond, the two errors we have discussed.

Research done by Weisinger and Salipante (1995) highlights serious misattributions between American and Japanese engineers who were asked to discuss the creation of joint business ventures. Parties on both sides tended to judge those of other cultures as less technically competent than they were due to different cultural norms about what competence was. Japanese engineers concluded that American engineers were not very good because they would not teach the Japanese engineers how they did certain types of analyses they employed. Such actions are valued in Japanese engineering culture because it emphasizes sharing responsibility and a team approach to design. However, in American engineering culture such actions signal disrespect for the professionalism of the other because fellow engineers are presumed to be competent due to their certification. There were also misunderstandings based on incorrect assumptions of shared "traits" of other cultures. For example, in a situation where Americans found out that the Japanese members of their joint venture had been solving joint venture problems among themselves parallel to work that the team was doing, the Americans attributed this to the "sneakiness" of the Japanese. Although cultures do share typical ways of thinking and doing things, there is little worth in such value-laden judgments. The Japanese were proceeding in a way common to their culture, thinking things through in a group, but the Americans, who valued open discussion and individual thinking, found this unacceptable and explained it in prejudicial terms. Note also that the Americans were engaging in the fundamental attribution error (attributing Japanese actions to bad intentions rather than to how they do things in Japanese culture), which compounded the misinterpretation.

Such misunderstandings are commonplace when people from different cultures and backgrounds come together. Attributions are made almost automatically, and generally people are not aware that their conclusions about others are based on faulty reasoning. When mistaken assumptions such as these drive behavior, they keep parties at a distance and feed negative conflict cycles.

Just as conflict is not static, the attributions made by individuals do not remain constant. As a conflict unfolds, attributions may change, thereby promoting use of different strategies. In this sense, the strategies a person uses are part of an emergent process mediated by ongoing reevaluation and attribution. Sillars and Parry (1982) found that as stress levels during conflict situations increase, other-directed blame due to the fundamental attribution error also rises. Spontaneous verbal statements that provide integrative understandings decrease as stress increases.

On the whole, research and theory in this area can be summarized by three propositions. First, people choose conflict resolution strategies based on the attributions they make regarding the cause of the conflict. Second, biases in the attribution process tend to encourage noncooperative modes of conflict. Third, the choice of conflict strategies influences the likelihood of conflict resolution and the degree of satisfaction with the relationship.

What do we do about attribution? Measures to enhance understanding and cut through mistaken assumptions are discussed throughout the remainder of the book. Chapter 8 discusses several structured problem-solving and communication methods that are particularly valuable in uncovering and correcting misunderstandings.

But one important step in limiting the impact of attributions on conflict is to remember that attribution errors occur all of the time and to be watchful for them. We have a tendency to make similar attributions in our conflict experiences across time, partners, and situations (Bono, Boles, Judge, and Lauver 2002). Research has shown that attributions, once made, are difficult to dismiss. In part this seems to be due to a lack of awareness of typical patterns. One useful corrective is to take such errors into account when we try to understand conflicts or disagreements. We need to remember that we are very likely to misinterpret the behavior of people from different cultures, genders, and socioeconomic backgrounds and that we should try to understand their behavior from their point of view. We are also more likely to find excuses for our behavior in the situation and have a tendency to blame others for their behavior. When this blaming occurs—when we assume others' behavior stems from their bad intentions toward us—we should remind ourselves that they may feel driven by the situation as well and look for ways to change the situation to encourage cooperation. Remember too that we tend to credit ourselves for good outcomes and blame others for bad ones. Hence, we should take a good hard look at our behavior to ensure that it is not causing the problem, and we should be more charitable toward others, not presume that they are creating the problems we face.

There is an important catch here, however. Despite the problems introduced by attribution biases, others may *really* have competitive intentions. If this is indeed the case, then our strategy in a conflict should be very different than if we are merely misunderstanding their behavior and assuming bad intentions when none exist. The challenge is sorting things out to determine which is the case. (See Case 2.4.)

Field Theory and the Concept of Climate

Kurt Lewin's field theory, developed in the 1950s, gave the concept of climate an important place in the study of conflict (Lewin 1951; Deutsch and Krauss 1965; Neel 1977). Lewin represented human behavior as movement through a life-space under the influence of various fields of force. The *life-space* consists of the person's conception of important goals and the barriers and requirements necessary to attain them. Figure 2.1 shows an illustrative space for a worker who wants to become chair of a committee. To reach this goal she must pass through or around four space regions, each of which corresponds to a requirement or barrier: region *a* representing the actions necessary to be elected to the committee; region *b* representing serving on the committee and becoming prominent; region *c* corresponding to opposition expected from Hank, a power-hungry member of the committee;

CASE **2.4**

Attribution Theory and the Parking Lot Scuffle

The parking lot scuffle exchange is characterized by conflict strategies that promote negative outcomes. Attribution theory describes Tim as using distributive tactics, including accusations, negative evaluations, insults, and physical aggression. Jay, on the other hand, is attempting to find answers to the dilemma, thereby engaging in a more integrative approach. Whether Jay's line 2 stands as a question or an accusation is open to debate. But given the context of Jay's justification in line 4, he deserves the benefit of the doubt.

If the attributional biases outlined in the theory are presumed true, then it can be surmised that Tim attributes both the accident and the escalating conflict that follows to Jay. Although we cannot say for sure, presumably Tim attributes these negative events to Jay's qualities as a person. This dispositional attribution casts Jay as generally uncaring of others' property and unwilling to accept responsibility. From this vantage, Jay is seen by Tim as the aggressor, one who deserves distributive tactics and violence.

According to the theory, Jay is undoubtedly guilty of the same attributional biases and probably is confused early in the encounter about why Tim takes such an aggressive posture. Toward the end of the episode, however, Jay may have concluded that Tim is generally an aggressive person and deserves the hostility he expressed in line 14.

Without knowing the perceptions of the parties, the attributions made can only be presumed. But attribution theory suggests that Tim's choice of distributive tactics, including the concluding violence, is a direct result of the attributions he made. Given Tim's distributive tactics, it is hard to imagine that a more positive outcome of this conflict was possible.

Discussion Questions

Consider a conflict wherein the strategies being used by one or both parties changed over the course of the interaction.

- *What prompted this change?*
- *Do you think that this change in strategy was due to a change in the attributions the parties were making?*

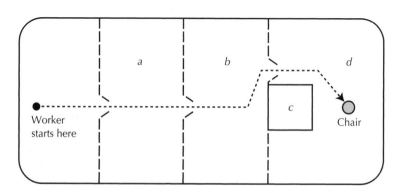

FIGURE 2.1   **A Sample Life-Space**

and region *d* representing the "politicking" needed to be elected chair of the committee. The dotted line represents one path the worker could take to achieve the chair. It includes cutting around Hank's opposition and therefore avoiding his field of force. This might be done by studiously avoiding Hank's challenges and instead concentrating on other members or issues.

A critical feature of the life-space is that it is determined by how the individual sees the world at a given time; the life-space is not determined objectively, but rather *psychologically*. Lewin and his co-workers identified a number of properties of life-spaces and of the forces that shape them. For the study of conflict, one of the most important properties is the overall character of the social field. As Lewin (1951, p. 241) puts it:

> To characterize properly the psychological field, one has to take into account such specific items as particular goals, stimuli, needs, social relations, as well as . . . more general characteristics of the field [such] as the *atmosphere* (for instance, the friendly, tense, or hostile atmosphere) or the amount of freedom. These characteristics of the field as a whole are as important in psychology as, for instance, the field of gravity for the explanation of events in classical physics. Psychological atmospheres are empirical realities and are scientifically describable facts.

Climate is a quality of the field "as a whole." As such it pervades all thought and action in the situation; it gives a "flavor"—for example, of warmth, safety, fear, or distrust—to everything that happens.

Perhaps the best analysis of the role of climate in conflict was provided by Morton Deutsch (1973), one of Lewin's students. In the opening pages of his discussion, Deutsch notes that "the processes of conflict resolution that are likely to be displayed will be strongly influenced by the context within which the conflict occurs" (p. 10). Deutsch argues that the critical contextual feature of conflict situations—the one that makes the difference between cooperative resolution and potentially destructive competition—is the type of *interdependence* established between the persons involved. For Deutsch, climates are defined by interdependence.

Deutsch defined two basic types of interdependence: (1) *promotive*, wherein the persons involved in the conflict perceive that gains by either one will promote gains by the other, while losses will promote losses; and (2) *contrient*, wherein everyone perceives that one's gain will be the other's loss. Perceptions of promotive interdependence, Deutsch argues, tend to promote cooperative interaction, whereas perceptions of contrient interdependence tend to produce competition.

Deutsch identifies several additional consequences of interaction occurring under promotive and contrient interdependence. Under promotive interdependence (cooperative climates), people will stress mutual interests and coordinated division of labor, exhibit trusting and friendly attitudes, perceive similarity in their beliefs and goals, and communicate more openly and honestly. Under contrient interdependence (competitive climate), people will focus on antagonistic interests and on constraining each other, exhibit suspicious and hostile attitudes, overemphasize differences, and communicate in a misleading and restrained manner. Studies by Deutsch and later researchers largely confirm these hypotheses and show that eventually these consequences "feed back" to influence interaction, thereby strengthening the dominant tendency in the conflict: "cooperation breeds cooperation, while competition breeds competition" (Deutsch 1973, p. 367).

Other research expands on Deutsch's analysis by suggesting additional climates that arise from and ultimately guide interaction in conflict. White and Lippitt (1968), for example, describe an individualistic orientation whereby members do not believe they are dependent on each other at all. It is characterized by a lack of common motives, autonomous behavior, rather indifferent attitudes toward others, and selfish preoccupation with one's own affairs. As a second alternative, Janis and Mann (1977) warn that overly cooperative orientations can lead to unthinking agreement among members, resulting in poor, unreflective group decisions. They propose instead a *vigilant* attitude, in which members are aware of common interests and trust and respect one another, but are wary of each other's ideas (see also Gouran 1982). Rather than easy cooperation, there may be sharp conflicts in vigilant groups, as members push each other toward the best decision through criticism and debate.

Deutsch's analysis is built on two assumptions that can be particularly useful in understanding the general direction and underlying coherence of conflict interaction. First, as described earlier, Deutsch stresses that the pervasive climate of a situation influences parties' conflict behavior. According to Deutsch, this generalized quality or force emerges as shared perceptions of interdependence develop. Perceptions of interdependence are generalized through parties' assumptions about their common interests, their level of trust, their friendly or hostile attitudes toward each other, their perceptions of similarity or difference in positions, and their communication. These perceptions constitute an overarching climate, a sense of the situation that shapes how parties calculate their moves and perceive each other.

Second, Deutsch points to the cyclical relationship between perceptions of interdependence and interaction. Deutsch suggests that generalized perceptions of interdependence arise from interaction, and once established, they in turn guide interaction. In other words, he assumes that interaction, cooperative or competitive, creates the climates just mentioned and, in turn, that parties' trust, attitudes, beliefs, and so on rebound to influence interaction and reinforce themselves. This cycle is common in groups and organizations. For example, a manager and an employee with a bad work record are likely to come into a performance appraisal interview with the expectation that it will be an unpleasant, competitive situation wherein the boss rebukes the employee and the employee tries to evade responsibility. It is this contrient, suspicious climate that causes both to interact mistrustfully and competitively to "protect" themselves. This reinforces the climate, which reinforces the interaction and so on, in a negative spiral. Similar positive spirals also work for cooperative, trusting climates, as discussed in Chapter 6.

Deutsch's two basic assumptions provide a strong footing for understanding the general direction that conflict interaction takes. However, there are certain limitations of his analysis. Deutsch isolates one feature of conflict situations:

interdependence, and he derives his entire analysis of cooperative and competitive processes from this feature. Although this has the advantage of permitting a simple, orderly description of cooperation and competition, it carries the disadvantage of an overly narrow focus. Other features of group situations, such as dominance or emotional relationships, are underemphasized in Deutsch's discussion. These omissions can lead to serious misdiagnoses of conflicts. Several features of climates discussed in Chapter 6, including dominance relations, supportiveness, group identity, and goal interdependence, are crucial aspects of group experience that are not directly accounted for in Deutsch's analysis.

A second limitation of Deutsch's analysis stems from his overemphasis on perceptions. Deutsch views participants' perceptions as the immediate cause of cooperative or competitive behavior. Although he recognizes that interdependence is exhibited in the interaction between people, he chooses to emphasize participants' perceptions of interdependence as the primary "cause" of conflict behavior. This leads to two problems. By focusing on perceptions of individuals, the analysis shifts away from a focus on a quality of the situation. This makes it very difficult to explain behavior in cases where individuals' perceptions disagree. Deutsch explicitly states that his analysis holds only for cases where both persons' perceptions are the same; when individuals' views differ, it is not possible to predict their behavior. This assumption may rule out a considerable number of important cases because individuals often have very different perceptions of what drives the group's interaction. Deutsch's focus also has the disadvantage of diverting attention away from behavior and toward individual psychology, thereby making it less likely to recognize the forces that shape conflict as they are produced during interaction.

Bearing these limitations in mind, several critical insights can be derived from Deutsch's work and field theory, including the importance of interdependence, the role of climates in conflict, and the cyclical flow between climate and interaction. (See Case 2.5.)

Summary and Review

What is perspectivism?

Perspectivism acknowledges that there is no one correct theory or viewpoint. A complex phenomenon like conflict is best understood if viewed from different angles, and employing diverse theories facilitates fuller understanding. This does not mean that everything is relative and that all theories are equally good. Social scientific theories must be evaluated against the evidence, and evidence may show flaws in any theory or even disconfirm it. Perspectivism recognizes that diverse types of evidence should be used in evaluating theories. It admits information and conclusions gathered from experiments, surveys, observational studies, qualitative research, clinical research, and pragmatic experience. Each theory is built on certain types of empirical study (for example, laboratory experimentation) and should be evaluated in terms of this type of evidence.

CASE **2.5**

Field Theory and the Parking Lot Scuffle

At the beginning of the parking lot scuffle, Jay was very uncertain about the situation. He had not expected the moped to be in his parking place, and he jumped out of his car, trying to make sense of what had happened. He was uncertain about the nature of his psychological field at this point, and the climate was full of uncertainty. When Tim registered his hostile comments, he became a barrier to Jay—a negative region in the force field. Jay attempted to bully his way through this barrier, probably because he interpreted Tim's remarks as indicating that Jay would be seen as a weakling if he gave in to Tim's attacks.

Tim's psychological field was thrown into disarray when Jay smashed his scooter. Jay represented a big negative region in this field, one that Tim saw as presenting a formidable barrier to attaining his goal of getting it repaired. So Tim went right after Jay, seeking to force him to make restitution. As the interaction progressed, Jay seemed a greater and greater barrier to Tim, and Tim continued to apply pressure, which ended in the scuffle.

The climate in this case was competitive and threatening for both Jay and Tim. Tim immediately felt threatened because of the damage to his personal property—even more so because vehicles are often an important part of our personal identity in modern U.S. culture. He adopted a competitive approach that created a sense of threat and defensiveness in Jay's life-space. Jay responded with a competitive move by line 8, which further reinforced Tim's tendencies to compete.

Discussion Questions
- *What factors created the perception of contrient interdependence between Tim and Jay?*
- *List some other conflicts in which climate played an important role. How did it function in these situations?*

How do psychological and interactional theories of conflict relate to each other?

The difference lies in the fact that the first set of theories centers on the inner experience of conflicts, whereas the second set looks to observable patterns of behavior. The term psychological is used broadly to include all approaches that deal with cognition, emotion, interpretation, and other mental processes. These processes are not instinctive or inborn, nor are they totally internally driven. They are influenced by social learning, physical and cultural context, and previous experiences with conflict. Psychological and interactional theories are related because inner processes influence behavior in important ways. In turn, interaction shapes inner processes such as attribution.

What is the psychodynamic perspective, and how does it explain conflict?

This perspective began with the work of Freud and has developed in the vibrant field of psychoanalysis. Fundamental is the premise that energy must be managed somehow, either by channeling it directly to the concerns at hand, by redirecting it to a different issue, or by expending energy to suppress the impulse. Two impulses, the aggressive impulse and anxiety, are particularly important in conflicts. Aggression can be handled through directly expressing it, but it may also be suppressed or displaced. Anxiety influences conflict by causing parties to be rigid and inflexible. The psychodynamic perspective is limited by its inability to explain which targets are chosen and how psychic energy is used.

What role does verbal aggressiveness play in conflict?

Verbal aggressiveness is a predisposition to engage in personalized attacks in response to conflict. It can be contrasted to argumentativeness, the tendency to enjoy the give and take of verbal argument. For obvious reasons, verbal aggressiveness has negative impacts on conflict management and interpersonal relationships. This theory explains conflict behavior in terms of more or less permanent traits, and thus differs from the other explanations, which focus on internal processes or interaction itself.

What is attribution theory? What tendencies does it encourage?

Attribution is the psychological process in which parties interpret and draw conclusions about others' behavior. It is a fundamental part of all interaction. Through lengthy study of the attribution process, researchers have identified several tendencies. Two that affect conflict are the fundamental attribution error and the self-serving bias.

The fundamental attribution error is a tendency to interpret others' behavior as intentional, but our own behavior as a result of the situation. Hence, parties are likely to interpret others' competitive behavior in conflicts as purposeful, selfish attempts to force others to comply; however, they interpret their own competitive behavior as simply a product of the situation in which they must contend with unreasonable others. This error sets up a situation in which parties are likely to respond to unreasonable and selfish competition with their own competitive moves that simply "respond" to what the other is doing—a dynamic that feeds into escalation cycles. The same process can also lead to cycles of avoidance.

The self-serving bias is a tendency to attribute negative consequences to external situational forces and positive consequences to our own behavior. Hence, parties are likely to conclude that the negative experiences they are having during conflicts are the fault of others, whereas the positive outcomes result from what they do. This error sets up a situation where others are faulted for negative feelings and outcomes a party may have, and the party has an incentive to punish others for creating this negative situation.

What contributions has Lewin's field theory made to our understanding of conflict interaction?

Field theory models human behavior as movement through a life-space that is influenced by various fields of force. An important feature of this life-space is its climate. Climate, which changes over time as a function of changes in the situation and the person's behavior, is the general quality of the field as a whole: its warmth, safety, or competitiveness. One important definer of climate is the nature of the interdependence between parties. Promotive interdependence exists when parties perceive that gains by one will produce gains by the other and losses by one will result in losses by the other as well. Contrient interdependence exists under the obverse conditions, when gains by one will produce losses by the other. The two types of interdependence set up different climates—cooperative in the case of promotive interdependence and competitive in the case of contrient interdependence.

Conclusion

Psychological theories offer explanations of conflict behavior based on thought processes and the dynamics of the human mind. The insights these theories offer can be both powerful and unsettling. They can be powerful because people's conscious thought processes have an enormous impact on their behavior. Rational thought processes influence how people decide to act and respond as conflicts unfold. But the insights from some of these theories can also be unsettling because they point to less-than-conscious influences the mind can have on behavior and communication. They suggest that at times we may respond to conflict without a complete awareness of our choices or why we make them. These unconscious influences help to capture the true complexity of people's responses and the real likelihood of escalation across many social settings in which conflicts arise. Gaining reliable access to both conscious and unconscious cognitive processes has been the focus of most research in the psychological, social psychological, and psychiatric fields. These disciplines provide useful perspectives from which to view conflict and to consider possible ways to manage it constructively.

3 Theories of Conflict Interaction

The interactional perspective contends that behavior is the source of meaningful understanding. Whereas the psychological perspective focuses on the mental processes that influence conflict behavior, the interactional perspective focuses on the behavior itself. According to the interactional perspective, actions or behaviors are a series of interconnected events. Interpretation is established through the patterns of those interlocked events. As an example, consider the pointed question: "How about sex?" Between an intimate couple on a late Friday night after holding hands and disclosing secrets, such a question probably stands as an invitation. On a survey questionnaire following a long set of yes–no questions, such a query undoubtedly serves as a request to respond with an appropriate category. After a painful physical examination and a long look of concern from a physician, the question probably means: "What should I know in order to treat you?"

The point is simple. Meaning cannot be discerned independent of context. Messages and behaviors are interpreted in the contexts within which they are embedded. What counts as context, according to the interactional view, is the general pattern of behavior. Perceptions and interpretations of context, such as restaurant, crowd, and quarrel, are important but are secondary to the behavioral patterns that define the context. In other words, that one perceives a setting to be a doctor's office is secondary to the behaviors constituting that experience. Action does not occur in isolation. Within the stream of behaviors, meaning becomes apparent.

The psychological perspective defines a given situation as the knowledge structure or schema people hold in their heads. As such, situations are firm, stable entities or activities with fixed labels, such as dining room, party, baseball game, conversation. Actors determine the situation by what they perceive. Perception of the situation then influences behavior and strategic choices made by actors. For example, someone may choose to defer to others when in a courtroom and dominate others when playing basketball.

The interactional perspective, on the other hand, regards situation as largely emergent. Although perceptions are important, the focus is on behavior. In this light, perceptions constrain but do not define situations. According to the interactional perspective, situations are constituted and sustained by actors through the behaviors they enact. Situation is seen as more fluid than fixed. Although people certainly create the situations they perceive, what they perceive is also influenced by what they do. For instance, imagine a common sales encounter in a retail outlet.

The service provider approaches the shopper and offers the standard opening: "Hello, may I help you?" As language is a creatively ambiguous code, the customer looks up and says in a highly suggestive tone: "You sure can help me. What are you doing Friday night?" What situation are these people sharing? Are they involved in what is typically called a customer-service encounter? Or is the situation more one of prospective dating? The interactional view suggests that it depends on how the conversation continues to unfold. The behavior, not the mental category, will define the situation and just as important, that definition will change when other behaviors are introduced.

Consistent with this position, the interactional perspective also embraces the idea of mutual influence. Communication is not so much a product as it is a process that is enacted. As an ongoing process, any given behavior is influenced more by preceding behaviors than by personality or situational constraints. Concepts of importance to conflict scholars—relationships, power, climate, dominance, and the like—are defined not by a single move or by a single actor but through interaction. In this sense, realities and meanings between people emerge and are negotiated through moves and countermoves during interactions. To be sure, how a particular interaction is accomplished will have an effect on the patterning of future interactions, but the golden rule is that what an interaction is about—its purpose and outcomes—are open to continuous negotiation by the participants.

The interactional perspective emphasizes several questions: (1) What patterns exist in conflict interaction? (2) What rules or structures do people use to make interpretations and construct social meanings in conflict situations? (3) How do people use messages to accomplish their goals in conflicts? (4) Which factors influence how sequences of moves unfold in conflict interaction?

The Human Relations Perspective and Conflict Styles

The human relations movement, which emerged during the 1940s and 1950s, has had a lasting impact on the study of organizations and on the field of organizational communication. This perspective assumes that the nature and quality of interpersonal relations in the workplace play a large role in determining employee motivation; satisfaction derived from work; level of absenteeism and resignations; management–employee relationships, and, ultimately, the productivity and success of the organization (Perrow 1986). Human relations research focused in particular on the work group, the site where most relationships develop and play out, and on the superior–subordinate relationship, probably the single most important work relationship (Conrad and Poole 2004).

With this emphasis on human relationships, it is no surprise that conflict was a major concern of the human relations researchers. From this concern came systems to identify recognizable styles or strategies people use in conflict and to determine how effective these styles are in different situations. The concept of style originated with Blake and Mouton (1964) and Jay Hall (1969) who identified five distinct types of conflict behavior. Their classification is based on two independent conflict behavior components (Ruble and Thomas 1976): (1) *assertiveness*, defined as behaviors intended to satisfy one's own concerns; and (2) *cooperativeness*, defined as behaviors intended to satisfy the other individual's concerns. These components combine to specify the five styles.

1. A *competing* style is high in assertiveness and low in cooperativeness: The party places great emphasis on his or her own concerns and ignores those of others. This orientation represents a desire to defeat the other; it has also been called the *forcing* or *dominant* style.
2. An *accommodating* style is unassertive and cooperative: The person gives in to others at the cost of his or her own concerns. This orientation has also been called *appeasement* or *smoothing,* and those who follow it attempt to avoid conflict for the sake of maintaining relationships. It is a self-sacrificing approach but may also be viewed as weak and retracting.
3. An *avoiding* style is unassertive and uncooperative: The person simply withdraws and refuses to deal with the conflict. In this orientation the person is indifferent to the outcome of the conflict and can be described as apathetic, isolated, or evasive. This style has also been called *flight.*
4. A *collaborating* style is high in both assertiveness and cooperation: The person works to attain a solution that will meet the needs of both people. In this orientation full satisfaction for all is sought. It has also been called the *problem-solving* and the *integrative* style.
5. A *compromising* style is intermediate in both assertiveness and cooperativeness: Both people give some and "split the difference" to reach an agreement. In this orientation both are expected to give up something and keep something. It has also been called *sharing* or *horse-trading.*

The five styles have been an enormously useful tool for understanding conflict (see Case 3.1). They provide a common vocabulary and almost every major writer on interpersonal or organizational conflict has referred to the styles extensively (Blake and Mouton 1964; Filley 1975; Thomas 1975; Wilmot and Wilmot 1978). In addition, this classification is grounded in experience: Blake and Mouton developed it from their own experience with organizational conflicts, and later research has supported the existence of the two dimensions and five styles (Filley 1975; Cosier and Ruble 1981). Chapter 7 identifies several variants of the five styles and discusses how these styles and their variants are useful in different situations and circumstances.

One labor mediator observed that during negotiations he is most confident that the parties will find a way to a settlement when they have no idea as to how to predict the others' behavior. Although the implications of this statement are intriguing in many ways, one point in particular has long captured the attention of conflict researchers. The mediator's observation implies that people enter disputes or negotiation sessions with set expectations about how others will react. Based on their past experiences, they assume that others will adopt predictable styles to deal

CASE **3.1**

Human Relations Theory and the Parking Lot Scuffle

From the outset Tim used a competing style, high in assertiveness and low in cooperativeness. This is indicated by his strong language, his demands for payment, and his refusal to consider Jay's point of view. Jay initially begins with a collaborating style; he does not apologize or give in to Tim, which would signal accommodation or, possibly, avoidance. He attempts to develop an understanding of what happened that could be the foundation for problem solving. Tim's continued confrontations are answered with firm resistance in line 8. Here Jay clearly states his unwillingness to accommodate ("Look, this is my spot.") and makes an attempt to reframe the situation when he says, "You're lucky I stopped when I did." This signals a continued attempt at collaboration that might have led to an integrative solution or a compromise had Tim followed this lead.

This in turn illustrates an important feature of collaboration: It does not necessarily mean that people are "nice" to each other. Often collaboration involves assertive moves that signal firmness and resolve. As indicated in Chapter 1, differentiation requires parties to acknowledge the validity of their differences, which sometimes requires one party to show the other that he or she will not be pushed around.

By line 10, Jay has abandoned collaboration and switched to a competing style ("You are the one with the problem. Do you work here?"). He may have concluded that Tim would never be reasonable and decided that the only way to obtain an acceptable outcome was to argue to a standoff. He may also intend to continue collaborating, in which case the point here was to further signal resolve and to register a mild threat

that Jay could attack right back if he wanted to. Or Jay may have just been sucked into the confrontation through a matching process. Aroused by Tim's anger, Jay's aggressive impulses and anxiety about the situation may have provoked a "fight" response whereby Jay becomes just as competitive as Tim.

Whatever the case, by line 12 Jay lashes back at Tim and attempts to leave the scene— "Who in the hell do you think you are? *(Starts walking away.)*" Taken out of context, this move might appear to enact an accommodation or avoidance style. In this context, however, it seems to be part of a larger strategy to win through retreat. Jay snarls at Tim and tries to have the last word by walking away. As Chapter 7 notes, there are variants of the five basic styles that identify different approaches to the same basic strategy.

Tim's reaction cements the competition when he grabs Jay. Jay continues with his retreat-and-win strategy, and Tim slugs him. Tim may have done this because he realized the situation was slipping away with Jay's impending retreat. Or, Tim may simply have been too incensed to "let go" of his attitude. If this was the case, he channeled his aggression into violence, which ended in the scuffle.

Discussion Questions

- *How did the styles adopted by these two feed into the conflict?*
- *Could Jay have taken a different tact that would have resulted in a more productive conflict?*
- *What other variations on styles have you observed?*
- *Are there different ways to collaborate or to avoid?*

---

with conflict. This is quite useful insofar as it encourages parties to focus on conflict interaction. However, as shown in Chapter 7, this is a somewhat oversimplified view of how people in conflict behave.

The human relations perspective has also been criticized because it emphasizes the resolution and elimination of conflict. This seems like a paradox at first sight because human relations theorists openly acknowledge conflict as a common occurrence and stress that it must be used productively. However, as Perrow (1986) notes, human relations theorists emphasize managing relationships so that cooperation results. Conflict is regarded as an inevitable part of human relationships, but an unnatural one that must be "managed" or "resolved" for the organization to run efficiently in its "natural" cooperative state. Human relations theorists do not entertain the possibility that conflict might be a basic building-block of organizations, impossible to remove completely—a positive and innovative force in its own right. As discussed in Chapter 4, low-power groups or minorities sometimes must foment conflict to make society more responsive to them. In this case, sustaining conflict is positive for these groups.

Experimental Gaming Research

The social exchange perspective and experimental gaming are two separate but closely related approaches to the study of conflict. Each has spawned a huge body of research, with more than a thousand experimental game studies alone (Pruitt and Kimmel 1977), and literally dozens of books summarizing social exchange research (for example, Thibaut and Kelley 1959; Homans 1961; Blau 1964; Roloff 1981). Despite the fact that researchers of either approach often seem unaware of studies conducted in the other, the two approaches are based on similar assumptions and lead to complementary conclusions. This section discusses the two approaches together. Because of the size and importance of these research traditions, this section is longer and more complex than some others.

Both approaches are based on a recognition of two important facts about conflict: (1) conflicts involve people who are interdependent, and (2) conflict behavior involves rewards and costs for participants. They attempt to explain conflict behavior, and, indeed, *all behavior* in terms of individual calculation of the potential rewards and costs associated with different actions. Both perspectives assume that people prefer those behaviors that promise rewards and avoid those for which costs are greater than benefits. Interdependence is critical because (as we noted in the Introduction) how others act and respond determines, in large part, an individual's rewards and costs. In both approaches, interdependence is defined as the degree to which two people can influence each other's rewards or costs. To show the relationship between the two approaches, the assumptions of the social exchange perspective must be explained and then how they translate into the assumptions of game research must be considered.

The *social exchange perspective* is built on two basic assumptions. First, it asserts that the guiding force behind behavior is *self-interest*. It is presumed that people monitor their rewards and costs during interaction and strive to achieve a relationship that meets their needs in terms of outcomes. Outcomes are defined as rewards minus costs. There are various ways to define what "meets" people's needs. The most obvious way is to assume that people attempt to maximize their profits regardless of others' losses (see, for example, Lewin's individualistic climate). However, social exchange occurs in the context of interpersonal relationships, and few relationships could survive for long in this dog-eat-dog situation. Instead, individuals often seem to seek outcomes that are fair in relation to others' outcomes. This rule of fairness, which has also been called *distributive justice* (Homans 1961) and *equity* (Walster, Walster, and Berscheid 1978), states that rewards should be proportionate to costs or contributions made to the relationship. Whether people seek to maximize their outcomes or to achieve fair distribution of outcomes, they are assumed to alter their behavior and to attempt to alter others' behavior to achieve desired outcomes. The social exchange perspective does not assume that rewards or costs can always be absolutely or objectively defined. People may be unaware of or mistaken about the consequences of their behavior. Rather, it is the parties' perceptions of benefits and costs that guide behavior.

Second, the social exchange perspective asserts that rewards and costs stem from *exchanges of resources* among participants during interaction. Roloff (1981, p. 21) defines social exchange as "the voluntary transference of some object or activity from one person to another in return for other objects or activities." A wide range of social resources can be exchanged during interaction, including liking, love, status, information, help, approval, respect, and authority. In the exchange perspective, it is assumed that people exchange or deny resources every time they interact. When Sherry compliments Herb on his new tie, she gives him approval; when Herb smiles back at Sherry, he gives her liking. In the same vein, when Sherry yells at Herb to pick up his socks, she gives him disapproval; when Herb refuses, he denies Sherry his cooperation.

A corollary to the two assumptions is that parties exchange resources to influence others to behave in ways that produce acceptable outcomes. Therefore, Sherry might compliment Herb so that he will wear his tie again; this will make him look attractive and be more pleasant for Sherry to be with. In the same way, Herb might refuse to pick up his socks in order to frustrate Sherry and show her that shouting will not work; if she stops yelling and asks him politely, Herb's outcomes will be better. From a social exchange perspective, interaction is a complex transaction in which individuals calculate present and desired outcomes and act in a manner that will maintain or improve the outcomes. It applies an economic metaphor to interaction.

This analysis suggests that conflict will emerge when one person (1) feels his or her outcomes are too low and (2) perceives or anticipates resistance from another when attempts are made to improve outcomes (Roloff 1981, Chapter 4). Outcomes may be too low because the person did not receive an expected reward, incurred an unexpected cost, or perceived inequity between his or her rewards and those of others. Conflict is triggered when the individual comes to believe that the others are responsible for unsatisfactory outcomes or that others stand in the way of future improvements. As we will show, both individuals can take several alternative paths in dealing with this conflict.

Because the social exchange perspective is based on an economic metaphor, it dovetails nicely with *experimental gaming* research, which is based on theories originally developed in economics (Von Neumann and Morgenstern 1947; Shubik 1987). The Thibaut and Kelley version of social exchange (1959; Kelley and Thibaut

1978) is strongly influenced by the economic theory of games and is often used in game experiments. Basically, the experimental gaming approach likens interaction, particularly conflicts, to games of strategy; for example, chess, in which the results of each player's moves depend on the other player's moves. In its most basic form the experimental gaming perspective includes the following assumptions:

1. The structure of a game is composed of choices (options) available to players and the rewards or costs (payoffs) they receive from selecting a given choice.
2. The choices available to players are limited in number, and players know what these choices are.
3. The payoffs associated with a given move depend not only on the player's choice but also on the choice made by the other.
4. Players know or can determine the payoffs associated with each combination of choices, and these payoffs are interesting and meaningful to them.
5. A player's choice is determined by calculation of payoffs (rewards and costs). Rational game behavior consists of the selection of choices that yield favorable outcomes, either the maximization of gain or the attainment of a beneficial norm, such as distributive justice.

Based on these assumptions the motivational structure of any conflict can be represented as a payoff matrix such as that shown in Figure 3.1. The particular game portrayed is sometimes called *Prisoner's Dilemma*, after a well-known situation. Consider two criminals who have been apprehended by the police. They are put in separate rooms and kept incommunicado. The police instruct each that they have two choices: confess or keep silent. If only one confesses, he or she can turn state's evidence and go free, with a reward for nailing the culprit; the other prisoner will "take the rap" and receive a heavy sentence. If both confess, they both go to prison with lighter sentences. If both remain silent, they go free because the police cannot make a case without a witness. Figure 3.1(a) represents a payoff matrix for this game, and Figure 3.1(b) expresses the payoffs in verbal terms. Note that within this structure there is incentive for each to betray the other and a lesser reward for remaining faithful.

The numbers in matrix 3.1(a) represent the values of outcomes for the prisoners for each pair of choices. In each cell of the matrix, the number in the upper corner is prisoner B's outcome and that in the lower corner is prisoner A's. To determine the outcomes associated with each combination of A's and B's choices, locate A's choice on the left side of the matrix and B's choice on the top of the matrix and then find the cell corresponding to the two choices. For example, if A confesses and B remains silent, the cell for this choice is the one in the lower left corner of Figure 3.1(a). (The entries in this cell are A's and B's outcomes.) So the possible outcomes shown are as follows:

1. If A remains silent *and* B remains silent, then A's outcome is 1 and B's outcome is 1.
2. If A remains silent *and* B confesses, then A's outcome is −2 and B's outcome is 2.

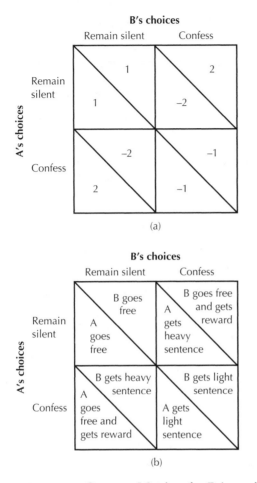

B's choices

FIGURE 3.1   **Outcome Matrices for *Prisoner's Dilemma***

3. If A confesses *and* B remains silent, then A's outcome is 2 and B's outcome is –2.
4. If A confesses *and* B confesses, then both have outcomes of –1.

All payoff matrices for experimental games can be understood in this fashion.

As this discussion shows, because the two prisoners are interdependent they each face a dilemma. If one confesses and the other does not, the first goes free. If both confess, they both go to prison. Can each trust the other to stand fast and not be a traitor? Misplaced trust may result in a severe penalty. The prisoners are therefore in a situation wherein there are incentives both to cooperate and to compete— a *mixed-motive* situation in the terminology of game research. Because almost all conflicts have incentives for both cooperation and competition, mixed-motive games provide good experimental models for conflict situations. Although the game is called the *Prisoner's Dilemma,* it applies to many other situations—that is, in almost any situation where each side has incentives both to take advantage of the other and to cooperate.

There are several ways in which the prisoners can attempt to resolve their dilemmas, and the particular strategies they choose for doing so provide the real interest of experimental game research. If each is only allowed one move, he could attempt to predict or infer what the other would most likely do and base his strategy on that prediction. However, in most experimental games, as in most conflicts, the parties are permitted to make more than one move. Hence each can use the other's previous moves as information for predicting the next move. Each can also use their own response to the other (competitive or cooperative) to tell the other what his choice should be. If, for example, A always confesses and B wants A to change, B can also consistently confess, which gives A *two* outcomes and an incentive to move toward cooperation. If the two sides are allowed to communicate with each other, each also has other strategies available for maximizing outcomes. For example, one might persuade the other to remain silent and then betray him. The numerous resolution strategies available to parties make it evident that a great many of the processes involved in conflicts—prediction, persuasion, interchanges of moves, bargaining—can be simulated with experimental games.

The versatility of games becomes even more apparent when other variations are considered. For one thing, many incentive structures other than the *Prisoner's Dilemma* can be built into the matrix. Figure 3.2 shows two other structures; matrix 3.2(a) shows a situation where cooperative *matching* is encouraged. Individuals receive rewards when they select the same choice and penalties when they make different choices. An example of this situation would be a couple very much in love who are considering whether to move to a different city or stay where they are. If one moves without the other, they both suffer—the mover somewhat more than the stayer.

Matrix 3.2(b) shows a game called *chicken* in which one party can win big if he or she can bluff the other, but loses big if the other calls the bluff. This matrix is illustrated by the game of "chicken" in which players drive their cars toward each other at high speeds. If one swerves and the other does not, the first is chicken and the other wins admiration for being brave. If both swerve, they lose face, but at least escape unharmed. If neither swerves, they collide. This game also has parallels to the thinking behind nuclear deterrence. Each nation must put itself in danger of annihilation to threaten the other. If the threat convinces the opponent to back down, the nation scores a great gain. If, however, the opponent responds in kind, the consequences for both are unthinkable. Many other matrices expressing almost any kind of incentive structure are possible (Kelley and Thibaut 1978). Game research assumes that all types of interdependence can be translated into these terms.

It is also possible to relax the assumption that members know all options or outcomes equally well. As Kelley and Thibaut (1978) point out, many behaviors can be interpreted as attempts to "explore" the outcome matrices. People ask others what they think of alternatives, observe them interacting with other people, and tentatively test certain alternatives to find out more about the outcomes they are likely to receive from interacting with another. It is also possible to expand the

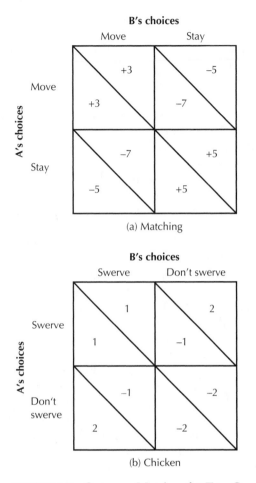

(a) Matching

(b) Chicken

FIGURE 3.2   Outcome Matrices for Two Conflict Situations

available alternatives to include mutually rewarding options. Just as people some-times narrow the options available to others with "either-or" type statements ("Either we go to that movie or I'm staying home!"), so too they can widen the range of alternatives ("Why don't we try *x*?"). As long as we can get a reasonably small set of options, the game approach is workable.

Finally, games do not have to be confined to the matrix format outlined before. As Pruitt and Kimmel (1977) note, there are three main types of experimental games: (1) *matrix games,* such as those just discussed; (2) *negotiation games,* which simulate formal negotiations over some issue such as an award in a legal case or the price of a used car (points are awarded on the basis of the final agreement); and (3) *coalition games* in which more than two subjects play a game or bargain and can form coalitions to defeat others (the coalition is awarded points and members then bargain to split their rewards). Although these games have different formats, for all practical purposes they are equivalent: Their outcomes are determined by numerical assignments, the choices available to players are limited, and multiple trials are run.

The similarities of the experimental game approach and the social exchange perspective are evident. As Thibaut and Kelley (1959) observe, game matrices can be regarded as explicit, numerical formulations of exchange principles. The advantage of games lies in the fact that the numerically specified outcomes allow easy control over experimental situations. This advantage has generated an immense amount of research on conflict and negotiation.

Experimental games have been used to study the effectiveness of various strategies to induce cooperation between parties. For example, one strategy a player might apply is called *tit for tat* or *matching*. The player matches each of the opponent's moves. If the opponent competes, the player competes; if the opponent cooperates, the player cooperates. The player might adopt this strategy to show the opponent that cooperation will be rewarded and competition punished. It turns out that this strategy is amazingly effective in inducing others to cooperate, as shown in Chapter 7. A complex study of various game strategies by Axelrod (1984) demonstrated that matching could potentially stimulate cooperation, even in situations where there were many competing parties.

Games have also been used to study the effects of variables, such as gender or time pressure, on conflict behavior. A number of studies have compared the behavior of men and women playing a series of rounds of experimental games. The results of these studies generally seem to indicate that men and women take different approaches to conflicts (Rubin and Brown 1975). The obvious hypothesis that men would be more competitive than women is not supported by these studies. Instead, women seem to vary a great deal in competitiveness, compared with men. In some studies women have been more competitive than men, and in others they have been less competitive. Women's strategies also vary more across different types of opponents than do men's strategies. Rubin and Brown (1975) conjectured that men respond primarily on the basis of the task at hand—that is, the incentive structure of the game itself. So when a game encouraged cooperation, men tended to cooperate, and when another game encouraged competition, men tended to compete. Women, on the other hand, paid more attention to their partners and responded based on partners' moves. Hence, they were more flexible in their responses and had more variation in strategies. Gaming research continues to study the impact of gender differences as well as other variables, such as the effects of different payoff structures, time pressure, nationality of the parties, and whether the parties are bargaining for themselves or representing another party.

Experimental gaming research and the social exchange perspective provide several important insights into conflict interaction.

1. *Both approaches focus on the role of strategic calculation in conflicts.* The approaches recognize that people usually play an active, controlling part in conflict interaction, as opposed to the passive, reactive role assigned to them by psychodynamic analyses. Moreover, in both approaches the principles governing peo-ple's choices, in this case the attainment of positive outcomes, are specified. These perspectives make it possible to identify factors that may predict others' behavior in conflict situations.

2. *The approaches serve to emphasize the importance of interdependence in conflicts.* The fact that conflicts almost never occur in wholly competitive or wholly cooper-ative situations is underscored. There is almost always a mixture of incentives to compete and incentives to cooperate. If parties focus on the former, they may be drawn into an ever-escalating spiral; if they recognize the latter, they have grounds for a productive resolution.

3. *The approaches provide a good picture of conflict as an exchange of moves and coun-termoves.* Both approaches show how later moves are shaped and constrained by earlier ones and how each party's power—in the form of control over the other's rewards and costs—determines the moves he or she can make.

4. *Both approaches show that rewards and costs associated with moves depend not only on direct, instrumental gains, such as a raise in salary, but also on the effects moves have on the relationship between parties.* The social exchange perspective asserts that resources obtained from relationships—love, liking, and self-esteem—are critically important sources of rewards and costs. People's calculations are based not just on gain, but on consequences for their relationships as well.

Clearly, game research and the social exchange perspective offer a powerful and useful analysis of conflict. Like all scientific approaches, however, they also have limitations. In effect, both approaches argue that conflict interaction can be reduced to a series of exchanges governed by participants' calculations of potential outcomes. This statement implies that other aspects of interaction may be interest-ing, but they are important only insofar as they influence the outcome structure or participants' practical reasoning. This is quite a claim. Can it be confirmed?

At least three problems revolve around the issue of human rationality. In both game and exchange perspectives, it is assumed that people (1) know their options, (2) know the outcomes associated with them, and (3) perform calculations of gains and losses. Consider these three assumptions in turn. First, one shortcoming of the gaming approach is that it does not take into account the extremely wide variety of choices people face in real life; game models are usually based on a relatively small set of options that remain stable over time. Consider the case of John and Steve who own a business together. Steve, who keeps the books, has let another check bounce because he does not keep up with deposits and balancing the account. The bank has just called John, and he is very angry about it. Here are just a few of his choices:

1. Ignore the problem.
2. Leave in disgust and go have a drink.
3. Shout at Steve.
4. Leave Steve a note so Steve will not see how angry John is.
5. Tell a mutual friend so he can let Steve know that John is angry.

    6. Call a financial consultant to help straighten out the books.
    7. Dissolve the partnership.

These are just some of John's choices. Depending on how Steve reacts to his move, John may face a totally different set of options later. John may, for example, choose response number four in the hope that things will cool off. But Steve may feel a note is impersonal and get angry. In the face of Steve's counteraccusation of his coldness, John faces a whole new array of problems. Real-world conflicts often are not fought using small, well-defined game matrices. The *options* problem becomes even thornier because parties often create entirely new options as they interact. The structure of options changes constantly as the conflict interaction unfolds.

    Second, these perspectives assume that parties know the consequences and outcomes associated with each option and make choices on the basis of expected outcomes. However, this is a much more complex process than it seems at first. Most resources or behaviors are neither totally rewarding nor totally noxious; instead, they have complex sets of properties, some of which are rewarding and some of which entail costs. For example, threatening to break up their partnership may be rewarding to John because he would be free of Steve's sloppiness, he could get out of a business that has become boring, he has the satisfaction of having shown Steve how he feels, and he would have more time to spend with his kids. At the same time, this threat may be costly because John would miss Steve if Steve agreed to the breakup and because bad feelings might arise, especially if they did not break up the partnership. If John considers all these possible consequences prior to acting, he would probably have trouble assigning positive or negative values to them. Is the reward of freedom from Steve's sloppiness greater than the cost of missing his friendship? How much greater? It is one thing to numerically rate rewards on a questionnaire concerning a hypothetical conflict; it is quite another to place values on possible consequences in the flux of an ongoing, highly emotional conflict. People simply do not know what they want sometimes.

    Third, these perspectives assume that behavioral choice is based on calculations of gains and losses. However, consider John's situation. If he considers three or four positive and negative consequences for each option, as well as the probability that the option will yield each consequence, he must perform a formidable calculation. This task, as Simon (1955) notes, is far beyond the available capacities of the human brain. It is simply impossible to weigh thirty to forty items of information for every act we undertake.

    There is an easy answer to the first three objections. It can be argued that people do not consider a wide range of confusingly similar options, consequences, and outcomes. Instead, they focus on just those few elements that they find salient in the given situation; they simplify issues to fit what they are capable of doing, and if they select a given outcome, it is because it is rewarding given their limited perceptions of the situation. This explanation, however, opens the door to the problem of circularity (Skidmore 1979).

    When we see someone doing something, we conclude that it must be because he expects rewards from doing it. Then we can identify the rewards or functions of this behavior; however, this is circular. Why is Bob doing X? Because it is rewarding to him. Then how do we know it really is rewarding? Because he is doing it. According to this logic *any* behavior is rewarding by definition. Skidmore (1979, pp. 105–106) summarizes the implications of this:

> "Reward" and "value" are indeed used as explanatory terms [in exchange theories]; but in every case they are used to explain something that has already happened, and they are used ad hoc. That is, we might observe a man doing something and, to explain his doing it, suggest that it might have been rewarding to him or else he would not have done it. Knowing nothing about the man's values or his previous state of reward or punishment, adding the concept of reward is really to add nothing. We could say, "He did it; I saw him." What more do we know, or what more can we predict, when we add, "It must have been rewarding to him"? Whatever he might do, the explanation remains the same. There is no way to prove the theory wrong, if it is.

Therefore, the choices are to try to define options and consequences in the full sense, which entails an impossible calculative task, or assume people "narrow their fields," which opens up to the charge of circular reasoning trying to determine how rewards motivate them. If the theory is accepted and it is assumed that people act because they feel rewarded by something, rewards can always be identified. Either way, however, there is a thorny dilemma if only this point of view is considered.

A final problem with the experimental game and social exchange perspectives is their oversimplification of complex issues. According to these approaches, options and outcomes are the critical explanatory factors in conflicts. Other variables, such as power, climate, and previous history, are assumed to influence conflict interaction through their effects on rewards and costs associated with options—that is, through their effects on the outcome matrix for the conflict. But this perspective seems to be an oversimplification. Climate does influence the rewards and costs associated with various moves; for example, in an open, trusting climate, being honest about one's feelings is not as likely to evoke ridicule as it would in an ordinary business climate. But climate also has other effects on interaction. It influences group members' perceptions of one another and their predictions of what others will do, as well as their attitudes toward the group. To focus exclusively on members' choices and not on other aspects of the situation seems too narrow and simplistic. This narrow focus could filter our perceptions too much and cause us to ignore or trivialize a number of important aspects of conflict interaction.

The limitations of the social exchange perspective and game research have been discussed here in great length. The purpose was not to refute these approaches. On the contrary, the two approaches provide what are probably the most important set of findings regarding conflict. It is important to consider the limitations of these approaches because they are so often accepted "whole cloth" as the correct way to look at conflict. Like the other perspectives considered in this chapter, exchange and game research provide a suggestive, but incomplete, view of conflict. Recognizing their limitations is important as is any attempt to build on their strengths.

Given their limitations, what is the ultimate value of experimental gaming research and the social exchange perspective? First, they serve as good *metaphors* for conflict. Even if they are not accurate in all particulars, the game and exchange metaphors bring out the important characteristics of conflict listed previously—conflict as a sequence of moves and countermoves, the active role of parties in the development of conflicts, interdependence, and the relational consequences of conflicts. These points are reexamined throughout this book.

In addition, there are cases where these perspectives are directly applicable; that is, cases wherein options are well-defined, outcomes are fairly clear, and parties are capable of calculating gains and losses. Conflicts in fairly advanced stages, after the parties have clarified their positions and have developed a working relationship, are probably the most important cases to which these approaches apply. For example, late stages of labor–management negotiations, wherein only a few options or proposals remain, can be modeled as games. So can conflicts in personal relationships once issues are heading toward a moment of truth—for example, to split up or stay together. A second case is when one party narrows the other's options with a statement such as "Either you move to California with me or I'm leaving you!" This can happen very early in an interchange, but it has the function of projecting alternatives into a few choices and pressuring parties to focus on them exclusively. Whenever choices are simplified or narrowed, game and social exchange approaches are applicable. (See Case 3.2.)

Intergroup Conflict Research

That conflict often arises between people of different nationalities, religions, races, ethnic groups, genders, or ages is not news. In Germany, the Nazis persecuted the Jews on the grounds that they were inferior to "Aryans"; in Yugoslavia, the Serbs and Croats fought savagely trying to settle "age-old" scores; in the United States, whites persecuted African Americans because of their skin color; in some large corporations, women are cut out of management by the "old boys," who control the front office, and respond with legal charges of discrimination. The list goes on and on. In all these cases, *differences* between these social groups are the alleged causes of conflict. The conflict is presumed to stem from the group's characteristics, which makes it inevitable. The groups are seen as "natural" or traditional enemies.

There are at least two problems with this explanation of intergroup conflict. In most cases one or both groups have economic or political interests in the conflict; one or both stand to gain from the other's defeat (Billig 1976; Tajfel 1978). Intergroup differences may be used by parties to justify the conflict, but they are certainly not its ultimate or original cause. Second, usually several other groups are different from the conflicting groups, but they are not drawn into the conflict. The theories of *natural* differences have no explanation for why these particular groups are in conflict and the others are not drawn in (Billig 1976). To explain this, it is necessary to go beyond group differences and to consider intergroup interaction.

Although they may not be the ultimate or original cause of conflicts, intergroup differences often contribute to the persistence, intensity, and violence of

CASE **3.2**

Game Research and the Parking Lot Scuffle

The parking lot scuffle can be analyzed as a social exchange situation in which Tim and Jay attempt to satisfy their self-interests. Tim seems to have set his primary goal as getting Jay to pay for repairing his scooter and a secondary goal as "blowing off steam" on Jay. Jay seems to have as his primary goal avoiding blame for the accident and a secondary goal as getting his day back on track and going to work.

Figure 3.3 indicates a possible incentive structure for the goals in this situation. This simplified set of goals suggests that Jay is somewhat less motivated to attain his goals than Tim is. The heated exchange shows Tim's strong motives to get Jay to comply with his reading of the situation; Jay is seen as slightly less invested in the outcome.

Jay and Tim adopt their respective conflict styles as they attempt to attain these goals. The payoff matrix in the figure illustrates the outcomes of various combinations of styles for the two based on the likelihood of attaining the goals given each combination. Notice that the matrix is set up so that the payoffs for Tim are higher for competition than those for collaboration no matter what Jay does. So Tim will compete no matter what Jay does; there is no

way that Jay can influence Tim's behavior. Jay would prefer that he and Tim collaborate because joint collaboration has the highest outcome (10) for Jay. But since Tim will always choose competition, the highest-yielding outcome for him, Jay should gravitate toward competition, which has a higher payoff if both compete than if Jay collaborates and Tim competes.

We can map the conflict styles chosen by the two combatants as follows:

- Moves 1 and 2: Tim competes, Jay collaborates
- Moves 3 and 4: Tim competes, Jay collaborates
- Moves 5 and 6: Tim competes, Jay collaborates
- Moves 7 and 8: Tim competes, Jay collaborates
- Moves 9 and 10: Tim competes, Jay competes (asks Tim if he works here, implying that Tim may not have a legitimate claim to the spot)
- Moves 11 and 12: Tim competes, Jay competes
- Moves 13 and 14: Tim competes, Jay competes

This sequence represents a tit-for-tat strategy in which there is a four-move latency of response on Jay's part; Jay takes four moves before he concludes that he cannot obtain the highest payoff cell for himself (collaborate–collaborate).

The irony of this situation is that following this payoff matrix gets neither Tim nor Jay their best outcome. Payoff matrices are defined by parties' perceptions of the degree to which moves can help them attain their goals, and this matrix reflects their estimates. In this case, the estimations are incorrect. The tensions between parties' perceived payoff matrices (Figure 3.3) and the real payoffs that

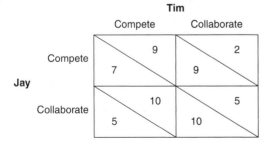

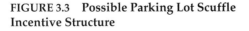

FIGURE 3.3   Possible Parking Lot Scuffle Incentive Structure

(continued)

CASE **3.2**   **Continued**

ensue from their behavior are something of an enigma for game theorists. One way to address this is to assume that parties begin with an outcome matrix that reflects their perception of payoffs and that this matrix changes as parties experience actual payoffs, coming more into line with real payoff values. At the end of the conflict, the payoff matrix for Tim and Jay may look very different from the one they started with.

Discussion Questions

- *Are the following conditions that are assumed in the classic versions of game theory satisfied for Tim and Jay? (1) They know their options. (2) They know the outcomes associated with these options.*
- *Do Jay and Tim seem to calculate what different moves will yield for them during their conflict? If they do not, is game theory still a good model for understanding this conflict? Why or why not?*

conflicts. Few things are as troubling as a persistent conflict that feeds on group prejudices. Small wonder that sociologists and social psychologists have devoted a great deal of time to the study of intergroup conflict. In the United States, the study of intergroup relations can be traced back to the late nineteenth century when sociologists Robert Park and W. I. Thomas were concerned with the problem of how to integrate multiethnic immigrants into the American melting pot. One of the most famous works in this tradition is Gordon Allport's study, *The Nature of Prejudice* (1954). In Europe, similar ethnic tensions and the horrors of the first fifty years of the twentieth century inspired social psychologists, such as Henry Tajfel and Serge Moscovici (1976), to investigate the roots of group differences. This research yields some important insights for the study of conflict.

The roots of intergroup conflict lie in the basic human need for identity. European researchers have explored the process of *social categorization*—a basic social process whereby people define themselves by identifying the groups they and others belong to (Doise 1978; Tajfel and Turner 1979). Starting in early childhood and continuing throughout adult life, a major factor in the definition of personal identity is the individual's perception of the social groups or categories he or she belongs to ("I am an American"; "I am a Minnesotan"; "I am a lawyer"). Moreover, identity is defined not only by the groups to which a person belongs, but by the groups to which they do *not* belong. For example, many Americans define themselves both as being Americans and as *not* being Mexicans or Japanese or some other nationality. Members of management can draw their identity as much from being opposed to the union as from being a manager. Every organization and society can be described as a network of complementary and opposing groups. For example, in a typical American factory there might be groups divided between labor and management, line workers and staff, male and female, white collar and blue collar, to name just a few. Each group is defined not only in its own terms, but also with reference to its complementary or opposite group. Social categorization is the process by which people determine to what groups they and others belong, creating identification and oppositions among people.

The social categories forming the dividing points of organizations and societies differ from case to case and throughout history. Although men and women have always been important social categories in the United States, the nature of the category "women" and the relationship between the categories "men" and "women" have changed radically. Plus, the men–women differentiation is quite different in Japan, the United States, and Ghana. The importance of social categories also changes through history. During the 1920s, whether one was in favor of or against the legal prohibition of alcohol was an important distinction. Today, it is not even an issue. There is no one set of universal social divisions; they are socially defined and negotiated in each culture and subculture.

Communication plays an important role in social categorization. It is the medium through which people are taught categories. When children hear talk about the general categories "boys" and "girls" or "blacks" and "whites," they are being taught social categories (Doise 1978). For adults such categorization is second-nature, and they learn and create additional categories. With each social category comes a characterization of what people in the category are like—their wants and needs, how they act, and so on. Of course, the characterization of each category differs depending on who is describing the category. A member of the social group "women" is likely to describe the characteristics of men differently from the way a "man" would. However, often communication barriers prevent people in different social categories from comparing notes—that is, recognizing the differences. Blacks and whites, for instance, sometimes keep their theories about the other group to themselves, only discussing them with other blacks or whites. The process of group differentiation, discussed later, adds additional communication barriers that keep people from refuting social characterizations.

A person's style of communicating often serves as a marker of the social group to which he or she belongs. Giles and Powesland (1975) summarize evidence that characteristics of speech, such as dialect or accent, are used as indicators of the social category to which a person belongs. During World War II, U.S. citizens with German accents were often branded as potential collaborators with the Nazis and kept under surveillance, despite the fact that they were loyal to the Allies.

When people accept social categories, they are likely to act toward those in other groups on the basis of these attributions. This sets up a self-reinforcing cycle that preserves theories about other social groups (Cooper and Fazio 1979). For example, if people in group A, which generally is politically unconcerned, are taught that people in group B are politically conservative, those in group A may never raise the subject of politics in discussions with members of group B. By so doing, they never give the people in group B a chance to show their true political beliefs. In turn, people in group B, who are actually somewhat centrist in their political beliefs, might think that the people in A are close-mouthed and manipulative in their political agenda. That members of group A never talk about politics might confirm this suspicion for many group B members. Thomas Scheff (1967) calls this state of affairs *pluralistic ignorance*—each side is mistaken about the other, but neither is aware that it is mistaken. So both sides act on their "true" beliefs and invite behavior that confirms their views.

Consider the influence of culture on how men and women communicate in conflict situations. Although differences can be found, more studies show that men and women respond similarly in conflict situations, resolving conflict in similar ways both at work and at home (Chusmir and Mills 1989; Renwick 1977; Turner and Henzel 1987). What is largely different between the sexes is what culture has shown us to expect from men and women in conflict. For example, researchers in one study (Korabik, Baril, and Watson 1993) found that men and women did not handle conflict differently but were judged as being less effective when their behavior was not gender congruent (more competitive for men and more accommodating for women). The stereotypes used are often self-fulfilling, creating differences in how we evaluate what we see. As a culture, we *gender-type* others with dramatic effects. In the workplace, for example, so called "good managers" are still seen as possessing largely masculine traits as opposed to more androgynous or feminine traits (Powell and Butterfield 1979, 1984). Hence, as a culture, we place pressure on women and men with less masculine personalities to conform or be judged as less. Not surprisingly, consistent findings surface in the research literature that match other gender stereotypes.

Evidence suggests that although men are generally thought to be more comfortable in conflict settings (Duane 1989), using assertiveness and reason with greater effect in the workplace (Papa and Natalle 1989) and approving of competition between parties (Baxter and Shepard 1978), they are also more likely to avoid conflict (Kelley, Cunningham, Grishman, Lefebvre, Sink, and Yablon 1978). Women, on the other hand, are thought to react more emotionally in conflict situations (Kelley et al., 1978) and to be more flexible than men in conflict, adjusting their behaviors to meet the needs of the situation with greater skill (Yelsma and Brown 1985). Both men and women report being more accommodating when in conflicts with female partners (Berryman-Fink and Brunner 1987).

Gender differences in conflict are largely the result of cultural influences rather than biological influences (Yelsma and Brown 1985; Eagly and Steffen 1986). This school of thought, known as *sex-role research,* presumes that behavior in a particular role is a product of the interaction and the situation as framed by cultural beliefs, not a product with primarily biological origins such as genitalia. A good example of this distinction is a common pattern of conflict found in many distressed marriages.

Several researchers have distinguished a common form of marital conflict— the *demand/withdraw pattern*—in distressed heterosexual marriages (Christiansen and Heavey 1990; Heavey, Layne, and Christensen 1993; Markman, Silvern, Clements, and Hanak 1993). The pattern is created when one partner pressures the other through emotional criticisms and complaints, which causes the other partner to retreat through withdrawal and passive inaction. Whereas evidence points to a gender linkage to this pattern with women demanding and men withdrawing, evidence also suggests that the pattern occurs in the opposite direction when it is the husband who is requesting a change from the wife and engages in emotional criticisms to achieve this change (Markman et al. 1993). In other words, demand is not a condition of women any more than withdrawal is a condition of men. Rather, demand and withdraw are reactions to a relational situation framed by a culture that stereotypes what men and women should be and do. Women often find themselves in a role, prescribed by culture, of changing relationships; men in the role of reacting to criticisms about relationships. This is not a biological call but learning that takes place over and over again in the language community we call *culture*. Although neither role is fixed, it is difficult for men and women to break the cultural mold, hence gender differences. But it is culture, more than biology, that exacts a charge on how genders should behave. Through culture we learn what roles we play, what behaviors are appropriate, what strategies are effective. Culture teaches us that genders differ, although research suggests that those differences are more a matter of expectation than orientation. In this way, culture reveals a powerful influence on the patterns we display in conflict situations.

Intergroup conflict stems from a second process that builds on social categorization—group differentiation. By itself, social categorization only creates neutral divisions that enable people to situate themselves within society. *Group differentiation* refers to the polarization between groups and the attendant stereotyping of other groups that trigger conflicts. A wide range of events, including economic and political problems, natural disasters, wars, and population movements, can create conflicts of interest between groups. Conflicts can also arise due to the structure of society, as groups are put into opposition by historical traditions, the structure of economic opportunity, the nature of the political system, changing demographics, long-term shifts in economic fortunes, and other large currents. When this happens, groups tend to attribute responsibility for their problems to other groups and to unite against them.

This *we–they polarization* is produced by several communication dynamics (Sherif, Harvey, White, Hood, and Sherif, 1961; Blake, Shepard, and Mouton 1964; Northrup 1989). When groups are put into competition, there tends to be an increase in members' expressions of loyalty and commitment to the group. This behavior can be seen in rival street gangs who trumpet their "groupness" with colors, graffiti, secret signs, and steadfast obedience to their leaders' demands. It is equally evident in the fierce loyalty expressed by employees of competing firms, who will work long hours and devote themselves wholeheartedly to creating the best product or the winning bid. In-group messages also slant positions in favor of the group and demean the claims and validity of the other group. U.S. news coverage of the Iraq–United Nations situation, for example, generally presented the UN's side of the issues as reasonable common sense; the Iraqi view was generally presented as illogical, arbitrary, and without merit. The one-sided nature of the coverage served to reinforce Americans' perceptions of the correctness of the UN stance and to invalidate the Iraqi position. This slanting of positions in favor of the in-group generally prevents reflection on the merits of the other group's claims; the other group may be perceived as the embodiment of evil, with no legitimate claims at all.

Internal communication processes move the in-group toward a narrow, oversimplified view of the other group and contribute to the development of stereotypes—highly simplified beliefs about characteristics of other groups. Examples of stereotypes include "Japanese people all work hard and have no fun"; "men do not care about feelings"; and "gays are promiscuous." In each case, all members of the other group are assumed to have the same threatening or undesirable characteristic. People who hold to the stereotypes may use them to interpret the behavior of a member of another group.

During the desegregation crisis that occurred in the Boston public schools during the late 1970s, newspapers reported the following incident (adapted from Cooper and Fazio 1979, p. 153):

> A white girl who wanted to make a change in her program was using the wrong entrance to the high school, when a young black man touched her arm to get her attention.
>
> She screamed.
>
> The school's headmaster, Boston's title for a high school principal, was nearby and stepped in immediately, averting what he thought might have become a major incident.
>
> "He grabbed me," the girl said.
>
> "I was just trying to help her and tell her to use the front door so she wouldn't get into trouble," the boy said.

Stereotypical interpretations, such as this girl's, can promote strong reactions, heightening tensions between groups. Ironically, the stereotyper's expectations may be confirmed by the response his or her interpretations provoke from the other. Had the headmaster not stepped in, a violent confrontation between whites and African Americans might have occurred. Whites would have come away with the conclusion that the African American student had attacked the white student, and African American stereotypes about whites would have been reinforced as well.

Other communication processes heighten perceived disagreements between groups and separate their positions. Discussions in the in-group minimize similarities between the in-group and other groups and exaggerate differences between the groups' positions. In the Iraq conflict, news items explaining the Islamic way of thinking emphasized its divergence from Western thought. In a study of conflicts between line workers and office staff, Dalton (1959) found that the two groups heightened perceptions of differences between them by emphasizing differences in education level, social skills, and dress. It is evident that the claims serve to differentiate the groups and emphasize the chasm between them. Polarization is heightened by suppression of disagreement in the in-group. In-group messages minimize disagreements between members of the group and present a common front. Members who venture the opinion that the other group may have some valid claims or a legitimate position are often charged with disloyalty (Janis 1972). This stance prevents members of the in-group from exploring possible common ground with other groups and preserves stereotypes.

These communication processes result in one group becoming strongly united against the other. As noted in the discussion of the psychodynamic perspective, Lewis Coser (1956) observed that this we–they relationship has useful functions for the in-group. It creates high levels of cohesion and turns attention away from conflicts or dissatisfactions within the group. However, these dynamics also can create self-reinforcing cycles of polarization and hostility between the groups. If members believe the other group is responsible for their problems, hear only bad things about the other group, and are not permitted to test perceptions and beliefs, there is no way to improve intergroup relations. Members of the in-group, expecting the worst from the other group, are likely to act in a defensive or hostile manner toward members of the other group. In effect, the in-group creates a self-fulfilling prophecy whereby its worst fears about the hostility of the other group seem to be confirmed, justifying further polarizing communication (Cooper and Fazio 1979; Northrup 1989).

Once two groups have been in conflict for a time, they develop intergroup ideologies to justify their positions (Volkan 1994; Ross 1993). *Intergroup ideologies* are organized belief systems that describe the differences between groups in terms that present the in-group in a favorable light and explain the conflict from the in-group's perspective. For example, in the ongoing Israeli–Palestinian conflict, each side has developed elaborate explanations of why it has legitimate claims and has been wronged by the other side. These explanations provide each side with a ready stock of justifications for aggression toward the other and for both's unwillingness to make concessions.

Gouldner (1954) describes a similar case in a gypsum plant facing a strike. A history of confrontation between union and management led management to conclude that the union was simply trying to control everything that occurred in the plant. As a result of this belief, management saw no need to consider the legitimacy of any issues raised by the union because managers thought that under all of them was the hidden agenda of control. Management's lack of response to worker concerns contributed to a wildcat strike, which might have been averted if the managers had considered the issues on their merits. Intergroup ideologies solidify the conflict between groups because they are taken as unquestionable truth. New members and children are taught these beliefs with the result that they can see the other group only in terms of the ideology.

Together, the processes of social categorization, group differentiation, and intergroup ideology development define social reality so that members transfer general beliefs about other groups and their differences into conflict situations. These beliefs can funnel interpretations and actions to produce longer and more intense conflicts.

Differences in culture, history, and experience between groups can also create misunderstandings that heighten divisions. It has been said that there are such fundamental differences between African American, white, and Hispanic cultures in the United States so that it is difficult for members to really understand each other. Shenkar and Ronen (1987, p. 268) discuss possible problems that can occur during negotiations between Chinese and U.S. citizens:

> The Chinese preference for restrained, moderate behavior suggests that one should avoid overtly aggressive behavior. The American task-oriented approach, which allows for the admission of differences in the positions of the parties to a negotiation so as to promote "honest confrontation" is viewed by the Chinese as aggressive, and

therefore as an unacceptable mode of behavior. . . . The Chinese tend to prefer to make decisions behind the scenes . . . and this contributes greatly to American anxiety as to where they stand as discussions progress. These differences in cultural preference can cause serious misunderstandings that contribute to escalation of conflicts.

The intergroup conflict perspective is useful because it reminds us that conflicts cannot be reduced to interpersonal terms. Larger social relations and the history of intergroup relations play an important role in many conflicts. Group identification is an important part of every person's identity, so it is inevitable that intergroup differences will be pulled into interpersonal conflicts. Indeed, sometimes people can be *forced into* a conflict by the structure of intergroup relations. In a community with racial problems, for example, it is difficult for people from different racial backgrounds to have an interpersonal conflict that is not in some way influenced by racial differences. Billig (1976) argues that the only way to prevent such conflicts is to change relationships between groups—a task that is often quite difficult to achieve. (See Case 3.3.)

The Coordinated Management of Meaning Theory

The Coordinated Management of Meaning (CMM) theory is an interactional theory that focuses on how individuals organize, manage, and coordinate their meanings and actions with one another (Pearce 1976; Pearce and Cronen 1980). The theory proposes that the interpretation of the meaning of a conversation or message is shaped by the context or nature of the relationship between the interactants as well as the self-concept and culture of each individual. Because each individual inevitably brings unique experiences and meanings to any conversation, meaning will always be to some degree idiosyncratic or unique. The more individuals share similar or complementary worldviews, self-concepts, and understandings of their relationships, the more likely they are to arrive at similar interpretations of conversations and messages. The theory provides a framework for explaining both how an individual attributes meaning to a message, conversation, or relationship and how interactants then come to coordinate both their meanings and actions in the course of a conversation. Meanings are important because they lead to decisions about what action to take and what action to avoid.

The theory proposes that individuals organize meanings hierarchically and use one level of meaning to determine meaning on another level (Figure 3.4). The seven levels of meaning described by the theory range from the broad and abstract to the concrete and specific. The hierarchy can be viewed as an inverted pyramid or triangle. At the bottom of the triangle is a specific message within a conversation. The hierarchy demonstrates the many layers of meaning that we coordinate and use to create coherence in interpreting specific messages and actions. Starting from the top, the first two levels of meaning are broad-based, cumulative ways of viewing the world and one's self.

CASE **3.3**

Intergroup Conflict Dynamics and the Parking Lot Scuffle

Jay and Tim are from the same cultural group, so intergroup dynamics do not explain the Parking Lot Scuffle very well. However, if Jay and Tim had been from different groups—for example, were different genders; had different sexual orientations; or were from different racial, ethnic, or national groups—these differences could have been salient. If they had, we would expect several dynamics described in this section to be set in motion.

We would expect that stereotypes about each group would surface and be woven into an interpretation of why Jay and Tim were reacting as they did. For example, if they were from different ethnic groups (say X and Y), then one might think of the other, "That's just how an X (or Y) would react here, always trying to get the upper hand." These simplified ideas would influence their attributions about each other and shape their behavior, perhaps making it more competitive than it would oth-

erwise be. As they interacted, the we–they polarization would get in the way of understanding, further complicating efforts at constructive conflict management.

After the scuffle, Tim and Jay might talk about it with members of their own group. This would promote ideological processes by which members further polarize opinions about the other group. In turn, this would strengthen Tim's and Jay's current competitive orientations and undermine their ability to collaborate in later discussions.

Discussion Question

■ *Although Tim and Jay are not from different groups, the Parking Lot Scuffle contains several statements that might contribute to stereotyping. Can you identify some of these and explain how they might function in an intergroup conflict if Tim and Jay did belong to different groups?*

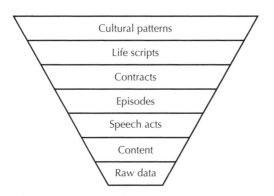

FIGURE 3.4   **Coordinated Management of Meaning: Hierarchy of Interpretive Contexts**

Cultural patterns refer to a socially shaped framework for viewing the world and one's roles and actions within it. This broadest context acknowledges the influence of one's particular cultural experience and how it shapes how all experience is viewed and interpreted. The second level, *life scripts*, specifically encompasses the individual's self-concept and expectations for what can and should happen to him or her. The next level of meaning concerns the specific individual or individuals with whom one is interacting at a particular point in time—*contracts* define and specify expectations of the particular relationship based on the kinds of episodes that occur within the relationship. *Episodes*—the next level of meaning—focus on the particular interaction taking place at a particular point in time. They define the kind of activity that occurs between individuals based on the kinds and sequencing of messages being exchanged. More specifically, the next three levels focus on a particular message that a speaker has produced in the flow of interaction: *Speech acts* identify the intent of the speaker ("What is the speaker trying to do by saying this to me?"), whereas *content* is the decoding of the substance of the message, and *raw data* concerns the audio and visual signals that reach the brain.

An individual coordinates meaning by using one level in the hierarchy to aid in the interpretation of meaning at another level. For example, if the intent of the speaker is unclear (speech act), then the receiver relies on the nature of the episode, the kind of relationship, and his or her life script and culture to help identify the likely intent. This logical relationship between levels produces *constitutive rules* for determining meaning. *Constitutive rules* stipulate how meanings at one level determine meanings at another level. For example, if an individual says, "You're looking good," you would rely on the nature of the relationship (for example, doctor–patient versus male–female strangers versus romantic partners), your self-concept (healthy, attractive), and the nature of the interaction between you (physical examination, chance encounter on a street, romantic interlude) to determine what this message "counts as." This interpretation then becomes a basis for action. Relying on regulative rules formed by one's culture, self-concept, relationship, type of episode, and speaker's intention, one determines an appropriate response. *Regulative rules* specify what is appropriate action given the nature of the relationship, the episode, and what the other person has said. Do you respond with relief to an indication that you are healthy? Or do you give the stranger an icy stare? Or do you return the compliment to your romantic partner? So, constitutive rules are means for identifying the meanings of relationships, messages, and so on, whereas regulative rules identify what action to take given these meanings. In this way, both meaning and action are determined.

An individual's meanings and actions become coordinated with one another as their rules become intermeshed. However, it is important to note that *coordinated* does not necessarily mean that individuals agree on the meaning of what is going on. Rules can be shared as individuals share meanings on a variety of levels. But rules may also differ, yet yield coordinated action. Consider the young college student who complains that he hates going home on the weekend because as soon as he enters the house his father starts interrogating him about his personal life at college. The son feels that he is independent and no longer needs to report to his father. The father, he believes, should respect his privacy. When his father asks him questions, he feels that he is treating him as a child and does not trust him. If the father were asked for his interpretation of these visits home, he would explain that he wants to be a good father and maintain a close and caring relationship with his son; therefore, he tries to show his interest and caring by asking about his son's life at school. The more his son withdraws, the more he feels he must persist because he does not want their relationship to deteriorate and become distant. And, of course, the more he persists, the more the son withdraws. The result is a very well-coordinated conversation, one in which the participants do not even suspect that the event has a different meaning for the other.

The coordinated management of meaning provides a basis for identifying and understanding how the same event can have different meanings for the parties involved and how these meanings affect their actions. The theory explains why participants sometimes seem vulnerable to escalating moves in interaction. According to CMM, people act according to the interpretive rules they use. Through interaction, participants create an interlocking rule system, which is considered interlocked because the *rule-guided behavior* of each party is interpreted and responded to by the rules of the other. In other words, each action becomes the condition of the next rule-guided interpretation. Because the type of interaction participants produce is a function of the rule system they create, certain patterns can be self-sustaining. Although most episodes vary widely, in some cases, people become so enmeshed in an episode as to be "out of control" (Cronen, Pearce, and Snavely 1980). In these situations, the rule system created by the participants produces unwanted repetitive patterns (URPs). The same patterns emerge again and again as participants interpret and respond to each other's actions in the same way. Once this pattern is established, we expect it to occur over and over. It is natural to make similar choices based on what we think our partner is likely to do (Berk and Anderson 2000). Such repetitive patterns for participants are difficult to recognize and hard to break.

The Coordinated Management of Meaning theory provides a framework for understanding one way in which intergroup differences influence conflicts. As social categorizations and stereotypes become salient through the processes discussed earlier, they highlight elements of contracts, life scripts, and cultural patterns that focus on group differences. Once these are activated and salient to parties, they influence interpretation of episodes, speech acts, and content. For example, if a male manager and female employee get into an argument and one registers a comment about the other's gender ["that's just what I'd expect from a man (woman)"], gender groupings would be highlighted. Subsequent remarks would be very likely to be interpreted in light of prevailing cultural beliefs about gender or gender-related parts of the parties' life scripts. In a real sense, the conflict becomes as much about gender as about the original issue because the framework of meanings emphasizes intergroup conflicts between genders. (See Case 3.4.)

CASE **3.4**

CMM Theory and the Parking Lot Scuffle

According to the CMM theory, each individual inevitably brings unique experiences and meanings to any conversation; hence, meaning will always be to some degree idiosyncratic. The more individuals share similar or complementary worldviews, self-concepts, and understandings of their relationships, the more likely they are to arrive at similar interpretations of conversations and messages. The lack of a common context in the Parking Lot Scuffle portends that interpretations of what is said will be especially problematic.

In this case, we do not have data concerning the individuals involved and their perceptions, so we must infer from their actions how they might see the situation. Furthermore, the individuals are strangers, so are more likely to see the situation differently and to not understand one another's perspective.

Tim aggressively confronts Jay over the accident. This strong opening may reflect a life script that includes a self-concept of standing up for himself to avoid being pushed around by others. In addition, as strangers, Tim's and Jay's relational contract is one totally defined by the situation of the accident, and each must use extraneous information to predict how the other might act. Given that Tim tells us that he cannot afford to have a moped fixed and that we know Jay has a parking place whereas Tim does not, it is possible that Tim perceives Jay as a higher-status person who may treat him poorly. These conclusions may produce the regulative rule that if one is in a threatening situation with a higher-status person, then one must stand up for oneself so that advantages will not be taken. Note how Tim continues to focus on the damage done to his scooter and how Jay must pay for it.

What counts as appropriate behavior in this situation is up to the participants. Because the nature of the relationship during the episode is relatively unfamiliar, other regula-

tive rules specifying appropriate action are also unclear. Constitutive rules are also contested. Both Jay and Tim struggle over how to interpret their speech acts, as displayed in lines 10 and 11, when Tim impugns Jay to explain what employment has to do with the accident. Only general cultural patterns help the actors interpret many of the remarks and questions they receive. In fact, it appears as though Jay may be slow on the uptake, taking questions in lines 1 and 8 on face value rather than as challenges.

It may be that the participants have created a rule system that encourages the use of escalating tactics. The redundancy of tactics in the episode supports this conclusion. Tim repeatedly threatens Jay, using a wide variety of speech acts to do so. Jay, on the other hand, who seems always to be on the defensive during the episode, repeatedly resorts to questions and justifications. Almost as if the episode is written to music, each accusation or threat by Tim increases in intensity, while each question by Jay responds with rising force. This result may suggest that Tim and Jay have created a repetitive pattern of caustic actions. From this vantage, we can see the same patterns emerge line after line as participants respond to each other's actions in the same way. In any case, the CMM theory would suggest that the Parking Lot Scuffle is more a conflict over how to coordinate necessarily ambiguous meanings than it is a conflict about the moped accident.

Discussion Questions

Analyze your own behavior in a recent conflict using CMM concepts.

- *What expectations did you have?*
- *What meanings did you assign to the other person's actions?*
- *Can you identify the source of those expectations and interpretations?*

The Confrontation Episodes Theory

Newell and Stutman (1988, 1991) offer a descriptive theory of social confrontation episodes. Their description of confrontation episodes is based on a view of communication as an activity performed cooperatively between two or more parties. According to the theory, an interaction is not simply talk about some topic but a purposeful event that participants co-create.

Social *confrontation episodes* involve conflict over conduct and rules of conduct. The confrontation episode is initiated when one participant signals the other participant that his or her behavior has violated, or is violating, a rule or expectation for appropriate conduct within the relationship or situation. The function of a social confrontation generally can be described as working through disagreement over behaviors and thus negotiating expectations for future conduct. The episode is recognizable as a sequence of behaviors moving from initiation to resolution.

The function of the episode appears to produce typical issues and sequences of interaction. Before the problematic issue can be explored in the episode, the participants must first agree to the social or relational legitimacy of the rule. Once this critical issue is settled, the behavior in question can be assessed with respect to the rule. For example, a person may confront a spouse over spending money for clothing beyond a budget limit. Once the confrontee acknowledges the legitimacy of this relational rule (budget), questions concerning the act of spending too much for clothing in relation to this rule can be explored. That is, did the confrontee perform the behavior in question? Does the behavior constitute a violation of this rule? Is there a superseding rule that takes precedence? Is the confrontee responsible for his or her behavior? The episode is then concluded with solutions ranging from remedy to legislation of a new rule.

Newell and Stutman (1988) provide a model of the social confrontation episode, which displays the various ways an episode can develop depending on the issues between the parties (Figure 3.5). The purpose of this model is to define the confrontation episode and to illustrate how confrontation episodes differ from one another in their lines of development. While action moves from initiation through development toward some sort of closure or resolution to the problem, the pattern of interaction can vary greatly. Although the confronter may perceive that the confrontee has behaved in a rule-breaking manner, how the problem ultimately comes to be defined and resolved depends on the interaction between the participants. Confrontation episodes are issue-driven. In other words, the development of the episode emerges from the points of controversy between the participants. The model then illustrates the major variations in how the problem is defined and resolved through interaction.

Constructed as an issue tree, the model in the figure displays the various issues likely to occur within confrontation (designated A–F), and the track or the line of development (designated 1–6) that any particular episode might take depending on the points of disagreement between the participants. The point of controversy determines the variation of a particular confrontation episode (tracks 1–6). The model serves as a visual display of the logical relationship between

A. Is the implied rule mutually accepted as legitimate?
B. Is this a special situation?
C. If invoked, is the superseding rule mutually accepted as legitimate?
D. Did the confrontee actually perform the behavior in question?
E. Does the behavior constitute a violation of the rule?
F. Does the confrontee accept responsibility for the behavior?

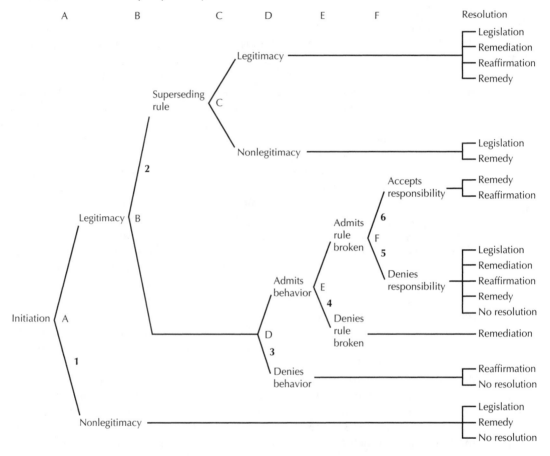

FIGURE 3.5   An Elaborate Model of Social Confrontation

Source: Adapted from Newell and Stutman (1988). Reprinted by permission of Taylor & Francis Ltd. (www.tandf.co.uk/journals).

central issues that can emerge in any particular confrontation. As such, it illustrates ways in which the episode may develop depending on the interaction between the participants.

The major split between tracks occurs over whether the confronter's expectations are explicitly or implicitly granted legitimacy by the confrontee, or whether the confrontee challenges the legitimacy of the expectations. The conversation moves along track 1, *nonlegitimacy,* if the confrontee challenges the legitimacy of the confronter's expectations, in essence arguing that the implied rule is not mutually acceptable or agreed on. If the confrontee does not challenge the legitimacy of the rule, a number of other lines of argument remain. On track 2, *justification,* the episode revolves around whether or not this is a special situation for which the confrontee invokes a superseding rule for the extenuating circumstances. This rule is also open to challenges of legitimacy, but this time by the confronter rather than the confrontee. On track 3, *denies behavior,* the question concerns whether the confrontee actually performed the behavior in question. On track 4, *denies rule broken,* the issue is one of interpretation as to what constitutes a violation of the rule. On track 5, *denies responsibility,* the issue revolves around the excuse offered by the confrontee to deny responsibility for the behavior. Confrontations that develop along the lines of track 6 stand out from the others because of the lack of controversy in defining the problem. On track 6, *accepts responsibility,* the confrontee accepts responsibility for his or her behavior and moves to reaffirm the rule or remedy the situation. The response of the "accused" to the confrontation determines the track the episode will take. Once on a particular line of development, the confronter is primarily left the job of evaluating the confrontee's response. The confronter's evaluation can either "hold" the interactants to a particular issue or allow them to move toward resolution. Resolution requires interactants to negotiate an acceptable response to the problem.

According to the theory, the social confrontation episode has a particular pattern—an imprint—which stands out from other communication episodes. Yet within this pattern is diversity; each enactment of social confrontation may display the uniqueness of a fingerprint. In particular, the initiating act serves to identify or define the episode that is to be enacted. Furthermore, the manner of the initiation sets the tone for the episode. The key for a social confrontation episode to occur lies in the receiver's willingness to honor the speaker's initiating act as a confrontation. This willingness can be described as conferring the act of complaining with social legitimacy.

Although the expectation or rule underlying the complaint may be arguable, the receiver accepts the right of the speaker to complain. Without this element a complaint may be ignored, a complainer requested to go away, or the message responded to as if it were some other complaining activity such as nagging or bellyaching. The receiver may even refuse, or be unable, to hear the message as a complaint. Actors negotiate the episodes they enact by first dealing with problematic initiatives in such a way as to satisfy their goals.

A complaint may be "heard" naively or strategically and receive a multitude of responses. For an example of the range of possibilities, let's consider the fairly straightforward statement, "You're late." A receiver might directly acknowledge this as a complaint, signifying a confrontation over rule infringement by responding: "I'm sorry. I forgot to set my alarm clock. I won't let it happen again." Or the receiver might respond in a manner that suggests the statement may simply be an assertion of a fact without a necessarily negative connotation. By asking, "Did I miss anything important?" the receiver at least opens up the conversation for confrontation should the sender decide to persist. Other responses simply add additional comment on the fact: "Everyone says I'll be late for my own funeral." "This is early for me." Alternately, responses may cast the statement as a complaint, but one requiring sympathy or commiseration: "Isn't it terrible? You just can't count on anyone anymore." "I know just how you feel. I hate waiting for people." Of course, the receiver may directly or indirectly challenge the sender's right to complain about the receiver's behavior: "You're not my keeper." "Your watch is keeping good time." Finally, the statement may be cast as an insult deserving reciprocation: "Not late enough to miss you."

The possible range of responses pinpoints the problematic nature of initiation. The receiver is always able to respond to the initial act in a manner inconsistent with its intent. Unwittingly interpreting a complaint as an insult or some other speech act is a common occurrence that forces the confronter to meet the resistance if confrontation is to occur. Such naive responses on the part of the receiver are not necessarily an issue of communication competence, but rather a function of the unique nature of communication episodes. To recast an episode is not a simple matter of reinitiation but one of gaining the cooperation of the other so that a confrontation will proceed. No single move can meet these conditions. Meaning is therefore negotiated by both parties even at the point of initiation.

Confrontation episodes theory illustrates how sequences of conflict interaction are coconstructed by parties. It gives a fuller picture of a point made in the Introduction: Conflict interaction is never fully controlled by one party but is a melding of two or more parties' actions to produce a larger episode. (See Case 3.5.)

Phase Models of Conflict

Other phase descriptions of conflict go beyond the two-phase analysis introduced in Chapter 1. The models rely on a multiple-stage characterization of how conflict develops. Phase descriptions are often developed from diverse conflict contexts, from broad societal and international models of conflict to much narrower accounts of small group decisions and intimate conflicts. They describe the emergence and progression of conflicts in terms of units larger than confrontation episodes.

Based on a study of international conflicts, Rummel (1976) suggests that conflicts pass through five sequential phases. In the earliest stage, Rummel says, conflict is *latent;* in other words, individuals hold different dispositions or attitudes that carry the potential for conflict. Differences in values, objectives, and outlooks are present and lay the groundwork for future behavior. During the *initiation* phase, some triggering event causes the individuals to act. At this point, the potential differences become the basis for interaction. After the conflict has been initiated, the interaction turns toward an attempt at balancing *power*. In this third phase, individuals assess each other's capabilities and willingness to use force, threats, rewards, and so on, and they actually confront the issue as they try to reach some accommodation or settlement. The accommodation leads to a *balance of power* phase in which the participants come to understand the consequences of the resolution and learn to live with the outcomes. This phase is characterized by the set expectations of indi-

CASE **3.5**

Confrontation Episodes Theory and the Parking Lot Scuffle

From the view of confrontation episodes theory, the Parking Lot Scuffle could be subtitled "Who Broke What Rule?" Tim and Jay each frame the problem differently and, thus, the responsibility for the problem differently. Ultimately, their failure to agree on the root problem leads to escalation and a physical fight. Tim focuses on the implicit rule that one should not hit a parked vehicle. Meanwhile, Jay focuses on the implied rule that one should not park in someone else's parking space. This rule provides backing to Jay's excuse that he did not see the moped in time to stop. Inevitably, what unfolds is competition over who gets to be the confronter in this episode.

Each is trying to establish that he has been harmed by the behavior of the other. Tim claims he was harmed by Jay running into his parked scooter. Jay claims that his car was damaged because Tim parked where he should not have. Their inability to negotiate the episode in terms of what is the relevant rule and who is the confronter and confrontee leads to a breakdown of conversation and the resorting to physical violence. Each party lays down different tracks for the conversation, riding different trains right past the other.

If we look at each of Tim's turns in the conversation, we see that his points are coherent with one another. He begins by confronting Jay for hitting his moped, then lists damage done, then seeks a remedy: "You're going to pay." Meanwhile, Jay only fleetingly follows Tim's lead by offering an excuse for his violation of the rule invoked by Tim: He could not see the bike in time to stop. But Jay immediately moves to shift to a different confrontation by counterconfronting Tim for parking in his space. Tim repeatedly denies the relevancy of Jay's counterconfrontation and returns to the damage done, seeking a remedy. When Jay attempts to shift the conversation by asking Tim if he works there and then to end it by walking away, Tim makes verbal and physical moves to continue the episode.

Discussion Questions

- *Using the following rules as starting points, map imagined conflicts on the confrontation episodes model from initiation through resolution/closure:*
  - *–Send a thank you note when you've received a gift.*
  - *–Clean up after your dog.*
  - *–Be prepared for class.*
- *Describe the possible controversies at each juncture of the model.*

---

viduals and may last for some time until significant changes in circumstances, attitudes, or goals arise. Such evolving changes lead to a *disruption* stage during which parties realize that circumstances are ripe once again for the emergence of potential conflict and eventual confrontation. This model implies a continual cycle—from latency to initiation to balancing power to a balance of power to a disruption, back to a new latency, and so on—until the issue is ultimately resolved.

In the organizational context, Pondy (1967) developed a somewhat similar phase analysis of the emergence and development of conflict. Pondy suggests that conflict passes through five stages. Conflict is first *latent* in that some set of conditions, such as insufficient resources or divergent goals, comes to exist but is not yet perceived or acted on. Then the conflict is *perceived* when the latent issues reach awareness. Pondy notes that conflict can be perceived when no latent conflict exists; that is, when parties misunderstand each other's positions. Parties then enter a stage of *felt* conflict in which the conflict changes one party's feelings for or effect on the other. It is here that the conflict becomes charged emotionally as parties feel anxiety, mistrust, or hostility toward a perceived opponent. *Manifest* conflict occurs when parties act on the perceived and felt differences. During this stage, behaviors are said to be conflictual if one or both parties perceive them as thwarting the attainment of goals. Finally, conflict enters an *aftermath* stage in which new relationships and arrangements are formed and assessments are made of outcomes. All through the stages, the development of conflict can be influenced not only by the moves of the parties but by changing the environmental conditions in the organization.

Analyses of formal negotiations suggest that the negotiation process unfolds in identifiable phases as well (Douglas 1962; Morley and Stephenson 1977; Putnam and Jones 1982b; Putnam, Wilson, Waltman, and Turner, 1986; Holmes 1992). One ground-breaking study of the interaction that occurs in union–management negotiations found that a three-phase framework described conflict development in this context (Morley and Stephenson 1977). In the first phase, called *distributive bargaining,* the parties test the feasibility of possible demands, establish criteria for appropriate settlements, assess the power of each side, and evaluate the strength of the cases being made. Here the parties see themselves fulfilling their roles as representatives of a "side" in the negotiations, building planned cases for constituents. In the second phase, *problem-solving,* the parties explore a range of solutions that might satisfy the criteria established at the outset. There is some tactical maneuvering but, by and large, the focus is on establishing a working relationship by proposing and evaluating solutions to identified problems. In the final *decision-making* phase, the parties come to agreement on some terms and explore the implications of their decision. The focus is on reality checking—assessing the feasibility and implementation of terms that both sides support.

All phase analyses of conflict are built on an episodic conception of how conflict interaction unfolds. Although somewhat different sequences of episodes are posited for different conflict contexts, the basic premise that conflicts travel through meaningful segments of interaction is common to all of the models. Phase theories offer several important insights about the nature of conflict interaction.

1. *Phase research suggests that conflicts have a definite pattern or rhythm.* The pattern often seems to depend on participants' expectations about likely directions conflicts will take. These expectations seem to be governed by an underlying logic of progressions that conflicts go through and serve to make even apparently confusing interaction understandable over the long run. Looking back and forward simultaneously, parties can see an ambiguous situation of latent conflict growing into a test of power and can anticipate the need to deescalate the conflict by compromise or at least by backing off. Phase models imply that an understanding of the direction and pattern of conflict behaviors can only be gained if conflicts are looked at broadly, with an eye toward the sequence of behaviors that occur over time. Phase models lead to a conception of conflict that includes not only confrontation and discussion of differences between parties, but also intermittent periods of equilibrium and calm when the parties settle into new arrangements resulting from the conflict (Christensen and Pasch 1993).

2. *The same patterns or forms of interaction can serve different functions in different conflict phases.* Each phase provides the broader, meaningful context that makes behavior understandable in light of what is going on at any particular conflict stage. Ellis and Fisher (1975) argue, for example, that ambiguous comments occur in both the beginning and end phases of decision-making conflict in small groups. At the beginning of a conflict, these comments reflect the ambiguity of indecision; people are unsure about their attitudes and are trying to orient themselves to the issue before the group. In the final phase, however, the ambiguous comments reflect members' moves from one position to another. Members are changing their minds so that agreement can be reached and a group decision can be made. So an understanding of the general phase guides interpretation of more specific comments, or sequences of acts, that occur at any moment in the conflict.

3. *Phase research also suggests that certain events can ignite confrontation.* This is not because they are particularly important in themselves, but because they occur at a critical point in the conflict interaction (Donohue and Kolt 1992). As a conflict ripens and people feel pressure to face up to the issues, seemingly common and inconsequential events can trigger rapid escalation. A misplaced criticism, teasing, or even a casual reference to a touchy subject can be tinder in a dry forest that soon ignites. Any comment can force parties to address an issue or to act on previously unacknowledged differences. While latent differences may influence interaction in subtle and destructive ways, the issues themselves are often hazy or ill-defined until the triggering event brings them out in the open.

4. *Conflict often includes a testing period before any direct confrontation occurs.* This testing period allows parties to reduce their uncertainty about what others will do if they make certain moves. For example, in the face of an impending conflict, one person may want to cooperate but fears being taken advantage of. By making certain subtle cooperative overtures, the individual can assess likely responses without taking big risks. By testing the waters, parties gain knowledge of the likely consequences of moves they might make. This knowledge enables people to develop broad strategies and to choose specific tactics as the conflict unfolds. Phase models suggest that these testing periods can play a critical role in determining the direction conflicts will take; they offer a chance for people to "flirt" with various approaches without overly exposing themselves.

The main weakness in phase models of conflict is that they are too simplistic. Recent research suggests that phasic analyses sometimes overemphasize the role of a *logical step-by-step sequence* in the development of conflicts. Poole (1981; Leveque and Poole 1998), for example, found that the assumption of a set sequence of phases was often not correct for decision-making groups. Instead of a single set of phases applicable to all decisions, he found numerous different sequences, depending on how the group chose to attack its problem. Sambamurthy and Poole

(1992) found that conflicts develop in several different sequences too. In a study of forty groups, they found four general patterns of response to differences. The first pattern was characterized by low confrontation on conflict issues. Instead of confronting, the group spent most of its time in phases of cooperative, *focused work* broken by *integration* phases consisting of tangential discussions or joking. Conflicts simply never surfaced in this first pattern. A second pattern was characterized by phases of focused work alternating with phases of *critical work* in which members raised alternative points of view but did not openly acknowledge opposition. In critical work phases, differences were aired in a low-key manner. This often proved to be an effective method of working out differences between members. In some cases, groups passed through three or four cycles of focused work phases, alternating with phases of critical work.

Neither of the first two patterns confronted conflict directly. A third pattern consisted of phases of focused work and critical work followed by a phase of *open opposition*, in which the conflict surfaced. Once the opposition was expressed, members resolved the conflict either by dropping the subject and reentering a phase of focused work or by one party giving in to the other. The first method of resolving the opposition corresponds to conflict avoidance, whereas the second method corresponds to a win–lose conflict resolution. A final pattern had phases of focused and critical work followed by opposition. In this case, however, the opposition was resolved by problem-solving or compromising. This final pattern corresponds to the entire *differentiation–integration sequence* discussed previously. Interestingly, Sambamurthy and Poole found that this fourth sequence resulted in better outcomes for their groups than did the first three sequences, consistent with predictions in the differentiation–integration model.

Phase theories point to the ways in which members' behaviors tend to perpetuate conflict cycles and illustrate how conflicts develop a momentum that leads interaction in constructive or destructive directions. Phase models of conflict suggest that conflict interaction is vulnerable to any force that can cause a redefinition of what the parties see themselves doing at any point in the conflict. When a disputant or a third-party intervenor changes the perceptions of what the parties see themselves doing, he or she can create changes in the moves and responses that follow. Disputants, in other words, will act in accordance with, or in defiance of, the episodic structure of the conflict as it is perceived. There are a series of techniques, often referred to under the general name *reframing*, that can create changes in perceptions of conflict episodes. (See Case 3.6.) Chapter 7 examines reframing techniques as a set of forces that can influence conflict interaction.

Summary and Review

What are conflict styles?

Human relations scholars defined five basic styles of conflict management, which represent how people in organizations can relate to each other during conflict. Conflict styles represent basic patterns of behavior that people tend to enact dur-

CASE **3.6**

Phase Models and the Parking Lot Scuffle

The Parking Lot Scuffle exhibits clear phasic structure. In terms of Rummel's model, there is no latent phase in this conflict. Because Tim and Jay do not meet each other until the accident, there is no incipient conflict. The triggering incident is the accident itself, which precipitates the interaction that leads to the conflict. The discussion up to and through the scuffle is a balancing of power between Jay and Tim. They test each other's positions and resolve and ultimately balance power through physical violence. The end of the scuffle finds the conflict in an unresolved state in that issues, such as who will pay for the damage and whether Tim and Jay can work out a shared interpretation of the situation, are undetermined. At the end of the scuffle, the conflict subsides, but it may break out again when Jay and Tim must discuss the accident, responsibilities, and liabilities later on. A new triggering incident may start another cycle of power bal-

ancing, and the conflict probably will continue until the parties attain a settlement that both accept.

In terms of Pondy's phase model, Tim and Jay pass through the perceived and felt conflict stages very quickly and move right into the manifest conflict stage. During this stage, they engage primarily in distributive behavior and emerge into the aftermath stage following the scuffle. Their assessments of the episode are likely to be quite negative, which could create latent conflict in future encounters. They are likely to quickly go through the perceived and felt conflict stages when they meet, precipitating a manifest conflict once again.

Discussion Question

■ *What could Jay and/or Tim do to break the cycles of conflict that are apparent in a phase theory picture of this conflict?*

---

ing conflicts. The five styles, which differ in terms of their concern with satisfying one's own goals and their concern for other's goals, can be distinguished: competing, accommodating, avoiding, collaborating, and compromising.

Why are experimental games used to model conflict?

Important influences on conflict behavior are the benefits and costs of various types of behavior for the parties. Experimental games depict the structure of benefits and costs for different combinations of moves parties might make, and therefore model this aspect of conflicts. The advantage of this is that interdependence can be clearly set up in experiments that explore behavior in conflicts. Many different kinds of games can be defined, reflecting different types of interdependence.

What are the assumptions underlying experimental game research?

In this approach, it is assumed that behavior is governed by social exchanges in which parties are motivated primarily by self-interest. Parties assess the costs and benefits of various behaviors and undertake the behavior that yields a satisfactory ratio of benefits to costs. In conflicts the exchanges occur in the course of selection of moves; the costs and benefits are displayed in the game matrix, which indicates the payoffs for each of the parties from each combination of moves. Game research assumes that the parties know the choices available to them, that they are aware of the payoffs of each choice, and that they make their choices based on calculations of gains and losses from each move.

What insights does game research provide into conflict?

It models conflict as a series of moves and countermoves, and experimental games give us insights into the tendencies people have in conflict interaction. Some of these insights are discussed in more depth in Chapter 7, which is concerned with conflict strategies and tactics. It also gives us insights into how people react to interdependence in conflicts.

What are some limitations of game research?

Game researchers assume limited, well-defined options, whereas in actual situations options are more varied and changeable. Game researchers also assume people are aware of outcomes associated with different behavior choices and can accurately assess their value. However, people often do not know or appreciate the consequences of their behavior. Game researchers also assume people are capable of some fairly complicated calculations. However, these calculations are often too complex for limited cognitive capacities and people shortcut them. One other limitation is that explanations based on social exchange are sometimes circular and insufficient.

How do intergroup dynamics influence conflict interaction?

Many social divisions characterize society, including possible divisions between genders, socioeconomic classes, ethnic groups, and cultures. When these division points become salient, they can start a process of self-reinforcing polarization that can fuel conflicts. A we–they division that distances the parties and promotes stereotyping is created through communication processes of social categorization, group differentiation, and intergroup ideology formation.

Social categorization defines different groups and makes the divisions between groups salient. Group differentiation processes highlight the value of and similarities among members of the in-group and exaggerate the negative qualities of the out-group. Both in-group and out-group are portrayed as more uniform and cohesive than they actually are, and individual differences among members of each group are downplayed. Group ideologies are developed to explain the conflict in a way that favors the in-group and demonizes the out-group. Differences and grievances between groups are explained in terms of qualities and characteristics of the group's members and one portrayed as inevitable and unchangeable. Other explanations of the conflict are downplayed, ignored, or refuted. The intergroup conflict perspective highlights the importance of social and cultural factors in conflicts and reminds us that conflicts cannot be reduced solely to the interpersonal level.

How does the coordinated management of meaning theory contribute to our understanding of conflict?

This perspective focuses on how individuals create and sustain meanings during communication processes. It proposes a hierarchical model with several levels of meaning: from highest to lowest they are cultural patterns, life scripts, contracts, episodes, speech acts, content, and raw data. When people try to understand communication at one level, they use other levels as context. For example, a joking comment is likely to mean one thing in a friendly conversation episode, but quite another during a conflict episode. The levels are used to specify two kinds of rules that govern communication. Constitutive rules indicate what an act stands for or indicates in a particular context, whereas regulative rules specify appropriate actions in that context. Parties use the two types of rules to interact. Each party invokes a particular set of rules as he or she interacts, and these may or may not be consistent. How the rule sets of the parties mesh determines how the interaction goes. If inconsistent rule sets are used, coordination becomes difficult and interaction may break down, or, in some circumstances, go out of control.

How does confrontation episodes theory model conflict?

This theory proposes a set of decision points, organized around key issues, that are likely to occur during a confrontation (see Figure 3.5). This figure defines several tracks episodes can follow, including nonlegitimacy, justification, denial of behavior, denial of broken rules, denial of responsibility, and acceptance of responsibility. This theory models conflict at the move–countermove level and provides a framework to help us understand the logic behind moves and countermoves. It represents a common way in which parties' rule systems mesh during conflicts.

How do the phase models relate to one another?

Phase models describe how conflicts unfold over time. Several models more complex than the two-phase model of Chapter 1 have been advanced. Rummel posits that conflicts pass through five stages: latent conflict, initiation, conflict behavior, balance of power, and disruption. This model, derived from studies of national conflict, is somewhat similar to Pondy's model of organizational conflict, which posits the following phases: latent conflict, perceived conflict, felt conflict, manifest conflict, aftermath. In both cases, conflict starts below the surface and then emerges into full-fledged struggle and then once again moves into a quiet period. Analyses of bargaining have tended to find three stages: distributive bargaining, problem-solving, and decision making.

Phase models depict the regular patterns during conflicts. These patterns form part of the context for moves and countermoves—they are episodes that frame conflict behaviors in terms of the Coordinated Management of Meaning theory. The same behavior means different things during different phases. A competitive move means something different during Pondy's felt conflict stage, wherein it is a trigger that moves behavior into manifest conflict, than during the aftermath stage, where it might be seen as inappropriate because the conflict has been resolved (or at least has subsided).

Phase models have been criticized as too simplistic because actual conflicts have a greater variety of behavior patterns than the phase models depict. Their simplicity is sometimes useful, however, because it provides a simple set of milestones to help us in navigating conflicts.

Conclusion

The theories presented in the preceding two chapters advance a variety of different explanations that point to a number of different features and processes in conflict. Differing treatments also lead to distinctive claims and conclusions. Whereas one theory may point to the perceptions as the key drivers of conflict, another theory ignores perceptions and focuses instead on the interpretive rules used by conflict participants. Whereas one theory makes predictions about the causes of aggression, another describes how conflict episodes are negotiated.

So what is to be learned from this exercise? At least three points are worth noting. First, different theories can complement, inform, or compete with each other. In many instances, theories serve to distinguish different issues in a conflict, thereby offering unique strengths and weaknesses. Depending on the premises they embrace, these multiple images furnish us with a well-rounded view of conflict. Occasionally, however, the premises found in theories compete, forcing us to choose one vantage point or another. For example, verbal aggressiveness theory informs us that aggression is largely a matter of situational learning and argumentation skill deficiency. In contrast, attribution theory suggests that aggression occurs as a result of perceptions, not traits or skills. We are likely to engage in aggression when we attribute incompatibility to the other party. On one level these two theories appear compatible. They are, after all, both concerned with the verbal tactics participants use and the consequences that result from their use. But the reason why a person behaves aggressively is markedly different for these theories. So much so, that intervention in conflicts is an entirely different matter depending on the explanation one prefers. Whereas one theory suggests teaching people how to argue, the other theory implicitly recommends changing participant perceptions.

The first impulse for many is to select one theory and reject the other on the basis of what rings true. Just remember that ringing true and being true are different matters. As suggested earlier, theories are rarely right or wrong. Nevertheless, explanations make more sense in some situations than in others. Do not accept one theory and reject another. Instead, collect them voraciously and use them as you would a hammer, wrench, or saw, selecting one or the other when the right project comes along.

Second, the practitioner must guard against an interpretation of theory that is so rigid as to render it useless in a specific case. A theory is a broad explanation, one that may not account for the intricacies and nuances of a particular case. To apply theories to cases with success, one must be creative, allowing the explanations to point the way, to frame inquiries, but not to complete them. The urge to use theories to create formulas, or "cookbooks," for assessing and managing conflict misses the mark entirely. If the complexities of conflict interaction could be boiled down into a few steps or how-to rules, there would be a great deal less destructive conflict in society and a great deal more optimism. Unfortunately, matters are not that simple. The riddle of human behavior is not likely to be solved anytime soon. Instead, it is best to apply theories believed to be useful and to manage conflict as these theories suggest.

Finally, theories should be evaluated on the basis of utility. As you read through this book, certain concepts and theories will speak to you and others will not. Some theories will confirm your already existing prejudices; others will stretch your thinking and supply you with new insights and avenues for conflict management. The ideas and theories presented here have stood the first test—utility. Scholars and researchers have turned them over time and time again, looking for flaws and searching for benefits. Although no consensus exists regarding the ideas presented in these pages, the very fact that they receive continued scrutiny suggests they hold promise. The real test, however, is for practitioners to use the ideas in the marketplace of everyday life. The best theories and concepts are the ones that allow you to understand and manage the conflicts within your relationships, family, organization, or team. No other measure of a theory can compete with that crucial test.

4 Power: The Architecture of Conflict

Power and the Emergence of Conflict

Chapter 1 noted that conflict is sustained by moves and countermoves in interaction and that these are dependent on the power participants exert. As we will see, the degree of power participants can bring to bear depends on having the resources and the skill to use these resources effectively to act and to influence others. A good way to understand how power functions in conflicts is to examine the emergence of a conflict—the turn a conflict takes from a latent awareness of differences to actions and reactions that generate conflict interaction.

Whenever people are in some way dependent on one another, there are likely to be differences, and people usually become aware of them before any conflict-related interaction occurs. As discussed in Chapter 3, Rummel and Pondy identified a series of steps in the emergence of conflicts. They found that before any observable conflict surfaces, there is usually a latent conflict phase in which parties become aware of opposing viewpoints, attitudes, or goals. A "consciousness of opposition" precedes conflict interaction and lays the groundwork for it. During this latent conflict phase, parties may note differences that actually exist among them, or they may incorrectly assume there are differences when none exist. At this point, however, parties do not attempt to act on these differences.

Case 4.1A illustrates a group whose unified purpose may be threatened by the members' awareness of differences in priorities. Knowledge of real or assumed differences stems largely from parties' experience with each other.

In relationships with a history, parties know the stands others have taken on various issues and the alternatives they have supported during previous discussions or decisions. Individuals come to expect some people to push for cautious or conservative choices and others to suggest or encourage major innovations. They know which people are allies and which are enemies. Each person's stand provides a general sense of where he or she would like to see the conflict head. In assessing and planning their stands, people try to forecast likely positions and anticipate where support or opposition will arise. This creates a consciousness of opposition when individuals foresee disagreement or incompatible goals.

In this case study, the Undergraduate Publications Board has a prevailing sense of an issue arising; members recognize likely differences in viewpoints and share an uncertainty about whether these differences will need to be addressed.

CASE **4.1A**

A Raid on the Student Activity Fees Fund

Imagine yourself as a magazine editor on this board whose publication may be threatened by the proposed budget cuts: What would be your likely response when you realize that there may not be sufficient funds to support all of the board's publications?

The Undergraduate Publications (UP) Board at a midsize university is responsible for overseeing five student-run publications: a weekly newspaper, an annual yearbook, and three magazines—a literary magazine, a political review, and a science journal—each published once a semester. The Board was created by the university to ensure comprehensive coverage of campus life and student accomplishments. Composed of two representatives from each of the publications (generally the editor and a senior staff member), plus a faculty advisor, the UP Board meets monthly to discuss a wide variety of issues. Together they make decisions regarding advertising and editorial policies, selection of the following year's editors, hardware and software purchases for the Board's shared computers, and nominations of individual writers for national collegiate writing awards. In addition, the group collectively determines the budgets for each of the publications, working from a lump sum allocation made to the UP Board by the student government at the beginning of each semester. As these issues are discussed, Board members' assumptions about the relative importance of each of the publications become apparent.

At one Board meeting shortly before the semester's allocations are made by the student government, the faculty advisor mentions that the university's administration is considering "raiding" the student activity fees fund to refurbish the student center. Because this fund is the sole source of money for the student government's allocation committee, it is possible that the UP Board budgets will be dramatically cut. After the meeting, members talk among themselves and with others about how the Board should handle potential cuts. Some members state their positions explicitly as they discuss the consequences of eliminating one of the magazines, reducing the length of the yearbook, or other choices.

Through these discussions and through recollections of how individual UP Board members have felt in the past, members begin to anticipate the suggestions that will be made to deal with the cuts. Because members sense that preferences will differ, an awareness of opposition mounts as the UP Board considers what it would mean to make any of these choices. The editors of the threatened magazines begin to assess how much support from the Board they and their magazine have and who their potential advocates and opponents are.

Discussion Questions

- *Why does the term "latent conflict" describe the situation that exists on this board?*
- *What could make this conflict move out of a latent stage and into an open conflict?*
- *What examples can you give of latent conflict phases in other situations (for example, family conflicts you have been involved in, neighborhood disputes, international conflicts you have followed)?*

There is, in other words, a *perception* of potential incompatibility of goals or objectives. At this point, however, the conflict remains latent because there is no immediate stimulus for the members to act on their positions.

What might make the UP Board members act on their expectations? In examining phases of conflict interaction, Rummel (1976), Pondy (1967), Walton (1969), and others have suggested that some critical event activates latent conflict. This *triggering* event turns a "consciousness of opposition" into acknowledged conflict. Obviously, any number of events are potential triggers in this case: the student government president could announce that the UP Board's budget will be cut by twenty-five percent, a member who has been appointed as next year's editor of one of the publications may request a special meeting on the subject to plan accordingly, or a Board member may write a formal letter that argues strongly for the elimination of the science journal if publication cutbacks are necessary.

Any of these incidents could be triggering events for conflict interaction by stimulating parties who perceive incompatible goals to move toward obtaining their objectives and to anticipate and elicit countermoves by those who hold opposing stands. Once parties are acting on behalf of their positions, conflict interaction can move through cycles of withdrawal, joking, problem-solving, heated arguments, proposals and counterproposals, and so on, in all their many forms. The triggering event signals a transition in the way people think and act about the conflict. Whereas latent conflict is sustained by perceptions of differences, conflict interaction is sustained by the moves and countermoves of the participants. In the latent phase, people think in terms of possibilities, while conflict interaction confronts them with real threats and constraints. Just as a critical incident changes the general tenor of the group's climate, a triggering event alters people's response to differences and shapes the particular form conflict takes. To illustrate how moves and countermoves might vary as a result of a specific triggering incident, consider two scenarios that might unfold with the UP Board (Case 4.1B).

It is easy to think of triggering events in negative terms, as "the straw that breaks the camel's back." However, a triggering event also carries with it an important opportunity. As noted in Chapter 1, a critical requirement of constructive conflict management is thorough and successful differentiation of conflicting positions. Before they can move to an integrative solution, parties must raise the conflict issue and spend sufficient time and energy clarifying positions, pursuing the reasons behind those positions, and acknowledging their differences. By bringing the conflict out, a triggering event sets the stage for constructive resolution. It opens the possibility of clearing away problems and tensions that undermine relationships or group performance. There is, of course, no guarantee that a constructive resolution will happen. As observed in Chapter 1, uncontrolled escalation and destructive avoidance can also develop during differentiation. How the parties handle differentiation is the key to whether it becomes destructive or constructive. In part, how people handle differentiation depends on individuals' ability to recognize and escape their trained incapacities and to diagnose and alter negative features of the prevailing climate. It also depends on specific responses to the triggering event, which are shaped by parties' access to and use of power.

In both scenarios in Case 4.1B, the letter was a move that fractured the latent conflict phase; one person acted on behalf of his own goals and others responded to the move. Once the UP Board members recognized and acted on the latent issue, the conflict entered a new phase of open engagement. How they reacted to this trigger set the stage for how the conflict was played out. In the first scenario, oth-

CASE **4.1B**

A Raid on the Student Activity Fees Fund (Continued)

Imagine yourself as one of the magazine editors attending a board meeting after the letter is written: What would be your likely response to each of the two scenarios?

Shortly after the faculty advisor mentions the possibility of cutbacks to the UP Board's budget, a member of the group writes a letter advocating the elimination of the science journal from the campus publications. This would fulfill cutback requirements without affecting other publications. The science journal is the clear choice, argues the letter writer, because it has the smallest circulation and has received no awards. As a result, two possible scenarios may occur.

Scenario #1: The letter is sent to the faculty advisor, with copies to other members of the Board. The members of the group assume that the letter will have no significant ramifications because the faculty advisor is not really a "player" in the group. The advisor reads the letter, acknowledges its receipt, and comments to the group as a whole that the issue will be discussed when the time comes.

Scenario #2: The letter is sent to the school newspaper, where it is published on the editorial page. The editor of the paper is the fraternity brother of two members of the allocations committee and has been known to use this connection to acquire special funding for the paper. In response to the letter's publication, some Board members request that a special meeting be called to discuss options for dealing with the cutbacks. Others write responses to the letter and submit them to the newspaper. Still others confront the letter writer and ask why such a proposal was offered when no cutbacks have yet been made.

Discussion Questions

- *How would you account for the different responses to the same letter?*
- *What benefits does the triggering event have for the group?*
- *To what extent did the following incidents act as triggering events: the Boston Tea Party, the bombing of Pearl Harbor, Rosa Parks's staying seated on a public bus, the "not guilty" verdict in the Rodney King beating case, the 9/11 attacks?*
- *What kind of power was used in each of the above to make the triggering event have more of an impact?*

---

ers did not believe the letter presented much of a threat. As a result, it did not elicit a strong reaction, and it did not begin a chain of moves and countermoves aimed at settling the issue. Members recognized an issue had been raised, but there were no drastic countermoves because its consequences were neither immediate nor threatening. The letter "set the agenda" for future discussions. In the second scenario, the letter began a lengthy series of moves and countermoves that would not only determine how the Board would handle any cutbacks, but could change the relationships among the Board members and alter its long-term climate.

Once a conflict is triggered, the moves people make depend on the power they can marshall and exert. Parties' ability and willingness to use power and their skills at employing it determine the moves and countermoves that will sustain the conflict. Available power establishes the set of actions that individuals may use and sets limits on the effectiveness of others' moves. Each move reveals to others how willing a party is to use power and what kinds of power that party has. The response to the move reveals whether the use of power will go unchallenged.

The most important difference between the two scenarios is the difference in power held by the Board member who wrote the letter. In both cases the letter could easily be construed as an attempt to sway attitudes by getting a "jump" on others. Laying out one set of arguments before other positions or proposals are developed or stated could give the writer a great advantage. Despite their common objective, only the second letter was perceived to have the potential to influence the outcome of the cutback decision. The second letter writer was perceived to hold power and had been known to use it on previous occasions: other Board members knew that this individual had strong persuasive abilities, was a fraternity brother of members of the allocations committee, and was willing to go public with his options before raising them with others on the Board. In responding to the letter, members had to rely on their own sources of power, such as the right to request a special meeting about an issue and the ability to build alliances, to prevent the letter from firmly setting attitudes before a full discussion of the issue occurred.

The shift from latent conflict to the emergence of conflict interaction inevitably confronts the participants with the issue of power. During latent conflict, parties may have a sense of the sources of power people hold and they may make estimates of how likely it will be for others to use power if the conflict surfaces. Once conflict interaction begins, however, each move and countermove confirms or challenges previous assessments of power. Individuals are caught up in an active process of testing and determining the role and limits of power in the conflict. But how, exactly, does this happen? The next section examines the nature of power more closely and points to several defining characteristics that make power a major influence on the direction conflict interaction takes.

A Relational View of Power

The everyday use of the term *power* often clouds or misrepresents its nature (Bachrach and Baratz 1970; Deutsch 1973; Janeway 1980). Expressions—such as, "He holds enormous power" or "The purchasing department's manager has lost the power she once had"—imply that power is a possession. That is, it is something that belongs to an individual, which can be increased or lost, and which, by implication, can be carried away from a group or organization. In this view, power is a quality of the strong or dominant, and something the weak lack. This view is dangerously misleading. Social philosopher Hannah Arendt (1969) points to the problem with this view when she states: "Power is never the property of an individual; it belongs to a group and remains in existence only so long as the group keeps together" (p. 44).

Chapter 1 defined power as the *ability to influence or control* events. What does it mean to say this ability "belongs to the group"? For one thing, it means recognizing that social *power stems from relationships* among people. Individuals have power when they have access to resources that can be used to persuade or convince others, to change their course of action, or to prevent others from moving toward their goals in conflict situations. These resources, which give power if used effectively, are controlled by individuals; it is easy to assume that the resources themselves equal power and that their owner therefore possesses power. However, this conclusion ignores the fact that any resource serving as a basis for power is only *effective because others endorse the resource* (Jewell and Reitz 1981). The resource only imparts power because it carries some weight in the context of relationships where it is used. The young child who throws a temper tantrum has power over her parents only if they are bothered (or touched) by the raucous fits and are willing to appease the child because the behavior is annoying (or heartbreaking). The boss who threatens to fire a worker can only influence a worker who values the job and believes his boss will carry out the threat. In both cases the second party must "endorse" the first's resources for them to become a basis for power.

Individuals can use a broad range of resources to exert power (French and Raven 1959; Wilmot and Wilmot 1978; Kipnis, Schmidt, and Wilkerson 1980; Boulding 1990). Potential resources include special skills or abilities, time, expertise about the task at hand, personal attractiveness or likability, control over rewards and/or punishments, formal position in a group or organization, loyal allies, persuasive skills, and control over critical group possessions (such as the treasury), to name a few. Anything that enables individuals to move toward their own goals or to interfere with another's actions is a resource that can be used in conflicts. Communication skills, such as being articulate or being able to construct effective arguments, can be power resources in themselves. However, for a move to have an impact on others' moves or on the outcome of the conflict, the resources it uses must be given some credence by others: either consciously or unconsciously others must endorse them. In this sense, power is always conferred on someone by those who endorse the resources.

At first glance, it would seem that the need for endorsement leaves an easy way out for weaker parties in conflict. Isn't it always possible to undermine the use of power by withholding endorsement of some resource? In principle, weaker parties always have this option. But the claim is misleading because the tendency to endorse power is deep-seated and based in powerful and pervasive social processes. At the most superficial level, we endorse power because the resources it is based on enable others to grant or deny things that are valuable. As Richard Emerson (1962) states: "[The] power to control or influence the other resides in control over the things he values, which may range all the way from oil resources to ego-support" (p. 11). This is an important, if obvious point, and it leads to a more fundamental issue: This control is exerted during interaction. Therefore, both the would-be controller and the controlled have a part in playing it out. One person makes a control bid based on real or potential use of resources, and the other accepts or rejects it.

Perhaps the most critical aspect of this process is the second person's acceptance or rejection of the legitimacy or force of the bid; in other words, the second person's *endorsement* (or lack of endorsement) of the first's resources and his or her ability to use them. This social process of endorsement is what underlies parties' perceptions of others' behavior as attempts to influence or control. If someone imitates the shape of a gun with her fingers, points them at someone else, and says, "Hand me your wallet," the "target" person may laugh at the joke, but he would not see this as a power move. If that same person picks up a gun and does the same thing, nearly everyone would see it as an attempt to influence or control. A person's endorsement of a gun as an instrument of force is a product of years of experience (education, television shows, firsthand encounters), which gives him or her an idea of its power and of how someone could handle it.

At the same time, even the power that a gun confers is not inherent in the possession of the gun itself. Because power is relational, the *effectiveness of any resource is* always *negotiated* in the interaction. If the person at whom the gun is aimed tells the assailant to "Move out of my way," this is an attempt to withdraw endorsement of the assailant's potential power. The response may or may not succeed—that is the nature of any unfolding negotiation—but, as the interaction proceeds, the perception of power can change. It is interaction, then, that changes perception of resources and the power they can ultimately generate. The influential powers of intangible social resources, such as a good reputation or persuasive abilities, are built in much the same way: People must endorse them if they are to carry any weight. The tendency and willingness to endorse power stem from several sources, including preconceptions about what makes a person weak or strong, an aura of mystery, the judicial use of authority, and evidence of valued skills or abilities.

Before these are examined in detail, consider the case of a unique and self-styled individual (Case 4.2). The Eccentric Professor case illustrates four factors, which the rest of this section describes, that influence endorsement.

1. The *social categorization process,* discussed in Chapter 1, creates strong preconceptions about what types of people are usually powerful and what types are generally weak. Erica Apfelbaum (1979) investigated the relation of social categorization to people's sense of their own and others' power. She notes that different resources and the ability to use them are associated with different social categories. Ranking executives, for example, are assumed by society to be wealthy, have connections, and be skilled in negotiation. Welfare mothers, on the other hand, are assumed to be poor and have little ability to get ahead in the world. An aura of competence and power attaches itself to the executive, something that the welfare mother does not have. Harold, being an Ivy League graduate with an upper-class background, might be ascribed by those around him with such characteristics as sophistication and worldliness. So it is with all social categories, Apfelbaum argues: Each is associated with a definite degree of power, with certain resources, and with certain abilities to use the resources available to them. These associations set up expectations that work in favor of or against endorsement of power moves by people from various categories: We endorse those we expect to be powerful and do not endorse those we expect to be weak.

These associations have several consequences. For one thing, they make the use of power easier for certain people and more difficult for others. During the 1960s, sociologists conducted a number of studies on the effects of members' status outside decision-making groups on member behavior within groups (Wilson 1978).

CASE 4.2

The Eccentric Professor

Imagine yourself as a student of this professor: Which of his characteristics might inspire you to respect him? How would your respect work as an endorsement of his power in the classroom?

In a large academic department, a professor became known as an exceptional intellect—a person who possessed unfathomable powers of insight and perspective. As a result of this perception, his colleagues and students often deferred to his judgment and looked to him to provide solutions to complex problems. In time, he came to hold the most powerful position in his college, choosing when he would teach and to whom.

The professor, Harold, was a prolific researcher and talented teacher. He held several advanced degrees from Ivy League universities and was a member of a wealthy, politically influential family. Perhaps his most singular trait was that he was fond of the unusual, the offbeat, the uncommon. He surrounded himself with objects and fashion from an earlier era, often wearing knickers, bow ties, and driving caps. He made it clear to anyone who inquired that he liked books and cats more than people. Because of his tastes, he kept to himself, shunning parties and all social gatherings. Harold maintained this interpersonal distance in his classes. He used seat assignments, a question period, forbade the wearing of hats or shorts in class, and never used first names, referring to students as Mr. and Miss instead.

The first words of each of his lectures were delivered as he crossed the threshold into the classroom and he concluded precisely as the hour ended, his final sentence often punctuated by the bell. Not many months after his arrival on campus, he was asked to address the faculty as part of the college's colloquium series. His lecture, on thinking and learning, incorporated NFL training-camp films and analogies from the history of the stock market.

In every conversation, from the important to the mundane, colleagues and students learned that Harold approached ideas and problems in unusual ways, from unusual angles. Whereas he was first ridiculed and avoided, he soon became an enigma to understand. And so the stories began.

He spent late evenings in the library and was seen carrying throngs of books. When asked by one bold student what he was after, Harold supposedly replied that he was committed to having read a portion of every book in the library. After Harold worked for months on a computer algorithm, a colleague supposedly learned that he was to use the program to make all his important decisions, from buying a house to selecting a wife.

After receiving a national award for one of his essays, he chose not to attend the award ceremony, claiming that he would not fly or take a train. When beseeched to attend, he finally agreed and spent a week riding a bus to and from the distant ceremony. Rumors spread that Harold had made a million dollars in the stock market and that he owned dozens of cats.

As the years rolled on, the stories grew and the mystery and power deepened. His image as an eccentric intellectual, capable of performing extraordinary feats, was perpetuated by attributions made by both students and professors caught up in the mystery of the man. In this way, Harold managed to gain considerable influence in his working environment, though in truth, he was more similar to his colleagues than dissimilar.

Discussion Questions

- *Given the influence he held, what might undercut this professor's power?*
- *What might prompt resistance to this professor's power?*
- *In what ways do political candidates hold influence over voters that is similar to the way this professor holds influence over his students?*

Consistently, members with higher status in society—for example, doctors, lawyers, university students—were more influential than those with lower status— such as, laborers and high school students—even if both members had exactly the same resources.

For example, a study by Moore (1968) had junior college students work in pairs to estimate the number of rectangles in an optical illusion. The experimenter led the students to believe that their partner was either a Stanford University student or a high school student. There was no difference in the ability of the students to estimate squares, but those who thought they worked with university students changed their estimates significantly more often than those who thought they worked with high school students. In other words, they allowed themselves to be influenced by "university" students and exercised influence over the high school students. The junior college students expected university students to be brighter and, therefore, to be better at the task. This assumption led the junior college students to endorse the university students' resources; the opposite assumption encouraged them to give less weight to the high school students' attempts to use their own resources. Whenever people from different social categories work together, similar preconceptions about their respective powers strengthen endorsement for some and weaken it for others.

Expectations about social categories not only shape members' perceptions of others' resources and abilities, but also influence their perceptions of themselves. People who belong to a social category generally expected to be powerful, and those who regularly receive endorsement for power moves, such as corporate executives, tend to see themselves as powerful and effective. They are confident when making future moves, and their confidence, in turn, is likely to lead to effective use of power, which reinforces their self-concepts. The same is true for those belonging to "powerless" categories. They expect to be ineffective and, therefore, give way before the powerful. Janeway (1980) argues that this is one of the major reasons women, minorities, and other low-power groups often take weak roles in conflict situations: They see themselves as having fewer resources than dominant groups, as being spectators rather than actors. Even though these groups have resources, including intelligence, social skills, and even sheer numbers, they do not realize their potential power. They believe they are weak and isolated and have little chance of competing with the "powers that be." In conflict, such people often do not assert themselves, and when they do, their efforts are not given the same weight of endorsement that people from powerful categories receive. Once again, there is a self-reinforcing cycle that serves to prove the weak are powerless and further strengthens other people's tendency to refuse endorsement.

Apfelbaum calls the socialization process that creates these perceptions of weakness *degrouping.* She argues that it is the most important mechanism by which the powerful maintain their positions. Here also is one of the roots of the common idea of power as a possession: If certain social groups are assumed to be consistently powerful, it takes only a small step to assume power is theirs by right; in other words, it is their possession. Because the process of learning social categorizations is very gradual and extends over years, it is easy to lose sight of their flexibility and forget that all social groups are, to a great extent, created by those within and outside of them. If the social definition of who is powerful changes, patterns of endorsement, and therefore of who can exert power effectively, can change radically.

When people perceive another party as a member of a group rather than as an individual, they may act more forcefully or aggressively toward them (Pruitt and Rubin 1986). This perceptual process is called *deindividuation* because it removes the personal and human characteristics normally associated with a party and replaces them with more global features. For example, it is not uncommon for people in conflict to refrain from using another party's name and to refer to him or her according to physical attributes or social roles, such as "that loud-mouthed boss" or "that aggressive lawyer." As the conflict and aggression escalate, so too does the degree of deindividuation. The opposing party may be identified by race or religion, denoting a more impersonal perception and label. Because people are seen as less human, the social inhibition on acting aggressively toward them disappears, or so we believe. Entire nations can get caught up in this pattern of deindividuation as a means to justify and absolve their citizens from being seen as aggressors. In every war in which the United States has been involved during the past century, examples of deindividuated names and labels for enemies, including the civilian populations, have surfaced. Such labels as "Krauts" and "Gooks" allow us to act aggressively without regulation or remorse.

2. The *use of power* also *carries a mystique* that reinforces endorsement of moves by powerful members. Janeway (1980) explores the childhood and adolescent experiences through which people learn to use and understand power. The actions of adults are incomprehensible to children and so, Janeway argues, children attribute to adults mysterious, unfathomable powers. As the rich fantasy life of childhood gives way to the mastery of adulthood, people learn how power works, but the aura persists, dimmed perhaps but never extinguished.

In addition to childhood experiences, the historical connection between kings and queens and the divine contributes to power's magical aura, Janeway (1980) observes. As a result, "even today, it seems, the governed are ready to accept the idea that the powerful are different from you and me, and not simply because they have more power. We grant them a different kind of power that contains some element of the supernatural" (p. 77). The unusual behavior and characteristics of Harold in the Eccentric Professor case was both mysterious and fascinating to all of those around him. The perception that he was unique served to increase his prestige on campus. This mystique functions to reinforce existing power relations: "for the powerful, the magic aura offers a validation of dominance over and above the consent of the governed; for the weak, a defensive shield against feelings of inferiority and ineffectiveness" (Janeway 1980, p. 126). After all, if power is a magical, unattainable possession, the strong must have special qualities and the weak cannot handle it and should not try. Kipnis (1990) notes that the supernatural mystique of power often carries with it reckless license: "Throughout history, we find a special divinity is assumed to surround the powerful so that they are excused from gross acts such as murder, theft, terrorism and intimidation" (p. 40).

The magical aura about power inspires a certain awe that facilitates its endorsement. It also tends to perpetuate power and weakness in the same hands over time. In groups, for example, more experienced, older members are often granted this aura or mystique. Although they may have more knowledge and information because of their longer stay in the group, the mystique assigned to them by newer members can linger and keep certain members in unwarranted influential positions.

3. *Interaction* in the immediate situation *is* the *primary* means through which endorsement is achieved. The response of other parties to a power move has a strong influence on an individual's endorsement. For example, if Harold, the eccentric professor, announces that hats and shorts are strictly forbidden in his classroom, and all members of the class obey without question, they are reinforcing one another's endorsement of the professor's authority. Each student observes the others obeying, and this lends additional weight to his or her own respect for Harold's authority. Assume, on the other hand, that a professor has been unfair in the past and that students have doubts about whether he deserves his authority. If one student refuses to go along with the professor's rules, it may very well undermine other students' endorsement of the professor's moves. Others see that some do not accept the professor unquestioningly, and their respect for his authority and his ability to use it may subsequently decrease.

The way in which someone executes a power move also influences its endorsement. Power involves the use of resources; successful power moves require skillful and appropriate use of resources. For example, when a leader or supervisor gives feedback and criticism to subordinates, it is more effective when (1) done privately rather than in front of co-workers, (2) positive points and improvements are discussed in addition to problems, and (3) raises or compensation increases are not tied to criticisms or the subordinate's attempts to solve his or her problems (Meyer, Kay, and French 1965; Downs, Smeyak, and Martin 1980). A supervisor who follows these rules is more likely to elicit cooperation from subordinates, partly because they offer a positive method of giving feedback, but also because they allow the subordinates to save face and do not push them into challenging the supervisor's authority. A boss who berates workers in front of their co-workers is likely to face a challenge or, at least, create resentment that may emerge later on. Exerting power in a socially appropriate manner that follows the path of least resistance is conducive to present and future endorsement by others.

Exactly what constitutes appropriate and skillful use of power varies from case to case. Research offers a few general principles, but they are sketchy, at best, and do not add up to a systematic theory.

4. Up to this point, we have emphasized what might be called the unconscious bases of endorsement. However, endorsements are often openly discussed and decided on. In these cases, *parties value certain abilities, knowledge, or personal characteristics and explicitly support the legitimacy of the resource.* A team might, for example, pride itself on always having sufficient information before reaching any final decision and compliment those who are most persistent in gathering and evaluating background material. One member could use this knowledge of the team's self-image as a basis for a move in a decision-making conflict. He or she could attempt to stop the team from adopting a solution by making the members feel guilty about not conducting an adequate search for information. In this instance, the powerful individual uses a resource that the team willingly endorses as a basis for a move. The move may or may not be successful and may or may not be intended for the good of the team, but it appeals to a resource that, as Arendt says, "belongs to the group."

Recognizing the relational nature of power forces us to acknowledge the status of resources. Regardless of how tight a hold someone has on any resource, the resource is always used in the context of a relationship. It is the other's view of the resource that makes it a basis for influence. Returning to the case of the eccentric professor, it might happen that Harold's ability to lecture unerringly and precisely for an hour is considered extraordinary by his students. They might look forward to class simply to see this feat performed. But if, over the course of the semester, students find reasons to leave class early, Harold's lecturing ability may wane as a source of power. If the other's view of the resource is altered during the conflict interaction, the basis of power shifts, and the possibilities for moves in the interaction are redefined. Because power is inherently relational, it is never entirely under one's control. The response to the use of power determines whether the resource that has been employed will remain a source of power as the conflict unfolds. The impact of power in conflict is constantly negotiated as interaction unfolds; it is interaction that changes perceptions of power.

As parties use resources, their moves renew, maintain, or reduce the weight a resource has in the interaction. A clumsy move can weaken endorsement of a resource and confidence in the abilities of the user. A well-executed move can enhance endorsement of a resource. The skills of the user, the response of other members, and the eventual course that the conflict takes all determine whether a resource maintains or loses its endorsement. Even the nature of the resource itself is important because some resources (for example, money or favors) can be exhausted and others (such as physical force) allow no turning back once employed. The use of resources is an extremely complex process, and we will return to it throughout the rest of this chapter.

Power and Conflict Interaction

The use of power imposes constraints on others. A power move usually brings about a reduction of others' options by limiting the moves they can make, by eliminating a possible resolution to the conflict, or by restricting their ability to employ countervailing power. These constraints influence the direction the conflict takes; they make certain behaviors or styles desirable or, alternatively, impossible. They shape parties' perceptions of each other, kindling hope or desperation, cooperation or competition. As the conflict evolves and changes, so do the constraints under which participants operate. The others' responses to moves set further constraints, the responses to the countermoves set still further constraints, and so on, until the conflict is no longer wholly controlled by either party but is a collective product. It is greater than—and in a real sense out of the control of—any single person.

To illustrate the relational nature of power, the influence of power on conflict interaction, and the multiplication of constraints, consider the case of a research and development committee in a large corporation (Case 4.3). This case is set in a corporate lab, but it could just as easily have occurred in other situations, such as a committee developing an advertising campaign, a team developing new software for a computer company, or a textbook selection committee in a university department. The case offers a clear illustration of the role of power in conflict interaction. During the early meetings members offered their reactions to various programs and tried to move steadily toward a final choice. Although there were differences of opinion about the programs in these early meetings, expertise and knowledge—resources used by members to exert influence and shape attitudes about the programs—were implicitly endorsed by the whole group. Members tried to articulate criteria for assessing the programs and to apply the criteria to the programs being considered. The moves parties made to keep a particular program under consideration were arguments based on knowledge and experience they had as researchers. Reasoned argument was the operating norm for the group, and as members worked together to make decisions through rational argument, they were, in effect, reinforcing the group's endorsement of expertise.

Once the list was narrowed to two programs and a consensus did not emerge through reasoned argument, members began to use other resources. The manager gave a strong indication that he might be willing to use his formal authority to force selection of the program by turning to each project director and asking, "How upset would you be if I chose the program I prefer?" This move was significantly different from any move that participants had made before, and it broadened the scope of the conflict considerably. The assumption that influence would rest on logical argument and expertise was now overturned. The project directors anticipated that Tom might exercise his right to choose the program. Although Tom's question was not the actual exercise of his right, it signaled the potential use of this power base to "resolve" the group's conflict. Tom was testing what impact the move might have if he disregarded the project directors' arguments and chose the program he wanted. In some ways, Tom's move was predictable. Research summarized by Kipnis (1990) suggests that people tend to use reason, logic, and simple requests until resistance occurs. At that point, beliefs about power guide the choice of tactics.

Tom's move marked a turning point in the conflict because it altered the resources members used. Tom moved from the use of expertise and knowledge, resources common to all members, to invoking his formal authority—a resource exclusively his. The project directors' response to Tom's move also invoked a new resource, their ability not to cooperate with their superior. The ability to run their projects independently was an "ace in the hole" for the project directors. Tom was responsible for productivity in all projects, and if his actions in this committee undermined the project directors' motivation or ability to work effectively, the outcome might reflect poorly on his ability to direct the labs. If projects were not productive, it would undoubtedly reflect on the project directors, but the reputation of the labs in the corporation ultimately rested with Tom. This reputation would be

CASE 4.3
The Creativity Development Committee

Imagine yourself as a project director serving on this committee: What resources do you, and the other project directors, bring to the committee that could be a source of influence? What constraints, if any, do your resources place on Tom, the Lab Manager?

Tom was the manager of three research and development laboratories for a large chemical and materials corporation. He supervised general operations, budgeting, personnel, and proposal development for the labs. Each lab had several projects, and each project team was headed by a project director who was usually a scientist or an engineer. Tom had been a project director for ten years at another of the corporation's labs and had been promoted to Lab Manager four years ago. Although he had to transfer across the country to take this job, he felt he had earned the respect of his subordinates. He had been regarded as an outsider at first, but he worked hard to be accepted, and the lab's productivity had gone up over the last two years. Tom's major worry was keeping track of everything. His busy schedule kept him from close supervision over projects.

As in most labs, each project generally went its own way. As long as it produced results, a project enjoyed a high degree of autonomy. Morale was usually high among the research staff. They knew they were on the leading edge of the corporation's success and they enjoyed it. The visibility and importance of innovative research were shown by the fact that project directors were regularly promoted. It was in this milieu that Tom decided that productivity might be still further increased if research creativity were heightened.

Research teams often met to discuss ideas and to decide on future directions. In these meetings, ideas were often improved, but they could also be killed or cut off. Tom had studied research on decision making, which indicated that groups often suppress good ideas without a hearing. The research suggested ways of preventing this suppression and of enhancing group creativity. Tom hoped to harness these findings by developing standard procedures through which idea development would be enhanced rather than hindered during these meetings. Tom asked four project directors if they would be willing to work with him to review the research and meet regularly over the summer to help formulate appropriate procedures. The four agreed to take on the task, and the group began its work enthusiastically.

During the first six weeks of the summer, the group met weekly to discuss relevant articles and books and to hear consultants. The group was able to narrow down a set of about fifteen procedures and programs to four prime ones. Eventually, two programs emerged as possibilities. However, as the list was narrowed from four to two, there was a clear split in how the group felt.

One procedure was strongly favored by three of the project directors. The fourth project director liked the procedure better than the other option but was less vocal in showing her support for it. In general, the project directors felt the procedure they favored was far more consistent with what project teams were currently doing and with the problems faced by the corporation. They believed the second program, which involved a lot of writing and the use of special voting procedures, was too abstract for working research scientists to accept. It would be difficult, they said, to use this procedure because everyone would have to fill out forms and explain ideas in writing before a meeting could be held. Because of the already heavy workloads, their people would not go along with the program. Researchers would ridicule the program and be prejudiced against future attempts to stimulate creativity.

Tom argued that the second program was more comprehensive, had a broader conception of problems, and would help develop more creative ideas than the first, which was a fairly conservative "brainstorming" process.

(continued)

Although discussion focused on the substantive nature of each program and its relation to the objective of creativity, the project directors knew that the program Tom favored was one he had been trained in at his former lab. Tom was a good friend of the consultant who had developed it. The project directors talked outside meetings about this friendship and questioned whether it was shaping Tom's attitudes. The climate of the group, which had initially been positive and enthusiastic, grew tense as issues connected to the power relations between the manager and project directors surfaced.

Although the project directors knew Tom could choose the program he wanted, the way in which the final choice would be made was never clarified at the beginning of the summer. The time that the project directors spent reading and evaluating the programs created an implicit expectation that they would have an equal say in the final choice. At the same time, the project directors had all worked at the lab for at least four years and had experienced firsthand the relative power of managers and project directors. They heard horror stories of project directors who had gotten on the manager's "wrong side" and been denied promotion or fired. When push came to shove, they expected the Lab Manager to have greater power and to be willing to use it.

At its final meeting, the group discussed the two programs for quite some time, but there seemed to be little movement. Somewhat hesitantly, Tom turned to each project director individually and asked, "How upset would you be if I choose the program I prefer?" One project director said he was uncomfortable answering. Two indicated that they felt they would have difficulty using the creativity program as it was currently designed. The fourth said she thought she could live with it. After these answers were given, Tom told the project directors he would leave a memo in their mailboxes informing them of the final decision.

Two weeks after this discussion, the project directors were told that the second program, the one the manager preferred, would be ordered. The memo also said that the other program would be used, on an experimental basis, by one of the eighteen projects. The decision caused considerable resentment—the project directors felt "used." They saw little reason in having spent so much time discussing programs if Tom was just going to choose the program he wanted regardless of their preferences. When it began in the fall, one of the project directors told his team that the program would be recommended rather than required, and he explained that it might have to be adapted extensively to fit the unit's style. This director made this decision without telling the manager. Although the move was in clear violation of authority, he knew Tom could not visit the teams often and was therefore unlikely to find out about it. Another project director instituted the program but commented afterward that he felt he had not integrated it into his unit well. He questioned how much effort he had actually invested in making the program "work."

The incident had a significant impact on the way Tom was seen by the project directors. Several commented that they had lost respect for him and that they saw Tom as someone who was willing to manipulate people for his own purposes. This opinion filtered to other corporate project directors and scientists through the grapevine and caused Tom considerable difficulties in a labor grievance during the following year. In this dispute, several researchers banded together and defied the manager because they believed he would eventually back down. In addition, the project director who made the program optional for his workers served as a model for similar defiance by others. Once the directors saw that "optional" use of the program would go unpunished, they felt free to do the same, further reducing Tom's control. Eventually, Tom transferred to another division of the corporation.

Discussion Questions

- *How do Tom's actions demonstrate the potential limits of the use of power?*
- *Can you think of organizational situations, such as corporate takeovers, strikes, where reactions to the use of power evoked more resistance than expected—and resulted in the removal of power?*

threatened if word got out that several project teams were unproductive and unruly.

In suggesting that he might use his power, the manager elicited the threat of a similar use of power by the project directors. The project directors signaled their potential willingness to act on their own power in responding to Tom's move; Tom's move elicited a reciprocal use of power in the conflict interaction.

It is instructive to stop for a moment and reflect on what this countermove meant to the project directors. They were well aware of the power their manager could exert because they had all been in the corporation for many years. They held the manager–project director dichotomy firmly in mind and were well aware that they had few resources in comparison to Tom. Moreover, because they themselves aspired to rise in the corporation, greatly admired the intellectual and political prowess of higher officers, and saw Tom's station as well beyond reach for the time being, Tom's acts held a certain magical aura for the project directors. The group operated in a fairly egalitarian and congenial manner, and this also reinforced the project directors' endorsement of Tom's move. Each project director saw the others going along with the process in apparent satisfaction, so there seemed little reason to question Tom's move. However, when Tom threw over the rational basis of influence and invoked the authority of his position, the project directors were jolted into considering countermeasures. They raised the argument of difficulty in using the program, but implicit in this was the threat that they would undermine it. This threat was probably not consciously planned. Their response was fairly weak because of the considerable endorsement they accorded to Tom's power. However, it carried the germ of an idea, and later, when their respect for Tom had waned even further, at least some of them would act against him.

The question–response exchange between Tom and the project directors illustrates how the use of power or, in this case, the indication of a willingness to use power, imposes constraints and thereby directs future moves in the conflict. When Tom asked for a response to the unilateral choice he might make, it reduced the range of appropriate moves his subordinates could make at that point in the interaction. It would not have been appropriate, for example, for them to comment on the relative academic merits of the two programs in responding to Tom's "How upset would you be . . . ?" question. The question sought an indication of how willing the project directors were to employ the power they had. If, in response to the question, one of them had said, "I think the program we want has the following strengths . . . ," the statement would not have been an appropriate response to the question (although it might have been effective as a strategy to change the subject and avoid the question altogether). The question—along with Tom's direct focus—created a subtle but strong pressure to respond on the manager's grounds.

The question moved the discussion away from a consideration of the relative merits of the two programs; information and expertise were no longer bases for influence at that point in the exchange. Tom's move constrained the project directors' options in the interaction and actually directed them toward a reciprocal use of power. Any statement that would have been a conversationally appropriate response to the question (for instance, "I'll walk out of the meeting," "I'll be very angry and notify your supervisor," or "I'd get over it") is a comment about the project directors' ability or willingness to use their own bases of power. Tom's remark interrupted the group's present direction and turned the interaction toward a series of moves based on alternative resources: It was a classic triggering event.

Tom's final decision to choose the program he preferred and the response of the project directors to this move illustrate the importance of endorsement. In moving away from a form of influence that the group as a whole endorsed, Tom relied on his right as manager to choose the program he wanted. Although the right was a "given" in the situation, it did not necessarily have to be endorsed or accepted once that power was exercised. A bid for influence may not be successful if other members do not endorse the basis for the move. The project director who decided to recommend rather than require the program and the director who said he did not use the program effectively did not fully endorse Tom's right to decide what program would be used. Although the project directors may or may not have been intentionally challenging Tom's power, in effect their responses were based on a belief that they had a greater say in how their projects were run than they had previously assumed. The project directors' decision questioned Tom's authority— his right to enforce the use of a program in the laboratories.

This does not mean that the project director did not fear reprisals by the manager. If Tom found out about this decision, he would either have to reestablish his power by imposing sanctions on the errant director or have to accept his diminished managerial role. It is likely he would have done the former. The project director was aware of this and gave credence to Tom's power, but he did so to a much lesser extent than he might have. After Tom's move, the project director saw him as unworthy of respect; he saw a way around Tom's power. The project director's original endorsement of Tom began to ebb.

The decline in endorsement of Tom's authority initiated in this incident continued through the labor dispute. Other subordinates saw that Tom could be defied successfully and heard disparaging remarks about him. They gossiped about "stupid" things they had seen Tom do and about his lack of respect for other project directors. The firm base of managerial respect was eroded and the project directors became more and more confident of their own resources vis-à-vis their manager. Tom's loss of endorsement clearly points to the dangers of using strength.

Use of Power in Conflict Tactics

Several researchers have developed extensive lists or typologies of conflict tactics (Sharp 1973; Roloff 1976; Wilmot and Wilmot 1978; Kipnis et al. 1980). A number of conflict tactics are discussed in Chapter 7. The variety and range of these tactics clearly show the many guises power can take in conflicts. Within this diversity, however, four distinct modes of power can be discerned.

1. Some tactics operate through the *direct* application of power: They are intended to compel others to respond regardless of what is wanted. These tactics bring physical, economic, and political resources directly to bear to force others to comply.

2. Other tactics involve a *direct and virtual* use of power: They attempt to elicit others' compliance by communicating the potential use of direct force. In direct and virtual use of power, parties openly display their resources and ability to employ them. Threats and promises are probably the best examples of this tactic.
3. Tactics can use power in an *indirect* mode: Someone may attempt to employ his or her power to shape interaction without ever making the use of power explicit. In the indirect mode, power or the potential to use it remains implicit and tacit.
4. Tactics may constitute a *hidden* use of power: In this mode, tactics use power to hide or suppress potential issues. The actual consequences of power are hidden because the issue is decided before it even develops or emerges.

Some tactics employ more than one mode of power. The particular mode(s) determine how open or explicit the influence attempt can be, the conditions it must meet to be effective, and the parties' general orientation and attitudes toward others. The modes in which a tactic operates indicate several important things about the tactic. First, they determine what skills and styles of behavior are necessary to use the tactic effectively. Making a threat, which involves direct, virtual power, requires a fundamentally different approach than does postponement, which uses the power indirectly. Second, power modes shape the type of resistance the tactic is likely to meet. Different measures are necessary to counteract different modes of power. Finally, each mode has different effects on the endorsement of power underlying the tactic. For example, direct uses of power are much more likely to undermine endorsement than are hidden uses.

We illustrate the fundamental principles and processes involved in the "nondirect" power modes by considering three important and common tactics: *threats and promises* (direct, virtual power), *relational control* (indirect power), and *issue control* (hidden power). For each we outline how the tactic can be used, some conditions governing its effectiveness, and the likely points of resistance it can meet. Because the three tactics are "pure" examples of each category, the principles and problems enumerated here can be generalized to other tactics employing the same power mode.

Threats and Promises

These tactics are discussed in more detail in Chapter 7, but are used as illustrations here. In one form or another, threats and promises appear in almost every conflict described in this book. A *threat* is defined as an individual's expressed intention to behave in a way that appears detrimental to the interests of another, if that other does not comply with the individual's request or terms; a promise is defined as an individual's expressed intention to behave in a way that appears beneficial to another, if the other complies with the individual's request or terms. Threats and promises then are two sides of the same coin—one negative and the other positive (Kelley 1965; Deutsch 1973; Bowers 1974).

Threats and promises are important not only because they are so common, but also because they are clear examples of the direct, virtual use of power to influence interaction. Threats and promises directly link resources—rewards and punishments—with influence attempts and therefore offer a clear illustration of the essential features of the implied use of power. Perhaps because of this, threats and promises have been researched more than any other conflict tactics (Tedeschi 1970; Bowers 1974; Rubin and Brown 1975; Gibbons, Bradac, and Busch 1992). Although this research is fragmented, sometimes contradictory, and often hard to grasp, it can be put into perspective by considering threats and promises as aspects of power—as moves involving the skilled application of resources with an impact that is dependent on the endorsement of the influenced individuals.

It is obvious that effective promising or threatening depends on one person's control over resources the other person values. A manager in a large corporation can hardly threaten an employee with dismissal if the employee knows the manager has no authority to hire or fire; nor will employees believe the manager's promise of a raise if they know the manager has no clout "upstairs." However, effective influence does not necessarily stem from the person's actual control, but rather the other's perception that the person controls an important resource. A person's *actual control* over a resource *becomes critical only if he or she has to carry out the threat or deliver the promise.* The effectiveness of threats and promises is thus dependent on the individual's skill at convincing others that he or she has the resources and willingness to use them.

As with all power processes, the very act of threatening or promising can create or dissipate others' endorsement of the resources being used. If a threat or promise is not carried out, it can suggest to others that the person does not have the necessary resources or the will to use them. This may in turn make others less likely to give credence to the person's resources and less likely to respond in the future. This development is particularly true of intangible resources such as authority. If the manager of a work team cannot carry out his or her promise to get a raise for them, the workers may lose respect and refuse to go along with the manager's future attempts to motivate or guide them (Pelz 1952; Stogdill 1974).

Carrying out threats or promises also has consequences for their endorsement. As might be expected, actually carrying out threats may cause others to resent that person and may ultimately undermine his or her resources. Promises have a unique advantage over threats in that carrying them out actually enhances others' endorsement of the person's power. The use of promises tends to make the party seem more likeable, trustworthy, and considerate in the eyes of others. These perceptions reinforce the very credibility needed to pull off a promise effectively. In an effort to combine the greater compliance created by threats with the credibility reinforcement of promises, Bowers (1974) has suggested that most people use *thromises*—messages that convey both rewards and punishments simultaneously. If a manager says "We really can't take Friday off unless we finish this report today," she is conveying a rewarding offer in language often used for threats. By doing this, she may be able to enhance her employees' liking for her by indirectly offering a reward, yet constrain their behavior effectively. In addition, by indirectly indicating that she wants Friday off, she may increase the workers' identification with her and further strengthen her credibility and their endorsement of her authority.

The basic properties of threats and promises apply for all direct tactics. Most important, they depend on the person's ability to project the potential consequences of a direct move. This requirement makes the person's credibility critical.

Relational Control

During any face-to-face interaction, people constantly define and redefine their relationships. In describing how this process occurs, Watzlawick, Beavin, and Jackson (1967) have noted that every message carries two levels of meaning. Messages have a report aspect that conveys the content of the statement (in other words, the meanings people understand because they know the semantics of the language) and a command aspect that carries relational messages. A relational message is a verbal expression that indicates how people regard each other, their relationship, or regard themselves within the context of the relationship (Burgoon and Saine 1978). In effect, a relational message says "I see us as having this type of relationship." Relational messages are always bids. They attempt to define a certain type of relationship, but may or may not be successful depending on the listener's response.

There are as many possible relational messages as there are different types of relationships. These messages can convey implicitly that someone feels inferior or superior to another person, that he or she is irritated, likes someone, or sees the relationship as one in which it is all right to discuss very personal feelings. Any of these relational statements sends information about the way the speaker wants the relationship defined. If the listener responds with relational messages that accept the speaker's bids, the speaker controls the definition of the relationship. A group member who continuously refuses to take stands on important issues could be sending a relational message that says, "Don't see me as someone who will share responsibility for decisions made in this group." If other members allow this person to demur, they have accepted the relationship for which the recalcitrant person has bid. Alternatively, people who "guilt-trip" others are also bidding for a certain definition of the relationship. They want to induce a feeling of indebtedness in others and to establish a relationship in which others will go along because they feel obligated to do so.

Having one's definition of the relationship accepted is an indirect use of power that can yield considerable control in a conflict. Relational control is indirect because it sets expectations about what can and cannot be said in future interactions without any explicit statements or directives to other people. Relational messages are, by nature, implicit messages. We generally have a good sense of what our relationships with others are like without them having to tell us explicitly. We know whether someone likes or dislikes us, treats us as inferiors, equals, or superiors. Although there are instances when people overtly discuss and define their relationships, even these discussions carry implicit relational messages about what the relationship is like now that the participants have decided to talk about their relationship. A relationship between two close friends, for example, often changes dramatically when they talk about whether they love each other. The mere occurrence of such a discussion, regardless of the actual content of the conversation, says something about what the relationship is currently like. The discussion is a turning point in the relationship because the friends have signaled to each other that these types of discussions are now possible, or impossible, on a relational level.

Relational control is an important form of influence because people often accept previously defined relationships without question. Their understanding of a relationship sets a frame or context that defines what can or cannot be said in a conflict as long as that frame is in place. The parties' relationship may prevent certain moves from being used either because they seem inappropriate or because they are inconceivable given the nature of the relationship. That is, the relationship itself would have to be renegotiated for certain moves to be feasible.

Because relational messages are implicit, they are often problematic. First, they can be easily denied, misinterpreted, or reinterpreted. Comments that seem condescending or demeaning to one person may be viewed as helpful or assisting by others. Second, conflicts that escalate over trivial or inconsequential issues are often fights over the implicit relational messages and definitions that these issues carry. For instance, fights over who will do a trivial task may reflect an unsettled relationship issue. Typically, the relationship issue centers implicitly around who has the right to assign such tasks. As long as the relational issue goes unacknowledged, escalation over such minor problems is likely to continue. The same struggle exists in team interaction. Members commonly embed the expression of relational conflict, such as equity, workload, and status, in the task issues confronting the team (Simons and Peterson 2000). Finally, the implicit nature of relational messages often masks the interactive nature of relational control. Like any use of power, relational control requires the endorsement of others. A relationship is not established until a relational bid has been accepted. Because relational messages are implicit, people often fail to recognize the ways in which they contribute to the definition of their own relationships.

Like other indirect tactics, relational control requires that the use of power remains undetected. If someone sees that there is an attempt being made to manipulate a relationship, the attempted control can be undermined (Tingley 2001). Indirect tactics, on the other hand, are often particularly effective as a means of control because they go unnoticed. They gain their advantage before they are seen. Relationships are defined and redefined with every message that speakers send. As a result, relational moves are second nature. We do not reflect on whether we are accepting or rejecting a certain definition of a relationship each time one is offered.

Issue Control

In an effort to clarify several power-related issues, Bachrach and Baratz (1962, 1970) criticized the available sociological and political studies of power. They argued that power researchers were blinded to the most important and insidious use of power by their emphasis on observing the behavior of parties in conflict. This emphasis constrained them to study only direct, virtual, and indirect uses of power to control decisions and prevented them from considering hidden uses of power, which resulted in what they called *nondecisions*. A decision is a "choice among alternative modes of action" (1970, p. 39). It is arrived at through interaction among the parties and, hence, is shaped by moves involving the direct, virtual, and indirect use of power. *A nondecision is the suppression or avoidance of a potential issue* that might challenge or threaten the values or interests of one of the parties. It is a *nonevent* that never surfaces and results from the hidden use of power by one or more members. Power is hidden in this case because there is no opportunity to observe its operation. If an issue never even materializes and nothing happens, it seems as though power has never come into play when, in fact, it is responsible for the lack of action.

Crenson (1971) illustrates "nondecision making" in a study of air pollution control in Gary, Indiana. He marshals impressive evidence that U.S. Steel prevented the adoption of air pollution standards not by directly opposing them, but by controlling the political agenda of the city. Because U.S. Steel was responsible for Gary's prosperity and had a powerful reputation, the issue simply was not raised for a number of years. When the issue finally did come up, the company was evasive. U.S. Steel did not take a strong stand for or against the issue, and most of the opposition was managed by community leaders with little connection to the company. As Crenson (1971, pp. 76–77) reports:

> Gary's antipollution activists were long unable to get U.S. Steel to take a clear stand. One of them, looking back on the bleak days of the dirty air debate, cited the evasiveness of the town's largest industrial corporation as a decisive factor in frustrating early efforts to enact a pollution control ordinance. The company executives, he said, would just nod sympathetically "and agree that air pollution was terrible, and pat you on the head. But they never did anything one way or the other. If only there had been a fight, then something might have been accomplished." What U.S. Steel did not do was probably more important to the career of Gary's air pollution issue than what it did do.

Its reputation for power and for benefiting Gary was sufficient to protect U.S. Steel from having to face the pollution issue for quite some time. Lukes (1974) and Bachrach and Baratz (1970) maintain that the hidden use of power is one of the most important and potentially dangerous power aspects precisely because it often goes totally undetected.

Issue control frequently occurs in face-to-face interaction. In many families, for example, some issues simply are not raised because one or both parents refuse to allow them to be heard. In families with domineering fathers, young children may not even try to voice their opinions because they know they will meet with strong disapproval. This prevents their concerns from becoming legitimate issues.

Two types of power resources come into play in issue control. First, parties may make definite moves that direct others' attention away from an issue. Control over what information people have access to is the most common means for accomplishing this. In his book, *Victims of Groupthink,* Janis (1972) notes that certain members of Kennedy's cabinet acted as "mindguards" to prevent the emergence of counterarguments against the CIA's plan for the Bay of Pigs invasion. As a result, the CIA's position was never challenged, which led to the ill-fated attack.

The information the parties have to work with can also limit the issues raised. Pfeffer's (1978) study of university departmental budget allocations illustrates this. Most people would agree that considerations, such as quality of teaching, level of scholarship, and general concern with social values, are the criteria that should guide decisions about where a university should spend or cut back its spending. However, with the advent of computerized information systems that provide "hard" numerical data on enrollment levels, number of articles published, and other performance measures, administrators have turned away from "soft" criteria judgments of educational quality, which cannot be numerically quantified. Although sheer number of students served is not nearly as good a criterion as educational quality, it determines decisions because it can be objectively measured. As a result, the hard, soul-searching questions about quality, which also may be threatening to some administrators and departments, are seldom raised and rarely dealt with. The form of information that groups use has built-in biases that preclude consideration of some issues by omitting them. If the group does not know that problems or alternatives exist, it cannot very well raise them or promote open conflict.

In other instances, people's attention is drawn away from conflict issues in more subtle ways. Bartunek and Reid (1992) and Fletcher (1999) illustrate, for example, how significant conflict issues in organizations never surface because they come to be cast as "personality conflicts" between members of the organization. Once seen this way, the underlying issues are often avoided.

The second type of resources involved in issue control function negatively: They suppress conflicts by creating fear of raising issues. One person's power and prominence may keep other people from even broaching a problem. Fear of the unknown—of whether raising an issue will create deep enmities with other members or upset the existing balance of power in the group—can also limit the issues raised. Even if there is no single overpowering person, people may fear an unpredictable collective reaction from the group if they transgress a strongly shared norm. Janis's *Victims of Groupthink* reports numerous cases where prestigious presidential advisors were subjected to ostracism, pressure, and even ridicule for disagreeing with the dominant sentiments of the cabinet.

There is also a skill factor in issue control. Because it operates tacitly, skillful issue control requires that the dominant person's power remains hidden. In the Gary pollution control case, U.S. Steel never openly agitated against the ordinance; to have done so would have aroused the community against it. As Pfeffer (1978) notes, this is one reason it is so hard to determine who holds power in organizations: Members do not want to divulge their strengths because they may become points of opposition for others.

Almost as effective, a dominant party may control issues by manipulating other issues indirectly related to the threatening issue. Pfeffer (1978) notes that one of the best means of influencing a decision is to control the criteria by which the decision is made. Because this is generally done very early in the decision-making process, its influence on the final outcome is often not apparent. Group leaders may shape members' evaluations by speaking briefly about what an effective decision might look like. These initial suggestions often have a strong influence on final decisions, despite the low-key manner in which they are delivered. Indeed, the frame or casting of the situation individuals offer may have a tremendous impact on what issues or ideas emerge in subsequent interactions (Putnam and Holmer 1992).

As with all tactics based on hidden power, how issue control is managed can undermine or strengthen the endorsement of the controlling person's power. If control is flaunted openly, others may band together to counteract the person's dominance. Hence, working quietly and through indirect channels offers the greatest chance to preserve and strengthen endorsement. Issue control tends to perpetuate itself as long as it operates tacitly because it *defines reality*. It restricts people's thought processes and the alternatives considered and therefore rules out challenges to the power base that sustains it.

The Balance of Power in Conflict

There is widespread agreement among scholars of conflict that any significant imbalance of power poses a serious threat to constructive conflict resolution (Walton 1969; Rummel 1976; Wehr 1979; Folberg and Taylor 1984; Pruitt and Rubin 1986). When one person can exert more influence than others because he or she holds greater power resources, or is more willing to employ his or her resources, the odds against reaching a mutually satisfying solution increase.

In the creativity development committee described in Case 4.3, the group initially acted under an assumption of equal power. The project directors believed the Lab Manager was holding his power in abeyance because he had called the group together to read, evaluate, and presumably select a new program for the lab. Interaction in early meetings was premised on the assumption of a balance of power. Members acted and reacted on the basis of their knowledge as researchers; because every member had experience with research, there was an assumption that all would have a say in the outcome. The project directors reported that it never occurred to them to refuse to use the program until after Tom indicated he might make the final choice himself. The shift from a recognized and self-endorsed balance of power to a state of potential imbalance when Tom acted on his managerial rights turned the course of the program selection away from the pursuit of a mutually satisfactory outcome. Tom asserted that he could make a choice that others would have little control over, and the project directors challenged that assertion.

Originally, Tom may have wanted to find a program on which the whole committee could agree; it is unlikely that he envisioned a split on the final options. Once the split occurred, however, the decision to act on a basis of power not available to project directors elicited their reciprocal use of power and triggered the beginning of a potentially destructive interaction. The relationship between Tom and his subordinates became strained; the quality of research could have been jeopardized, and the project directors' careers could have been threatened if Tom chose to retaliate.

When significant power imbalances exist, acting on those imbalances can escalate conflicts and promote the kind of destructive consequences no one on the creativity development committee believed were even remotely possible. Stronger and weaker parties in conflict are both in precarious positions as they make moves in a conflict interaction. Although the dangers and problems of being the weaker party may seem more apparent at first glance, stronger parties face as many dilemmas as weaker ones when trying to act in a conflict where a significant power imbalance exists.

As a case in point, consider large organizations in which scores of conflicts occur daily. Because employees in large companies are sometimes without the power to exert influence directly, they often resort to coercive tactics to "even the score." For example, Tucker (1993) has shown that temporary employees often pursue grievances against employing organizations by engaging in gossip, theft, sabotage, and noncooperation, even when legal and other formal channels are available to them. The lesson is clear: When a severe power imbalance exists, both parties are often victim to destructive consequences.

The Dilemmas of Strength

Power doesn't corrupt people; people corrupt power.
William Gaddis

. . . control of other people's behavior and thoughts encourages
the belief that those we control are less worthy than ourselves.
David Kipnis (1990, p. 38)

Holding more power than others in a conflict is usually seen as a competitive advantage. However, the use of power in conflict interaction is often far more complex and self-threatening than is commonly assumed (Boulding 1990). To demonstrate this complexity, we consider three dilemmas that the more powerful party in a conflict typically faces.

First, the moves that a more powerful party makes in a conflict are sometimes self-defeating because *any source of power can erode once it is used.* Because power must be endorsed by others in the group to be a basis for successful influence, using the resources one holds can prompt others to begin withdrawing their endorsement of those resources. Bachrach and Baratz (1970) suggest two reasons why this erosion tends to take place. First, they note that the use of power can cause "a radical reordering" of the values in the coerced person and undermine the power relationship (p. 29). The person who is the target of a power move may reshuffle his or her values so that the stronger party becomes less consequential. This clearly happened in the creativity development committee case. The project director who decided not to require the program in his unit made a value decision about the relative importance of his role in the laboratory. He placed a higher value on his right to work as he thought best than on honoring his manager's right to assign the decision-making procedure. The project director had never considered counteracting his superior's orders before the summer committee met. It was Tom's use of power that prompted the project director to question it. Did Tom actually have the power of his position once he used it? In a real sense, he did not. The basis of his power eroded, in his subordinates' eyes, when he used the unique source of power he held in this situation. Tom still held the legitimate authority of his position, but that authority was weakened: The endorsement that gave it force over his subordinates was undermined.

Bachrach and Baratz also suggest that power may be exhausted because the constraint or sanction imposed by a powerful party "may prove in retrospect far less severe than it appeared in prospect . . . " (p. 29). The threat of power may be more effective than its actual use because the actual constraint may be more tolerable than was ever expected. Future attempts to influence the "weaker" party or gain compliance may fail because the power has been used once, and the weaker party has "lived through" its consequences. This is illustrated by the case of a new employee who is required to work alongside a powerful colleague (Case 4.4).

Sometimes parties realize that using their power advantage may exhaust it. One tactic in this case is to make bogus power moves that only appear to employ power. To protect specific resources, the stronger party follows the "rule of anticipated reactions" (Bachrach and Baratz 1970): the party anticipates the reactions or preferences of the weaker party and tailors any demands to these anticipated

---

CASE **4.4**

The Copywriters' Committee

Imagine yourself as Jan: At what point would you have reacted to Rosa's behavior?

In the advertising department of a large company, a committee of all the copywriters normally approves the ads being released. One member of this committee, Rosa, often dominated discussions. Rosa was extremely forceful and had a habit of making cutting remarks about others who disagreed with her. Sometimes she shouted them down. This forcefulness initially cowed Jan, a new copywriter for the department, and she generally went along with Rosa's positions, however unwillingly. Jan finally decided to defy Rosa when Rosa attempted to revise an ad on which Jan had worked for several months. She attempted to refute Rosa's objections and received what she described as "a torrent of abuse" questioning her qualifications, competence, and loyalty to the department.

Jan reported that once Rosa's attack started, she realized it was not as bad as she had thought it would be. She recognized that Rosa was simply trying to manipulate her. Jan stood firm and, after some discussion, managed to work out a compromise in the committee. After this incident Jan was much less fearful of Rosa and became one of Rosa's leading opponents in the group.

Discussion Question

■ *How are the dilemmas parents face in disciplining children similar to the dilemma that Rosa found herself in?*

preferences. When this happens, the weaker party appears to be influenced by the stronger, but the stronger party has actually tailored any demands to the behaviors he or she knows the weaker party will accept. When bogus power moves are made, they often reflect the stronger party's fear of exercising power. The use of the power is forestalled but, ironically, the base itself is protected because it has not been put to the test. There is no risk that weaker parties will withdraw their endorsement of the power.

Not only do powerful people face the dilemma of losing power with its use, they also run a second risk—the *risk of making false assumptions about the weaker person's response*. Raven and Kruglanski (1970) suggest, for example, that stronger people often anticipate that those in a less powerful position will resent the power they hold or dislike them personally. This assumption gives rise to an image of the weaker person as unfriendly or hostile. This image, in turn, "convinces" the stronger person that an even tougher stand must be taken to defend against possible counterattack. The stronger person moves as if the weaker person intends to undermine or challenge his or her power base, regardless of the weaker person's actual intentions or feelings. In conflict situations, this assumption can quickly promote hostile escalation and remove the possibility that people will act without using force or threats (Babcock, Waltz, Johnson, and Gottman 1993).

False or untested assumptions about a weaker party are also likely when the more powerful party is successful. In research on how people explain their ability to influence successfully, high-status individuals who were able to change others' opinions were likely to believe that the change occurred because of ingratiation (Jones, Gergen, and Jones 1963) or because the weaker party is not in charge of his or her own behavior (Kipnis 1990). Stronger people tend to believe, in other words, that people change their minds because they want to win an influential person's favor or because they are incapable of greater self-determination. Similarly, Walton (1969) suggests that in unbalanced power situations, the stronger person's trust in the weaker is undermined because the more powerful person may assume others act out of a dutiful sense of compliance rather than by choice (Pruitt and Rubin 1986). This belief can encourage a stronger person to mistrust the behaviors of less powerful individuals and can prevent powerful people from recognizing instances where others act, not out of a sense of duty, but because they see that the more powerful person is worthy of a receptive response. As Case 4.5 shows, power imbalances can exist in intimate relationships and undermine the stronger party's trust in the weaker.

A third dilemma of strength stems from the stronger person's ability to set the terms for reaching a settlement. *In conflicts with significant differences in power, the stronger individual frequently controls how destructive the conflict interaction becomes* (Komorita 1977). This control may stem not from the stronger person's power moves, but from failure to make deescalation an attractive alternative to the weaker person. A weaker individual may have little motivation to stop destructive interaction cycles and begin searching for some workable solution to the problem, unless the stronger person demonstrates that this approach may be worthwhile. If the weaker person believes that compromising on an issue will mean "total loss"

CASE **4.5**

Unbalanced Intimacy

Imagine yourself as Tara: Is there anything you could do to enhance the trust you have in Jameel's feelings toward you?

A college-aged couple (Jameel and Tara) had been dating for almost two years, and, according to both of them, they had a fairly enjoyable relationship. They shared many interests, liked each other's friends and families, and had relatively few disagreements. Tara began to feel, however, that the relationship was unbalanced in a fundamental sense—Jameel was an unusually insecure person. He felt that he was unattractive and was just plain lucky to have Tara interested in him. He often said that if she ended the relationship, it would be unlikely that he would ever meet anyone again. Tara enjoyed Jameel very much and wanted the

relationship to continue but also felt secure enough to think that if this relationship ended, in time she would probably meet someone else.

The difficulty for Tara was that she began to mistrust Jameel's expressions of love for her. She said she could never be sure that Jameel actually cared for her. She kept thinking that his feelings were simply based on his own insecurities rather than a real attraction to her. She ended up leaving the relationship because of these nagging doubts—doubts that ultimately stemmed from the much stronger position she held in the relationship.

Discussion Question
- *What advice might a couples' counselor give to Jameel and Tara?*

---

because the more powerful person can obtain "total gain" once the weaker person begins making concessions, the weaker person has little incentive to begin negotiating. If the more powerful person demands total capitulation, continued fighting or avoidance of the issue may be more attractive to the weaker person than an attempt to resolve the conflict through negotiation or problem solving.

In many conflict situations, it is easy for the stronger person to lay an implicit or explicit claim to a desired solution to the conflict and to create an impression in the weaker party that nothing short of that outcome will be acceptable. This impression can be enough to dissuade a weaker person from pursuing constructive approaches to the problem. The subtle ways in which a more powerful faction in a group can deter a weaker member from working on a conflict are illustrated in the case of a three-person office group (Case 4.6).

Because this office had little organizational structure and few direct lines of authority to evaluate performance formally, the two newer workers at this agency developed a considerable power base. Their friendship and similar views about what the agency should be doing made the pair a strong coalition, capable of making Kathy's situation unbearable. In taking an early hard-nosed stand and concluding that Kathy had to leave, they provided no incentive for Kathy to change her behavior. It is surprising that Kathy did so little to change in the face of her co-workers' criticism because, as a self-supporting parent, she needed the job badly. Although the two newer employees may have had a valid criticism of Kathy's work,

Job Resignation at a Social Service Agency

Imagine yourself as a board member for this agency: What observations could you make regarding the relative power of the three employees?

A small social service agency employed three women to coordinate and plan projects that a large group of volunteers carried out. The agency was a fairly informal, nonhierarchical organization. The employees did not have written job descriptions; instead, an informal set of expectations about the agency's objectives guided their day-to-day work routines. The co-workers assumed that they had an equal say in the projects that were conducted by the office. None of them held the role of director or boss; all three answered to an agency board.

One of the workers, Kathy, was a single parent in her mid-forties who had worked at the office for a little over three years. The other two workers, Lois and Janelle, were in their early twenties, had just graduated from college together, and were good friends when they were hired. They had been at the office for less than a year. The younger employees had a great deal of energy to devote to the agency, in part because they had few personal commitments outside work that would direct their time or attention elsewhere, and in part because they had a well-developed and somewhat idealistic view of the path they wanted the agency to follow. Kathy, on the other hand, found it difficult to support and raise a child while working. Also, because she had been working at the agency for three years, she did not have as much enthusiasm for her work as the other two staff people. The job had become more routine for her and was primarily a way of making ends meet.

Over a period of several months, Lois and Janelle became increasingly dissatisfied with Kathy's work at the agency. They felt she did not complete project reports on time or in sufficient detail, and as a result they tried to complete or revise a considerable amount of her work. They felt that Kathy had a different perspective on what their jobs entailed and what the goals of the agency should be. They

were frustrated by the additional work they were forced to do and by their belief that Kathy was not allowing the agency to change and move in new directions.

A fairly short time later, Lois and Janelle became more vocal about their dissatisfaction with Kathy's work. Although they would occasionally give specific criticisms about her performance, the larger issue of how much say they would have in moving the agency in new directions brought them to a quick, defiant stand against Kathy. The issue that "Kathy is not doing her work right" quickly became "we want Kathy out." Kathy was aware of her co-workers' feelings and realized that they had different conceptions about the agency and their roles in it. On a day-to-day basis, however, she tended to avoid confronting the issue as much as possible. When questioned about her work, she would typically respond with a question that mirrored the resentment and hostility of Lois and Janelle: "How could I do all that when I've been trying to deal with a sick child at home all week?" Kathy felt that the two women had very little understanding of her situation. She knew that the two younger workers saw her as a "bad person," and she felt they did not seek the kind of information that would allow them to see why her view of the job and agency differed from theirs.

Lois and Janelle eventually confronted Kathy with the problem by bringing it up to the agency board. They told the board that, in their view, Kathy was not fulfilling her job requirements and that she was resisting efforts to improve the agency. When questioned about the situation, Kathy tried to defend herself, but soon became conciliatory. Feeling enormous pressure from the two other workers, Kathy resigned from the agency within a few weeks after the board meeting.

Discussion Question

- *As a board member, what could you have done to try to resolve the agency conflict constructively?*

their belief that Kathy had to leave the agency was, in effect, a demand for total capitulation. Kathy became convinced that there was little reason to work through the issue. Even if the board had decided she should stay on, it would have been difficult for her to work closely with the other employees. The women had the ability to pressure Kathy to resign and, by leaving the impression that they indeed wanted this outcome, they discouraged any initiatives to work on the conflict constructively.

The Dangers of Weakness

One way to analyze a conflict is to define parties' needs and determine which of the needs are incompatible. In the social service agency described previously, for example, the needs of the two newer staff people were basically twofold: to move the agency in new directions and to have the office run efficiently while maintaining an equal division of labor among the three workers. Kathy's needs centered around the necessity of balancing a difficult home life with a demanding job. This general concern lay behind her need to continue with established programs rather than begin new ones and to work at a slower pace than her co-workers at the office. Although the issue spread fast and became highly personalized, the "problem" underlying this conflict centered around the apparent incompatibility of these two sets of needs. A collaborative or problem-solving orientation to this conflict would have set the participants in determined pursuit of a solution that could have met both sets of needs simultaneously. However, problem-solving approaches to conflict are premised on an assumption that participants recognize the legitimacy of each other's needs. When the needs themselves are held in question, there is no reason for the participants to search for some way of satisfying those needs.

In a situation *where power is unbalanced, the greatest danger for weaker parties is that their needs will not be viewed as legitimate,* that they will not be taken into account when the conflict is resolved. When more powerful parties discount others' needs, the solutions they seek, such as firing Kathy, are ones that by definition are unacceptable or unsatisfying for other parties. This is more than just a case of the stronger person's needs winning out over those of the weaker. The stronger person can often determine what needs are relevant through his or her ability to define what the conflict is about—in other words, to exert issue control.

The social service case just mentioned provides an excellent example of the effects of issue control on the weaker party. When the issue was brought before the board, it was defined as a conflict over whether Kathy would or could hold up her end of the agency's work and adapt to its new directions. This put Kathy in a defensive position. Several possible alternative definitions were not considered: The conflict could be (1) over whether the agency should expand, (2) over whether fair and reasonable demands were being made of Kathy, or even (3) over quality-of-life issues (Kathy claimed the job took away family time, and the two new members wanted the work to play a big role in their lives). Each of these definitions implies a different focus for conflict interaction than the definition presented to the board. Definition 1 defines the conflict as a problem common to all three members concerning the agency's goals, whereas definition 2 questions the behavior of Lois and Janelle, and definition 3 reorients concerns to external issues such as members' overall satisfaction and life plans. Clearly it would be easier for Kathy to respond to any of these issues than to the issue presented before the board, but they were not raised. Lois and Janelle used their power and momentum to press their attack before the board and, by "getting the first word in," set an agenda to which Kathy had to reply. Kathy had little choice but to attempt to defend herself, and this response no doubt made her look bad in the eyes of the board and undermined her already shaken confidence.

A danger of weakness is that *stronger parties may be able to define the terms and grounds of the conflict in their own favor* (Sheppard, Lewicki, and Minton 1992; Geist, 1995). Even the language a powerful party uses can have a significant impact on the way an issue is perceived or it can be used to legitimize and maintain the status quo (Deetz and Mumby 1985; Giles and Wiemann 1987; Conrad and Ryan 1985). This type of definition not only puts the weaker member at a disadvantage, but it may also hurt both people by resulting in an ineffective or harmful solution. The more powerful person often only understands one side of the conflict and his or her grasp of the underlying causes may be imperfect. As a result, the definition of the conflict advanced by the stronger person may not state the problem in terms that would lead to an effective solution. For example, in the social service agency, Lois and Janelle defined the conflict as Kathy's lack of cooperation. This definition pressured Kathy to resign. The social service agency lost Kathy's experience and talent and had to pay for hiring and training a replacement.

The outcome might have been different had the situation been defined as a conflict over whether the agency should expand. This definition recognizes both sides' concerns by emphasizing the agency, not the members. Although the same issues would probably have come out—Kathy's lack of energy, Lois and Janelle's desire to innovate—they would have been discussed in terms of a common issue, and much of the pressure would have been off Kathy. Perhaps, if managed correctly, a problem-solving approach could have generated solutions all could have lived with, while preserving Kathy's talents for the agency.

A second danger of weakness is its *tendency to become self-perpetuating and self-defeating*. As mentioned before, weak parties tend to perceive themselves as powerless. These perceptions can discourage parties from attempting to resist or make countermoves to a powerful person's moves. The end result is a reinforcement of the powerful person's control and further proof of the weak person's impotence (Kipnis 1990; Kritek 1994; Eisenhardt, Kahwajy, and Bourgeois 1998). This process simply reproduces both parties' positions. Research on dating partners (Roloff and Cloven 1990) supports this self-perpetuating tendency in unequal power relationships. There can be a "chilling effect" on the expression of conflict when perceived power differences exist between dating partners. When one person feels that his or her partner has superior alternatives to the current relationship (for example, has more power), the weaker person is less likely to express conflict issues. Weaker parties who are influenced by the chilling effect are reluctant to raise issues because they fear that conflict escalation might damage the relationship further and put it at risk. Similarly, research on marital partners (Kelley 1979) suggests that the more dependent partner attends more to the care of the relationship than the less dependent partner. The effect of such moves by less powerful parties is to preserve and reinforce existing power structures in relationships.

People who are convinced that they have little influence and who are threatened with loss of a particularly valued goal or possession may feel pressure to commit acts of desperation. As noted in the previous section, sometimes the weaker person may be convinced that he or she has little to lose by resisting, and a serious attack—one that threatens the existence of the relationship or organization—may appear to be the only course with a chance of success. For example, in a charity fund-raising committee, one man with very little power faced the loss of the money necessary for the survival of his "pet" project, a community development loan corporation. If the project fell through, the member stood to lose his job as director of the corporation as well as his position on the committee. Believing the committee was about to veto his project, the member threatened to go to the local newspaper and state that the committee gave no support to the local economy. This would arouse a great deal of controversy around the committee and possibly hurt its major fund-raising drive, which was to begin in two months. The committee ultimately forged a compromise that gave the project partial funding, but considerable anger was caused by the member's move. The committee's cohesion was undermined, and the project was canceled two years later. The desperation of weakness can motivate "absolute" acts with the potential to destroy relationships or groups or lead to worse retributions later on.

Cultural Differences in Values

The preceding discussion assumes that maintaining equality is an important value. Although it is certainly important in most Northern European–derived cultures, *equality is not a central value in all cultures.* Hofstede and Bond (1984) define power distance as a characteristic of cultures that reflects the "extent to which the less powerful members of institutions . . . accept that power is distributed unequally" (p. 419). The higher the power distance in a culture, the more its members accept unequal distributions of power. Ting-Toomey (1999) notes that power distance is low for Austria, Israel, Denmark, Ireland, Sweden, Norway, and Germany. Canada and the United States are moderately low on this dimension. Power distance is high in Malaysia, Guatemala, Panama, the Philippines, Arab nations, India, West African countries, and Singapore.

In these latter cultures, lower power parties do not expect to be part of the decision process, and the value of respect between parties of different status is taught from a young age. Ting-Toomey (1999, p. 71) observes:

> People in small power distance cultures tend to value equal power distributions, equal rights and relations, and equitable rewards and punishments based on performance. People in large power distance cultures tend to accept unequal power distributions, hierarchical rights, asymmetrical role relations and rewards and punishments based on age, rank, status, title, and seniority. For small power distance

cultures, equality of personal rights represents an ideal to work toward in a system. For large power distance cultures, respect for power hierarchy in any system is a fundamental way of life.

Parties in high power distance cultures are likely to employ either the harmony or regulative models of conflict management rather than the confrontative model. For both models, and especially for the regulative model, balancing power is not as important as other considerations. Hence, power imbalances do not influence conflict interaction as strongly in these cultures as they do in cultures that favor a confrontative model of conflict management.

Working with Power

There are a number of barriers to accurate diagnosis of the role of power in conflicts. For one thing, people are often unwilling to talk about power or to provide honest and accurate assessments of their own or others' power for several reasons. Given our culture's emphasis on democracy and equality, the open use of power is not socially sanctioned. Parties may be unwilling to admit that they use force or that a group is controlled by only a few members because they believe it makes them look bad. Furthermore, because power depends on endorsement, powerful parties often try to keep their power unobtrusive in order not to alienate those they influence. If weaker parties cannot see the power, or if they do not understand how it works, they can do nothing to upset the present balance. Additionally many moves, such as issue control, use power indirectly, and it is hard to determine who is having influence. Finally, power and endorsement processes depend on relationships between parties rather than being properties of individuals, so it is often hard to determine where the source of power is. If power stems from relationships, it is misleading to try to identify a particular person who holds power. The more important question may be who assents to the use of power or who withholds endorsement.

These barriers make the assessment of power a complex process for which there can be no set formula. It is best to try several approaches. One way to assess power is to *determine the possible power resources in the situation and identify who holds them.* This involves identifying both obvious resources, such as status, knowledge, personal attractiveness, or formal authority, and more subtle sources of power, such as confidence or the ability to predict another's behavior. A second, complementary approach is to *identify power through its effects.* Those whose preferences consistently win out and who are accommodated by other members are generally those who control resources and use them effectively. As Frost and Wilmot (1978) note, the ability to label the conflict is also a sign of power. If a conflict could be interpreted either as a minor difference of opinion or as an important matter of principle, and it ends up being interpreted as a minor difference, the members who favored this view are likely to hold the high ground. A third indicator of power is *conservatism.* If power is relational, then changes in existing relationships generally alter the balance of power, while stability preserves it. People who are against changes are likely to believe they will lose by it. These are often the people who hold substantial power under the status quo.

None of these three indicators is foolproof, and each can lead to mistakes; however, they are a good starting point. Judgments about power ultimately rest on knowledge of relationships among parties, their particular history, and the nuances that signal dominance and subordination. Diagnoses cannot be programmed and must be continually refined.

Another important diagnostic tool in analyzing power is the *ability to recognize when parties draw on unique or shared power resources as a basis for influence in conflict.* Parties can attempt to influence a conflict by drawing either on the unique resources they hold or on sources of power commonly available to everyone and explicitly endorsed as a legitimate basis for influence. When parties use unique power sources, integration is more difficult and escalation more likely. Each move premised on unique sources of power "tells" others that an attempt may be made to resolve the issue by means not available to everyone. In effect, use of unique power resources is an attempt to exert unilateral control. This message can promote escalation by prompting other parties to use their own resources to counter moves they cannot reciprocate.

The creativity development committee case (refer to Case 4.3) provides an illustration of people moving from the use of shared to individual resources. In the early meetings, parties' actions were contained by boundaries that the group as a whole accepted. The project directors and the manager drew from a set of resources they all shared and saw as a legitimate basis for changing opinions and determining possible outcomes. When he indicated that he might make the final choice based on his position as the Lab Manager, the emphasis shifted to the unique sources of power that individual parties held. Similarly, in the Job Resignation case (refer to Case 4.6), the conflict drew on unique power bases. The two newer staff people used their friendship and agreement on agency policy to move against Kathy. Kathy drew from her seniority and experience as an older worker to justify her position in response to the challenge she faced. The three women never developed an implicit agreement about what resources could be used to influence each other. There was not, in other words, a mutually endorsed set of resources that could be used to work through the conflicts over the quality of work and the long-range objectives of the agency. Although differences of opinion on these issues may have been difficult to resolve, the staff's inaction prevented a group assault on the problems. In making moves based on their unique sources of power, parties worked on the problem from their own standpoints and discouraged give and take on common ground.

To safeguard against the dangers resulting from unbalanced power, parties need to forestall power moves based on unique resources. Individually held resources become less salient and are less likely to be invoked when all parties have established a mutually endorsed power base. But how do parties promote the use of shared power? Although there is no cut-and-dried answer to this question, research and practice suggest some guidelines.

Fostering Shared Power in Conflicts

Three primary conditions encourage reliance on shared power in conflicts. First, *if all members agree on the primary goals of the group, team, or organization, unique sources of power are less likely to be used.* A shared sense of purpose gives members a common orientation, which encourages interchanges on common ground (Mansbridge 1980, 1990; Larson and LaFasto 1989). A common goal gives the group a center that encourages members to identify with each other. When they identify, members are likely to think in similar terms about how to influence each other. They are not as likely to resort to unique resources that could underscore potential divisions among them.

Of course, this is easier said than done; members must be able to articulate what the general goals of the group mean when they are applied in particular situations. An organization can easily say it intends to work for the community good, but what does this mean exactly? When members look at any given problem and examine alternatives, and perhaps incompatible, proposals in light of the group's general purpose, they are engaging in behavior that promotes constructive conflict interaction. This process enables people to check each other and to articulate the group's purpose again; to build cohesion around that purpose; and to consistently steer itself, on a decision-by-decision basis, toward common goals (Eisenhardt, Kahwajy, and Bourgeois 1998).

Classroom teams that are formed to complete a project assignment often fail to attain a common goal or purpose. Some students see the team's major aim as education; they accept the premise that going through the trials and tribulations necessary to complete the term project will be a good learning experience. For these students, the general purpose of the team is to learn how to collectively carry out assigned tasks. Other students do not buy into this educational objective. Their goal is simply to complete an acceptable assignment that meets the basic requirements for the course and to get a good grade without expending too much effort.

When two different goals exist in a project team, differences over how the project should be accomplished, how often they should meet, or how much time should be spent on each task are ripe for escalation into full-blown conflict. *Without an overarching goal to guide them, members are likely to feel disconnected from others and to turn to unique sources of power to influence the team's choices on the issues.* When all members buy into the same goal, there can still be considerable debate over how long meetings should run and so on, but the team is working toward the same conception of success as it tries to reach agreement on issues. Members may have to spend considerable time defining what success entails, what the best means for achieving success are, and how much time is needed to reach the goal, but this discussion is constructive. It points the team toward a more well-defined conception of itself, and it allows members to set explicit standards for what behavior is expected from them. In terms of power, it forms a basis for common effort that encourages members to operate on the same level when they try to influence each other (Jehn & Chatman 2000).

In the Job Resignation case, the three women never reached agreement about what the primary goals of the agency should be. There were implicit differences that the two factions never tried to resolve or meld into one shared mission for the office. As a result, differences over an issue, such as what constituted quality work at the agency, were "settled" when members turned to the unique sources of power they held. Sticking to the shared definition of their problem—should the agency expand?—might have helped the three women to identify common goals.

It is important to note that a common goal does not guarantee that shared power bases will be used. Many teams with clear goals also have strong leaders who have access to resources, such as formal authority, different from those of other members. The point here is that a common goal encourages member identification, which may predispose the team to use common resources.

A second condition conducive to a shared power base is the group's or organization's willingness to make power resources accessible to all members. A resource truly shared by the membership is an attractive alternative to unique sources. If, for example, knowledge of the history of the organization is endorsed as an important resource for influencing decisions, settling differences about policy matters, and so on, then all members—even new people—must be given access to this knowledge. New members, of course, will be less influential than others at first because they do not enter the team with a full history in hand. However, if the relevant information is made available on a decision-by-decision or issue-by-issue basis, newer members can draw on the same sources of influence that long-standing members use. In some teams, this is done through formal channels such as orientation sessions, training in skills valued by the group, and written histories.

Even when all information is available and access is given to all members in principle, certain members may consistently be more influential than others because they are more skillful. Some members may be more powerful than others because they are better able to articulate positions the team recognizes as appropriate or consistent with its direction. Ensuring access to all does not mean that all members will be equally able to use a resource. Some members may be able to apply the resource more quickly or insightfully as new issues arise, and therefore their power, their ability to influence the direction of conflicts, will appear to be greater. The difference is, however, that the power these members exercise is legitimate because the group as a whole continues to endorse the resources regardless of who uses them.

The importance of equalizing the power resources available to all members is clear in the Job Resignation case. In their coalition, Lois and Janelle had a source of power unavailable to Kathy. If Lois and Janelle had not taken advantage of their alliance and had instead tried to deal with Kathy one-on-one, they might have been able to work out a more constructive solution. From one-on-one conversations, Lois and Janelle might have been able to understand Kathy's needs and feelings better. They might also have seen her potential and the problems that kept her from contributing. Kathy, on the other hand, would not be intimidated by the united front of Lois and Janelle's and might herself have seen the merits in their case. Once each side understood the other's needs and problems, working out a solution would have been easier. Moreover, once Kathy was assured that the other two would not use their superior power to force her, she might have become less reactive and more willing to work on improving the agency.

A third condition underlies the first two: *The group should recognize that its members are the source of power and that they participate continually in the exercise and renewal of power.* The group must work to see through the myth of power as a possession to the process of endorsement necessary for any move to be effective. It must acknowledge that this endorsement occurs in members' interaction and that therefore, as Janeway (1980) argues, all power is grounded in *community* among members. This is what democratic nations try to do in their constitutions, and this is what groups must do to build a shared power base. However, just as governments often have trouble remembering their popular roots, so too do groups and teams have trouble remembering the roots of their power. As noted before, the endorsement process operates to hide the source of power from members. Long socialization, the mystique of power, and subtle interaction processes veil members' roles in endorsement. To achieve a balance of power, groups must adopt structural measures to counteract these forces. Groups have done this in a variety of ways, including rotating leadership regularly, appointing "process watchers" to comment on members' moves and group interaction, setting up retreats and evaluation periods to help members discuss power-related problems, and forcing their leaders to adopt a nondirective style. Whatever the specific steps, these moves tend to be effective because (1) they make members aware of their community and their responsibilities to the group and to each other, (2) they emphasize admitting all members into discussions on an equal basis, and (3) they deemphasize the prominence of any particular individual.

This section has emphasized the need to develop shared power bases. This is meant as an ideal or goal to strive for, not as the only effective or justifiable use of power. Some groups have such deep-seated discrepancies that weaker members have no choice but to develop and use unique power bases. In such instances, the use of force or countervailing resources may be the only way to check or get the attention of the controlling members. The literature on teams and organizations is full of examples of groups with authoritarian leaders who became so oppressive that members saw no choice but to band together and to rebel. A forceful countermove was the only way these parties could get their message heard. Although cases exist in which unique sources of power can be used beneficially, it is important to remember that doing so creates unstable situations over the long run. One side may topple the other, but, in time, the toppled side is likely to strike back. Moving to a shared power base greatly enhances the likelihood of a constructive and mutually beneficial solution.

In one sense, these suggestions are preconditions; they must be in place in a group if members can hope to develop shared power resources and to use them as a basis for moves in any conflict interaction. In another sense, these suggestions offer long-term intervention strategies; they are areas that the group can work on to establish general expectations for how it operates. They can govern what members consider doing when they try to sway each other's thinking about issues.

What happens, however, when these preconditions have not been established or when someone uses unique resources in a conflict that is particularly important to him or her? Although no intervention is foolproof, several approaches may help prevent escalation in such instances.

First, it may be helpful if people discuss their likely reaction to the use of unique resources. For example, members might acknowledge that they will see someone who uses seniority to justify job assignments as "out for themselves." Open discussions can effectively raise the group's consciousness about power moves. It can help the group learn that certain resources will change conflict interaction dramatically. It also alerts the group to possible dangers or pitfalls that might result.

A second approach is aimed at developing structural changes in interaction when power moves are based on unique resources. One of the most effective tools for changing the influence of power in conflicts is to increase people's awareness of the role they play in creating and sustaining others' power. If members become aware of how their endorsement is shaped by social categorization, the mystique of power, and their own interaction, they are well on the way to seeing through the existing power structure. The value of consciousness raising is illustrated by the support groups that spring up in professions undergoing rapid change and coping with the struggles that result. These groups, which range from female executives in male-dominated corporations to nurses and medical orderlies attempting to have more input in hospital's decisions, give their members a chance to share problems and fears and to give each other advice. People help each other understand how those dominant in their professions maintain their positions. They also work out ways of being more effective, and build resolve and courage to face difficult situations. They encourage members to question what was previously unquestionable— the taken-for-granted relations of authority and obedience, strength and weakness. Formal support groups are not the only thing that can serve this function: A conversation over dinner or after work can generate important insights. Just realizing one is not alone and sharing experiences are often important steps.

As Janeway (1980) observes, in addition to awareness, mutual support is another way for weaker members to counterbalance stronger ones. People generally associate coalitions with open shows of strength and solidarity, as in a union vote, but such displays may be ineffective in many contexts. Raising the flag of defiance can threaten stronger people and cause them to overreact, sending the conflict into an escalating spiral. Those who have greater resources stand to lose if the current balance tips in a new direction, and they will resist such moves. A coalition is more likely to be successful in moving a conflict in a productive direction if it is unobtrusive. The pact between people should not be openly displayed, and, if possible, any coordination or support should not be obvious. In addition, a coalition is more likely to turn conflict in a productive direction if it aims for a balance of power than if it tries to win. If the powerful people's interests are not threatened, and if they do not face serious losses, they are more likely to cooperate with efforts to achieve a balance of power.

Summary and Review

What is power?

Power is the ability to influence or control events. It depends on resources parties can employ to influence others and attain their goals. A wide variety of resources can serve as sources of power, including material resources (money or strength), skills, likability, and formal position in a group or organization.

What gives resources their empowering nature?

Resources are not valid in any absolute sense. The effectiveness of a resource as a basis of power depends on its endorsement by other parties. If a resource is not valued or validated by others—or if they do not believe the party's use of the resource is legitimate—then the resource will not motivate them to comply. As we will see in Chapter 7, even direct physical violence cannot necessarily force someone who does not endorse it to comply.

How does the process of endorsement work?

Endorsement is negotiated during interaction. This negotiation is influenced by four factors: social categorization, the mystique of power, values attached to certain resources, and the degree to which resources are used skillfully. Because it is produced in interaction, the endorsement of power moves differs across situations and may change during an episode. These differences tend to remain hidden, and the fact that power is produced through the collaboration of all parties is obscured by the tendency in U.S. culture to avoid open discussion of power in interpersonal relationships.

The effective power in a given situation is a product of the give-and-take in which parties employ resources to place constraints on each other. One party's constraint is answered by another's countermove, and the resulting web of constraints gives the conflict direction by favoring certain moves and making other moves less productive. Each move—or power bid—places a certain resource into play, and the four factors mentioned in the previous paragraph influence whether the bid is accepted or not. When bids are accepted, the resource is endorsed for future use, and bids that are rejected decrease the endorsement of the resource.

How does power operate when a conflict tactic is employed?

Power may operate in four distinct modes. Direct power employs resources to compel others to comply in an open power move. Direct and virtual uses of power imply the potential use of direct power, but do not actually put the resources into play. Indirect power moves use resources to influence interaction, but do not make the use of power explicit. Hidden power is employed to frame or limit the discussion of issues behind the scenes; tactics that use this mode of power keep issues from being contested and predetermine the outcome of conflicts.

Some tactics use more than one mode of power, as we will see in Chapter 7. We discuss three that exemplified more or less pure modes of power. Threats and promises employ direct, virtual power. To use them skillfully, a party must make the threat or promise credible. Relational control employs indirect power by defining the nature of the relationship between the parties, thereby making certain moves likely and constraining the use of other moves. The endorsement of indirect power depends on its remaining under the surface—hidden from view. If one party senses that the other is trying to manipulate him or her, the relational messages that define and constrain behavior become less effective, and the relationship itself—the key resource in relational control—may be endangered. Issue control employs hidden power to set the agenda for a conflict, enabling some issues to be raised and suppressing others. As with indirect power, hidden power needs to operate under the surface and in the back rooms. If it is brought into the open, issue control is generally viewed as improper manipulation, and endorsement of this channel of power decreases.

Why is the balance of power among parties important?

Imbalances of power result when parties possess different resources that are endorsed at different levels. For most cultures in the United States, maintaining equality of opportunity is valued. When parties do not have equal control over the situation, several problems can result. Although being the stronger party may seem desirable, it creates certain dilemmas: Using the very resources that contribute to strength may undermine their endorsement due to the resistance and resentment of weaker parties. Stronger parties also tend to assume that the weaker party is complying only because he or she is forced to. This creates a sense of distrust of the weaker party and encourages the stronger party to continue forcing, further undermining the relationship between the two. Imbalances of power also encourage the weaker party to give up on cooperative solutions, effectively guaranteeing repeated cycles of forcing. A continuing imbalance of power may encourage the weaker party to feel powerless and devalue his or her resources. This further cements control of the stronger party because his or her resources are endorsed by the weaker party, who also "dis-endorses" his or her own resources.

It is important to note that balancing power is not a key value in cultures with high power distance. In such cultures, the dynamics of power in conflicts are likely to be quite different.

How can we work productively with power in conflicts?

The first prerequisite to working with power is to understand how it is operating in the situation. Indicators of who has power and the impacts it has on the conflict include who controls power resources and might use them, conservatism, and the effects of power. One important aspect of power is whether the parties have unique resources. Once parties (and third parties) understand how power is operating, they can move to change the situation.

How can parties foster shared power?

Shared power is more likely when: (a) parties are in agreement about broader goals and a shared sense of purpose overarches the conflict; (b) key sources of power are accessible to all parties, rather than distributed unequally; and (c) parties understand their own role in the creation of power and actively work to manage how power is used in the conflict.

Several steps may be taken to encourage a move toward shared power from a situation in which unique sources of power are used. First, parties can openly discuss their reactions to certain power moves, indicating which sources of power are acceptable to them and which are threatening or negative. Second, parties can change the structure of the situation so that certain types of power resources are encouraged and other resources disallowed. Third, weaker parties can support each other to resist a more powerful party with the goal of reaching a stalemate that can promote discussion or structural changes.

Conclusion

Power is the architecture of conflict interaction. The moves and countermoves in a conflict are based on parties' ability and willingness to use power. Power moves are based on resources people hold that serve as a successful basis of influence. These resources can range from material goods to time, physical attractiveness, communication skills, and other talents. Power must be viewed as a relational concept because in order for resources to be a basis for influence, the resources must carry the endorsement of others. Power is thus always conferred on people by those who endorse the resources, and it is conferred through interaction.

At first glance, the relational nature of power seems to suggest that weaker parties in a conflict always have a way out: They can withdraw their endorsement if more powerful parties apply pressure. There are, however, strong social forces that encourage or sustain the endorsement of various forms of power. Whatever the distribution of power may be, its balance is critically important in determining the direction of conflict. When power is unbalanced, the stronger and weaker parties both face dilemmas as they make moves and step through difficult conflict situations. Stronger parties can exhaust their power by its use, consciously or inadvertently set settlement terms that encourage continued escalation, and make faulty assumptions about the likely response of a weaker person. Weaker parties may have to live with a definition of the problem that ignores their real needs because they have no hand in determining what issues get addressed.

CHAPTER

5   Face-Saving

Imagine that you are so absorbed in reading a new movie review while walking to class or work that you fail to notice a stairwell. Just when you reach a particularly arresting section in the review, you notice something is not right. You are off-balance, falling on what should be level ground. Thanks to superior coordination skills, you keep from going head over heels down the steps, but do jerk and jump down the jagged cement. Your belongings fly into the air, but you make a remarkable recovery, landing on both feet and catching one of your things before it spins into a bush. Just as your nerves and heart settle, you notice that a group of your co-workers is watching. In fact, it is obvious from the expressions on their faces that they have watched the entire embarrassing event.

A million thoughts race through your brain. What do you say or do? Do you walk on and ignore them? What about your things? You are struck by a sudden desire to say something intelligent, something that reflects you are not the clumsy boob you appear to be. Instead, you stoop down to pick up your things. You look at the steps and curse them, as if they possessed a human quality that consciously decided to trip you. With a newfound composure, you turn to your colleagues and say, "What are you looking at?" You immediately realize this is a moronic question, so you add, "I was reading, didn't see the steps." They laugh. You turn red. One says, "Hope you didn't break your newspaper." He probably meant it as a joke to ease the moment. Somehow, though, this joke stings. They turn and walk away. Half-jokingly, you vow to hate these people for the rest of your life. You are amazed at how bitter you feel. Hours later, you wonder what the big deal was. How could you have gotten so flustered and bent out of shape over a simple misstep and comment? The answer lies in what scholars, and now practitioners, commonly refer to as *face*.

Face is a central theoretical concept used in a wide array of disciplines and is defined in as many ways. Yet most definitions concur that "face" is concerned with identity needs. People have identities or public images they want others to share. Although the attributes vary, people want to be seen by those they encounter as possessing certain traits, skills, and qualities. They constantly position themselves in interaction with others (Harre and Van Langenhove 1999). In short, *face is the communicator's claim to be seen as a certain kind of person.* As one scholar in the area puts it, face is "the positive social value a person effectively claims for himself [*sic*] by the line others assume he has taken during a particular contact" (Goffman 1955).

The concept of face can be traced to fourth century B.C. China. The Chinese distinguish between two aspects of face, *lien,* and *mien-tzu* (Hu 1944). *Lien* stands for good moral character. A person does not achieve *lien,* but rather is ascribed this quality unless he or she behaves in a socially unacceptable manner. To have *no lien* means to have no integrity, which is perhaps the most severe condemnation that can be made of a person. *Mien-tzu* reflects a person's reputation or social standing. One can increase *mien-tzu* by acquiring social resources such as wealth and power. To have *no mien-tzu* is simply to have floundered without success, an outcome that bears no social stigma.

The Dimensions of Face

Although scholars generally concur that face is a universal characteristic of being human, there is less agreement as to the common identities or face wants people share. Brown and Levinson (1978, 1987) propose the most popular view in their theory of politeness. *Politeness theory* conceives of face as something that can be lost, maintained, or enhanced and must constantly be attended to in interactions. Specifically, the authors propose two dimensions of face: *Positive face* refers to a person's desire to acquire the approval of others; *negative face* is the desire for autonomy or to not be imposed on by others. Conflict may arise because many communicative acts, especially instances of social influence, are face-threatening. For example, a request to "get busy with that report" may interfere with the hearer's negative face wants or the desire for autonomy. According to the theory, the degree to which face is threatened by a request is a function of three factors: the social distance between the parties, the relative power of the parties, and the intrusiveness of the request or act. The greatest potential face threat is found when there is greater social distance between the parties, the listener has more power than the speaker, and there is a great degree of imposition placed by the communicative request or act. The authors refer to the theory as "politeness" because the degree of face threat is thought to determine how polite a speaker will be. Brown and Levinson propose that people use five general strategies to perform a *Face-Threatening Act* (FTA), represented in Table 5.1.

The strategies and examples in Table 5.1 are presented from most to least polite. The most polite strategy is to *avoid* the FTA completely—the speaker makes no request. The next strategy is called *going off-record.* This is when the FTA is performed in such an ambiguous manner that it could be interpreted as some other act by the hearer. Going off-record is stating a request indirectly or implicitly. The third strategy is the use of *negative politeness.* This strategy attempts to mitigate the threat to the hearer's negative face by giving him or her autonomy. *Positive politeness* is the fourth strategy—the speaker performs the FTA with attention to positive face needs (the want of approval). The least polite strategy is a *bald on-record* FTA with no attempt to acknowledge another's face wants. Politeness theory contends that speakers employ the strategy that fits the situation. The more serious the FTA, the more polite the speaker will attempt to be.

TABLE 5.1   Politeness and FTA Strategies

Example Request: Begin Fixing the Dinner Meal

Politeness	FTA Strategy	Example
High	Avoid—do not perform	No request is made.
	Going off-record	I'm really getting hungry.
	Negative politeness	I know you are busy, but could you start cooking dinner?
	Positive politeness	You are such a good cook. I can't wait until you start dinner.
Low	Bald on-record	Would you fix dinner?

Source: Adapted from Brown and Levinson (1978).

Lim and Bowers (1991) extend the Brown and Levinson concept of positive face (the want for approval) because it compounds two different human face needs: the need to be included and the need to be respected. The need for inclusion, they maintain, is the need to have one's person and personality approved of, whereas the need for respect is the need to have one's abilities and skills approved of. As a result, Lim and Bowers distinguish between three types of human face needs: the want to be included or *fellowship face,* the want that one's abilities be respected or *competence face,* and the want not to be imposed on or *autonomy face.*

Face-Loss as It Relates to Face-Saving

When face wants are not addressed during interaction, one or both of the parties may experience a loss of face. People are said to *lose face* when they are treated in such a way that their identity claims are challenged or ignored. Given the strong need to maintain a favorable image, face-loss can lead to an impasse in interaction and exacerbate or create conflict between parties. Goffman (1955) describes several face-loss consequences. First, face-loss often causes a person to be momentarily incapacitated or confused. The shock that one's identity is facing attack sometimes takes a moment to adjust to. Second, the individual may feel shame or embarrassment. This feeling is often accompanied by a host of common symptoms that reflect this social distress, including blushing, sweating, blinking, fumbling, stuttering, and general nervousness (Sharkey 1988). Third, the person may feel inferior or less powerful. In sum, face-loss is an unpleasant experience, seen from the eyes of the harmed party as social humiliation. Not surprisingly, research shows that people are willing to retaliate and sacrifice rewards at great costs when they perceive the threat of humiliation (Brown 1977).

Face-saving behaviors are defensive attempts to reestablish face after threats to face or face-loss. In other words, face-saving is what a person does to regain the image he or she believes has been dismissed. The remainder of the chapter explores the consequences of face-saving strategies for parties in conflict.

A Threat to Flexibility in Conflict Interaction

Continued change is often a good sign in conflict. Changes in a person's positions and styles, as well as more general shifts in the climate and emotional tenor, indicate that a person or group is successfully resisting tendencies toward rigid perpetuation of conflict interactional patterns. They also decrease the likelihood that the parties will lock into the destructive cycles that trained incapacities often produce. As uncomfortable as it sometimes is, people should be encouraged by change because it usually means that others are still working on the issue and that a breakthrough is possible. Change requires energy; the use of energy to move the conflict interaction in new directions suggests that there is still some level of motivation to deal with the unresolved issue. Any signs of stalemate or rigidity can easily paint the first gray shades of discouragement on a colorful, although difficult and emotionally draining, conflict.

The emotional side of conflict is intimately connected with a person's flexibility. As noted in Chapter 1, every move in conflict interaction affects relationships, liking or disliking for each other, mutual respect or lack of respect, beliefs about each other's competence, and a score of other beliefs and feelings. *Face-saving is an attempt to protect or repair relational images in response to threats, real or imagined, potential or actual.* It can limit a person's flexibility in taking new approaches to the conflict issue. In addition, because of its relational consequences, face-saving often carries an emotional "charge" that can greatly accelerate destructive escalation or avoidance in conflict. Like the effects of trained incapacities, face-saving issues often redefine conflicts. Once face-saving becomes a concern, people's perceptions and interaction patterns can lead to a progressive redefinition of the conflict, which changes a potentially resolvable difference over some tangible problem into an unmanageable issue centering on the relationships between the parties and the images people hold of themselves.

Before exploring face-saving in detail—its causes and its consequences—it is useful to consider a few illustrations. Cases 5.1 through 5.3 show three diverse conflict situations wherein the ability to be flexible and to change approaches, positions, or interaction styles are in jeopardy. At the heart of each case lies a concern with saving face.

- In Case 5.1, a university professor became increasingly concerned about the way students would be likely to see her if she changed her mind about a decision she had recently made.
- In Case 5.2, a group had fears that an outspoken, quick-thinking member would have trouble backing off from a position once she took a stand on an issue. To the group's surprise, she had little concern about being seen as

CASE **5.1**

The Professor's Decision

Imagine yourself as the English professor: Why might you be so concerned about your image?

An English professor at a Midwestern university was called by the academic appeals referee and told that a student in her introductory writing course had filed a grievance about a grade he received last semester. The student was given a "D" in the class because he did not take the final exam in the course. On the day of the exam, the student had left a message with the department secretary saying that he was ill and would not be present for the test. Although the professor received this message, the student did not get back in touch with her until after the grades had to be submitted. When the student did get in touch with the professor, he told her that he had three other final exams scheduled that week and had decided to take those tests to stay on schedule rather than making up the English final immediately. He said he had thought he would be able to contact her again before the grades had to be reported, but, as it turned out, he was too slow in doing so. On hearing the student's explanation, the professor decided to stick with her earlier decision to give him the grade he received without any points on the final. The student's grades on the earlier tests and writing assignments were good enough that if he had received a "B" on the final exam, he would have finished with a "B" in the course.

After receiving the call from the appeals referee, the professor began to question her decision. Originally she had felt justified in taking the tough stand because she had stated a very clear policy about missing tests and assignments early in the term. She began to believe, however, that she might have been somewhat dogmatic in this case and was leaning toward allowing the student to take a make-up exam and using that score in recomputing his final grade. But as she entered the meeting with the appeals referee and student, she became increasingly concerned about changing her mind. She knew that word travels fast among students, and she was worried that soon she would have a reputation for changing grades or class policy when the right pressure was applied. She was also increasingly bothered by the student's decision to register a formal complaint against her in the college.

Discussion Questions

- *How could an understanding of the professor's concern for her future image assist the appeals referee in this case?*
- *Can you think of examples of conflicts in which you felt someone's concern about image contributed to his or her inflexibility?*

"wishy-washy" and changed stands once a better argument was made by other members.

- In Case 5.3, three staff members felt their face was threatened by one person who "took charge" without the team's endorsement.

In each of these cases, some form of face-saving was a central concern and could have undermined the parties' ability to successfully deal with the conflict. In the grade dispute, the professor had taken a stand on an issue and was reluctant to

CASE **5.2**

The Outspoken Member

Imagine yourself as Rhonda: Why do you think you are so willing to change your position? What is the image of yourself that you are protecting?

A group of twelve leaders and activists in the antipollution movement of an eastern city began meeting to discuss strategies for dealing with an attack on water standards that was currently being made in their area. A local business executive was mounting a campaign that could have jeopardized water and waste treatment standards if it gained sufficient support. The group of twelve met to determine what could be done to counteract the business campaign and to coordinate the efforts of environmentalists who wanted to work on the project. They saw their main task as building an effective alliance of people in town who wanted to work for environmental quality at this crucial time.

The people in the group were from a wide variety of backgrounds and professions: Some headed smaller civic organizations, some were students, one worked for a local newspaper, one was an elected city official. One member, Rhonda, was an attorney in her thirties and a long-time activist in local politics. She was an outspoken person who took the floor several times early in the first meeting and spoke in a loud and confident tone of voice. She came to the meeting with well-developed ideas about what the group should do and she was able to argue her position clearly and forcefully while other members, on the other hand, still seemed to be thinking about what the current situation was like and calculating what should be done as an immediate plan of action.

When Rhonda made a strong case for what the group should do in the first part of the initial meeting, the climate in the group grew uneasy and tense. Several people looked at each other uncomfortably and most people seemed hesitant to speak. The group seemed to be "holding its breath" and anticipating that Rhonda would be difficult to work with. Although she was obviously bright and had good reasons supporting her suggestions, members feared that Rhonda had set ideas and would not budge from the proposal she had just articulated so forcefully. The group thought she would feel as if she had lost face if she moved away from her stated position.

After several people made comments that were not related to Rhonda's proposal, one man in the group began pointing to possible complications and problems with Rhonda's suggestion. She listened intently and when he was finished speaking, Rhonda said that she really had not thought of the points he had raised and that she felt they posed a serious set of problems. She asked the man if he had an alternative suggestion, listened to it, and then shortly began arguing for it. She made stronger and more well-reasoned arguments for the man's proposal than he himself had made, and Rhonda was able to clarify questions other people in the group had about the proposed plan without dominating the interaction or intimidating people further.

The group soon saw Rhonda as one of its most valuable members. She could carry a line of thought through for the group and lay out a well-reasoned set of arguments for a stand she was taking, but at the same time, she was not hesitant to turn 180 degrees on an issue if new information or evidence was presented that she had not previously considered.

Discussion Questions

- *What are the dangers of assuming that someone would be threatened if you argued with them?*
- *Can you describe a situation where you felt someone was not changing a stated position even though you felt he or she had had a change of mind?*

CASE **5.3**

The Controversial Team Member

Imagine yourself as one of this case's three staff members: In what ways is your face threatened by your co-worker? Why would you want to talk to your supervisor?

Four staff members in a personnel office at a large computer corporation were assigned to a rather demanding recruitment project in addition to their regular job of interviewing and placement. They were asked to design and implement an effective program for minority recruitment and placement within the corporation. The project was viewed as one of the top priorities for the department, and the workers knew that the success or failure of the project would have a significant impact on their advancement in the organization.

About a month before the project was due, one of the team members asked her immediate supervisor if they could meet with him. The supervisor agreed, but when the team arrived, only three of the four members were present. The team had not asked the fourth member to attend the meeting with the supervisor. The problem the team faced was that the fourth member repeatedly made decisions and completed tasks that all had not endorsed. The three staff members felt that these decisions and actions were threatening the quality of the entire project.

The fourth member was a man who had been in the personnel office a year longer than the other three. He felt he had more knowledge and experience than the other staff members, and he made this point on several occasions. He also told them that he did not want this project to interfere with the time he needed to complete his normal work routine, and so he was willing to make certain decisions about the project on his own to move things along faster.

Although the three felt intimidated by their co-worker's outspoken and evaluative style, they felt that he was bright, hardworking, and did have some experience that they lacked. In most cases, however, they felt this additional experience was unrelated to the current assignment. They saw the man's concern about the project taking time away from his normal work as pure arrogance; they all had the same work schedule to complete each week and needed to find time to work on the recruitment project. The team felt particularly insulted because, on several occasions, the man did not show up for meetings that had been scheduled. He did not let the group know that he would not be attending nor did he offer any explanations for his absence afterward. He made no attempt to get information that he held to these meetings. Thus the team's work was often delayed. When he was present, meetings were tense and antagonistic, and the motivation of the team had plummeted because of the problem.

When the supervisor asked the team if they had discussed their reactions openly with the "problem" person, the three members said they had not. They had wrestled with the idea but decided that the issue was just too emotional to air openly. They were, however, mad at the co-worker, felt intimidated by him, and wanted the department management to hear about the problem.

Discussion Questions
- *Is there a "downside" to having face concerns addressed by someone not directly involved in the conflict?*
- *In what ways does "gossip" sometimes function as an attempt to receive face support?*

move from that position because she might be seen as indecisive or unsure of herself. When she reconsidered her decision, she recognized that the student may have had a good case and that she may have been too harsh in enforcing her no make-up policy. As she entered the meeting where the conflict was to be addressed, however, there was a great likelihood that her current beliefs on the problem would not be stated unless something was done to ease her concern about the image she might acquire by following her inclinations. Part of her reluctance to move also stemmed from an already existing threat to face: The image she had of herself as a fair professor had already been called into question publicly by the student's decision to contact the college official.

In the environmental group, the face-saving issue was anticipated by members who heard Rhonda make forceful arguments early on. A tense and uneasy climate arose because most members assumed Rhonda had a strong commitment to her position and would be very hard to move. There was a general sense that Rhonda would be a "problem" because others assumed a strong public defense of her position meant Rhonda's self-image would be at stake if the group challenged her suggestions. The group was surprised and relieved to find that Rhonda's intellectual and verbal abilities could provide information and clear reasoning for them without being tied to Rhonda's self-image. If no one in the group had run the risk of questioning Rhonda's initial stand because of the fear of embarrassing her, the group could easily have become dissatisfied with the decision-making process but remained silent, perhaps eventually splintering into pro- and anti-Rhonda factions.

Face-saving was at least one of the concerns of the staff on the personnel project as they entered the supervisor's office. Although the team feared the emotional strain and potential long-range consequences of raising the issue with their coworker, they felt this person had treated them unfairly. They were made to feel as if their input on the project was unnecessary or even harmful. At least part of their motivation for contacting the supervisor was to restore face: They did not want to think of themselves as incompetent; nor did they want to see themselves as people who would accept unfair treatment without resistance. If the supervisor agreed with their accusations and assessment of the situation, their face would be restored.

When face-saving becomes an issue, it threatens parties' ability to remain flexible and shift their modes of conflict interaction. Face-saving reduces flexibility and the likelihood of change in group and interpersonal conflict situations for two reasons. First, the emergence of a concern with saving face inevitably adds an issue to the conflict. The additional problem tends to take precedence because it stands in the way of getting back to the main issue (Penman 1991; Wilson 1992). Energy and attention are drawn away from the central issue and are spent on peripheral matters; work may stop on the issues that count most as people deal with a threat to face. In each of the three previous cases, face-saving added issues to the conflict that diverted attention—and interaction—away from the central concern, or exhausted the parties before an adequate resolution was reached (Table 5.2).

In the grade dispute in Case 5.1, for example, the main conflict was over the professor's policy on make-up exams and her decision to enforce that policy in the current situation. The professor's reputation as indecisive or soft was really a sec-

TABLE 5.2   Possible Consequences of Face-Saving in Conflicts

- Reduces parties' flexibility
- Adds an issue to the conflict
- Turns attention away from more tangible concerns
- Increases the likelihood of impasse
- Encourages an all-or-nothing approach to resolution
- Prompts parties to turn to outside people to address concerns

ondary, although related, issue. In the environmental group, members' attention started to shift from a concern with how the group should go about protecting water standards to how the group was going to deal with a member who appeared to be dogmatic and would likely be threatened by criticism. In the personnel project team case, the central conflict was over decision-making rights in the group. By not addressing this issue, the three workers added a face-saving concern: They felt unjustly intimidated by the man and spent considerable time trying to feel better about the situation and attempting to decide whether they had somehow helped elicit the man's arrogant behavior. These additional issues can easily displace the team's focus if they remain salient concerns or if the members fail to address a face-saving issue that is influencing members' behaviors.

Besides multiplying issues, face-saving makes inflexibility likely because face-saving concerns usually include the real possibility of a future impasse in the conflict. Motives to save face are difficult to alleviate in conflicts and tend to foster interaction that heads toward stalemates and standoffs. After examining face-saving in a variety of formal bargaining settings, Brown (1977) notes that issues related to the loss of face are "among the most troublesome kinds of problems that arise in negotiation" (p. 275). Several factors contribute to the tendency for face-saving issues to head toward impasse.

Face-saving issues often remain highly intangible and elusive because people are reluctant to acknowledge that their image has been threatened. People can sense that something is going wrong and that positions seem to be tightening, but the face-saving motive may never be raised explicitly. To acknowledge a threat to one's image is in some ways to make that threat all the more real. One can maintain a desired self-image despite what others think as long as one can somehow deny what others think. To openly state what the threat may be and risk confirmation of the belief is in some cases to remove the possibility of denial. Therefore, the threat to one's image may be real and may be influencing the conflict interaction, but it often lies beneath the surface where it will go unrecognized or unaddressed.

The professor in the grade controversy, for example, might go through the entire meeting with the student and appeals referee without raising the issue of her image or without noting that she felt put off by the student's decision to contact the referee about the matter. Although these concerns may never surface, they could prompt her to make strong arguments in favor of her original decision, even though she now doubts its fairness, or to make unreasonable demands on the student before moving from her initial stand. An effective third-party appeals referee might anticipate these face-saving concerns and make suggestions that alleviate them but not require that the issue be stated explicitly (Shubert and Folger 1986). Often the mere presence of a third party allows someone to move from a position without losing face because they can attribute any movement they make to the other party: "I never would have settled for that if the appeals referee hadn't pushed for it" (Pruitt and Johnson 1970; Brown 1977).

There is another reason why impasses are likely outcomes of conflicts complicated by face-saving issues: *Conflict interaction becomes highly vulnerable to an all-or-nothing approach to resolution when face-saving issues arise.* A gambler who loses all evening at a casino table may feel a need to bet big at the end of the night to restore face with those who have watched her struggle for a missed fortune. When an issue becomes heavily steeped in establishing or protecting face, it is often easier for participants "to go for broke" or walk away than to remain in a situation that, in an important sense, undermines their self-concept or sense of self-worth. Face, in many instances, is seen as an issue on which no compromise was possible. Personal honor and a commitment to oneself can take precedence over any continued involvement with or commitment to the relationship.

The staff who worked on the personnel recruitment project were all too willing to let the one man make decisions for them even though they were insulted and upset with his behavior. The members expected further embarrassment if they brought the issue to the man's attention; they thought he would defend himself by pointing to his own experience and chide them for ignoring their daily work tasks to work on this project. Rather than risk the confrontation and a further affront to their self-image, members were willing to walk away from the issue even though it meant continued frustration with the project.

Conflict Interaction as a Face-Saving Arena

Face-saving messages are concerned with an image the speaker is trying to maintain or reestablish in the interaction. Because this image depends on others' reactions, any attempt to save face is an attempt to negotiate the speaker's relationship with other parties in the conflict. Face-saving messages offer information about how the speaker wants and expects to be seen in the exchange. Studies of how communication is used to define interpersonal relationships have noted that this type of *relational comment* (in other words, "This is how I see you seeing me" or "This is how I want you to see me") is carried by any message a speaker sends (Watzlawick et al. 1967). In the case of face-saving messages, however, the relational comment is more salient because it is under dispute; the face-saving message is a defensive response to a perceived threat. The speaker has reason to believe that his or her desired image will not be accepted by other members. As a result, the speaker feels a need for assurance or confirmation and engages in various behaviors, such as those in our examples, to "restore face." Interaction usually cannot proceed without resolution of the face problem and will often be dominated by this problem until the speaker feels satisfied that enough has been done to establish the desired image. It is clearly the speaker's perception of how others are taking him or her that determines when the face-saving issue is lifted from the interaction.

If a person rushes into an important meeting fifteen minutes late and says, "Back-to-back meetings never seem to work out," the comment carries a face-saving message. It asks the group to see the person as someone so busy that he or she may have to overschedule meetings and end up being late at times. This relational message serves a face-saving function because it supplants a potentially threatening image others could hold; it asks people not to see the speaker as someone who is inconsiderate of others' time or is unconcerned about what may go on at the meeting. Being busy, hardworking, or overtaxed is a positive image; being inconsiderate, slow, or careless is an image the person wants to avoid.

In an insightful analysis of face-saving work in everyday interactions, Goffman (1967) describes how people try to conduct themselves in social encounters to maintain both their own and others' face. Goffman emphasizes that the mutual acceptance of face is "a condition of interaction not its objective" (p. 12). Interaction ordinarily proceeds on the assumption that the faces people want to project are, in fact, the ones that are accepted as the exchange unfolds. There is a noticeable strain or a recognizable problem when face maintenance becomes the objective rather than a precondition of interaction. Even in ordinary interaction, then, people feel a need to amend the situation when a face-saving issue arises so that the exchange can unfold without the concern.

In group conflict there is a noticeable difference in interaction when face-saving issues arise and become the objective of the interaction. There is a shift away from group-centered and group-directed interaction toward interaction focused on the experience of the individual member and his or her relationship to the group. Conflict interaction is group-centered when all parties take into account their membership within the group and continuously recognize that any movement made on an issue must be made with other parties in the conflict. Individual positions and stands can be argued, and indeed must be, if adequate differentiation is to occur. However, when the interaction remains group-centered, there is a continual recognition that individual positions are being offered and that all comments are geared toward issues that result from differences in members' needs or goals. Members never lose their identities and concepts of self when interaction is group-focused; the commitment to self and the sense of personal identity become secondary to the awareness that the conflict is a shared experience and that change or movement in the direction of the conflict will be *with* other members.

The emergence of face-saving as an issue undercuts the group-centered focus in conflict interaction. By its very nature, face-saving gives prominence to the individual members and their sense of self in the group. Attention is turned toward the experience of the individual because face inevitably raises a question about the way some member is seen by others in the group.

Face-saving issues cross the line between group- and individual-centered interaction. This crossing reflects an ambivalence about the role of individuals in groups that has been noted repeatedly in analyses of group experience. Several researchers have observed that the individual's fundamental attitudes toward group membership are "characterized by ambivalence. . . . The basic antagonism is between the individual's commitment to himself—to his own needs, beliefs and ambitions—and his yearning for psychological submersion in a group, for an obliteration of those qualities that make him unique and thus distinct and separate from others. . . . Submersion brings a measure of security and a sense of connectedness and belonging, but it also undermines individual autonomy . . . and may in other respects demand a sacrifice of individual wishes to those of the group" (Gibbard, Hartman, and Mann 1974, p. 177).

When face-saving becomes an issue, individual concerns begin to outweigh those of the group or the substantive issues in the conflict. The commitment to self and, in particular, the commitment to establishing a desirable self-image take precedence over the sense of belonging and cohesion that exists when members more fully "step into" the group.

Face-saving produces a qualitative change in the nature of the group's conflict interaction. Group-centered interaction is founded on the assumption that all are acting and responding primarily as group members. In this sense, everyone remains at the same level in the interaction because they all take into account their membership in the group and act on that awareness when they speak and respond to others. When interaction becomes individually focused, one person steps into an "official role" that he or she holds as an individual. Obviously, such a role is always available to each member but it can easily remain dormant while members try to sustain group-centered interaction. The role of the member as an individual raises concerns about what the person looks like to the group, what impact that person in particular is having on the outcome of a decision, what place he or she holds in the group's power structure, and so on. In a sense, the individual adopts an authority position and wants to be seen as the authoritative representative of an image he or she wants to maintain or a role he or she wants to play in the group's process. There is an awareness of someone carving out an individual figure from the composite interaction that the group has molded. This separation lays the groundwork for the inflexibility discussed before.

The following example, which is an actual transcript of a discussion among four graduate students, illustrates a turn from group- to individual-centered interaction. The students in this discussion were given a topic as part of a class assignment. Believe it or not, their task was to clarify Plato's conception of truth. In the interaction just prior to this segment, the students, who were from the same department and knew each other quite well, joked about the seriousness of the topic and were somewhat eager to go off on a tangent before leaping into the task at hand. As this segment of interaction begins, Kathy asks Peggy about her research on gender differences in people's thought patterns. The group recognizes that the question is somewhat off the assigned topic, but they are more than willing to pursue it and delay their discussion of truth. The group eventually ties the issue of gender research back to the main topic, but that part of the exchange is not included here. Watch for the turn the interaction takes toward individual-centered interaction.

KATHY: (*to Peggy*) Are you doing any more work on differences in male–female thinking?

PEGGY: (*answering Kathy*) Uh, hum.

DAVE: I have an article.

PEGGY: Collecting data as a matter of fact.

DAVE: I have an article that is so good. This is off the subject, but let's talk about it for a few minutes.

PEGGY: That's right, let's forget truth. I'd rather talk about males and females than truth.

KATHY: Mhmmm.

GARY: Mhmmm.

DAVE: Candice Pert is into, got into, pharmacology and is now in neuroscience. She is the discoverer of what's called the opiate receptor in the brain. Those are the brain cells that opium has an effect on. The ones they're attracted to.

PEGGY: Hmmmm.

DAVE: And they've, they've gone from opium receptors to ah Valium receptors to any tranquilizer. And she's working now on a marijuana receptor, that the cells hit. And it's so neat . . . (*Some laughter while Dave is talking; Gary mimes something and Kathy makes a comment under her breath and laughs.*)

DAVE: (*laughing slightly*) Now wait a minute, wait a minute. This is fascinating. (*General laughter*)

GARY: I've already heard it, so I'm spacing off on my own here.

DAVE: She made this discovery when she was a grad student.

KATHY: Then there's hope for me yet.
(*General laughter*)

PEGGY: (*pointing to the back of her head*) Ah, here are my opiate receptors.

DAVE: She's first author, and her male mentor and advisor and teacher is second author.

PEGGY: Hmmmmm.

DAVE: There was an award given called the . . .

KATHY: (*interrupting*) And he got it, right?

DAVE: (*continuing*) The Lasky award, which is seen as a stepping stone to a, to a Nobel prize, and ah . . .

KATHY: What do opiates have to do with men and women?

DAVE: Now wait a minute.

PEGGY: (*jokingly*) Wait, wait—have patience, have faith.

DAVE: Here's, here's your politics in it to start with.

KATHY: All right.

DAVE: She was first author on this paper when this Lasky award was given; it was given to four men.

KATHY: Mhmmm.

DAVE: And she was invited to the awards ceremony. That's the extent of it. And she talks about it a little bit.

PEGGY: Oh, marvelous.

DAVE: But in the interview she talks about the, you know, I can be known as a scorned woman here, but I've done some other things since then that are really important to me. And she, she uses the analogy of the brain as a computer. And although she doesn't talk about what we would commonly call software, that's what you learn, she really, she's looking at what she calls the hardwiring. The circuitry in the brain. And the differences in male/female circuitry.

PEGGY: And she's found some?

DAVE: She's found some possibilities. Some probable areas. Now there are differences, there are some other differences that are not just male and female. There are differences, say, between what we would consider healthy, normal personalities and, say, schizophrenia.

PEGGY: Mhmm.

DAVE: (*There's a three-second interruption here as someone enters the room, then Dave continues.*) Ah, you look at the evolution of language instead of being male-oriented and thinking that men had to learn how to use language so that they could coordinate hunting down a large animal. It was women who were the ones who were staying home.

KATHY: (*sarcastically*) To get them out of the cave.
(*General laughter*)

PEGGY: To talk to the walls.

DAVE: Yeah, you know talk to walls, talk to the kids.

PEGGY: Well, that's interesting. I'd like to read that.

DAVE: And from the beginning. Yeah, it's really fascinating because there are detectable differences in male and female brains.

KATHY: Hmmm (*makes a face*).

PEGGY: Yeah, I'd like to read that.

DAVE: (*to Kathy*) You act like I'm being chauvinistic.

PEGGY: No.

KATHY: No, I'm just, I'm . . .

DAVE: (*interrupting*) Oh boy, this is terrible.

GARY: She'd act a whole lot worse if you were being chauvinistic.

KATHY: Do I act like you're chauvinistic? Yes.

DAVE: You made a face.

KATHY: (*laughing*) I'm trying to see inside my brain to see if there are any differences. That's all.

DAVE: Differences. What, from mine?

KATHY: Yes.

DAVE: But how can you see mine?

KATHY: Oh, I don't know. I can't see in mine either. Let me be successful here first. No, I was thinking of brains, young Frankenstein you know.

DAVE: (*laughing*) Oh yeah.

KATHY: Twelve years dead, six months dead, freshly dead.

DAVE: Yeah, yeah.

KATHY: Sorry, Dave, I'm just not on that level today.

DAVE: No, no.

PEGGY: Well, I think there are some very definite differences in language use and that would be some clue as to why. I've always talked about it being culture, socialization, and that sort of thing, but, ah . . .

GARY: I wonder if there's a change coming in that with the revolutionary changes in men and women's roles in society—they're now becoming different—and if that will have an effect on this too.

PEGGY: Go back far enough and actually you can see that the species will evolve differently. . . .

Initially, the group's interaction in this exchange consisted primarily of offering and evaluating information about research on gender differences. Although Peggy did not elaborate on her research when Kathy asked her about it, Dave's comments about the brain's sensitivity to drugs held the group's interest and prompted continued interaction on this topic. It became the focus of questions and jokes in the group, and it also raised the issue of how sexual politics becomes involved in research. Dave's summary of the article he had read and his commentary about the possible implications it might have for understanding the evolutionary development of male and female language use set the stage for the turn toward individual-centered interaction that took place in this discussion.

After Dave says "Yeah, it's really fascinating because there are detectable differences in male and female brains," the next twenty speaking turns are focused on Dave's image in the group. These comments deal with Dave's relationship to the group rather than with the topic that had surfaced and engaged the group as a whole. Kathy's facial response to Dave's statement made Dave concerned about whether Kathy or the other group members saw him as a chauvinist. Peggy, Gary, and Kathy all attempt to reassure him, although sometimes lightheartedly and perhaps unconvincingly, that he is not seen as a chauvinist because of the way he summarized the article and reacted to it. In the main, the group handles the face-saving concern by joking about the article, becoming somewhat ludicrous (with the references to young Frankenstein's brain) and finally treating one of Dave's major points (about the possible value of an evolutionary explanation for language differences) seriously. When Peggy and Gary make their comments in the last three speaking turns in this segment, the interaction is turned back to a group focus. The interaction is no longer focused on Dave's experience in the group and the way he is seen by others. Dave lets his concern about his image drop and the group continues with an exploration of the merits and problems with research on gender differences.

Because people are always concerned about their self-concepts and roles within a group or dyad, interaction, conflict or otherwise, tends to teeter somewhere between group and individual emphases. It is possible to achieve a healthy balance that eases the basic antagonism between individuals' commitments to themselves and the need or desire to work in the group or dyad. This balance can allow the group or dyad to remain a cohesive unit able to settle disputes, yet, at the same time, minimize the threat to individuals and meet individual needs. Needless to say, this balance is difficult to maintain when conflicts occur.

Conflicts provide an arena where the balance of group- and individual-centered interaction is easily tipped toward the concerns of individual members, making face-saving likely to occur. Several factors, in combination, may lead the group away from group-centered interaction once conflict arises. First, the process of differentiation is, as noted in Chapter 1, one that temporarily associates individuals in the conflict with sides of an issue and reveals the main differences between members. This differentiation is desirable because it articulates individual stands and creates an understanding of the differences between members. *Clarifying individual positions is, however, a powerful thrust toward individual-centered interaction.* People hear themselves argue for a position in front of others and may be hesitant to leave their initial positions once they make a public statement.

Second, *there is a tendency for members to point a finger at others and assign responsibility for the emergence of the conflict to a single individual or faction in the group.* Sometimes this arises from displaced aggression as discussed in Chapter 2. This tactic ignores the fact that conflicts always lie in some incompatibility of goals or needs among all concerned. It also focuses attention and interaction on the roles or behaviors of individuals in the conflict. The accused are put in the paradoxical position of, on the one hand, having to defend themselves against the charges, thus giving continued prominence to their individuality, while, on the other hand, needing to move the interaction toward a group focus if real progress toward reaching a resolution is to be made.

Third, as observed in Chapter 4, *parties in conflict often turn to unique sources of power during conflict interaction.* Any move based on unique power sources gives prominence to the characteristics of individuals in the conflict and promotes countermoves that are also based on unique sources of power. The moves work against members being able to construct and use group-endorsed bases of power as a means of influence. When people use unique sources of power to try to influence the group, they put an important part of themselves on the line. If the move is not successful, their image, not the image of the whole group, is threatened and may need to be redeemed through the use of threats, force, or deception.

Besides the effects of differentiation, the tendency to attribute conflict to individuals, and the use of unique sources of power, *interaction in groups can also tip toward an individual focus because of decision-making procedures that groups employ in conflict settings.* If members know that decisions will be made and conflicts settled by, for example, a voting procedure, a group often "walks" through conflicts with an expectation that the vote will settle things. Voting labels people as winners or losers. Each person knows whether he or she is on a winning or losing side as issues are discussed and solutions chosen by the group. This awareness can heighten people's sense of themselves as allied with, or against, others and promote comments and responses that defend individual positions and self-images: "I lost out this time, but you can bet it won't happen again soon."

In sum, conflicts are likely arenas for establishing and defending people's images of themselves. These concerns can easily turn interaction away from constructive work on the conflict issue and toward secondary, but troublesome, issues that stem from the individual's relationship to the group. When these concerns arise, they tend to promote inflexibility in interaction and prevent the group from approaching the conflict from new directions.

Although these destructive tendencies are likely, it should be noted that there may be times when a turn toward individual-centered interaction is useful or necessary. Some individuals may need certain images of themselves confirmed, even though the images may not have been questioned by other people in the group. Someone may, for example, have a strong need to know that his or her contributions are valued by other people. To fulfill this need, the interaction would have to center on the person's relationship to the group. This in turn could serve a useful function, *if* it provides valuable feedback about a member's performance or an incentive for someone to continue with his or her work and involvement in the group. In most cases, this type of interaction occurs outside conflict situations, so it rarely becomes problematic.

Face-Saving Forms in Conflict Interaction

Although there are many ways in which concerns for self-image can surface in interaction, three general forms of face-saving can be distinguished. Each reflects a different interpretation the person trying to save face might assign to the situation. These interpretations act as "mind-sets" to promote defensive, face-saving behavior. Each type of face-saving has recognizable symptoms that distinguish it from the others and each requires different corrective measures. Two of these forms have been studied by researchers who focused on competitive contexts such as negotiation and bargaining settings: resisting unjust intimidation and refusing to step back from a position. They have been alluded to in the earlier cases, but deserve more explicit attention because they pose a serious threat to constructive conflict interaction. A third form of face-saving that has not been studied by previous researchers also is discussed: suppressing conflict issues. This form is unique to more informal conflict settings (like most work or group decision-making contexts) where the interaction is premised, at least initially, on the assumption that people will act cooperatively to make decisions and settle differences. Few researchers have studied these noncompetitive contexts.

Resisting Unjust Intimidation

Brown (1977) and others (Deutsch and Krauss 1962) have suggested that face-saving often results from a need to "resist undeserved intimidation in order to guard against the loss of self-esteem and of social approval that ordinarily results from uncontested acquiescence to such treatment" (Brown 1977, p. 278). When people feel they are being treated unfairly or pushed in a way that is unjustified, they are likely to make some attempt to resist this treatment. Interaction can turn toward a defense of one's self-image as the individual tries to establish that he or she will not be intimidated. It carries an "I don't have to take this" or "Any fair-minded person wouldn't stand for this" message to the other party.

When this form of face-saving message is sent, it always carries two components. First, there is an accusation that others are in fact treating the person unfairly or aggressively. In some cases, the other party will recognize (although perhaps not admit) that there may be some grounds for the accusation. The other's response in this case is likely to be a defense of his or her behavior or accusation. For example, in a local health department, an assistant administrator conducted several surprise inspections that made employees very nervous and defensive and came near to causing a labor dispute. When one supervisor confronted the assistant administrator with this problem and challenged her fairness, she refused to discuss the issue. Her responsibilities, she argued, forced her to "tighten up the ship" and to increase work quality by whatever methods she had available.

In other instances, the accusatory face-saving message can take other parties by surprise and elicit either an initial defensive response ("We never did that to you") or avoidance because people are unaware or do not believe they have attacked. This type of face-saving message requires some type of reaction because it carries an accusation. The accusatory nature of the message makes it a force that redirects interaction. Even the indirect response of active avoidance means that the parties have decided to allow future interaction to be influenced by the unacknowledged but real effects of an issue that they had decided to ignore.

The second important component of this type of face-saving message is the sense of adamant resistance it conveys. The speaker suggests, in effect, that "business as usual" cannot continue until the concern has been addressed. This sense of resistance often accompanies messages sparked by a perceived threat (Gibb 1961). Such messages have the potential for altering the climate of the relationship or group. Once this type of face-saving message is sent, others may feel that it is no longer safe to allow the interaction to continue in the present direction or to suggest new questions or issues for discussion. The defensive party has claimed the right to define the immediate topic of conversation until he or she is satisfied. Others can challenge this claim, but the move would be immediately recognized as a challenge and thus contribute to an air of threat; it would increase the chance that the relationship would be adversely harmed or that the group may splinter. Messages that suggest unfair treatment, such as those sent by the workers in the personnel department, may also imply that people are not committed to one another. It hoists a warning flag signaling problems with trust and responsibility. If this issue is not met head-on, the parties may have difficulty sustaining an image that they are committed to each other.

Face-saving triggered by what the party perceives as unjust intimidation can have destructive consequences. In one case, a woman who had planned to leave a job in a food distribution company for unrelated personal reasons decided to stay on six months longer to "fight it out" with her uncooperative co-workers. She did not want to leave with the feeling that she had been driven away. In Case 5.3, the three intimidated workers spent considerable time and effort trying to feel better about themselves. This time could have been spent on the project if the issue had been addressed at an earlier point.

When this type of face-saving issue goes unaddressed, it is also common for the threatened person to contact an outside party for help, hoping that a neutral outsider might understand and perhaps exonerate him or her. Although a third party can help in many instances, if the person trying to save face contacts the outsider, it may subvert any legitimate effort to mediate the problem. The parties have to recognize the problem and agree on a need for outside help before any intervention is likely to be successful. Finally, if this type of face-saving issue is not confronted, the parties trying to save face often feel a need to explain the causes behind the unjust or intimidating treatment. Because others have not supplied any reasons or denied that they intended to intimidate, the party may make unfounded attributions about the causes of others' intimidating behavior. These unchecked attributions can shape the comments the party makes from that point on and lead to a more serious set of impenetrable problems. For example, in the food distribution company mentioned before, three people were involved in the conflict, including the woman who stayed on six months. All three incorrectly assumed that the others hated them and were attacking them for reasons of personal incompatibility. Actually, all three were merely responding to the others' aggressive behavior, and their responses fed on each others', thereby escalating the conflict.

The key to alleviating face-saving concerns that emerge from perceptions of unjust intimidation lies in parties' ability to give feedback without eliciting further animosity. Parties who feel they are being unjustly treated or intimidated must be able to state their perceptions in a way that does not prejudge others or discourage them from explaining their behavior. Escalation and standoffs are likely when criticism is handled poorly as a face-saving issue is addressed. Although many prescriptions have been given for constructing feedback, most discussions of constructive criticism stress that feedback must be timely (Maurer 1994). In other words, it should be offered at a point that is both relevant and the least disruptive. It should also be centered on descriptions of the party's own feelings rather than assumptions about what others intend—for example, "When you didn't show up for the dinner, I felt put down"; rather than "You wanted to teach me a lesson by not showing up for our dinner."

Face-saving concerns that stem from feelings of unjust intimidation can be managed the best if the parties have set aside time for regular evaluations of the process. Setting aside five or ten minutes at the end of each meeting or day for evaluation can allow people to raise issues early before they become impasses and to give positive or negative feedback to each other without interfering with work or other obligations. Resentment and hostility are less likely to build and affect other issues if the parties know time has been set aside to address relational issues or concerns about interactions.

Refusing to Step Back from a Position

A second form of face-saving is based on people's fears that they will compromise a position or stand they have taken on some issue (Pruitt 1971; Brown 1977). People often remain committed to a stand or solution even in light of convincing refutations, not because they still believe it is the best option but because they believe moving away from that position will harm their image. This form of face-saving emerges when someone believes that reversing his or her stand, or stepping back from a position, is unsafe.

There are many reasons why this may be a real fear for people involved in a conflict. In their analysis of the forces governing commitment to decisions, Janis and Mann (1977) suggest that people may remain committed to an undesirable decision because they believe that they will look indecisive, erratic, or unstable if they retract or reverse their choice. "To avoid perceiving himself as weak-minded, vacillating, ineffectual, and undependable, the person turns his back on pressures to reconsider his decision and sticks firmly with his chosen alternative, even after he has started to suspect that it is a defective choice" (p. 283). For example, Epstein (1962) reports that novice parachutists, fearing loss of face, often go through with their decision to jump even though, as the time draws near, their desire to skip what may seem a dangerous and senseless endeavor increases. Fear of losing face is a stronger motive in this case than their judgment at the moment. If others place a higher value on consistency than on accuracy, fear can prevent people from changing their minds or remaining flexible as new information and proposals are considered.

Janis and Mann also suggest that there is a certain momentum behind reaching a decision or articulating a position in public. This momentum stems from the difficulty of reversing a decision once it is made or retracting a position once it is stated. It simply takes more work and effort to explain why one has changed one's mind than it does to stick with a previously stated position. The destructive consequences of leaders being overly identified with their stated viewpoints and with their organizations in general have been well documented (Finkelstein 2003). Having personal identity linked too closely to professional identity is a road map for rigidity and its negative effects.

Goffman (1967) discusses a similar motive for this form of face-saving. He indicates that people's fears of moving from a position can rest on a belief that they will not be taken seriously in the future if they step away from a position they have taken. In this case, the party believes that his or her credibility will suffer if he or she moves on an important issue or decision. Others have established a climate—or at least it is believed that a climate exists—where reversal will be costly in future situations. Ideas or suggestions the person makes will be overlooked or considered less seriously if others believe that ideas are not developed fully enough to warrant continued commitment. There is a fear that future suggestions will be seen, in all cases, as potentially problematic so they will be given less weight in the discussion when they are offered.

Finally, Brown (1977) and other researchers (Tjosvold and Huston 1978) point to a somewhat different motive for this type of face-saving in adversarial contexts, such as bargaining and negotiation sessions. When people make initial settlement offers then try to negotiate an agreement, they are often reluctant to move from their initial position because they might be seen as weak bargainers. In a negotiation context, people often want to appear tough as long as it is to their advantage. If the opposing side believes they will give in easily, the opposition may hold their ground because they believe they can obtain concessions (Stevens 1963). When conflict interaction becomes competitive, and people believe that the outcome will produce winners and losers, this belief becomes a possible source of face-saving concerns. If people believe that their goals are inherently incompatible and that they cannot find a solution that meets everyone's needs, then the appearance of strength or weakness influences the moves people make in the conflict.

Whatever the motivation, whether people feel comfortable in changing a stated position is ultimately tied to expectations they have about how ideas (in other words, suggestions, information, proposals) are treated. The climate, to be discussed in the next chapter, tells people how ideas should be proposed and, perhaps more important, how they will be perceived once they are offered. People have a sense, for example, of whether exploratory questions will be valued or discouraged. In the same vein, others may welcome or discount suggestions that are not fully developed. Ideas that are offered tentatively can be seen either as a waste of time or as a sign that people feel comfortable making comments that may not be complete but could spark ideas. Some parties seek or value authoritative statements—statements well supported by reliable evidence or proposals that have known consequences. If the other party expects authoritative statements, the person may feel more closely bound to any position already taken or idea offered. Because the parties work under this shared expectation, once an idea is offered it is easy for people to convince themselves that they would not have offered it unless the idea was worth continued support.

Statements such as "I really haven't thought this through but I'd like to suggest . . . " or "I don't know exactly how I feel about this but we could try . . . " may be an indication that people feel they have to apologize for half-baked ideas. They may indicate that the other party does not encourage or accept tentative suggestions. At the same time, however, these types of phrases may promote a more exploratory climate. In effect, speakers who use such phrases are attempting to establish that it is all right to offer tentative ideas. The statements can provide a frame or context for the interaction, which says, in effect, that the parties are in an exploratory frame of mind. Ideas can be offered and evaluations can be made without committing an individual to any suggestions. This sets a tone that helps preserve flexibility and the possibility of continued change when conflicts arise.

Suppressing Conflict Issues

In situations that assume people should be able to reach agreement without conflict or that people can handle any conflict without seeking outside help, we may strongly discourage others from admitting that a conflict exists or is beyond our control. If a person attempts to acknowledge the existence of a conflict or to raise the possibility that they seek third-party assistance, he or she may lose face in the eyes of others. The person may be seen as someone who causes problems or is eager to find fault with the way the other party operates. This threat may deter people from engaging in adequate differentiation, and it may promote prolonged and destructive avoidance of an issue.

If someone decides to raise an issue in such a climate, conflict interaction can turn in a negative direction. A turn toward inflexibility and stalemate may be imminent if the person feels his or her image must be defended at all costs ("I don't care whether this hurts you or not, I think we need to address it"). These complications may mean that the parties cannot differentiate successfully or that integration is unattainable.

Academic appeal referees at colleges and universities are assigned the task of mediating disputes that arise between students and faculty about grades, financial aid, discrimination, enactment of departmental or university policies, and so on. One referee at a large university reports that students are often reluctant to raise conflict issues and, as a result, conflicts are not addressed until the issues have gotten out of hand. Students are often hesitant to raise concerns with a third party because they fear loss of face in the eyes of their mentors. In university settings, student–faculty relationships are premised on a cooperative assumption: Students (especially graduate students) and faculty are expected to work and learn together to advance knowledge in their academic fields. When a conflict arises over issues, such as grading or interpretation of departmental policy, students feel that if they take the issue to a third party (even one the university endorses), they may threaten or destroy their relationship. A student fears that the faculty will see him or her as someone who is unwilling to work through difficulties cooperatively and is trying to make the professor look bad in the eyes of a representative of the institution. Third-parties who work in this context need to address face threats and help restore an atmosphere of cooperation so that the relationship can continue after the specific issue has been resolved.

In these types of conflicts, the threat to face stems from a fear of being seen as someone who is willing to jeopardize a good relationship by bringing a conflict out in the open. This fear is almost inevitably founded on a belief that the very emergence of conflict is always harmful or destructive.

Face-Giving Strategies

After exploring the destructive nature of face-saving, this chapter now turns its attention to how people help others avoid taking such extreme measures. This section examines the dynamics of face-giving.

Face-giving refers to the strategic moves that support the other's image or identity claims. To fully grasp how people "give face," we must first examine how people orient to face in everyday interaction.

Goffman (1957) identifies two strands of face-orienting, or face-giving, strategies: corrective and preventive practices. As the names imply, *corrective practices* are what people do after a face-threatening act or loss of face. Face-saving strategies are corrective practices. In contrast, *preventive practices* are what people do to avoid threats to face. Preventive practices are either defensive or protective. Defensive strategies involve actions to prevent threats to one's own face. For example, people often ask the hearer to suspend judgment by using disclaimers, such as "Now some of my best friends are professors, but. . . ." Protective strategies consist of actions that prevent or minimize threats to another's face. For example, people often provide normative accounts for others, such as "The traffic must have been horrendous. I'm surprised you got here so fast."

Defensive strategies can be seen as alignment actions (Stokes and Hewitt 1976). *Alignment actions* are verbal efforts to resolve discrepancies between people's conduct and cultural expectations. Essentially, these actions or messages align a person's behavior with cultural norms. For example, imagine you are late to a very important meeting. Just as you slink into your chair, the group pauses and your colleagues turn to greet you. Feeling that your absence has clearly violated expectations, you say, "I'm really sorry. My car would not start." Such an alignment message demonstrates that you are not eccentric and allows you to manage your social identity in the group (Table 5.3).

Researchers have identified several types of alignment actions used in everyday speech (Cupach and Metts 1994). The largest group of alignment actions falls

---

TABLE 5.3   Types of Face-Giving Alignment Actions

- Account: giving reasons for a behavior
- Apology: expresses regret
- Quasi theory: provides adages, simplistic explanations
- Excuse: admits action and denies responsibility for it
- Justification: admits responsibility, denies consequences
- Disclaimer: asks for a suspension of judgment
- Counterclaim: denies negative intentions
- Conversational repair: corrects or restates a conversational error
- Remedy: offers a reparation to an offended party

under the rubric of accounts. *Accounts* are reason-giving descriptions that presume one of the parties has committed an offense. They serve as devices to make failure or inappropriate behavior sound reasonable (McLaughlin, Cody, and Rosenstein 1983). In addition to descriptive reasons for behavior, common accounts include apologies, quasi theories, excuses, and justifications. An *apology* expresses regret over an earlier action. Statements—such as "I'm sorry," "I will never do that again," "What can I do to make up for this?"—acknowledge responsibility and express remorse (Fraser 1981). When speakers use apologies they presume that others recognize that a failed and face-threatening event has occurred. *Quasi theories* are simplistic formulas or adages used to explain away complex situations. "Boys will be boys" and "We had a falling out" are examples of quasi theories.

The most common accounts are excuses and justifications, which attempt to shift the burden of accountability. When people admit that their actions may be wrong or inappropriate, but deny responsibility, they are employing an excuse. *Excuses* such as "I didn't feel well," "I couldn't resist," and "The phone was busy" readily acknowledge a mistake but resist responsibility because of mitigating circumstances (Shaw, Wild, and Colquitt 2003). Researchers classify excuses into three types: (1) statements that deny harmful intent, (2) statements that deny volition and assert lack of bodily control, and (3) statements that deny the party performed the action (Tedeschi and Riess 1981). Whereas excuses focus on responsibility, justifications focus on the consequences of the actions. *Justifications* are statements in which the party admits personal responsibility but denies negative consequences, usually by relating the action to some socially acceptable rule of conduct such as higher authority, self-defense, company policy, or situational norms. Statements such as "It was necessary in the long run" and "If we had held the meeting, it would have been a disaster" are examples of justifications. They claim a behavior was appropriate given the circumstance.

Other types of alignment actions include disclaimers, counterclaims, conversational repairs, and licenses. *Disclaimers* ask the hearer for a suspension of judgment to prevent a negative typification (Hewitt and Stokes 1975). Statements, such as "I realize you might think this is wrong but. . . ." and "This is only my opinion but. . . ." defeat in advance doubts and unfavorable reactions. *Counterclaims* are devices used to deny unfavorable intentions (Stutman 1988). People intuitively know that a speaker with persuasive goals is considered less trustworthy by others. When one party may benefit from a persuasive exchange, such as during sales encounters, the hearer naturally becomes more resistant to messages he or she receives. As a result, when people pursue persuasive goals they often deny that intent by stating the opposite. Because they counter the perceived goal of the message that follows them, these devices are called counterclaims. Statements such as "Now I'm not trying to persuade you but . . . ," "I don't want to change your mind but . . . ," and "This isn't an excuse but. . . ." deny unfavorable intentions.

When people make conversational errors, they often attempt to revise what was said with corrections, restatements, or requests to ignore earlier actions. Statements such as "Oh, I didn't mean that" and "You get the just, eh, gist" serve as *conversational repairs*. Repairs serve as "detours" and "time-outs" for people to correct utterances they have employed (McLaughlin 1984). Interestingly, what gets repaired may not appear wrong or in need of correction; sometimes only the speaker perceives that a conversational misstep was made.

A *remedy* is often proposed to make reparations to an offended party. This sometimes occurs even when the offense is unstated or unknown. For example, imagine a scenario where, at the beginning of a joint assignment, a co-worker mistakenly misplaces a file that may be useful for the project. Even though the other has neither requested the file nor knows of its disappearance, the co-worker feels guilty. The co-worker then begins to offer a series of remarks that can be seen as remedies: "I think I should keep a list of all files that move through the office." "My organizational skills are not up to par. I should probably seek training." "It's time I reorganized my desk." Remedies, like other alignment actions, signal that a party is attempting to preserve face.

Grice (1975) maintains that people follow four implicit rules or maxims during conversations. Speakers cooperate with each other by (1) offering accurate or truthful information, (2) maintaining economy in speech by being neither too brief nor too lengthy, (3) offering relevant and topical points, and (4) refraining from overly obscure or ambiguous speech. When speakers anticipate breaking one or more of these rules, they often employ licenses to forecast the rule violation (Mura 1983). *Licenses* give the listener notice that a violation will occur or is occurring but that the infraction is necessary or unusual. For example, a speaker who breaks the rule of speech accuracy may qualify the statement: "I love your new car. I don't know much about cars." Words and phrases, such as "in fact," "actually," "really," and "of course," are often used to signal qualification. After being verbose and breaking the rule of speech economy, a speaker may say "I told you everything so that you could decide for yourself." A license used for breaking the rule of relevancy might sound like this: "I went off on a tangent because I need a plan for tomorrow." Breaking the rule of not using ambiguous speech might be followed by: "I know that sounds confusing, but it's really not." As alignment actions, licenses serve to defend the face of the speaker by reframing the rule-breaking event.

The devices used to prevent threat to one's own face can also serve as flags or markers that attention to face wants is desired. At the very minimum, such markers signal that the hearer is experiencing or anticipating a threat to face, and further challenge will result in a face-saving strategy. Protective strategies basically consist of the same alignment actions. The only difference is that we align for the other party. When people preface statements or evaluations with any of the alignment actions, they are essentially protecting the face of others. Consider the possible ways a superior might protect the face of a subordinate while communicating that an improvement in work quality is needed. One might use an excuse: "You have been working hard the last few weeks, but let's talk about where this effort gets you." One might use a justification: "With all the assignments I throw at you, it's no wonder I have noticed a problem with quality." Or a disclaimer might be used: "Heaven knows quality is impossible to define, but. . . ." The options are diverse and plentiful. The key point is that protective strategies provide the listener with a means to protect face.

Goffman (1955) maintains that all interaction is potentially face-threatening; whenever people interact, they are making identity claims. Tracy (1991) notes that these claims may be quite general as opposed to personalized and specific. For example, in a grocery line we often want to be seen as patient; in a car, that we can drive with skill. Because people care deeply about how they are perceived almost all the time, there is always some potential for a threat to face.

Inadvertently, people walk on each other's identity claims. Social situations involve tensions between cooperation and competition, between one's and others' face. Even in situations where it is in the best interest of the speaker to cooperate, people employ messages that are threatening and antagonistic (Craig, Tracy, and Spisak 1986). The need to protect another's face is ever present. Related research suggests that some people seem to be better at face-giving than others.

A wide body of research on communication has been aimed at understanding how communicators design messages that promote relational harmony and facilitate goodwill between parties. This work can loosely be described as investigating *person-centered* speech—any communication intended to support, comfort, or otherwise confirm the hearer can be considered *person-centered*. Such speech consists of prosocial behaviors and displays a willingness on the part of the speaker to verbally express his or her thoughts and feelings in a way that takes the other into account. Essentially, researchers conclude that this message design is driven by an ability and by a desire on the part of the speaker to adapt his or her communication to the hearer to achieve one or more strategic goals (Applegate and Delia 1980).

To engage in person-centered speech, research demonstrates that the speaker must possess an ability to take on other perspectives; *perspective-taking* suggests a skill to adopt the psychological viewpoint of the other. It allows the speaker to anticipate the behavior and reactions of others. Perspective-taking presumes that the motivations, intentions, and feelings of any individual are unique. Moreover, it presumes that the character of each situation is equally original. Once a speaker understands the psychological viewpoints of others, he or she can then adapt their communication to achieve any of a number of strategic goals, such as task (persuasion, instruction, entertainment) or identity (credibility, social status, intent). Of the many strategic goals a speaker might pursue, person-centered speech highlights the importance of relational maintenance. Hence a focus on the unique characteristics of others, or the situation, to promote the relationship is highly personal or person-centered.

In contrast, many communicators assume the identities of others, and the meaning of their actions can be understood in terms of assigned roles, contexts, and topics. Communicators working from this mode need not understand others' perspectives, nor adapt to other actors. Instead, they focus on the assigned roles of the participants, the authority that inheres in those roles, and the norms surrounding such role relationships. This is known as *position-centered speech,* which expresses feelings through nonverbal channels rather than elaborating them through verbal codes. Such speech often appears to focus on the topic or the task at hand at the expense of others' feelings. It is not that communicators who use position-centered speech are insensitive to others, but rather that they assume individual identities, such as image or motivation, can be dispensed with by following fixed rules of social conduct.

Whereas person-centered speech promotes relational harmony and facilitates goodwill between parties, position-centered speech encourages defensiveness and caution. Communicators who employ person-centered speech generally exhibit the following patterns:

1. Speech that is more indirect so as to lessen the degree of imposition placed on the hearer, but not to the point of inhibiting understanding.
2. Use of face-sensitive messages that attempt to protect the desired image of the hearer.
3. Ability to align others' behavior to situated norms.
4. Reliance on information-seeking through questions.
5. Refraining from overt evaluations and attacks on others' self-concepts.
6. Sensitive use of challenges, directives, and demands.

There is a good deal of variation across cultures in the propensity to engage in face-giving interactions. Ting-Toomey (1999) notes that parties from collectivistic cultures are oriented more toward giving face and avoiding face-threatening incidents than are members of individualistic cultures. So in Asian, African, and Latin American cultures, face-giving is expected and more common than in an individualistic culture such as that in the United States.

Working with Face-Saving Issues

The key to diagnosing face-saving issues successfully lies in parties' ability to recognize its symptoms in interaction. When face-saving is occurring, the interaction becomes centered on a secondary issue rather than on the substance of the conflict. The substantive problems that parties must resolve are buried by statements and reactions indicating resentment or by arguments that defend individual positions but do little to advance parties' understanding of the problem. Because the face-saving issues are related to the more substantive problems, they can come to dominate the interaction before parties realize it.

For example, people may defend alternative positions in what appears to be a heated debate. They may do so, however, only because they feel that if they back away from their positions, they will not have credibility in future discussions or decisions. In this case, the most pressing issue, the one that has the greatest influence over the interaction, is "How will others treat someone who changes his or her mind?" However, the content of the discussion remains focused on a substantive point, disguising the face issue. If parties fail to realize that a secondary issue is driving an interaction, face-saving can produce destructive escalation and seriously threaten relationships.

Establishing climates that prevent face-saving concerns from emerging is probably the most effective means of eliminating their destructive influence. The climate within a team, organization, or relationship plays a critical role in determining whether face-saving concerns will emerge and become problematic. People have shared expectations about whether it is safe to move away from a stated position, whether conflict issues can be raised without threatening the relationships, and whether someone's feelings of unjust treatment can be discussed openly. Although establishing a *healthy* climate is something people can work toward using methods discussed in Chapter 6, the difficult interventions are those that are needed when a preventive climate has not been established or when some event calls the climate into question. For example, when something happens that makes parties unsure about whether they can step back from a position and still be seen as credible, even the most comfortable atmosphere can begin to disintegrate.

In group decision making, we know intuitively that an absence of credible explanations can lead people to react. In fact, research has shown that the absence of reasonable explanations is linked to a decrease in cooperation (Colquitt 2001), increased levels of retaliation such as litigation and theft (Wanberg, Bruce, and Gavin 1999), and withdrawal and interference (Shaw, Wild, and Colquitt 2003).

As already suggested, during conflict situations people become explainers, and teams are no exception. Decision makers are quick to elaborate on exactly what they did, why they did it, or why it was unavoidable, so as to dampen any potential assault on their competence. The most common of these explanations are excuses and justifications. Individuals judge decisions by comparing what happened to what might have been (Folger and Cropanzano 2001). Research suggests that when confronted with questions about what happened, the choice between excuse and justification is critical. Whereas excuses demonstrate that a mitigating circumstance made the decision necessary or unavoidable, justifications demonstrate that the decision was appropriate in light of the circumstances. In reexamining decisions made to protect face, excuses are preferred over justifications because they are seen as more reasonable by those on the outside looking in. Excuses create a reasonable climate where honest mistakes could have been made. Justifications sound honorable in that they accept full responsibility but impugn integrity by suggesting the decision wasn't that bad after all.

Interventions that attempt to stop the destructive effects of face-saving must recognize that face-saving centers around the negotiation of one's image. The alignment actions that people use to prevent loss of face serve as flags or markers to the other party that attention to face wants is desired. When one hears an alignment action, bells and whistles should go off. These devices signal that the hearer is experiencing or anticipating a threat to face. Further challenge will result in a face-saving strategy. At this point, the use of protective strategies to align the other party's actions may help to prevent their face-saving measures.

Several face-saving forms discussed here threaten to impose an undesirable image on the speaker. Consider the following statements, which various forms of face-saving behavior make:

- *Resisting unjust intimidation:* "Don't see me as someone who accepts unfair treatment or intimidation."
- *Stepping back from a position:* "Don't see me as someone who is indecisive" (easily beaten, weak, and so forth).

■ *Raising unacknowledged conflict issues:* "Don't see me as someone who is willing to cause problems by raising conflict issues."

Each of these statements reflects a guess that the party has made about others' likely reactions, and each indicates that the person feels threatened by the image he or she assumes others will assign. However, each statement is founded on an assumption about others' interpretations and reactions, which can either be confirmed or refuted by subsequent events. The interaction that occurs when face is an issue is always a negotiation; it is an attempt to settle what image others can assign to someone.

Interventions that treat face-saving as a negotiation process may have the greatest chance for success (Ting-Toomey and Kurogi 1998). Three steps can be taken to help facilitate this process. First, the negotiations can occur with less chance of continued escalation if defensiveness is reduced. A person trying to save face always perceives a threat—the threat of having an undesirable image assigned to him or her by others. Defensiveness is a likely reaction to perceived threat (Gibb 1961). People feel they must be on guard because a mistaken move on their part can result in some undesirable consequence. Research by Rapaport (1960) suggests that defensiveness can be reduced by having an opponent indicate an understanding of another's position and by recognizing some area of validity in the other's position. Parties can show that they understand why another feels unfairly treated or worried about appearing weak or indecisive; they can also recognize ways in which the belief may actually be legitimate. If the parties have handled similar incidents poorly in the past, acknowledging these can show a sympathetic understanding for the person's concern. Acknowledging another's position as legitimate and indicating an understanding of it do not ensure that the issue can be settled easily, but they do allow for the possibility of an open discussion as the negotiation unfolds (Roth 1993).

Second, the negotiation of a face-saving concern can be facilitated if the parties open the door for an exchange of concessions on the issue. Pruitt (1971) demonstrates the importance of letting both parties in a negotiation tell each other, either implicitly or explicitly, that an exchange of concessions is possible and safe. The parties need to know that there will be some reciprocity if one side begins making offers. Although face-saving issues are not the same as formal bargaining situations where offers can be made in increments, it is useful to think of the negotiation of a face-saving issue in the same general terms. Take as an example the face-saving situation where someone is hesitant to step back from a position. The person who is concerned about losing face needs some assurance that moving away from a position is safe; when afraid of losing face, he or she needs to know that shifting positions will not reduce his or her credibility. Comments, or reactions, that give individuals a way out of fear is likely to reduce the concern for face that may be keeping parties from conceding a position they themselves no longer want to defend.

In Case 5.4, a supervisor in a large recordkeeping office at a corporation recently dealt with a difficult face-saving issue by trying to reassure an employee that it was safe to move away from a position. Signaling that an exchange of concessions is possible is important in other face-saving situations, although the way

CASE 5.4

The Productivity and Performance Report

Imagine yourself as Ron's supervisor: What cues did you pick up that enabled you to handle this situation successfully?

Ron, an office worker, was assigned the task of putting together an extensive report that described the productivity and performance of people in various divisions of a corporation. When the report was printed, a copy was sent to each division head for his or her inspection before it was distributed generally in the corporation. One division head called the research office after reading the report and was irate about an error that he found in the description of his department. He saw the mistake as a significant problem that could cause considerable damage to his division's reputation and future.

The complaint was discussed by several supervisors in the research office before it reached Ron. When he was told about the error, Ron became very defensive and argued that the information that appeared in the report was accurate. It was clear to his supervisor that the information was in error and that the employee was trying to save face. Ron was defending his position, not because he firmly believed that it was correct, but because acknowledging that

he had made a mistake could mean that he would be seen as incompetent.

The approach Ron's supervisor took in handling this situation was to point out that compiling the report was an immense and difficult task because the information had to be drawn from so many different sources. Often it had to be inferred from sketchy notes or letters that various people in the departments submitted to the records office. She congratulated Ron for putting together a report that had 10,000 pieces of correct information. These comments allowed Ron to admit the error because they reduced the threat of being seen as incompetent. More important, they allowed Ron and his supervisor to begin discussing possible ways that the error could be handled so that the irate division head would be satisfied and accurate information about the unit would be disseminated.

Discussion Question

- *Identify a specific situation in which a disputant is more interested in face issues than in moving ahead cooperatively. What suggestions would you make?*

---

signaling occurs would be different. The person trying to save face because of perceived unfair treatment is often preoccupied with making this known. Broadcasting perceived slights can take precedence over any desire to discuss issues per se. To address this, others must provide some assurance that the issue of mistreatment will not be lost or forgotten if the party stops emphasizing it, which is often more difficult than it may appear at first glance. If a person feels that he or she has been treated unfairly in the past, believing that others actually want to address the issue may be difficult. Until such assurance is given, the face-saving issue may continue to escalate as the party criticizes others without allowing for a productive discussion of the issue.

A party who raises a conflict in a situation where parties typically avoid potentially divisive issues—or actually believe that none exist—may also show a concern for face. This party may believe that others see him or her as the cause of the problem rather than as someone who raised an issue that needed to be addressed. At least one other party must step forward and say that he or she believes it is an important issue to discuss—that someone else is beginning to own the conflict. If such a signal is not sent, the person who raised the issue may become defensive, assuming others hold him or her responsible for the conflict.

If defensiveness cannot be reduced, or if parties cannot facilitate negotiations through an exchange of concessions, a third step can be taken to help stop the possible destructive effects of face-saving interaction: One or more parties can stress the consequences of not settling the substantive issue. This tactic is frequently advocated as a way to sharpen conflict so that members will become more motivated to deal with the issue (Walton 1969; Stulberg 1987). When face-saving is an issue, increasing tension by pointing to the consequences of an unresolved conflict can encourage a party who is concerned about face to care more about the substantive issue than the potential threat to image. It can, in other words, help direct the interaction away from a personal focus toward a substantive focus.

Benjamin Franklin was an early proponent of face-giving in his discussion club with fellow tradesmen, the Junto, and gives us some good advice concerning setting up nonthreatening situations. Franklin's first rule was to display humility during conversations and to put forth ideas through suggestions and questions, using (or pretending) naïve curiosity to avoid contradicting people in a manner that could offend them. In the discussions held by the Junto, Franklin observed: "All expressions of positiveness in opinion or of direct contradiction were prohibited under small pecuniary penalties." Franklin later tried to bring a similar approach to the Constitutional Convention (without the monetary penalties!) and has been remembered as a moderating force in the deliberations of this great founding body.

Summary and Review

What is face?

Face is a communicator's claim to be seen as a certain type of person; the positive social value a person claims for himself or herself. Two dimensions of face can be distinguished. Positive face refers to a person's desire to gain the approval of others. This dimension has two subcomponents; the need to be included and the need to be respected. Negative face refers to the desire to have autonomy and not be controlled by others.

How does one lose face?

People lose face when their identity claims are challenged or ignored by others. Mutual acknowledgment and cooperative maintenance of face is one of the major concerns in everyday interaction. Challenges to face, which can occur during conflicts and other nonroutine episodes, are unusual and threatening. A threatening experience can drive conflicts in negative directions. Face-saving behavior represents attempts by the party to save or to restore face, and it is a major source of inflexibility in conflicts.

How does face-saving affect issues in a conflict?

When face is threatened, saving face may supplant substantive issues for one or both parties. When this happens, unrealistic conflict (defined in Chapter 1) is likely to predominate. Face-saving also inhibits a group-centered approach to a conflict in which parties try to work out resolutions that are satisfactory for the group as a whole. Parties become individually focused and are concerned primarily with their own image and status; this promotes destructive conflict.

What forms does face-saving take in conflict interaction?

Three basic forms of face-saving occur during conflicts, depending on which interpretation the party places on the face-threatening behavior. First, parties can assume they must save face by resisting unjust intimidation. In such cases, people are concerned that they will be seen as weak and be treated unfairly, and their behavior is oriented toward just treatment and not giving in to a threatening other. Second, parties may engage in face-saving because they assume that if they back down from a position they will be seen as weak. In this case, parties adamantly defend their positions in the face of resistance. Third, people may attempt to save face when they try to suppress a potentially damaging conflict. In this case, parties are afraid to confront a conflict that they believe may result in a humiliating defeat. The three forms of face-saving involve different behavioral patterns and each must be handled differently. To avoid damage due to face-saving, it is important to recognize what form it takes and to address the concerns implicit in that form. For example, when parties see themselves as resisting unjust intimidation, this can be counteracted by behaving fairly and equitably and signaling respect and autonomy to others.

What is face-giving?

Face-giving occurs when parties support others' face claims and work with them to prevent loss of face or to restore face. Corrective and preventive face-giving can be distinguished: Corrective face-giving occurs after loss of face, whereas defensive face-giving is intended to prevent loss of face in the first place. Studies of interaction moves, called alignment actions, have uncovered a number of moves that give face, including accounts, apologies, quasi theories, excuses, justifications, disclaimers, counterclaims, conversational repairs, and licenses. These moves are not only used to give face—parties who use them are sometimes signaling their sensitivity to face concerns.

How does person-centered speech contribute to face-giving?

Person-centered speech is communication intended to support, comfort, or otherwise confirm the hearer. As such, person-centered speech gives face and support to parties' attempts to maintain or to restore face. Perspective-taking skills make engaging in person-centered speech more likely.

How can face-saving be used to promote more constructive conflict management?

Several measures are useful. First, it is important to promote a safe, nondefensive atmosphere. The discussion of climate in the next chapter suggests some ways to do this. Second, parties can promote face through exchanging concessions. Third, parties can actively give face to others.

Conclusion

Face-saving concerns are, at base, concerns about relationships. When interaction becomes centered on these concerns during a conflict, people are negotiating how they will see each other. Each message and response establishes whether a desired image will be allowed to stand in the eyes of others. Because these images are closely tied to people's self-concepts, face-saving interaction has a strong influence on how comfortable people feel and how successful the parties will be at resolving conflicts constructively.

Teams and relationships often benefit when the role of individuals and their sense of self become the focus of interactions. Relationships can be improved and people can feel better about themselves because others have confirmed self-images they value. When the need to save face emerges, however, interaction can head toward destructive escalation because a person's self-image may be under attack. Uncertain that a desired self-image is accepted by others (or certain that an undesirable image has been established), a person seeks confirmation of a new relational image. If the acceptance of this bid is problematic, moving on from the issue can be difficult. Attempts to redirect the topic or shift back to group-centered or person-centered interaction can be thwarted by feelings of resentment or a preoccupation with the other party's resistance to changing his or her view. When face-saving issues go unresolved, making any decision or addressing any issue can be a highly volatile task. Unsettled issues about images can be played out in other more substantive contexts with potentially disastrous effects for the relationship or team.

CHAPTER

6 Climate and Conflict Interaction

Perhaps because we live in the scientific age, most people prefer well-defined, straightforward explanations for the way things are. Ideally we should be able to isolate the forces that shape conflict and then define, measure, and study them to come up with a fairly complete explanation. Unfortunately, however, the world seldom lives up to our ideals. There is simply more there than is dreamed of in this simple scientific philosophy. Conflict behavior cannot be reduced to a small set of well-defined variables. People also act on the basis of their general "feelings" about a situation, feelings that generally cannot be precisely defined or boiled down to a simple explanation.

People often speak of "getting the feel of" a situation or "learning the ropes." Managers, labor leaders, and politicians observe an "air of conflict" or "a mood of compromise" among their employees, colleagues, or opponents. Planners and consultants assess the "climate for change" in the organizations or teams they try to influence. These people are responding to the general, global character of the situation, to what has been called the "climate" of the situation. *Climate* represents the prevailing temper, attitudes, and outlook of a dyad, team, or organization. As the meteorological name implies, social climate is just as diffuse, just as pervasive, as the weather.

Climate is important in understanding conflict interaction because it provides continuity and coherence to mutual activities. As a general sense of a relationship, team, or organization, climate enables members to ascertain their general direction; what it means to be part of the group; what actions are appropriate; how fellow members are likely to react; and what other information is necessary to guide people's behavior and to help them understand the social unit. In The Columnist's Brown Bag (Case 1.1), the open and relaxed climate encouraged participants to exercise their curiosity and to be receptive to each others' comments. Questions, answers, and discussion flowed freely and spontaneously for most of the session. When the columnist was challenged, the atmosphere grew tense, and participants became hesitant and defensive.

The challenge seemed out of place, given the openness of previous discussion. It introduced great uncertainty and some hostility into the proceedings. People reacted to the challenge as a violation of appropriate behavior, and subsequent interaction was colored by this. Eventually, rather than risk escalation of the challenge and permanent collapse of free, relaxed exchange, the leaders chose to terminate the session. By evoking certain types of behavior and discouraging others, the open climate gave the discussion direction and held it together. It united the diverse styles and concerns of individuals by providing a common ground for acting together and for reacting to a "crisis."

Implicit in any climate is an attitude toward conflict and how it should be handled. Climate constrains and channels conflict behavior; it lends a definite tenor to interchanges that can accelerate destructive cycles or preserve a productive approach. During the brown-bag session, the questioner's challenge was hastily cut off because the group was in "guest speaker mode," which implied a respectful and friendly attitude toward the editor. The challenge raised the specter of open and prolonged disagreement and potential embarrassment of the speaker. The group's open, nonevaluative climate made the challenge seem inappropriate. Rather than allow disagreement to ripen, those in charge were eager to end the session. Interestingly, the reaction of others to the challenge contributed to the sudden shift from an open climate to a tense and evaluative one, even though this is the last thing they would have wanted. The interplay of concrete, specific interactions and generalized climate is a critical force determining the direction of conflicts. A large part of this chapter explores this relationship.

At first glance, climate is an uncomfortably vague concept. To get a handle on it, it is tempting to define a set of variables or properties that "make up" climate and classify different climate types, such as cooperative versus competitive climates, on the basis of whether they have various combinations of properties. Most social scientists have tried to do just this (Deutsch 1973; James and Jones 1974). The utility of this approach is limited, however. Climates are extremely complex and diffuse. As a result, it is difficult, if not impossible, to isolate a few defining variables that can capture all the varied forms and nuances of climates. More important, the concepts we use to explain and understand human behavior should be equivalent to those used by people in the situation. Our explorations of climate should take into account its diffuse, general quality. Therefore, while some properties of climates are defined to help people analyze their own groups, we will always operate from the assumption that climate is a holistic, general characteristic. This chapter emphasizes how climates are created and sustained because climate can best be understood and controlled if we can clarify how it is produced, maintained, and changed by people's actions.

Climate is a characteristic of social units, such as relationships, families, work teams, crowds, and organizations. When not exploring specific examples, the general term *social unit* is used to indicate climates across situations.

A Definition of Climate

To get a grasp on this elusive concept, it is helpful to consider a specific example of how climate develops and operates in a work team. Case 6.1 was reported by a third party who was called to intervene in a thorny conflict.

CASE **6.1**

Riverdale Halfway House

Imagine yourself as Carole: How much of an impact do you perceive yourself having on the organization's climate? How would you describe and explain the change in climate that occurs? How might descriptions and explanations be different for different people in this group?

Riverdale Halfway House is a correctional institution designed to provide low-level security confinement and counseling for male youth offenders. It houses about twenty-five second- and third-time offenders and for all practical purposes represents the last stop before prison for its inhabitants. Residents are required to work or look for work and are on restricted hours. Counseling and other life-adjustment services are provided, and counselors' reports on a prisoner can make an important difference in both the length of incarceration and the conditions of release. Because the counselors are also authority figures, relationships between staff and prisoners are delicate and touchy. Staff members are subjected to a great deal of stress as the prisoners attempt to manipulate them.

The staff of Riverdale consists of a director who handles funding, general administration, and external relations with other agencies, notably the courts and law enforcement offices; an assistant director who concentrates on external administration of the staff and the halfway house; three counselors; two night caretakers; and an administrative assistant who handles the books and paperwork. The director, George, was the newest staff member at the time of the conflict. The assistant director—who had also applied for the director's slot that George filled—and the three counselors had been at Riverdale for at least a year longer than George. They described George's predecessor as a very "charismatic" person. Prior to George's arrival, relations among the staff were cordial, morale was high, and there was a great deal of informal contact among staff members. The staff reported

a high level of respect for all workers under the previous director. Workers felt engaged by an important, if difficult, task that all would work on as a team.

With George's arrival, the climate at Riverdale changed. Right before he started, the staff changed offices and rearranged furniture, leaving the shoddiest pieces for George, who regarded this as a sign of rejection. He believed the staff had "worked around him" and had tried to undermine his authority by rearranging things without consulting him. He was hurt and angry despite the staff's attempts to explain that no harm was meant. Added to this was George's belief that Carole, the assistant director, resented him and wanted his job. Carole claimed she did not resent George, although she did fear that he might have her fired. She tended to withdraw from George in order to avoid conflict. Her withdrawal was interpreted by George as a sign of further rejection, which reinforced his suspicion of Carole.

The previous director left pretty big shoes for George to fill, and this showed especially in his working relationship with the staff. The staff felt George was not open with them, and that he quizzed them about their work in a manipulative fashion. Several staff members, including Carole, complained that George swore at them and ordered them around; they considered this behavior an affront to their professionalism. George's attempts to assert his authority also angered the staff. In one case, he investigated a disciplinary problem with two staff members without consulting Carole, who was ordinarily in charge of such matters. George's investigation did not reveal any problems, but it embarrassed the staff members (who had been manipulated by prisoners) and made Carole feel George did not respect her. George admitted his mistake and hoped the incident would blow over.

Ten months after George arrived at Riverdale, the climate had changed drastically.

Whereas Riverdale had been a supportive, cohesive work group, now it was filled with tension. Interaction between George and the staff, particularly Carole, was formal and distant. The staff had to some degree pulled together in response to George, but its cohesiveness was gone. Informal communication was down, and staff members received much less support from each other. As the third-party mediator observed, "the staff members expected disrespect from each other." They felt stuck with their problems and believed there was no way out of their dilemma. There was no trust and no sense of safety in the group. Members believed they had to change others to improve the situation and did not consider changing themselves or living with others' quirks.

The staff wanted George to become less authoritarian and more open to them. George wanted the staff to let him blow up and shout and then forget about it. There was little flexibility or willingness to negotiate. As Carole observed, each contact between herself and George just seemed to make things worse, "so what point was there in trying to talk things out?" The consultant noted that the staff seemed to be unable to forget previous fights. They interpreted what others said as continuations of old conflicts and assumed a hostile attitude even when one was not present.

The third party tried to get the group to meet and iron out its problems, but the group wanted to avoid confrontation—on several occasions, scheduled meetings were postponed because of other "pressing" problems. Finally, George found another job and left Riverdale, as did one of the counselors. Since then, the staff reports that conditions have improved considerably.

Discussion Questions
- *At what points in this conflict could a significant change in climate have occurred? What alternatives were available to staff members at these points?*
- *To what extent do you feel that this group's climate was inevitable?*

The following definition is offered: *climate is the relatively enduring quality of a social unit that (1) is experienced in common by members, and (2) arises from and influences their interaction and behavior.* Several aspects of this definition require explanation and can be illustrated from the case.

First, climate is not psychological—it is not an intangible belief or feeling in members' minds. Climate is a quality of the social unit itself because it arises from interaction among members. For this reason a climate is more than the beliefs or feelings of any single individual (Fink and Chen 1995). The climate of Riverdale was hostile and suspicious not because any particular member had suspicions about or disliked another, but because of how the group as a whole interacted. Members were hostile and suspicious toward each other, and these interchanges built on themselves until most group activities were premised on hostility.

This is not to say that individual members' perceptions of climate are not important. People's perceptions play an important role in the creation and maintenance of climate because these perceptions mediate the effects of climate on people's actions. However, climate cannot be reduced to the beliefs or feelings of individual members. Various individuals in the Riverdale case had different perceptions of the hostile situation. George thought the group was hostile because Carole wanted his job and the staff resented him. Carole felt the hostility was because George cursed at her and went around her in making decisions. It is clear that neither George nor Carole had the "correct" or complete view, but they were reacting to a common situation. Their beliefs and feelings represent a particular sampling and interpretation of experiences in the group.

Members' perceptions of climate are strongly influenced by their positions in the team or relationship, as a study by Albrecht (1979) illustrates. Albrecht compared the perceptions of organizational climate by "key" communicators (active communicators who link large groups of people) with those of "non-key" communicators (those more isolated from the communication flow). She found that key communicators identified more with their jobs and were more satisfied with their communication with superiors than were non-key communicators. Albrecht explained these differences as a function of greater frequency of communication (greater activity leads to a more positive image of the organization) and greater amount of information obtained by the key communicators (more information creates greater involvement on the job). Numerous other studies have also shown different perceptions of organizational climate depending on the members' positions in the authority hierarchy (Schneider and Bartlett 1970), the type of work done (Powell and Butterfield 1978), and how long the member belonged to the team or organization (Johnston 1976). Clearly, different experiences and different day-to-day interaction patterns create different perceptions of climate. Hence George, as a new manager, and Carole, as his "old-hand" assistant, had somewhat different views of Riverdale's climate. These different perceptions were one reason George and Carole reacted differently in the conflict.

George's and Carole's perspectives on Riverdale's climate can be viewed as individual interpretations of the group's climate, which is "experienced in common by members." However, individual perceptions provide only a partial picture of the climate itself. A social unit's climate is more than any individual's perceptions and can only be identified and understood if the unit's interaction as a whole is considered (Poole 1985). Individual's perceptions of climate play an important role in maintaining or changing climates, but they are different from climate at the most fundamental level.

A second feature of the definition is its characterization of climate as *experienced in common by members.* As the preceding paragraph suggests, because climate emerges from interaction, it is a shared experience for the parties. This implies that there should be some common elements in members' interpretations and descriptions of the group, even though there will be differences in specific details and concerns. Therefore, the staff at Riverdale all agreed that the group was tense, hostile, and hard to manage. Although each person focused on different evidence—George on the furniture incident, Carole on George's cursing—and had somewhat different interpretations, a common theme emerged; the consultant was able to construct a unified picture of the climate from the various members' stories. Common experiences do not mean identical interpretations, but they do mean a unifying theme.

One common experience important to the study of climate, for example, is the concept of trust. *Trust* is a vulnerability we extend to others (Rousseau, Sitkin, Burt, and Camerer 1998); we trust when we believe others have earned our vulnerability through past interactions. As such, we give those we trust more latitude, we require less information, we reveal more of ourselves and our opinions, and we give people the benefit of the doubt when credibility is in question. In organizational settings, trust between parties results in a myriad of positive benefits, including increased commitment, enhanced job satisfaction, and improved job performance (Dirks and Ferrin 2002). In virtually every environment, critical actions can foster trust and a conflict-positive climate. For example, showing concern for employees and encouraging open communication about sensitive issues promotes trust between managers and employees (Korsgaard, Brodt, and Whitener 2002). When our actions form a common experience of trust, the climate is changed, usually for the better.

Third, because climates are products of interaction, *no one person is responsible for creating a climate.* In the Riverdale case, it would be easy to blame George for creating the hostile atmosphere but closer consideration shows that all the others contributed too. The counselors rearranged the furniture without considering that George might be insecure in a new job. Carole withdrew when George confronted her, which prevented an airing of the issues and may have increased his suspicions. The hostile atmosphere at Riverdale was so pervasive because most members acted in accordance with it. Their actions reinforced each other and created an expectation of hostility in most interchanges.

Climates are also *relatively enduring;* that is, they persist for extended spans of time and do not change with every change in interaction (Tagiuri 1968). In some social units, the same climate may hold for months or years. At Riverdale, for example, the hostile climate built for ten months before a mediator was called in. Members of a community consulting group reported a consistent atmosphere of support and cooperation extending for several years. Although many disagreements and controversies arose during this time, they were worked out in a constructive and cooperative manner. Furthermore, employees of some corporations have observed a consistent "tone," "flavor," or "attitude" in their work environment that evolved over months or years and seems likely to persist into the future (Dalton 1959; Roy 1959; Kanter 1977). In other cases, a climate has a shorter life, as in the brown-bag discussion, where a challenging, hostile climate supplanted the generally relaxed climate after only an hour.

Both long- and short-lived climates represent periods wherein definite themes and directions predominate in a social unit's interaction. The "life span" of a climate is determined by the relative stability of its themes, and this in turn depends on whether the themes are reinforced in day-to-day interaction (Poole and McPhee 1983; Poole 1985). In some teams or dyads, the climate is firmly established in fundamental assumptions of group operation and therefore changes very slowly. For example, in the community consulting group, cooperative means of decision making were built into the meeting procedures, and cooperative activity was therefore reinforced whenever conflicts arose. In other groups, interaction remains more unstable; there is little consensus on basic assumptions, and the overall sense of the group shifts relatively easily. Shifts in interaction can shift the underlying assumptions of the group rather quickly. The brown-bag discussion, which brought together a group of relative strangers, is one such case. Because climate reinforces the patterns of interaction from which it arises, the longer a climate holds, the more entrenched and enduring it is likely to become (Poole and McPhee 1983). Climates are changed by changes in interaction that "break the spell" and reroute the interaction.

Climate Themes

But just what is the "content" of climates? What do climates tell members that helps them make specific projections? *Climate can best be described as a set of general themes running through interaction.* At Riverdale, for example, one theme was the lack of respect members had for one another. This was clearly reflected in the behaviors of Riverdale's staff: George cursed at people and worked around Carole's authority; staff members excluded George from their office improvements and talked about him behind his back. Identifying these themes permitted the consultant to understand some of the dynamics at Riverdale.

A barrier to the identification of climates is the amazing diversity of themes. If 100 social units are observed, 100 different sets of themes will probably be found. In some social units we might find a cooperative atmosphere based on dedication to a common task or mission and in others cooperation based on warm and supportive friendships. At Riverdale, hostility and mistrust were grounded in suspicions about the possible misuse of authority, whereas in another group hostility might be grounded in competition for scarce rewards such as raises or promotions. The variations are endless. From the many specific variations, however, it is possible to identify general categories of concerns addressed by climate themes. The four general themes discussed next arise from "universal" features of human relationships identified by a number of previous studies (Wish and Kaplan 1977; Bales and Cohen 1979; LaFasto and Larson 2001). These themes, shown in Table 6.1, emerge repeatedly because they relate to problems and concerns faced in every social unit. Although they certainly do not cover every theme, the ones here offer useful guideposts for the identification of climates.

One category of themes revolves around *dominance or authority relations.* These themes are concerned with a set of questions concerning how a social unit ordinarily deals with the distribution of power and respect. Is power concentrated in the hands of a few, or is it accessible to most or all people? How important is power in decisions: to what extent are power and influence used to mandate decisions or resolve disagreements, as opposed to open discussion and argument about the issues? How rigid is the power structure: can people readily shift roles and assume authority, or are the same people always in control? Related to this: Are the differences in power, status, and respect accorded to leaders greatly different from those accorded to followers? Answers to these and related questions are important in understanding how people are differentiated in the social unit and how they act together.

At Riverdale, for example, power was part of the day-to-day interaction. George used his directorship to berate staff members. His attempts to circumvent

TABLE 6.1   Four Important Climate Theme Categories

Type of Theme	Examples of Issues Associated with Each Theme
1. Dominance and authority relations	Is power concentrated in the hands of a few or is it shared?
	How important is power in decisions?
	How rigid is the team's or dyad's power structure: Do people shift roles?
	How are power, status, and respect distributed among people?
2. Degree of supportiveness	Are people friendly or intimate with one another?
	Can people trust one another?
	Can people safely express emotions in the group, team, or relationship?
	Does the team or dyad tolerate disagreements among members?
	To what degree does the team or dyad emphasize task versus socioemotional concerns?
3. Sense of relational identity	Does the team or dyad have a definite identity?
	Do people feel ownership of accomplishments?
	How great is the commitment to each other?
	Do people share responsibility for decisions?
4. Interdependence	Can all gain if they cooperate, or will one's gain be another's loss?
	Are people pitted against one another?

Carole and her opposition created a climate in which the use of power and opposition were taken for granted, with predictable consequences for the group's interaction. Dominance themes are important determinants of conflict behavior because they enable members to draw conclusions as to how differentiation will be handled by others and how differences will be resolved. If, for example, members perceive domination of the group by one or two members and they disagree with the dominant position, it is logical to assume that they believe they have to use force to bring their own views into prominence. This reasoning may lead a member to avoid conflict because there is too much to lose, or to state his or her case in extremely forceful terms in an attempt to fight a dominant member. Just such an assumption about George kept Carole from confronting him about the issues that were undermining their relationship.

A second category of themes concerns the *degree of supportiveness* in the social unit. This category covers a cluster of related issues. Are people friendly toward each other? Can they trust one another? Can people safely express their emotions?

Is there tolerance for disagreements and different points of view? What is the relative degree of concern with tasks and members' socioemotional needs? Answers to these and related questions give people an idea of their safety in the social unit and the level of commitment they have to one another. At Riverdale there was very little emotional safety. Members distrusted one another, and there was little tolerance for disagreement. Members dug into entrenched positions and assumed they were right—that it was up to others to mend their ways. People protected themselves and showed little concern for others' feelings. Although emotions were expressed to some extent (at least by George), they were perceived as levers and not as a means for deeper understanding. Emotionality themes are important in conflict because they allow members to draw conclusions about whether needs and feelings should and will be addressed in managing the conflict. In cases where emotional expression is not safe, there often is a tendency to conceal needs or address them indirectly (Bartunek and Reid 1992; Van Maanan 1992; Roth 1993). This veiling can make successful conflict management much more difficult.

Consider Case 6.2 and the impact that supportiveness, or lack thereof, can have on emotional conflicts. The organization in question is a small cooperative bakery with seven staff members. Although these workers were generally congenial with one another, they did not have sufficient intimacy or trust to air an emotional crisis, and therefore this lack of trust made the conflict much worse than it should have been.

A third category of themes concerns members' *sense of relational identity* (Wilson 1978; Smith and Berg 1987). It covers questions such as the following: Does the social unit have an identity of its own or is it just a collection of individuals? Do people feel ownership of accomplishments? How great is their commitment? Do people know about and trust in each other's decisions? Themes related to these questions give members information that allows them to project the consequences of conflict for the social unit. For example, if a group does not have a definite identity, and member commitment is low, the group may fracture into subgroups if conflict comes into the open. Members with an interest in preserving the group might try to hide conflict to prevent this. An important reason the staff at Riverdale was unable to manage its conflict was because members believed raising the issues again "wasn't worth the hassle" and would only worsen an already unpleasant situation. The group's cohesiveness had been so disrupted by its problems that members feared they would not be able to do their jobs if the conflict advanced any further.

A final category of themes concerns the type of *interdependence* that exists among members, which addresses the motivational set of a situation. Can all gain if they cooperate, or will one's gain be another's loss? Do people normally take a competitive attitude toward each other? The themes in this category are closely related to the climates discussed by Deutsch (1973). As noted in Chapter 2, at least three types of interdependence can be identified—cooperative, competitive, and individualistic—each having quite different effects on interaction. Answers to questions revolving around motivational interdependence are important because they can influence whether working habits predispose members toward destructive redefinition of conflicts into win–lose terms. A competitive climate can encour-

CASE **6.2**

The Breakup at the Bakery

Imagine yourself as a staff member at this bakery: Why would you be reluctant to share your emotional reactions with the others?

A group of seven people had established and run a bakery for two years when a severe conflict emerged and threatened the store's existence. Two workers had been in a committed intimate relationship for several years but were now going through a difficult breakup. During this time, neither the man nor the woman could stand being around one another, but neither could afford to quit his or her job. The store needed both members' skills and experience to survive financially.

Over three months the climate in the workplace grew more and more unbearable. Workers had to deal with the tension between the couple while working under daily time pressures and the constraints of having a minimal staff. Many believed that they could not work effectively if the situation got much worse. Important information about bakery orders and deliveries was not being exchanged as workers talked less and less to each other. The group decided to call in a third party to help improve the situation. In discussing the problem with individual staff members, the third party realized that the workers strongly resented having to deal with the "relationship problem" at the bakery. They felt they were being forced to choose sides in the conflict or

risk losing the friendship of both. At the same time, it was painful to see two friends endure a very difficult emotional trauma.

Although the staff members were eager to share these feelings with the third party, almost nothing had been said to the man or woman about their conflict. The staff was not willing to discuss the emotional issues because they seemed highly volatile and might lead to the breakdown of the work group. The climate had prevented them from expressing emotional reactions, which might have helped the couple understand how their breakup was affecting everyone. As a result, tension heightened, and the bakery was about to go under. The third party was able to increase members' feelings of safety, and eventually all were able to talk about the problems. It was finally decided that the man would train his successor and leave the bakery within three months, while the woman would stay on.

Discussion Questions
- *To what extent can one person improve the supportiveness within an organization through communication and action?*
- *Could this group have shifted the climate without the help of a third party?*
- *Do you think that climate is necessarily affected when some co-workers have an intimate relationship?*

age this tendency, whereas a cooperative climate can discourage it. For example, interaction at Riverdale was premised on a competitive assumption. George and Carole were each trying to protect their own "turf" from the other. The others were resistant to George and regarded him as an opponent who would try to defeat them by browbeating and by using his authority.

We have advanced these four categories to illustrate common climate themes, not as a complete description. Although these themes capture important aspects of climates, climates are much more complex and dynamic than the categories themselves imply. The categories represent general types of climate themes and, taken in isolation, give only a "frozen" picture of climate. They cannot mark the ways in which climate is constantly being renewed in an interaction. Moreover, the four categories omit many features of climates. To adequately understand the climate of a team or relationship, it is necessary to identify the specific combinations of themes in the particular unit under consideration. Even if all themes happen to fall into the four categories, the specific combination very likely will be unique to the social unit in question. The unique combination of climate themes influences the patterns of conflict that emerge.

The four climate theme categories are not totally independent. The same theme can cross more than one category, as the Riverdale case shows. The suspicious and hostile relationship between George and the rest of the staff, notably Carole, had consequences related to both the dominance and supportiveness categories. As this also implies, not all the categories of themes are important in every social unit. In some units one theme may dominate all the others. For example, at one office, the boss was so authoritarian and angered his employees so much that they organized against him. When the boss was not around, they ridiculed him and fantasized about revenge. They slowed down their work and covered for each other so the boss would not find out. The office was preoccupied with authority relations; other concerns were less of an influence over people's behavior.

Climate and Conflict Interaction

The key to understanding the impact of climates on conflict is to explore the reciprocal influence of climate and interaction. *Climate affects interaction, and interaction in turn defines and alters climate.* Both sides of this relationship need close examination in order to understand the role climate plays in conflicts. Once we understand this better, we can posit some methods for creating productive climates and avoiding nonproductive ones. The following section examines how climate constrains and channels conflict interaction. The next section considers the other side of the coin: how interaction shapes climate.

The Effects of Climate on Conflict Interaction

In all interaction, and particularly in conflicts, one of the key problems parties face is their uncertainty about how to act and about what the consequences of their actions will be. Uncertainty is natural in conflict because many people are not as accustomed to conflict as they are to other sorts of interaction. Perhaps due to a cultural tendency toward avoiding or ignoring undesirable situations, many people simply do not think or learn much about conflicts. Even for those who are accustomed to conflict, every conflict presents specific problems and choices never faced before. Even if it is a dreary rehash of a long-standing argument, each conflict holds the potential for change, for better or worse.

There are two ways in which members can respond to this uncertainty. As noted in Chapter 2, the psychodynamic perspective posits that some people reduce their uncertainty by becoming rigid—that is, by responding to all conflicts in the same way regardless of circumstances. Rigid behavior can take many forms, but two of the most striking examples provide good illustrations. Most of us have seen people who get defensive and lash out at anyone in their way. Others try to ignore or avoid all conflicts regardless of how important they are. Both forms of behavior tend to perpetuate themselves and they can be maddening for those who have to deal with them, but rigidity has definite benefits in both cases. There are numerous ways that an attacker can intimidate potential opposition into giving in or never registering a complaint (Donohue 1981; Simmons 1998). In the same vein, the avoider can often stifle issues that are threatening to him or her. Rigid responses also have the psychological benefits of reducing internal tension and enabling the person to mount some response to a potentially paralyzing situation. However, like permanently fixed working habits, rigidity can result in destructive escalation or avoidance cycles because it encourages stereotyped, repetitive responses. If the counterattacker cannot intimidate others or if the avoider cannot successfully stifle issues, rigid behavior quickly accelerates negative spirals of conflict interaction.

Rubin and Brown (1975) summarize evidence suggesting that men are more likely to fall prey to this type of rigidity than are women. They believe this is because women are more responsive to others' interpersonal cues than men are and therefore tend to be more flexible: They call it "interpersonally oriented." Men, on the other hand, tend to interpret conflicts in win–lose terms and approach all conflicts with whatever strategies usually result in a win for them. Although these explanations are somewhat debatable, they are certainly thought-provoking.

More numerous—and also more effective—are those people who attempt to cope with their uncertainty by diagnosing the situation and reacting in a manner appropriate to it. Because exact prediction is impossible, people must project their actions and estimate how others will respond to them. This projection can occur consciously (as when a member plots out a strategy for the conflict), or it can be unconscious (as when a member takes a reactive stance and only looks ahead to the next act), but it always involves estimations and guesswork about the future. Climate is indispensable in this process.

People use their sense of climate to gauge the appropriateness, effectiveness, or likely consequences of their behavior. The prevailing climate is projected into its future and sets a standard for behavior in the conflict. At Riverdale, for example, the firmly entrenched climate of hostility and suspicion led Carole to expect hostile interactions with George, and therefore she came into situations with her guard up, tended to interpret most of George's actions in an unfavorable light, and tended to act in a hostile or defensive manner toward George. Unable to predict the specifics of a conflict, people use their general impressions of a situation (in other words, of its climate) to generate specific expectations about how things should or will go. Because climate is so diffuse and generalized, it is difficult to trace the particular reasoning involved in these projections; for this reason, it is often called *intuition.*

The preceding paragraph concentrated on people's projections of their own behaviors, but equally important is their understanding of others' behavior. Here again, climate plays a major role. Especially critical are the attempts to deduce the intentions of others. For example, at some point early in the conflict, Carole decided

George intended to undermine her authority and maybe even force her to leave Riverdale. As a result, she was uncooperative and withdrew whenever George confronted her, answering what she perceived as hostility with hostility. Carole may have been right or wrong about George; that she drew conclusions at all was enough to stimulate her hostile behavior.

As discussed in Chapter 2, several biases can influence the attributions parties make about others during conflicts (Sillars 1980a, 1980c). Recall that self-serving attribution leads people to exaggerate their own cooperativeness while at the same time exaggerating their opponent's competitiveness (in other words, responsibility for the conflict). These findings imply a bias toward overestimating others' competitive tendencies (Pruitt and Rubin 1986). This bias can have important effects on conflict interaction. Remember that Sillars (1980b) found that subjects who attributed responsibility for the conflict to others were more likely to use avoidance and competitive strategies and less likely to use collaborative strategies than were those who did not make this attribution. However, the bias reported by Thomas and Pondy (1977) does not show up in some situations. In particular, studies of trust have found a bias toward assuming cooperativeness on the part of others once trust has been established (Zand 1972; Deutsch 1973).

These different outcomes can be understood in view of our discussion of climate. In the Thomas and Pondy study, the business workers were asked to talk about a recent conflict. It is likely that they chose instances in which there was open controversy, in line with the common conception of conflicts as fights. In such cases the climate is very likely to be competitive and at least somewhat hostile, and the participants are thus primed to see others as competitive. The studies on trust specifically tried to induce a climate of cooperation by instructing participants to be concerned about how the outcome of a game affected their opponents. Therefore, it is not surprising that people perceived each other as friendly and cooperative. In both cases the direction of the bias toward attribution of either competition or cooperation was determined by the climate of the situation. Interestingly, the studies of trust also postulate that people's perceptions of others as cooperative caused them to behave more cooperatively and reinforced the trusting atmosphere. The same self-reinforcing cycle is also presumed for situations in which distrust and competition prevail: perceptions of competition breed competitive behavior and reinforce hostile reactions (Sillars 1980c). *The prevailing climate of a conflict situation colors members' interpretations of one another, thereby encouraging certain types of behavior and reinforcing the situational climate.*

To this point we have considered the uses of climate for individual members. But people's actions, each guided by climate, combine and build on one another to impart a momentum in the social unit. At Riverdale, for example, individuals picked up on the hostile climate, and their defensive and unfriendly actions thrust the group into a tense spiral of hostile exchanges. This process can also work to the benefit of social units. Friendly and responsive actions encouraged by an open climate also tend to create a chain reaction and to give the conflict a positive momentum. The influence that climate exerts on individual members' behavior translates into a more encompassing influence on the direction of the unit as a whole.

The Effects of Interaction on Climate

The definition of climate points to the critical role of interaction in creating and sustaining climates. People's immediate experience of climate comes from interaction; by observing how others act and react, a person picks up cues about others' sense of the climate. Because each person acts on an interpretation of climate based on observations of other people (and their reactions to him or her), the prevailing climate has a *multiplier* effect—it tends to reproduce itself because people orient themselves to each other and each orients to the climate in projecting his or her own acts (Fink and Chen 1995). For example, in a friendship, people tend to be cooperative because they assume that is "the way things should be" between friends. When one person sees the other being friendly and cooperative, this reaffirms the relational climate and probably strengthens their inclination toward cooperativeness. Because this is happening for everyone, the effect multiplies itself and becomes quite strong.

However, the multiplier effect can also change the climate under some conditions. If a member deviates in a way that "breaks" the prevailing climate, and other people follow the lead, the direction of the interaction can be changed. If the change is profound and holds on long enough, it can result in a shift in the overall climate. Take the cooperative relationship just mentioned. If one person selfishly starts to press her interests, the other may conclude that he must do the same. Once individuals begin to act only for themselves, the underlying assumptions may shift to emphasize competition and taking advantage of others. This reflects a radical shift in the relational climate, the result of a single person's shift multiplied through the actions of the others. Obviously, this is a very complicated process.

Case 6.3A explores how conflict interaction both reflects and reproduces climate, and how a psychological evaluation unit at a large hospital responded to several controversies and disagreements surrounding an important decision. Three themes set the climate of this group. The first pertains to dominance and authority relations and can best be described as a dilemma. On the one hand, operation of the group is premised on Jerry's dominance. Partly as a result of his leadership, Jerry has evolved a forceful, take-charge style, and others in the group seem to expect this of him. On the other hand, full, relatively equal participation by all is necessary for the unit to be effective. However, Jerry's dominance discourages participation in the decision-making process by the social workers and psychologist. This aspect creates a paradox. If all of them insist on a strong voice, the unit will be less effective, because the power Jerry needs to negotiate with the bureaucracy is undercut and because Jerry may resist sharing power and disrupt the group. But if weaker members do not assert themselves, the unit will also be less effective because representatives of all disciplines are not contributing. Members' behavior is colored by their responses to this dilemma.

The second theme pertains to supportiveness and concerns the safety of being open in the group. The unit emphasizes a high level of professionalism. In some areas this code implies that members should hold back; for example, expression of anger is seen as unprofessional, as is making a "half-baked" suggestion in

CASE **6.3A**
The Psychological Evaluation Unit

Imagine yourself as Laura, one of the psychiatrists: How might the climate of this group affect the way you engaged in conflict?

The psychological evaluation unit at a large hospital is composed of three psychiatrists, a psychologist, and two social workers. The unit was purposely designed as a multidisciplinary cross section, with competent professionals from all "helping" areas: psychiatry, psychology, and social work. Each profession must exert its influence if the unit is to function properly. The unit emphasizes a high level of professionalism for its members and, because of this, presentation of oneself as a professional is very important. The unit is charged with diagnosing disturbed patients and with running a training program for newly graduated doctors interning at the hospital.

The unit was created at a time of budget surplus for the hospital. The services it provides were originally provided by staff psychiatrists, but the unit was created to consolidate diagnostic techniques and leave the staff psychiatrists free for therapy. However, a budget crunch set in the last year and the hospital board is looking for services and units to cut. Because the evaluation unit is new, it is high on the list of departments to be scrutinized. Members are worried about the unit's survival and most decisions are made with an eye toward making the unit look good, or, at least, not look questionable to outside observers.

The psychiatrist who heads the committee, Jerry, chairs most meetings and represents the unit in the hospital bureaucracy. He is a "take-charge" person, and the psychologist and social workers are intimidated by his forceful style. He tries to be open, but, partly due to Jerry's strength and partly due to uncertainty about their own status, the three have relatively little input in group discussions. The other two psychiatrists, John and Laura, sometimes provide a balance, but they are not as aggressive as Jerry and therefore tend to be overshadowed. John and Laura are aware of Jerry's take-charge tendencies and have tried to encourage the psychologist and social workers. However, all tend to hang back in the face of Jerry's initiatives.

Discussion Questions
- *How would you describe the climate of the psychological evaluation unit?*
- *Consider the climate of a group, team, or organization of which you are a member. Does the climate influence the way you interact with others? Does it influence the way conflict unfolds?*

a decision-making discussion. In other areas this implies full openness; for example, when researchers come in to present new therapeutic ideas to the unit, members are encouraged to ask questions as part of the learning process. Therefore, whether it is safe to be open is determined by whether the specific instance of openness is regarded as "professional" or not. For most of the meeting, as we will examine, openness is not considered to be professional.

The third theme concerns the unit's identity and can be described as the "problem of survival." Members are concerned with legitimizing the functions of the unit to the hospital.

These themes were identified from observation of a number of group meetings and form the backdrop for the controversy to be considered. Case 6.3B

CASE **6.3B**

The Psychological Evaluation Unit (Continued)

Imagine yourself as Laura: Why might it be difficult for you to change the existing climate?

Jerry introduces the issue at hand: The unit is evaluating a psychiatric intern who has repeatedly missed his turns of duty at evaluation clinics. Talking for about five minutes, Jerry gives a brief history of the intern's problems and summarizes his attempts to talk to the intern. In particular, Jerry asked the intern what a proper attendance rate should be. The intern ventured a ten percent absentee rate as an adequate figure. Jerry introduces this figure as a standard and then asks the others, "What do you think?" The psychologist and one social worker, Megan, ask what the intern's excuse is, and Jerry responds with a lengthy answer detailing the excuses and offering commentary on them.

[One thing Jerry does here that reinforces his position of strength is to talk at length when he introduces the problem. The amount of time spent talking in a group has been shown to be both an indicator and a determinant of dominance in the group (Hayes and Meltzer 1972; Folger 1980; Folger and Sillars 1980). Moreover, Jerry defines the problem based on his own perceptions and opinions, thereby keeping any conflict that might arise on his own "turf." Laura, who also knows about the problem, does not introduce it; although Jerry asks Laura if he is presenting the case accurately, he dominates the floor when the discussion is set up.]

Laura then speaks, arguing that an absence rate of one day every two months is more than enough. Megan, one of the two social workers, jumps in, and this exchange follows:

MEGAN: You shouldn't even give him that *(once every two months)* . . . I mean, if an emergency comes up that's one thing. If you say you're gonna get off . . .

JERRY: *(interrupting)* This is not . . . This is not time that we expect him to take. This is how often we expect emergencies to occur.

MEGAN: But he's going to interpret it as if we're gonna give him a day or two every two months if we say it.

JERRY: *(shaking his head as Megan speaks and speaking immediately on her last word)* It depends on how we want to say it, but what we had in mind was, if you look at how often he's here or not here—it's sort of a gross way to do an evaluation, but it's one possibility. And one could say, "If emergencies come up with more frequency, you need more time to attend to your emergencies, and we could make an exception." How you word it might vary, but I think what we need is some kind of sense for what's tolerable.

FRANK: *(the other social worker)* What about the things he has done when he shows up—expectations as far as staying or leaving early. Which is . . . I think, one of many things. After his last patients, five or ten minutes later he's gone. And yesterday that happened and five minutes later we had a walk-in who really needed medical help, and I was the only one there and I could have used (help) . . . that was, you know, it was like 11:15 and he didn't show up. Don't we expect the interns to check to see if there are any walk-ins before they leave?

JERRY: *(interrupting)* We can talk about that as another issue.

FRANK: *(interrupting)* Well, it's another expectation that needs to be addressed.

At this point Laura clarifies her position on the intern's attendance, and the issue raised by Frank is dropped. In both cases Jerry cuts off the social workers, redefines the issues they raise, and turns the discussion back in the direction he has defined. That the other two psychiatrists tacitly support his approach reinforces the

(continued)

CASE 6.3B   Continued

social workers' uncertainty and hesitancy. [In effect, Jerry and the others are reproducing the suppressed climate of the group. This also allows Jerry to use the presumption of his dominance to "win" the argument.] Laura and Jerry then pursue a long exchange in which they try to define an acceptable level of participation for interns. Jerry's participation in this interchange is marked by his attempts to define criteria for evaluating the intern. For example:

LAURA: *(after a long speech)* . . . to vanish from sight (when patients need him), I just don't find that acceptable. *(pause)*

JERRY: On the other hand, if it's 11:15, and you don't have any patients . . .

LAURA: *(interrupting)* That's a different issue.

JERRY: We don't have to provide any options. We can say that we recognize that over a year and a half your participation has been mitigated because of unusual circumstances, and that's the end. I mean, we don't have to make a deal at all.

[In this sequence Jerry attempts to help by raising another option available to the group. As decision-making research has shown, the more options a group considers, the better its decision is likely to be. However, notice that Jerry still controls the definition of the issue. He does not respond to Laura's disagreement, but shifts the discussion to another alternative, an alternative that he dismissed as a legitimate topic for discussion earlier. Because other members generally go along with these shifts, Jerry unwittingly maintains control. Moreover, because the way in which issues are defined is in line with Jerry's style of thinking and his particular concerns, other members of the group are caught off balance in discussions. They are not as prepared to work issues through to their conclusions as Jerry is, and so they come across as less competent or as having little to say. This is especially likely to be true of the social workers, who have very

different backgrounds and less administrative experience than Jerry. The other two psychiatrists and, to a lesser extent, the psychologist raise their own issues, but these issues are usually redefined and commented on by Jerry. When Jerry raises an issue he has the advantage of forethought; he can think things through before the discussion because he dictates when it will begin.]

As the discussion progresses, they try to set an acceptable number of absences for the intern. After arguing back and forth, the group determines that setting an ideal attendance rate is impossible. Rather, members decide to talk to the intern in order to make him aware of the problem and then to reevaluate the situation in two months. Throughout this process Jerry moderates the discussion. He is responsive to concerns but still sets the tone of the decision, as the following excerpts from the discussion suggest.

LAURA: I guess I agree. I want to give him time off . . . but if he's gonna be there, then he has to be there.

JERRY: But we have to come up with some kind of sense that if he exceeds we have to say "thank you, but no thank you."

LAURA: I'd say more than once in two months, or maybe twice in two months more than an hour late. Nobody else does that . . . that I know of . . . in terms of missing times.

MEGAN: *(talking over Laura's last sentences)* Rather than just specifically making a case for him, maybe we should decide what's appropriate—what the expectations are for all the residents.

JERRY: *(interrupting)* I think we are. I think you're right that the kind of sense we're generating is not necessarily specific. . . . It turns out that he's going to be the one for whom it's an issue . . . and we also have to acknowledge that there will be individual circumstances that . . . change. We may need to face that. But I need to have some type of sense of what we expect of him and at what point we should acknowledge that he should or should not participate. And one way—it's sort of simple and artificial—is to do attendance, to say "How many hours are you late? How many times are you late?" That avoids in part coming to grips with, you know, an overall kind of evaluation, and maybe we don't want to use a numerical scale. I'm open to lots of different suggestions. The one that I wasn't willing to accept was that if others in the subspecialties used their own internal sets I wasn't going to ask them to change (such as, other departments could evaluate the intern according to their own criteria).

Jerry continued to elaborate this position for another minute. Note that he interrupted Megan and gave a summary of how he sees the issues and what he is willing to accept. Note also that he spoke much longer than Megan.

JOHN: I think there's a double-barreled threat *(from the intern's absences)*. Dr. Jacobs *(director of the hospital)* is coming and casual conversation says *(the intern)* is OK when he's here, but he's never here, then clearly that's another, that's a threat . . .

JERRY: *(interrupting)* That's been defined. That one seems clear and has been addressed.

[In this passage, Jerry attempted to move the group on to another issue. He did so by interrupting John to tell him his first concern (of two) has been addressed. John never raised the second concern. The discussion moved on to another topic after Jerry's interruption.]

JERRY: *(summarizing the group's decision)* I'm comfortable if what the group wants to do, then, is take it back to (the intern) and say we have a set of expectations—they include your participation—your full participation—in this program. That we will reassess our impression of that participation—and we hope you will assess it—on a monthly basis or something and that if we need to—because there's some question of whether or not your participation is complete—then we'll meet and we'll need to talk about it.

[This is a fair summary of the group's decision, but it is cast in terms of what Jerry is comfortable with. He personalizes and takes charge of the group's decision.]

Discussion Question
- *How is climate reproduced in this interaction?*

discusses disagreements that emerge as the unit makes its decision. Because it is the members' talk that creates and sustains the group's climate, close analysis of the transcript is necessary.

The inhibited climate of the group is not a result of total control over decisions by Jerry: Jerry eventually gives in to the arguments of others and shifts his position away from setting a figure for absences. The climate results from the way in which the group manages its decision-making process, particularly actual or potential disagreements. Jerry's attempts to lead the unit to an effective, efficient decision end up controlling the discussion. By persistently stepping in to restate, redefine, summarize, and comment, Jerry channels the discussion. The others, with few exceptions, respond by following Jerry's lines of thought and thereby reinforce his control over the discussion and his resolutions of disagreements. The end result of this process is to create a sense that Jerry can and will jump in and redirect the discussion at any time, that he is an arbiter of opinions and suggestions, and that lower-status members do not have as good a grasp of the priorities of the unit as Jerry does. The social workers and the psychologist are hesitant and tense during meetings, and outside meetings they complain to each other and spend a good deal of time planning how to "get heard" in meetings.

Another striking feature of this decision is how much disagreement and frustration there are yet how little of this actually emerges during the discussion. Members, especially the weaker ones, are very restrained and try to speak in "reasoned, measured tones." Disagreements are rarely admitted, much less sharpened. Instead, Jerry (and to a lesser extent Laura) incorporates dissenting ideas into the final solution insofar as they fit. If dissenting opinions do not fit, they are cut off. Other members of the unit do not seem to play an active role in changing the original proposal; they introduce ideas and passively allow them to be incorporated, relying on Jerry's willingness to cooperate. This pattern is in part due to the professionalized climate, which works against strong expressions of disagreement, and in part due to members' acceptance of dominance relations in the unit. But subdued behavior also reinforces these qualities of the group's climate: by assenting to professionalism and Jerry's leadership the members are reproducing it.

None of these effects are necessarily intentional. Jerry makes honest attempts to be open to others' suggestions and often changes his stand in response. He asks others for ideas and uses a lot of open questions (such as, "What should we do here?") in an attempt to elicit participation. However, Jerry's style—even when he is seeking only to clarify—translates ideas into his own terms and tends to stifle different points of view. His interruptions and lengthy answers "disenfranchise" members with less forcefulness or less skill at managing interaction, preventing them from taking the initiative. Reactions to Jerry do little to counteract these tendencies and, in some cases, even reinforce them. Although the excerpts do not show it, when people speak, they direct most of their comments to Jerry. As noted, they also pick up on Jerry's comments and defer to him when he interrupts and generally are unaware (or only marginally aware) of these tendencies. They see themselves as trying to contribute—and perceive Jerry as trying to cut them off—without recognizing their own complicity in the process. The entire unit "works together" to create and sustain the suppressed, hesitant, uncomfortable atmosphere.

This example has focused on how a climate is reproduced in interaction. However, interaction can also change climates. One bit of advice often given to lower-status members is simply to be more assertive, to speak up when issues concern them, and to resist interruptions. This advice is sound, for the most part. To shift the climate of their unit toward a less suppressed direction members could, for example, make Jerry aware of his tendency to interrupt; they might also support each other when they attempt to redefine the problems facing the unit. If Jerry is sincere about opening up the group, he will not resist these moves. This lack of resistance should, in turn, encourage further moves that will open up the group even more and reproduce the open climate. This opening up should not, however, be done in a fashion that threatens Jerry's authority. In the face of an openly divisive challenge, Jerry is likely to strike back in order to save face, and this could promote bitter, open conflict.

Moves that depart from the patterns implied in the prevailing climate function as bids for change. If people follow up on these bids, they become institutionalized and have the potential to alter the climate of a team or relationship. At least two studies have shown that clear and unambiguous changes in behavior could quickly change climates from cooperative to competitive or vice versa (Lindskold, Betz, and Walters 1986). More often, however, bids are rejected. Sometimes people simply fail to support an action that departs from accepted patterns, whereas in other cases dominant individuals actively suppress a bid for change. When people look back at successful bids for change, they often identify them as critical incidents (or turning points) in the life of the team or relationship. *Critical incidents break up climates, either because they make members more aware of themselves or simply because they are so striking that members unconsciously pick up on them and perpetuate new patterns.* Once interaction patterns are changed, they generalize to climates, and if they are changed for a long enough period, the prevailing climate changes. Unfortunately, we do not know enough about critical incidents to specify what allows a bid to become a turning point. In general, however, the bid must catch the attention and imagination of people, it must address some deep-seated problem, and it must not move powerful people to organize against it.

The interaction–climate relationship is a complex one and works on several levels. Climates are maintained and changed through specific actions that are relevant to particular issues and concerns. Jerry's tendency to jump on people implicitly told members who wished to enter into the discussion that the group (specifically, Jerry) was judgmental and therefore likely to criticize or reject their contributions.

Donald Roy's famous case study of a factory work team, "Banana Time," provides another good example (Roy 1959). In his study Roy took a job in a factory assembling plastic raincoats so that he could observe how workers dealt with boring and repetitive work. He was assigned to a work unit with three other workers who soon "taught him the ropes" and included him in their social circle. Games, jokes, and teasing provided the major escape for Roy's comrades. Usually all would participate with enthusiasm in these incidents, but Roy observed one instance when a joke backfired and disrupted the team's congenial atmosphere. When one person, Ike, teased another with higher status, George, about his son-in-law (who was a college professor), George blew up and withdrew from Ike. George would not speak to Ike, with whom he had formerly been very close, and Ike's apologies were ignored. The normally pleasant atmosphere was poisoned. The team gradually returned to normal, but George's message was clear: There were limits on teasing. George's outburst defined, and perhaps narrowed, the latitude members had in their relationships, and thereafter the team was more restrained for some time.

Because climates are generalized, interaction influences climate on a second level: Changes in one theme can influence other related themes. In the psychological unit, Jerry's controlling moves during discussions directly maintained dominance relationships. However, they also influenced the members' sense of the safety and supportiveness of the unit. If one's contributions are likely to be overruled or ignored, he or she is unlikely to feel highly regarded or safe in a team or relationship. George's reactions to Ike pertained not only to emotional relationships but indirectly to the team's sense of its own identity. Roy commented that the unit fell apart for all practical purposes when George refused to speak to Ike. The lack of supportiveness threatened the team's effectiveness and called its sense of itself into question.

At a third level, interaction can create a climate that temporarily overshadows the more enduring qualities of a social unit. In the psychological evaluation unit, a meeting several weeks after the one examined previously exhibited a much more relaxed atmosphere. The group discussed a schedule of inservice meetings that would be presented over the next year. Interaction was relatively uninhibited, and both social workers contributed freely on topics that fell in their areas of expertise. Jerry talked no more than anyone else, and the other two psychiatrists facilitated the meeting in a noncontrolling manner; for this one meeting, the tensions disappeared. Perhaps due to differences in topic, perhaps due to a fortunate conjunction of moods, the interactions cast an altogether different spell. For the time being, a more spontaneous, open atmosphere prevailed, and the joking and excitement evident in the meeting reflected this more fraternal attitude. At the next meeting, people were more inhibited, although not as tense as before. The previous climate, marked by quandaries about power relations and safety, had reasserted itself.

Because they are sustained by interaction, climates are vulnerable to temporary shifts due to temporary alterations of interaction patterns. These shifts can be beneficial, as in the evaluation unit, or they can present problems—for example, when a normally harmonious group is disrupted by a "no holds barred" fight between two members. The shifts, however, are also vulnerable to the reassertion of the former climate. The longer the climate has been sustained, the deeper its grooves are worn, and the more likely the traditional quality of the social unit is to reassert itself. It is only by hard work that a temporary improvement in climate can be institutionalized.

As this chapter has shown, climates are created and maintained by particular events in interaction. However, because climates are generalized and diffuse, it is easy to forget this. People are often aware of a change in the tone of the team or relationship soon after a critical incident occurs. It is hard, for example, to miss the connection between an insult and increased tension. However, if the tension persists and becomes a part of the prevailing climate, the climate tends to become second nature. They forget that climate depends on how individuals interact and assume that the social unit is "just that way," that the enduring qualities are independent of what people do. In failing to realize that they themselves hold the key to maintaining or changing the climate, people are thereby controlled by the climate. Like the social workers in the psychological evaluation unit, members may assume they have to keep acting as they do because there is no alternative. This assumption is responsible for the tendency of climates to reproduce themselves rather than to change.

In closing this section, it is necessary to introduce an important qualification: throughout this discussion we have spoken as though every social unit has a well-defined climate. This is not always the case. *Climates are generalizations from interaction, and they can only emerge insofar as interaction has at least some consistent, characteristic patterns in the social unit.* Most social units exhibit such patterns, however sketchy. Even though most of the attendees at the brown-bag lunch (Case 1.1) had never met, the group developed a definite atmosphere because participants freely entered into the exploratory, question-and-answer format. The group evolved a pleasant climate that was threatened by the challenge to the speaker.

However, if a social unit's interaction patterns vary frequently and unpredictably, there is no foundation for a coherent climate. Groups of people thrown together for an "exercise" in a class or workshop are often chaotic because they have no knowledge of each other and no commitment to future interaction. As a result, they act only for themselves and the group as a whole develops no coherent themes. Even more difficult are social units beset by a crisis, often in the form of an unexpected and bitter fight between two important members. In conflicts of this type, people often feel that their relationship, team, or organization is falling apart. They lose their bearings because the situation gives them no clues for predicting what will happen next. This is in part because the conflict introduces a whole new situation, one that is incompatible with the traditional climate, but not clear enough to institute a new climate.

How definite a climate is depends on the degree of structure in the social unit, which ranges on a continuum from very rigid and structured to almost chaotic; climates can vary accordingly. This should not imply, however, that change in a social unit is synonymous with a lack of structure. In fact, most changes use existing structures and do not require a radical break in the prevailing climate. Even fundamental alterations in climate often occur gradually and result in relatively little disruption. Only when change calls the existing basis of the social unit into question all at once does it throw the unit into chaos. This does not happen often, but it is important to recognize that it can happen, and that when it does, all bets are off as far as climate is concerned.

Identifying Climates

Because climates are so diffuse, yet so important, it is critical for people to be able to identify them. Unless people can detect and work on climate, it will remain a nebulous, "untamed" force, always liable to "get away" from people and impart a harmful momentum to interaction. Our discussion implies several guidelines for the diagnosis of climates.

   1. *Climate themes are best identified by observing the entire social unit for an extended period.* Although exchanges between key members—for example, George and Carole at Riverdale—can play an important role in the team or dyad, they must be generalized and influence others' interchanges to become part of the unit's climate. To become a relatively enduring feature of a social unit, interchanges "with the same feel" must occur repeatedly and be recognized as characteristic by members.

This implies that climate themes should permeate interaction and that those that are most enduring and significant will tend to emerge most frequently over time.

2. *To diagnose climate, it is necessary to focus on interaction.* Talking with people is a critical part of diagnosis. The consultant got most of her initial ideas about Riverdale by interviewing the staff involved in the conflict. However, members' ideas will always be somewhat biased. One may be angry at another and therefore attempt to cast that person in a negative light by claiming he or she causes problems. In other cases, people bias their accounts to make themselves look good. Thomas and Pondy (1977) interpreted their finding that business employees reported their own conflict behavior as generally cooperative to be a tendency on the part of their subjects to perceive themselves more favorably than they perceived others. In some cases, people's reports will be biased because they are unaware of their own behavior and therefore do not see themselves as part of the problem. In the Riverdale case, neither George nor Carole was aware that their behavior contributed to the conflict; each blamed the other and believed the other had to change to resolve the conflict. Because individual oral or written accounts are thus "contaminated," they cannot be the sole source of evidence on climate. Accounts can give initial insights, but these must be checked by observing how people interact. If observations based on interaction are consistent with reports, then the conclusions in the reports can be trusted, at least to some extent.

However, if interaction is inconsistent with reports, the inconsistency itself can be an important source of information about the organization, team, or dyad. One of the authors was working with a citywide charitable group to try to resolve arguments over its budget. The secretary of the group had confided that he believed the president always favored funding proposals from groups in which she had special interests. However, on observing several meetings, the consultant noted that the president was fairly objective, whereas the secretary pushed his interests very strongly. This suggested that the secretary had trouble monitoring his own behavior and had projected his personal tensions and biases onto the president, who was threatening because she stood in the way of his priorities. The consultant took the secretary aside in a confrontational manner to discuss the problem, and, for a while, the secretary was able to take his biases into account. (The group later reverted to its old bickering, however, because of problems in following the third party's advice.)

To make an accurate estimate of climate, it is valuable to cross-check individual oral or written accounts, minutes of meetings, other historical records, and actual observations. This has a particularly important implication for those trying to diagnose their own relationships or groups: They need to talk to other members, and to outside observers, if available, to get their views. One's own views represent only one perspective and may yield biased perceptions. There is no privileged vantage point; even the external observer can be subject to misperceptions: All views must be cross-checked to identify climates accurately.

3. *The four categories discussed earlier supply some ideas of the types of themes likely to emerge in climates.* Most of the themes (see Table 6.1) can be interpreted as answers to questions of concern in these categories—for instance, is power evenly distributed? *Metaphors* are a particularly fertile source of themes; often they contain unconscious associations capable of telling us more about the social unit's sense of itself than anyone's account. For example, one college department we are acquainted with described itself with a "family" metaphor. Members repeatedly referred to the department family, and people being interviewed for faculty positions were told the department was like a "big family." In line with this metaphor, several faculty members filled the slots reserved for father, mother, uncle, and aunt. Even the problems and conflicts in the faculty related to issues of authority and independence often associated with parent–child or parent–parent relationships. Patterns of conflict behavior in the department reflected the family metaphor to some extent: the "father" tried to take charge of the situation, and the "mother" tried to soothe those involved and sympathized with them. The "children" were rebellious but unsure of themselves and tended to knuckle under when the father applied pressure. Of course, the family metaphor should not be carried too far because it was not the only force affecting conflict behavior. However, it did give some insights into the workings of the department that could not have been gleaned from direct questioning of the faculty. Because the precise details of meaning are only implicit in a metaphor, people will often use metaphors, whereas they would not provide an explicit description carrying similar meaning. This makes metaphors very valuable as a means of understanding a relationship, team, or organization.

In some cases, a metaphor or theme will be expanded considerably into an entire fantasy. Bormann (1986) discusses the dynamics of fantasy themes and their roles in holding groups together. In particular, he argues that *fantasy* themes often develop as a drama, with a definite plot, scene, and distinguishable heroes and villains. These dramas provide a deeper meaning for group life and help people understand their world and guide their actions. Building on his work, Cragan and Shields (1981) analyzed fantasy themes in a fire station in St. Paul, Minnesota. The firefighters saw themselves as heroic, courageous professionals acting in dangerous situations. To do so, they needed to be dedicated, competent team players, able to get along with others and get the job done. They emphasized self-confidence and "were willing to let their actions do the talking." An integral part of the fire station's climate was also the belief that the public thought of firefighters as having a soft job, being reckless in fighting fires, and being undependable and slow. So the vision emerges of courageous, professional people performing heroic and hazardous duty, but who are misunderstood and disliked by the very people they save. This interpretation of their world is likely to promote the supportiveness necessary to carry the firefighters through their hazardous duties. It also promotes a sense of the fire company as a misunderstood and badly treated group, setting firefighters off against an ignorant and ungrateful public. Clearly this may have important effects both on how firefighters interact with each other in conflicts and how open they are to citizen complaints. This perception of distance from the ungrateful public is likely to cause firefighters to use avoidance strategies and "stonewall" any citizen complaints.

Some metaphors that influence interaction in dyads, teams, or organizations stem from broad cultural expectations and trends. The increasing reliance on the legal system in our culture has led to "legalistic" thinking and structuring of situations (Meyer 1983; Selznick 1969; Yudof 1981). The legal process is not only an option for addressing problems but has become a metaphor for how to think about them. The process is circular: Recourse to legal means in our society leads to an infiltration of legal language into organizations. The legal language creates a conventional metaphor that then structures how individuals think about situations in the workplace, increasing reliance on legalistic processes (Stutman and Putnam 1994). Even when official legal channels are not used, other channels for managing problems are modeled after them. This tendency to view conflict and the means to addressing problems within a legal frame in our culture represents a spreading conventional metaphor, which structures thinking about how to address problems and affects actions and sanctions.

Litigation has infiltrated organizational life not only as a formal system for guiding and enforcing behaviors but also as a way of managing informal relationships. This infiltration is evident in the language of organizational disputes. Relationships are "contractual." When expectations are violated, people claim, "You broke our agreement." An individual reacts to an "accusation" by claiming that he or she is not "the guilty party." Organizational disputes are legitimate if they are "grievable" and are evaluated in the following ways: "You don't have a case." "You need to document the problem." "What are the facts?" A disagreement is only "alleged" until all the facts are in. Consequences of ill-begotten behaviors are expressed as "damages." Actions may be taken for "damage-control." If a "contract is broken," then "punitive measures" can be taken or a "deal cut." Communication is also structured by legal metaphors: Individuals are "cross-examined," "statements" are "on or off the record," and decisions are described as "impartial." Decisions may be put off until someone has a chance to "deliberate" and until that time the "jury is still out." Labels for behaviors can become threatening in and of themselves because of their legal connotations: "That's harassment."

As an example of the litigation metaphor, consider a dispute about the use of employer records in performance evaluation. Teachers in a union system complained that principals were using information collected in their personnel files as evidence in evaluation reports. An infraction, such as being late for lunchroom duty, would appear on the evaluation form without informing the teacher that this data was in his or her file. Teachers viewed this practice as an abuse of the current appraisal policy, a lack of openness in superior–subordinate interaction, and ineffective downward communication. If the teachers adopt a legal metaphor to manage this dispute, they might treat the principal as their adversary and highlight the "violation" of the contract, obtain "facts" and "proof" that the notes were used in evaluations, link the proof to the "right to know," decry the lack of "due process" in evaluating employees, and seek "redress" for past actions and for "breaking contractual obligations." They could set up a public dispute process with a verdict to be determined by a jury of peers or by an impartial judge selected by both sides.

In some organizations, the metaphor of negotiation replaces litigation as a prevailing influence on conflict. Negotiation embodies a different set of language patterns and metaphorical structure than does litigation. Organizational members form agreements through "making deals" or "driving a hard bargain." These agreements imply that disputants find a "middle ground" or a "compromise" from their initial positions. Negotiators regard each other as "fitting opponents" or "skillful players" rather than as adversaries who must be defeated.

The process of negotiation also adheres to rules and procedures. However, unlike litigation, the rules are normative and negotiated between the disputants, who engage in an "exchange of offers" that may follow a tit-for-tat pattern. Norms of "reciprocity" imply that both sides are expected to "trade offers" and that one party's actions are adapted to the moves and expectations of the other side. The parties indicate their desire to negotiate through a willingness "to meet at the table" and adherence to "bargaining in good faith." These standards form a normative base for appropriate behavior, one determined by the participants rather than by objective legal criteria. Negotiation involves confrontation or a direct management of problems, an activity that superiors and subordinates value in the workplace (Lawrence and Lorsch 1967; Wheeless and Reichel 1988). By directly confronting one another, disputants reveal their expectations and make them open for affirmation or denial, negotiation or change (Morris and Hopper 1980; Newell and Stutman 1988, 1989/1990, 1991).

A negotiation metaphor for managing disputes would follow a different approach in the teacher evaluation example previously cited. Rather than treat the principal as an adversary, the teachers might view her as someone who may have ignored, misunderstood, or misinterpreted the contract; or as someone who had different concerns that could be met in alternate ways. In this approach, the contract is not an objective document but rather an agreement open to interpretation. That principal's actions may violate the initial agreement between the teachers and administration, but both the violation and the interpretation of the contract are open for discussion.

The teachers might confront the principal about what she sees as the problem and try to negotiate a change in the practice. If this approach is unsuccessful, the teachers might take the problem to formal negotiations. In both instances, the teachers would make arguments about the harms or disadvantages of putting notes into their files and offer alternatives for obtaining the principal's goals without the notes. The principal might counter the teachers' proposals. This argumentation process, however, differs from rules for providing evidence, making legal claims, and sticking to the issues in dispute.

4. *Intuition can and does play an important role in the diagnosis of climates.* Because most individuals have spent considerable time in relationships, teams, or organizations, people have experienced climates firsthand and therefore know at least what some of them "feel" like. The problem is developing our intuitions (unverbalized knowledge) to the point where they can be verbalized and worked with.

The rest of this chapter is designed to help in this process; *practice* in becoming attuned to climates as we experience them is the real key.

Working with Climate

So far we have discussed ways to diagnose climates. This section advances three measures for changing climate. Earlier analyses of climate clearly imply a first principle: *Small, cumulative changes in interaction can eventually result in major changes in climate.* For example, in team or organizational contexts, many people report that their first feeling of belonging to their social unit occurred when members began using "we" when talking about activities. This subtle difference signals a change in identification from "individual" to "member"; it promotes a more relaxed climate in the group by indicating to members that others are well disposed toward them and that they are on common ground. In the Psychological Evaluation Unit case, Jerry maintained his dominant position as well as the group's authoritarian climate through a series of moves that enabled him to control the issues on which they worked. In this case, members could have changed the climate by being more assertive and making bids to have a say in controlling the unit. Jerry might not have noticed these changes, but they would have gradually altered the climate to encourage more equal participation by members.

A second tactic for working on climates is to *openly discuss themes that trouble parties.* Much of the climate's influence on interaction depends on parties' inability to recognize it. If they can bring its effects out in the open and consciously move to counteract them, climate can be used to channel conflict interaction in constructive directions. Often this *consciousness raising* is done by one insightful person (Case 6.4).

There are also formal procedures for evaluating a social unit's climate and functioning (Auvine, Densmore, Extrom, Poole, and Shanklin 1977). Self-evaluation questionnaires on which members of teams or organizations rate their own and others' performance and weaknesses are often used (see Johnson and Johnson 1975, for several good forms). Questionnaires provide a structured and legitimate way to raise criticisms and open them up for discussion. This "survey–feedback" process can be used to set goals for changing a social unit's interaction and, ultimately, its climate (Case 6.5).

A third tactic for altering climate is to *create a critical incident that shifts the entire direction of the climate.* Recall the example in Chapter 1 of the faculty brown-bag discussion wherein the student suddenly challenged the speaker: The climate shifted from congenial to tense. In the same vein, parties can attempt to create critical incidents to alter unfavorable climates. Several considerations must be taken into account to do this effectively.

For one thing, *timing is critical;* people must be able to recognize propitious moments for acting on the climate. Bormann (1972) gives a good example of the importance of timing. In the groups he studied, he found a certain point in discus-

CASE 6.4
The Consulting Agency

Imagine yourself as Karen: Why might you hesitate to intervene in this way?

Imagine yourself as Joe or Juanita: How might you feel when Karen first brings up this issue?

In a small, twelve-person consulting agency, two important members, the program coordinator, Joe, and the publications manager, Juanita, were having serious problems getting along because their five-year marriage was failing. Joe and Juanita decided not to bring up their problems in front of the group because they believed it would only disrupt the operations of the ordinarily harmonious group. Suppression of the problems certainly kept their antagonism from becoming an open issue, but it did not prevent their tensions from influencing the group's climate. The agency's weekly meetings were marked by uncomfortable pauses and evasions of pressing issues. Relationships became cautious and artificial; authority relations were also ambiguous because two important members

were reluctant to talk to each other and fought over small issues.

Finally, at one tension-filled meeting, another member, Karen, openly stated that she felt uncomfortable and that she wanted to talk about Joe and Juanita's problems and their effect on the group. In the ensuing discussion, many issues and feelings emerged. Members were relieved to talk openly, and both Joe and Juanita were able to unburden themselves and get support from the group. The tension between Joe and Juanita did not subside as a result of Karen's intervention (in fact, it continued until Joe left the agency), but the group's climate improved markedly and members were better able to cope with their co-workers' relationship problems.

Discussion Questions
- *What were the risks Karen took?*
- *Why do you think the overall climate improved despite these risks?*

sion at which one member would venture a favorable comment or joke about the group. In cases where others responded with more favorable comments or followed up on the joke, the group generally developed an open, inclusive climate. When people let the favorable comment drop, the group usually took a much longer time to develop cohesion, if it did so at all. Timing is vital; if the critical moment passes, it is gone and there may not be another chance.

Along with timing, *salience is also important.* The move must hold the parties' attention if it is to serve as a watershed. The student's attack on the brown-bag lunch speaker captured the attention of other people; thereafter, they were reacting to the student's move and their reactions reinforced the tension his statement originally interjected. There are many ways of enhancing the salience of a move—including raising the volume of one's voice, using colorful or symbolic language, being dramatic, or saying something surprising. Used properly, these tactics increase the probability that the move will prove effective.

The Expanding Printing Company

Imagine yourself as an employee of this company: What fears might you have of having consultants come in to assess the organization's climate?

A small but prosperous printing company had been experiencing tremendous growth in a relatively short period of time. New equipment, expanded services, new employees, and expansions in sales territories and clients were just some of the changes that accompanied this growth. Older employees noticed a gradual change in the working climate in the company. What had once been a playful, relaxing atmosphere had quickly become somber and tense, at least in the eyes of several outspoken critics of the changes. Open conflicts became more frequent. For the first time, employees began to hold informal gripe sessions. Verbally aggressive behavior among employees was no longer kept behind closed doors. Perplexed, the company's president turned to a team of communication consultants to assess the situation and recommend strategies for improving the climate.

The consultants conducted in-depth interviews with the president and a select number of employees to discern their perceptions of the company. This interview process was guided by a series of questions geared toward understanding the working climate—for example: (1) What kind of people work here? (2) Do people respect each other? (3) How do they show respect or disrespect? (4) Describe the leadership in this organization. (5) How are decisions made in the company? (6) What types of conflicts surface with regularity? (7) How does information travel through the company? (8) What role does the grapevine play in disseminating information?

After reviewing the information obtained through these interviews, the consulting team elected to survey the entire organization with a self-report instrument measuring sixteen dimensions thought to be important to the working climate. Dimensions, such as work space, performance standards, managerial structure, job pressure, and employee morale, were assessed through this instrument. Within days of administering the survey, the consultants led a "town meeting" to report the results.

The meeting allowed employees to share opinions about the change openly and to compare perceptions. Key issues uncovered through the interviews and the climate measure were raised and discussed. Although the president of the company resisted competing views at first, she soon began to listen and inquire about the employee feedback. With the help of the employees, the consulting team had identified three issues central to the company's climate.

First, employees believed that the expectations and standards for performance were too low, especially for new recruits. The president was flabbergasted. The employees wanted higher performance standards for everyone—something she thought could never occur without a fight. Second, the group perceived a threat to the physical surroundings. They were worried that new equipment and expansion in the same physical space would create poor working conditions. Third, many employees felt that the opportunity to participate in decisions was reduced as more employees were added. This resulted in frustration and struggles over many of the new decisions passed along during the recent changes. The consultants, the president, and the employees drafted a set of policy and procedural changes that addressed these and other issues. A follow-up survey a few months later reflected a much healthier organization, a company with a working climate described in one report as "robust."

Discussion Questions

- *Were consultants necessary in this case?*
- *What kinds of things, if any, could the president have done to "manage" the climate of the organization effectively during this period of time?*
- *Imagine yourself as the consultants. Why would you take the approach that you did, and ask the questions that you did?*

Finally, a party who aspires to create a critical incident should have *credibility and respect* in the eyes of other people. The actions of a respected group member, for example, are likely to receive attention from others and therefore have a good chance to influence the interaction. In addition, making an effort to change climate can be interpreted as manipulation; moves of a respected and trusted member are unlikely to be rejected as self-serving.

Of the three approaches for changing climate, creating a critical incident is the most uncertain. It is difficult to do, and it has the potential to backfire—others may reject the person who attempts to maneuver the climate. When effective, however, the critical incident tactic gets results quickly and it can be initiated by a single person. Small, cumulative changes and open discussion are more certain to work but also have problems. Small changes operate piecemeal through day-to-day interaction; it is easy therefore to lapse back into old patterns. To use this technique successfully requires a clear sense of purpose and patience. It does not work quickly and is of limited utility in situations where climate is causing an immediate crisis in a social unit or relationship. Open discussion works much more quickly than cumulative change, but it can add fuel to a conflict by introducing a new issue: People satisfied with the present climate may side against those who are dissatisfied. The emotions associated with discussions of power relations or supportiveness may generalize to the conflict and intensify disagreements on other issues. In using any of the approaches discussed here, it is important to be aware of possible problems and take measures to circumvent them.

Creating Constructive Climates

To this point, a discussion of any sort of "ideal" climate has been studiously avoided because the complexity and diversity of climates needed to be emphasized. However, several writers have described an "ideal climate" that is likely to lead to productive conflict management. The most famous description comes from an article by Jack R. Gibb titled "Defensive Communication" (Gibb 1961). He addresses the problem of how to create a climate that prevents defensive behavior. To define this climate, Gibb contrasts two types of climates: defensive and supportive. A *defensive climate* is one in which parties perceive or anticipate threats. A defensive person devotes a great deal of energy to protecting himself or herself and focuses on defeating the other. Defensiveness prevents one from listening fully to others' messages. The defensive person often distorts or misinterprets messages to confirm his or her own sense of threat and danger. Moreover, defensiveness causes the person to behave in a way that makes others defensive too. Gibb comments that "defensive behavior, in short, engenders defensive listening, and this in turn produces postural, facial, and verbal cues which raise the defense level of the original communicator" (p.141). Conversely, a *supportive climate* tends to produce accurate communication and to reinforce supportive behavior in others. Producing a supportive climate gives a conflict its best chance to move in a productive direction.

All this should sound pretty familiar in light of earlier discussions. However, Gibb takes this one step further and describes how to communicate in order to produce a supportive, as opposed to a defensive, climate. He discusses six categories of behavior on which defensive and supportive climates contrast.

According to Gibb, a defensive climate is produced by communication that is *evaluative,* whereas a supportive climate is encouraged by *descriptive* language. For example, an evaluative statement—"You are messy and inconsiderate!"—might be reframed as the descriptive message—"Your things were scattered around the living room this morning." No one likes to be judged, and evaluative language implies judgment. Once a judgment is made, the one judged cannot try to reason with it; it is final. The only option is to reject the judgment, thereby erecting barriers between the parties. Evaluation also implies that the communicator does not grant legitimacy to the person's arguments or position. By contrast, descriptive language leaves the field open for discussion. The one judged can explain that the room is not really cluttered by his or her standards.

Descriptive statements tend to open up dialogue, whereas evaluative statements tend to close off communication, leaving resistance or avoidance as the primary options. The wording of statements plays an important role in determining whether they are evaluative, but nonverbal communication is also important. As Gibb (1961, p. 142) puts it:

> Anyone who has attempted to train professionals to use information-seeking speech with neutral affect appreciates how difficult it is to teach a person to say even the simple "Who did that?" without being seen as accusing. Speech is so frequently judgmental that there is a reality base for the defensive interpretations which are so common.

A second type of characteristic of communication that encourages defensiveness is that it is *controlling;* speech that attempts to control often fosters resistance, especially in conflict situations. This can be contrasted with supportive communication, which is more **problem oriented.** Rather than trying to get someone to do what the speaker wants, *problem-oriented* messages try to define a problem on which both can work. So instead of saying "Stop talking so loudly!" which attempts to tell the other what to do, we might say, "You are talking too loudly and this is making it hard to hear Jack," which designates this as a problem to be dealt with. The accused can dispute the definition of the problem, or explain why he is talking loudly, or apologize, but the choice is left to him based on the way the statement is phrased. Of course, the history of a relationship influences whether a statement will be taken as controlling or not. Even statements phrased in a problem-oriented fashion may be perceived as controlling if one person has used them to manipulate the other in the past.

Third, defensive climates are promoted by statements that seem *strategic.* Supportive climates are promoted by *spontaneous* messages. "When the sender is perceived as engaged in a stratagem involving ambiguous and multiple motivations, the receiver becomes defensive" (Gibb 1961, p. 145). If a message that seems to be a sincere request on the surface is really a tactic to get us to do something we would not otherwise want to do, we are likely to react defensively. Deception promotes reaction. On the other hand, if "what we see is what we get"—if the other is sincere and open—then one is likely to respond more spontaneously as well. People are not always reluctant to give others what they want, but they may be reluctant to be forced to do so.

A fourth speech characteristic that creates defensiveness is apathy toward us by the other. If another's speech is *neutral,* it often conveys the message that they do not care about us. On the other hand, *empathetic* speech styles, which indicate true concern for others, promote supportive climates. To create a supportive climate it is important to acknowledge the legitimacy of others' emotions and needs—to empathize with them. This does not imply agreement with others' demands, merely acceptance of them as real, legitimate concerns.

Defensiveness can also result when others' messages convey a sense of *superiority* in position, power, wealth, intelligence, family background, education, or physical attributes. Gibb reasons that such statements cause defensiveness because they cause the listener to "center upon the affect loading of the statement" rather than its content. "The receiver then reacts by not hearing the message, by forgetting it, by competing with the sender, or by becoming jealous of him" (Gibb 1961, p. 147). To promote a supportive climate, it is important that sender and receiver perceive common ground, a shared, problem-solving relationship. Communication should convey *equality* between the parties. Although differences may exist between sender and receiver, it is important to attach little importance to them in the situation.

Finally, defensiveness is encouraged by messages that seem *certain* and dogmatic. Statements that assert they are the final word on an issue leave others with little control over the interaction and may provoke resistance. Anyone who has talked in a dogmatic "know-it-all" way has experienced the reactions to certainty that create a defensive climate. Messages that convey the attitude that one is willing to experiment with ideas and to change one's position are more likely to create a supportive climate. So ideal messages should have a *provisional* quality. Rather than saying "You are always late for meetings," it may be better to say something like, "It seems like you've been late quite a bit lately." A less absolute and more provisional message encourages others to think over your comment and leaves room for a constructive response.

It is difficult to ensure that our communication style avoids the six characteristics of defensive communication and fits the six characteristics conducive to supportive climates. Most of us habitually communicate in ways that provoke defensiveness, but a more supportive style can be learned. To start, you might try to write down what you said in a case when someone else became defensive and evaluate this according to the six categories. Think of how you might rephrase your comments in a more supportive fashion. There is no guarantee that adopting a supportive communication style will cause others to be supportive as well; however, it offers the best chance for success and is well worth trying.

Summary and Review

What is climate?

Climate captures the overall feel of the situation for parties. It is experienced in common by members of a team or dyad and is a product of interaction. It also influences interaction because it shapes the attributions parties make about each other, their predictions about how interaction will unfold in the situation, and the behaviors they engage in.

How can we describe the climate in a social unit or interpersonal situation?

Climate can be described in terms of themes that express beliefs and feelings about the social unit and its leading problems or concerns. The four major categories of themes discussed are those that (1) concern dominance and authority relations, (2) relate to the supportiveness that people show toward one another, (3) express the team's or dyad's sense of its own identity, and (4) concern the type of interdependence among members. These general categories do not exhaust the variety of possible conflict themes, but they do represent the areas most commonly found in climate analyses.

How does climate affect conflict interaction?

Climate shapes interaction by facilitating parties' prediction of how the episode will unfold and their interpretations of others' words and deeds. Through this, it influences how parties act. As we saw in Chapter 2, interpretations are also influenced by attribution processes, which tend to favor competitive over cooperative orientations. It is important to understand the influence of attribution processes because they make it more difficult to establish a cooperative climate and tend to dampen the impact of cooperative climates.

How does interaction affect climate?

Climates are the product of interaction. Climatic themes shape conflict interaction, and conflict interaction moves in a cyclical fashion to shape climates. This multiplier effect can set climates in place by influencing parties to act in a way consistent with the climate, thus reproducing the climate. However, this same cycle leaves an opening for those who would like to change the climate. Changes in interaction and critical incidents can alter climates by creating new behavioral precedents and by making parties aware of undesirable ruts into which the team or dyad may have fallen. Changes in interaction set up new expectations for the future and raise new issues that may persist and change the climate if sustained by people's actions.

Climate and interaction influence each other on several levels. At the most elementary level, climate influences individual actions, which in turn have a role in building climate. At a second level, influences on one climate theme can spread to other themes, insofar as these are connected (for example, parties' feeling of safety may be connected to how they think power will be used in the situation). Third, a temporary climate may overshadow the general prevailing climate of an organization. For example, a sharp fight may break out in a generally cooperative organization, temporarily creating a competitive climate with little supportiveness for people.

What are some tips for identifying climates?

Climates are best identified by observing an entire social unit or dyad for an extended period of time. This observation should focus on their interactions because this is where climates are enacted. The four categories of climate themes suggest what to look for in interaction. Themes that constitute climate are often found through identifying the metaphors used in a group. Finally, your own feel of or intuition about the climate is a useful guide. Climates are often felt more than directly spelled out.

What can parties do to change a climate?

At least three things can be done to change climates. First, undertake small changes in interaction; if parties are persistent and consistent in these changes, they often generalize to change the climate as a whole. A second tactic is to discuss troubling themes openly. When troubling aspects of climate are surfaced, parties often realize that they were all bothered by them and can then act together to recreate the climate of the team or dyad. It is also useful to discuss the themes that are useful and constructive so that parties can continue building on them. A final option is to intentionally create a critical incident that alters the climate in "one fell swoop." This is a riskier strategy, but in some cases can be used to good effect.

How do we create a constructive climate?

A supportive climate is one in which people feel safe and valued. It can be contrasted to a defensive climate in which parties perceive threats to their interests and identities and do not feel valued. Supportive climates can be created through communication that is: descriptive rather than evaluative, problem-oriented rather than controlling, spontaneous rather than strategic, empathetic rather than neutral, equal rather than superior, and provisional rather than certain.

Conclusion

On sheet music, composers describe the emotional tenor of the piece they have written in a short phrase above the first measure. Phrases such as "allegro agitato," "appasionato," or "tenderly" are instructions that tell the performer what mood the piece should convey to an audience. In some ways, climates are like these musical instructions. They do not specify the "notes," the specific behaviors members undertake; instead, they give an indication of the expected tone or temper for interaction. Climates reduce people's uncertainty about how to act and about how to interpret others' actions by providing a simple, general idea—a feel—of the situation and of whether things are right or wrong, appropriate or out of place. This is particularly important in the uneasy uncertainty of conflict; the general temper of the situation surrounding a conflict is a critical determinant of whether it takes a productive or destructive direction. A hostile, tense climate can make escalation inevitable; a cooperative climate can turn the same situation toward problem solving. As the "composer" of its own interaction, a social unit can change the instructions on how behaviors will be played out and interpreted. These shifts in climate come as the people hear their own changes in emotional pitch; they come to have a strong influence on the direction conflict interaction takes.

7 Doing Conflict: Strategies, Styles, and Tactics

What is the best way to handle conflicts? Should we stick to one approach, or be flexible? Should we let others have a say, or try to control the situation? Should we carefully plan how we will react, or improvise? And how do we avoid getting caught up in spiraling escalation or avoidance cycles?

A common recommendation is that we should try to plan a conscious *strategy* for the conflict. One example of strategic planning is when people rehearse what they are going to say. Along with the well-planned strategy would come carefully selected *tactics*—actions for carrying out the strategy. Although sound advice in general, this approach overemphasizes the degree to which anyone can plan interactions. The key to an effective strategy is the ability to control the situation. However, conflicts are the product of two or more parties' interaction, and often they move in quite different directions. In the face of the others' moves, it is often hard to stick to plans, even if we can remember them after someone has succeeded in flustering or upsetting us. Also, it is often difficult to determine which tactics will serve a given strategy. An openly belligerent approach, for example, can serve strategies of avoidance (by scaring the other so much that he or she avoids the conflict) or integration (by convincing the other that you are serious enough to want to fight over the issue), as well as forcing.

Rather than overemphasizing planning, it is more useful to work on mastering various styles of doing conflict. The notion of *style* emphasizes a consistent, specific orientation toward the conflict, an orientation that unifies specific tactics into a coherent whole, yet does not stress planning and foresight too much. Research indicates that people have characteristic conflict-handling styles, which they tend to apply regardless of differences in situations. You can, however, teach old dogs new tricks; people can learn new behaviors if they are aware of alternatives. Moreover, there is evidence that people change styles as disputes develop. Therefore, it is useful to consider conflict and negotiation styles as a repertoire of options that one can learn to apply.

There will always be an element of strategy in the selection of styles, but it is important to emphasize the emergent nature of conflict interaction. Interactions can take many directions, and about the best one can hope for is to be responsive to changes as a conflict unfolds. Of course this still leaves all of the original questions intact. How do we select an appropriate style? When should we change styles? What are the long-run consequences of various styles? How do we select the proper tactics to carry out styles?

It is also important to remember that strategies, or styles, are not the only things to which we have to attend. The development of conflicts is also shaped by individual actions or tactics. Many of us have experienced this firsthand: A conflict seems to be moving constructively, but then someone says "the wrong thing" and everything falls apart. Another example of this is when individual acts set up a cascade of escalation moves, creating the type of self-perpetuating conflict discussed in Chapter 1. So, you also need to consider tactics and their possible influence on conflict interaction.

Conflict Styles

To be able to choose conflict styles, it is important to know what they require and what their potential consequences are. This section describes conflict styles—their meanings, variations, and effectiveness; cultural and gender influences; and styles within organizations or social units. It specifies rules for shifting and selecting styles.

Describing Styles

To understand styles it is useful to consider some basic concepts that describe styles and their effects on the other party. Chapter 3 briefly described the five traditional conflict styles—competing, avoiding, accommodating, compromising, and problem-solving. It was noted that they can be distinguished along two dimensions: *assertiveness*—the degree to which the style attempts to satisfy the party's concerns with respect to the issues—and *cooperativeness*—the degree to which the style attempts to satisfy the other party's concerns. Four additional dimensions of style can be identified. Sillars, Coletti, Parry, and Rogers (1982) define *disclosiveness*—the degree to which a conflict style or tactic discloses information to the other party—as a basic dimension of conflict behavior. Disclosiveness is closely related to the maintenance of an open communication climate. Styles also differ in *empowerment*—the degree to which they grant the other party some control or power. Some styles hinge on the party's control of the situation, others share control between two parties, and others give control to the other party. Hence styles can have an effect on the balance of power and its impacts on conflicts, as discussed in Chapter 4. *Activeness* (Riggs 1983) represents the degree of involvement with conflict issues. Parties' activeness can range from very intense concern to apathy. Finally, styles can differ in *flexibility*—the degree of movement the party is willing to make in working out the conflict (Ruble and Thomas 1976; Riggs 1983). Some styles allow for considerable pliability in parties' positions, whereas others are quite rigid in their insistence that the initial position not be changed.

Thinking in terms of these six dimensions can clarify the differences among styles. The dimensions also help us link tactics to various styles because they can be used to classify tactics. The section on tactics later in this chapter discusses general sets of tactics in terms of these dimensions so that they can be matched to respective styles.

Each of the five styles introduced in Chapter 3 has a unique set of values on the six dimensions, as the bold headings in Table 7.1 show. So, for example, parties who adopt a competing style place a great deal of emphasis on their own concerns and little on those of the other party; they are not very disclosive or flexible; and they are highly involved in the conflict and attempt to maximize their control over the situation and to minimize control by others. Table 7.1 is a starting point for understanding the styles and the consequences of using them.

TABLE 7.1   Conflict Styles and Their Variants Rated on Six Dimensions

Conflict Style	Assertive	Cooperative	Disclosive	Empowerment		Active	Flexibility
				Other	*Self*		
Competing	High	Low	Low to moderate	Yes	No	High	Low
Forcing	High	Low	Low	Yes	No	High	Low
Contending	High	Low	Moderate	Yes	No	High	Moderate
Avoiding	Low	Low	Low	Varies	No	Low	Low to moderate
Protecting	Low	Low	Low	Yes	No	Low	Low
Withdrawing	Low	Low	Low to moderate	No	No	Low	Moderate
Smoothing	Low	Low	Moderate	No	No	Moderate	Moderate
Accommodating	Low	High	Low to moderate	Yes	No	Low	High
Yielding	Low	High	Low	No	Yes	Low	High
Conceding	Low	High	Moderate	No	Yes	Low to moderate	moderate to high
Compromising	Moderate	Moderate	Moderate to high	Yes	Yes	Moderate to high	Moderate
Firm compromising	Moderate	Moderate	Low to moderate	Yes	Yes	High	Moderate
Flexible compromising	Moderate	Moderate	Moderate to high	Yes	Yes	Moderate	Moderate
Problem-solving	High	High	Moderate to high	Yes	Yes	High	High

Much research has been directed to defining and measuring conflict styles. The articles in Putnam (1988) examine five different instruments designed to measure conflict styles: Hall's (1969) Conflict Management Survey, the Thomas and Kilmann (1974) Management-of-Differences (MODE) Survey, Rahim's (1983) Organizational Conflict Inventory-II, the Putnam and Wilson (1982) Organizational Communication Conflict Instrument, and the Ross and DeWine (1988) Conflict Management Message Style Instrument. Each of these instruments identifies somewhat different styles or dimensions underlying conflict, but in general their styles can be related to the five defined here. The instruments by Putnam and Wilson and Ross and DeWine specifically focus on communication behaviors in conflicts and are therefore of special interest.

As the plethora of measurement instruments suggests, there are several different ways to conceive of conflict styles. The following sections attempt to sort out several different interpretations of conflict styles.

The Meaning of Conflict Styles

Some writers, such as Filley (1975), define style as the way a person usually *responds to conflict.* In this view, styles identify types of people—the "tough battler," the "friendly helper," "the problem solver"—who are predisposed to handle all conflicts in the same way. This tradition has strongly influenced how the tests that measure a person's predominant style of conflict-handling behavior have been interpreted. Although the way the tests are scored allows people to fall under more than one style (for instance, people are often classified as compromisers and problem solvers), styles are interpreted as a relatively *stable aspect* of the individual's personality. Several studies have yielded evidence that people develop habitual styles of responding to conflict that are consistent across situations (Gormly, Gormly, and Johnson, 1972; Jones and Melcher 1982; Sternberg and Soriano 1984). This view is somewhat misleading, however.

Although people certainly develop habitual ways of responding to conflict, they also have a capacity to change or adapt their behavior from situation to situation. There is abundant evidence (Phillips and Cheston 1979) that people change their conflict behavior during the conflict process (Phillips and Cheston 1979; Sillars 1980b; Papa and Natalle 1989; Sambamurthy and Poole 1992). There is also evidence that more effective people are more flexible in their responses to situations (Hill 1973; Stogdill 1974; Phillips and Cheston 1979). In the larger view, an extensive body of research on personality traits has shown that they do not lead to consistent behavior in all situations (Mischel 1968; Endler and Magnusson 1976). Two recent studies (Jones and Melcher 1982) show very low correlations between conflict styles and personality traits such as dogmatism, deference, and Machiavellianism (manipulativeness). People can and do adapt and change, and denying this capacity through the assumption of fixed styles denies an important human potential.

Taught to large numbers of people this view could even be harmful. If people assume their styles are stable traits, they may not be motivated to change in order to break out of destructive patterns. If a supervisor assumes an employee is a tough battler and will always be one, he or she is likely to go into any disagreement with the employee with a belligerent "he's-not-going-to-run-over-me" attitude that greatly increases the possibility of destructive escalation. Alternatively, the supervisor may just give in to avoid the employee's wrath but later resent this act of submission. Neither response is a good one; not only do both responses increase the probability of destructive conflict and bad decision making, but they also deny the worker's ability to change. Assuming that the other person is inflexible may discourage parties from trying different approaches. The anticipatory attack of the boss may make the employee respond as a tough battler as a defense, even though he would actually have preferred to discuss the issue quietly. Expectations about "how people are" too easily turn into self-fulfilling prophecies that can lead individuals to act toward people in ways that cause others to respond with the undesirable but expected behaviors. The attitudes freeze others into a mold that prevents the flexible and responsive behavior needed for effective conflict management. This problem is compounded when people believe they themselves have a characteristic personal style. "I'm a battler," they say and assume they cannot or do not have to be flexible because "that's just the way I am." Thus, conflict training programs and tests that purport to identify "characteristic styles" may escalate the very conflicts they are intended to help. People do fall into habits, but they can also change.

A second view of style turns away from personal characteristics and defines styles as *specific types of conflict behavior* (Cosier and Ruble 1981). In this view, any behavior intended to defeat the other (for example, making a threat) is competitive, while a behavior designed to achieve a mutually acceptable solution (for example, restating the conflict in problem-oriented terms) is collaborative. The styles refer to categories of behavior, not types of people. This definition is an improvement over the previous one because it neither assumes nor encourages inflexibility. However, it too has a problem: The same behavior can fall under different styles. A threat, for example, can be classified under competing, but it could also be classified under avoiding if it were intended to keep an opponent from raising a conflict ("I'll leave if you bring that up again"). Postponing a conflict is often advocated as a problem-solving tactic because it gives both sides a "cooling off" period, but it can also be an avoidance tactic if used persistently. An offer to "split the difference" is certainly a compromise, but it can also be accommodating if what one is offering is of little value and he or she did it simply to avoid losing. There is a good deal of truth in the definition of styles as behaviors, but another interpretation offers a more accurate conception of styles.

The third, and most useful, position defines styles as *behavioral orientations* people can take toward conflict (Thomas 1975). In this view, a style is a general expectation about how the conflict should be approached—an attitude about how best to deal with the other party. A competing style is oriented toward defeating the other, toward achieving one's own goals without regard for others, and it dictates certain behavioral choices to achieve these ends. A problem-solving style reflects an orientation toward mutual benefit; it favors moves that enhance cooperation and creative thinking toward this end. The definition of styles as orientations solves the problem of classifying specific behaviors under one style or the other—the same tactics can serve different intentions and attitudes. Moreover, this definition is true to the observations showing that people exhibit definite, consistent strategies, or thrusts, during conflicts without denying their capacity to change. Choosing an orientation is making a decision about the principles that will guide one through the conflict; it is choosing the degree to which people will be cooperative and/or assertive.

According to this definition, behavioral strategies and general orientations are bound up with each other because behaviors are not meaningful outside the context of the style they represent. So the behavior of postponing the conflict can be seen in one way if it is part of a problem-solving style and in another if the party is avoiding. Although Conrad (1991) usefully discusses the distinction between behavioral strategy and styles, it does not seem possible to draw a clean line, as he tries to do. This book has chosen to emphasize that *strategy is a planned sequence of behaviors,* whereas *style is a general orientation* that does not require explicit behavioral planning.

The ultimate problem with this definition (or with any definition of style for that matter) is its focus on the individual. Style refers to the *orientation of the individual* during conflict; it reflects one person's approach independent of the other person. Certainly, any action starts with an individual's behavioral choices. However, in the long run, it is inaccurate to stay at the level of the individual. The interlocking actions of all parties must be taken into account. Styles represent the "mind-sets" that parties have in the conflict, but what another person does often changes one's attitudes and intentions, often without the individual realizing it. Someone may go into a disagreement with a firm intention to problem solve, but if the other person betrays, or viciously attacks, or refuses to talk about the conflict at all, it is difficult to keep on problem solving. The other's reactions make one want to defend oneself, or strike back, or scream in exasperation, or withdraw completely. Whatever the response and reaction to that response, it makes no sense to talk of strategies or styles as if they were independent of another's actions. Conrad (1991) summarizes substantial evidence that the actual behaviors people engage in during conflicts differ from how they expect to behave. He attributes this largely to the influence of others' behavior.

In line with this concern with style as behavioral orientations that interact with others' orientations, gerunds have been used to name each style because the "-ing" form indicates the *active process* involved in using a style. Styles are not something people simply put on and forget about, but something they must perform. Descriptions of styles will refer to the parties who carry out styles with the "-er" or "-or" suffix—a party using *competing* will be called a *competer;* a party using *accommodating,* an *accommodator;* and so on. This is purely for ease of expression and not because the styles are perceived as traits of the people who use them.

Variations on Conflict Styles

Riggs (1983; see also Savage, Blair, and Sorenson 1989) suggests that there may be variations on styles that are consistent with the general orientation but represent different ways of carrying out the style. This is illustrated in Figure 7.1, which shows the five styles not as single points but as regions on the graph. So, for example, a supervisor using a competing style may "pull out all the stops" and push for his own goals, showing no concern at all for his staff, or he may use his authority to gain staff members' compliance but acknowledge their feelings and explain the necessity for his orders. These are very different ways of carrying out a competing style, and they are likely to have different consequences for the supervisor's future relationship with the staff. In general, styles take a limited range of values on each of the six dimensions rather than a single value. As we turn now to defining styles, it is important to try to identify variations (refer to Table 7.1 on page 215 for styles and their primary variants).

Competing.   This style is marked by a primary emphasis on satisfying the party's own concerns and disregard of others' concerns. It is a closed style, low to moderate in disclosiveness; parties make their demands apparent but often hide their true motives and any other information that might weaken their position. Competers are quite active and highly involved in the conflict. Competers aggressively pursue personal goals, taking any initiatives necessary to achieve them. Flexibility is generally low in the competing style. Competers attempt to avoid sacrificing any goals, instead using any effective means to compel others to satisfy their concerns. This requires that competers attempt to control the situation and deny others power or control. A notable exception exists when competers are working *within a team* against another team. Competitive people can be surprisingly flexible and cooperative with their teammates when engaged in a competition with an outside group (Carnevale and Probst 1997).

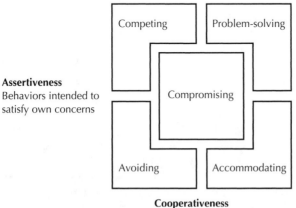

FIGURE 7.1   **Styles as "Regions" on the Graph**

There are two major variants of the competing style. In *forcing*, parties exhibit very low flexibility and disclosiveness and simply try to get others to go along with them by virtue of superior power. There is no expression of concern or understanding for the other's position, nor any effort to build or to preserve a future relationship. The silent treatment described by Baxter, Wilmot, Simmons, and Swartz (1993) is also a type of forcing intended to wear others down and compel them to deal with issues on the individual's terms. *Contending* is a "softer" form of competing. A contending style is somewhat flexible, as long as flexibility does not threaten to prevent the party from attaining his or her goals (Pruitt, Rubin, and Kim 1994), and is also moderately disclosive. Contenders may try to explain why they are compelling others and express understanding and sympathy for others' feelings. A contending style is concerned with future relationships.

Research indicates that using authority to compel others to accept a resolution to a conflict is more effective if the superior explains why the decision was made (Phillips and Cheston 1979). Bies, Shapiro, and Cummings (1988) add that the explanation must be based on "objective" factors, such as company norms or budget constraints, rather than on the superior's preferences. This suggests that contending may be more effective than forcing in long-term working relationships. However, forcing is less time-consuming than contending, and it does not require the effort of maintaining a good relationship with others; in some cases, this may be a low priority.

In general, competing styles tend to be selected by people when the outcomes of conflicts are important to them and when achieving an agreement through other means seems unlikely (Phillips and Cheston 1979). Competing, especially forcing, is often advantageous when there is pressure to come to a resolution quickly, because competers can push their own agendas through. However, when employing a competing style, it is important to bear in mind that it may create resentment that leads to resistance later on. This may be a significant problem if the cooperation of others is critical in implementing a decision. Moreover, as noted in Chapter 4, use of a power resource in competing may ultimately undermine one's power base.

Avoiding.   Parties who avoid conflict show low levels of concern with both their own and other parties' concerns. Avoiding prevents these concerns from being aired and addressed. There is, of course, one exception: When parties use avoiding to get out of conflicts they fear they will "lose." But even in this case, issues remain unresolved and can resurface in the future. Avoiders choose a low level of activeness, sometimes bordering on apathy. They exhibit a low level of disclosiveness as well, because avoiding prevents parties from communicating about concerns or positions. An avoiding style varies in terms of the party's level of control, but it attempts to disempower others by denying them the possibility of dealing with the conflict.

The first variation of avoiding is protecting. The *protecting* style emerges when parties are determined to avoid conflict at all costs. They are so concerned that the conflict will surface that they build a shell around themselves, and in some cases they respond to attempts to raise an issue with a strong counterattack designed to warn others off. A protecting style involves very low activeness and flexibility: Protectors do not want to work with the conflict at all and will accept no attempts to surface the conflict. Protecting is also very low in disclosiveness, except for the information that the party is determined to avoid conflict. Protectors' motives for avoiding generally remain hidden. A softer version of avoiding is withdrawing. In *withdrawing*, parties work to keep issues off the table, but they are somewhat more flexible than with the protecting style. Withdrawers may be apologetic, or address some aspects of the issues while avoiding others. They may find ways to change the subject or to leave the conversation, but these will not carry warnings. Withdrawing is more subtle and flexible than protecting. A third variation of avoiding is *smoothing*, in which the party plays down differences and emphasizes issues on which there is common ground. Issues that might cause hurt feelings or arouse anger are avoided. In essence, smoothing tries to emphasize the positive, to keep the topic on subjects that will take up the time that could be spent on conflict.

Avoiding styles may be useful if chances of success with problem-solving or compromising are slight and if parties' needs can be met without surfacing the conflict. For example, avoidance has been shown to improve team effectiveness by eliminating a distraction that would otherwise derail progress on an issue (deDreu and Van Vianen 2001). Avoiding can also be effective if the party has a very weak position or faces a formidable opponent. It may enable him or her to save face. However, avoiding leaves the issues behind the conflict unaddressed, and they may fester and eventually surface with destructive consequences. Wall and Nolan (1987) report that an avoiding style led to relatively low satisfaction among students describing their conflicts. Avoiding can become destructive if issues are skirted—"walking on eggs" by mutual agreement. Avoiding can also impede development of relationships. As noted in previous chapters, successfully dealing with a conflict can enhance relationships and increase mutual knowledge.

Protecting, in particular, may incur all the disadvantages associated with forcing. It can anger others and encourage them to compete because it has a surface resemblance to competing. Protecting has an advantage over withdrawing in that it is not likely to make one seem vulnerable, whereas withdrawing may. However, withdrawing and smoothing are more likely to promote a good relationship with other parties than protecting does. All three variations can be frustrating for a party who sees the conflict as important.

Accommodating.   An accommodating style permits others to realize their concerns but gives less attention to the party's own concerns. Accommodators basically give in to others. Often this is designed to improve a bad or shaky relationship or to preserve a good one, especially when the issue is less important than the relationship. Accommodators are highly flexible; they are willing to accede to the other's demands and to change their own positions. Accommodators' level of activeness is low because they are not involved in the issues per se, but rather in their relationships with others. Accommodating involves a low to moderate level of disclosiveness; accommodators learn much about others' positions and concerns but generally disclose little about their own. Accommodators generally empower the other party and suspend their own control; they "go with the flow" of others' agendas. There are two variations of accommodating: yielding and conceding.

In *yielding* parties exhibit apathy toward the conflict, show no concern with their own needs, and accommodate others entirely. Yielders are very high in flexibility and very low in activeness. They allow the other to control the situation and to define the outcomes of the conflict. The passivity of yielding does not encourage others to be concerned with the relationship. Yielders disengage themselves from the situation and go along with what others want. A "firmer" version of accommodation is conceding. In *conceding* the party still accommodates others' concerns but is more involved in the conflict. Conceders maintain contact with the issues and accommodate in order to build a better relationship with others. Conceders have a mixture of motives, including real concern for others and a tactical concern for building a relationship that may be useful in the future. Conceding generally is higher in disclosiveness than yielding because conceders are more involved in the conflict and others become aware of their willingness to build relationships.

Accommodating is a useful strategy when one is more concerned with future relationships with others than with the issues behind a conflict. Skillfully employed, an accommodating style can convey the party's understanding of others' needs, improving relationships. Withdrawing and smoothing are more effective than yielding in doing this. Accommodating is also useful when one party is weaker than another and will lose in any competition. The other party may take accommodating as a sign of weakness. This may encourage the other to take a more competitive approach on the assumption that he or she fears confrontation. The complementary relationship of dominance and submissiveness is quite common (Millar and Rogers 1987). Once such a pattern develops, breaking it may require considerable effort.

Compromising.   This style has moderate levels of assertiveness and cooperativeness because it requires both parties to give up some of their needs to fulfill others. Compromising attempts to find an intermediate position or trade-off through which parties can achieve some important goals in exchange for foregoing others. Compromisers are moderate to high in activeness: In some cases, a great deal of energy and involvement are required to arrive at an acceptable compromise, while in other cases parties settle for compromise because finding an optimal solution seems unlikely. Compromising is in the moderate range of flexibility because compromisers are flexible enough to give in on some of their demands, but not so flexible that they will rework their positions to allow problem-solving or accommodating. Compromising involves moderate to moderately high disclosiveness: Compromisers let others know what they are willing to trade and their evaluations of other positions, but they do not always explain the reasoning or needs that underlie their offers. Compromisers attempt to empower both themselves and others because shared control is essential to the give-and-take necessary for compromise.

One variation is *firm compromising,* which offers trade-offs but exhibits limited flexibility of position and low to moderate disclosure. In this case, compromisers push other parties somewhat, showing a rather tough approach designed to motivate them to cooperate, hopefully on the compromiser's terms. Firm compromisers are highly involved in the conflict, working actively and taking the lead in hammering out the compromise. A somewhat more cooperative variation is *flexible compromising;* flexible compromisers have less well-defined positions than their firm kin. They exhibit moderate to high disclosure because sharing thoughts and positions is an important requirement for the evolution of compromises from flexible positions. Flexible compromisers may be less actively involved in the conflict, in some cases following others' initiatives.

The compromising style is often confused with the problem-solving style (Cosier and Ruble 1981). Trade-offs and exchanges are many people's idea of integrative behavior (Putnam and Wilson 1982). In many cases—especially those in which there are two equally strong parties who are locked in an impasse—compromises are the best that can be achieved. As Filley (1975) notes, however, compromises often attain a low level of commitment from parties because they force them to give up something they value. With the satisfaction of achieving some goals comes the bitterness of having to give up others. This does not happen with the problem-solving style, which tries to find solutions that meet everyone's needs.

Problem-Solving. This conflict style has received the most attention because its goal is to develop a solution that meets all of the important needs of both parties and does not lead to any significant disadvantages. This is a tall order, and it is doubtful that any problem solvers achieve this goal, but they generally believe they have done so. In part this may be due to the fact that the parties redefine their goals during the integrative process, emphasizing those that are achievable. Following successful problem solving, people are generally pleased and often enthusiastic about the resolution; this can promote implementation of the solution. It is exhilarating to discover a creative solution through joint effort. Parties learn about themselves and new possibilities open up for the future.

Burke (1970) lists a number of characteristics of the problem-solving style:

1. Both people have a vested interest in the outcome.
2. The people involved believe that they have the potential to resolve the conflict and achieve a better solution through collaboration.
3. Parties recognize that the conflict or problem is mainly in the relationship between the individuals, not in each person separately. Therefore, if the conflict is in the relationship, it must be defined by those who have the relationship. In addition, if solutions are to be developed, the solutions have to be generated by those who have the responsibility for seeing the solution work and making the relationship last.
4. There needs to be a concern with solving the problem, not accommodating different points of view. This process identifies the causes of reservation, doubt, and misunderstanding between the people confronted with conflict

and disagreement. Alternative ways of approaching conflict resolution are explored and tested.

5. People are problem-minded instead of solution-minded, taking fluid instead of fixed positions. Both people together search out the issues that separate them. Through joint effort, problems that demand solution are identified and later solved.

6. There is a realization that both aspects of a controversy have potential strengths and potential weaknesses. Rarely is one position completely right and the other completely wrong.

7. One needs to try to understand the conflict or problem from the other's point of view and from the standpoint of "real," or legitimate, needs that must be recognized and met before problem solving can occur. There is full acceptance of the other.

8. It is important to look at the conflict objectively rather than in a personalized sort of way.

9. One's own attitudes (hostilities, antagonisms) should be examined before interpersonal contact on a less effective basis has a chance to occur.

10. There should be an understanding of the less effective methods of conflict resolution, such as win–lose.

11. It is important to prevent face-saving situations. Allow people to "give" so that a change in one's viewpoint does not suggest weakness or capitulation.

12. People should try to minimize the effects of status differences, defensiveness, and other barriers to working together.

13. Everyone needs an awareness of the limitations of arguing or presenting evidence in favor of one's own position while degrading an opponent's position.

Problem-solvers are highly concerned with both their own and others' needs. They are very involved in the conflict, actively pursuing every issue to increase their understanding and probe possible integrative solutions. They are also flexible, not rigidly adhering to positions. However, this does not mean that problem-solvers give in to others: They are firmly committed to achieving their goals and do not sacrifice them. Problem-solving works best when parties have high aspirations for the outcome of the conflict, firmly insist that their goals and needs be satisfied, but are flexible about the means by which this is done (Pruitt 1981, 1983). Problem-solvers are also moderately to highly disclosive. Problem-solving requires a high level of information about the issues and about parties' needs, and this requires an open communication climate. Problem-solving also requires parties to share control over the emerging solution. Hence problem-solvers attempt to empower others while not sacrificing their own power bases. As noted before, this is most easily done when both parties have common power resources.

The problem-solving style is not without its problems. It requires a great deal of time and energy. Creativity is not easy, and parties may have to spend a considerable amount of time exchanging offers and ideas before an acceptable solution can be hammered out. So problem-solving tends not to work well in cases where there is little time or great pressure to act immediately. Parties' enhanced aspirations can also become an issue. In some situations, problem-solving can give greater advantage to a stronger party (Pruitt, Rubin, and Kim 1994). During the problem-solving process parties get their hopes up. If a problem-solving approach fails to deliver a timely solution, they may give up on the process and decide that only forcing or some other style can work. Indeed, people in a stronger position may make a show of problem-solving, set things up so that it fails, and then justify use of force with the argument that they "tried everything short of force."

Shifting Styles During Conflict Episodes

It is tempting to think of styles as more or less stable choices people make, but it is common for parties to change styles as conflict unfolds. Several studies have documented changes in conflict styles (Sillars 1980c; Papa and Natalle 1989; Conrad 1991). Case 7.1 illustrates several styles two women adopted during a protracted conflict.

Jill and Rachel use several different styles in this conflict. Jill starts with a forcing style during the kitchen incident and Rachel responds with the protecting remark, "Do whatever the hell you want!" As often happens after protecting, Rachel moves into a withdrawing style, giving Jill the silent treatment. This type of withdrawing also contains elements of competing, because the silent treatment is often used to punish others and "show them how upset I am." During this period Jill continues forcing, talking to the other roommates about how unreasonable Rachel is being. Finally, Jill shifts to a problem-solving style, telling Rachel that they have to talk. Rachel at first responds with protecting ("I didn't realize I was supposed to talk. Sorry.") Jill persists with problem-solving, trying to get Rachel to talk about the issue openly. Rachel goes along with her, and the two have an open discussion about their problems. The discussion does not resolve the issue, however, and it ends with a compromise: Both apologize and Rachel says that she thinks she can forgive Tina and Jill. However, this resolution is not wholly satisfactory—to Rachel, at least. She reports that she and Jill "have never been as close as they once were." In part, this is because Rachel and Jill do not work out a solution that addresses the sources of the conflict. Merely forgiving Tina and Jill is not the issue; Rachel wants Jill to spend more time with her, and it is not clear that Jill is willing to do that.

The styles each woman adopts change as the conflict unfolds. Shifts in styles are common when a conflict stretches over time. As the dialogue at the end illustrates, it is also possible to shift styles within a short discussion. If one style does not "work"—as the problem-solving style does not in the discussion between Rachel and Jill—parties often shift to a related style—compromising in this case. Another thing to notice is how Rachel shifts between protecting and withdrawing while remaining in the same overall style—avoiding. These shifts are common in the ebb and flow of conflict as parties bring issues to the fore and then back away from each other.

Selecting Conflict Styles

In choosing a conflict style, parties should consider several factors. First and foremost, consideration must be given to how effective the style is likely to be in the

CASE **7.1**

College Roommates

Imagine yourself as Jill: At what points in your interaction with Rachel did your style change?

Jill, Rachel, Connie, and Tina decided to room together during their sophomore year at college. Jill and Rachel, best friends, decided to share one bedroom, and Connie and Tina the other. After a couple of months Rachel noticed that Jill and Tina spent a great deal of time together, doing laundry together, fixing their hair in the same style, shopping together, going out. Rachel had little in common with Connie, and she was "a little hurt" that Jill had abandoned her.

More seeds for the conflict were sown right after Christmas break. Jill decided to try to lose some weight and went on an "oatmeal diet" in which her main food consisted of five bowls of oatmeal a day. Rachel did not think Jill needed to lose weight and teased her about her diet. Jill joined in the laughter and asked Rachel for nutrition advice. But Jill kept up her oatmeal regimen, and Rachel dropped the subject after about a week. During this time Jill and Tina continued to spend a lot of time together. Rachel reported being somewhat resentful because she had introduced Tina to Jill.

About a week later, Jill began to make sarcastic remarks whenever Rachel mentioned her diet. For example, Rachel walked into the kitchen and saw Jill standing and eating cottage cheese out of the carton. Rachel asked Jill if she was planning on eating the whole carton, and Jill replied harshly, "I will if I want to!" Rachel had meant this as a joke, but Jill's reply made her mad and she replied, "Do whatever the hell you want!" and walked out of the room.

Rachel gave Jill the silent treatment after the incident. Within earshot of Rachel, Jill complained about Rachel's behavior to the other two roommates. Rachel talked to Connie about the situation, but Connie did not offer much insight: She interpreted the whole conflict as a result of personal attacks between Jill and Rachel.

Rachel reported that she had decided to give up on her friendship with Jill. However, Jill felt differently and decided to confront the issue. Two weeks before spring term was over, Jill approached Rachel and told her that the two of them needed to talk. They went into the bedroom and closed the door. The following dialogue ensued:

JILL: What's going on between us?

RACHEL: I don't know. What do you mean?

JILL: I mean why won't you talk to me anymore? You won't even say "Good morning" to me when you walk past to go to the bathroom.

RACHEL: I didn't realize I was supposed to talk. Sorry.

JILL: Were you planning on not speaking to me for the rest of the year and leaving without ever seeing me again?

RACHEL: That was not what I meant to do . . . but I figured, why bother saying anything? Every time I open my mouth, I get a sarcastic remark back. I just didn't need that anymore, so I shut up.

JILL: I'm sorry, but I was hurt, and the way I handle it is by getting defensive and making sarcastic remarks. I didn't really mean to hurt you.

RACHEL: Well you did.

JILL: Well, you hurt me too, and I didn't know what to do.

RACHEL: How did I hurt you?

JILL: I didn't like it when you made fun of my eating habits, like eating oatmeal five times a day. I also didn't appreciate it when you would make fun of my exercising or my big butt. How would you like it if I started teasing you about your thighs?

RACHEL: Jill, I had no idea you were so upset about those remarks. Why didn't you tell me this a long time ago? It certainly would have saved a lot of hurt feelings and resentment.

JILL: I figured you would stop making them sooner or later. I thought you would realize you were hurting my feelings.

RACHEL: Jill, how could I? You were always going along with me and even making fun of yourself. Do you think if I had known I was hurting you I would have continued? I'm not that mean.

JILL: I know you're not, and I'm sorry I made so many rude remarks when I was hurt. I really want to get things straightened out between us. Doesn't our friendship mean anything to you anymore?

RACHEL: Yes, it means something to me, but I didn't think it meant anything to you. I've been feeling really hurt lately by your behavior with Tina. I feel like you guys just run off and forget that I even exist. You are always doing everything together without including me. I figured she was just more important to you than me. Therefore, I would just finish out the year and go home and let you two have each other. I felt like I wasn't needed anymore.

JILL: I feel bad that you felt this way. I realize I have been spending a lot of time with Tina, but you've been pretty busy with your boyfriend. I didn't think you had much time for me either.

RACHEL: Yes, I have been spending a lot of time with my boyfriend, but that doesn't mean I don't need your friendship too. We have been friends for quite a while, and it was hard for me to see you turn away like you did. I started spending so much time with my boyfriend because of that. Now, don't get me wrong. I realize what you and Tina have is special. However, that doesn't ease my pain at being rejected or excluded from everything you guys do.

JILL: I'm not rejecting you as a friend or picking Tina over you. It just so happened that Tina and I have a lot in common and we have fun together. This naturally leads us to spending more time together. We didn't really think you wanted to do everything with us.

RACHEL: You're right. I probably wouldn't have. But, I felt like you didn't need me for a friend at all anymore.

JILL: Well, you're wrong. I still value our friendship, and I hope we can keep it going.

RACHEL: I feel better for having talked it over, and I'm sorry for having hurt you.

JILL: I'm sorry too—I hope you can forgive Tina and me somehow.

RACHEL: I think I can.

Discussion Questions
- *Which of the moves or shifts in styles had the most impact on the ultimate direction this conflict took?*
- *Think of a conflict you have been involved in where the patterns of style changes were similar to the changes in this conflict.*

immediate situation. The effectiveness of styles will vary depending on the characteristics of the situation, which will be discussed shortly.

Second, parties should consider the long-term consequences of a style. Styles can improve or worsen relationships with others, and this may come back to help or haunt if parties must work with each other in the future. Then too, the styles that parties adopt may change them. If a style is used often enough, it becomes habitual. So a party who accommodates often may develop a reputation for so doing, and others may assume they can get what they want by competing. Repeatedly seeing themselves accommodating, parties may define themselves as relatively weak, ignoring their unique resources and setting up a self-reinforcing cycle of accommodating behavior. Over the long term, conflict styles shape definitions of self. A final long-term consequence is that two or more people may develop complementary styles that they fall into more or less automatically. For example, one person may engage in competing and the other in accommodating. In effect, the two people become prisoners of each other's style. Because it is rare for one style to be appropriate for all situations, this inflexible interdependence can prevent parties from meeting their needs and cause long-term problems.

Third, parties should consider the ethical implications of selecting a style. Although no single set of values can be applied in all conflicts, individuals should assess their own values with respect to the styles. Some people are uncomfortable with styles that do not take others into account; this would indicate a preference for problem-solving, compromising, and accommodating and a dislike for competing and avoiding. Others may believe it is very important to be assertive, favoring competing, problem-solving, compromising, and the more active forms of accommodating and avoiding. All styles involve value choices. Although style choice is discussed from a situational standpoint, ethical imperatives can override concerns with short- and long-term effectiveness.

Fourth, it is important to bear in mind that when parties enact a style, they may provoke responses from other parties. Others still have latitude to choose how they will respond, and in many cases they are attempting to be strategic too. However, Cosier and Ruble (1981) found that there was a tendency for people to reciprocate competing, compromising, accommodating, and problem-solving styles. This is particularly important in light of the tendency noted in earlier chapters toward matching and the development of nonproductive cycles of behavior.

Evidence on the Effectiveness of Conflict Styles

Several studies have evaluated the effectiveness of styles in various situations. Cummings (reported in Filley 1975) studied the consequences when pairs of different styles interact. Among other things, he found that competitive versus competitive styles generally resulted in stalemates in bargaining and that competitive versus collaborative styles led to mutual agreement in many cases, though the competitive person still won in more than fifty percent of the cases. In a related study of group decision making, Jones and White (1985) found that groups composed of problem-solvers were more effective in terms of task accomplishment, while groups composed of accommodators were less effective. In general, the more group members differed in their preference for the problem-solving style, the less effective the group was. This was not found for either competing or accommodating styles.

Phillips and Cheston (1979) compared the effectiveness of forcing (competitiveness) and problem-solving (collaboration) strategies in fifty-two conflict cases reported by middle managers. Managers used forcing twice as often as they used problem-solving but also reported more "bad" solutions with forcing than with

A Procedure for Selecting Conflict Styles

Building on existing evidence, we can propose a procedure for selecting conflict styles (Thomas 1975; Musser 1982; Ebert and Wall 1983; Savage et al. 1989). The procedure takes the form of a *decision tree*—a diagram that supports the selection of options based on answers to a series of questions. The diagram presents a question to someone and, based on the answer to this question, the party traces different branches of the tree, which lead to other questions and branches, and finally to a recommended style. In the conflict style decision tree shown in Figure 7.2, the party would have to answer a maximum of five questions to arrive at a style selection. The questions, as described next, are arranged in logical order, prompting the party to consider the factors that studies and common sense suggest are important.

   1. *How important are the issues to the party?* An importance dimension has long been used to define conflict styles (Thomas 1975; Pruitt, Rubin, and Kim 1994). If the issues are important, the decision tree indicates that the party should pursue "firm" strategies that focus on realizing the party's interests; that is, forcing, contending, firm compromising,

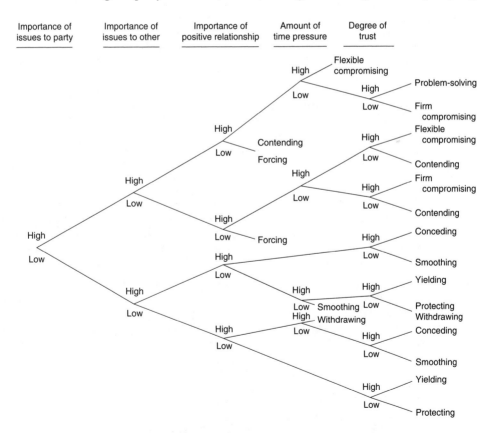

FIGURE 7.2   Style Selection Decision Tree

(continued)

Continued

flexible compromising, and problem-solving. If the issues are unimportant, however, less assertive strategies, such as yielding, conceding, smoothing, withdrawing, and protecting, are recommended because they can be less costly in time or energy.

2. *How important are the issues to the other?* This question reflects a second dimension in the classic conflict style diagram—concern for others. The decision tree assumes that if the issues are important to the other, each party will benefit most by choosing strategies that take the other into account; that is, flexible compromising, firm compromising, problem-solving, yielding, or conceding. If the issues are not important to the other, then it is more efficient to choose strategies that place less emphasis on the other's needs; that is, contending, forcing, protecting, withdrawing, or smoothing.

3. *How important is maintaining a positive relationship?* How conflicts are managed affects the long-term relationship between parties—their degree of trust and liking for each other and whether parties nurse grudges or hard feelings. In some cases, it is important to maintain a good relationship with the other. This is true when people must work together in the future, or when one may control or influence the other's fate at some future time. In this case, it would be best to choose styles that build, or at least do not undermine, trust and positive feelings; that is, flexible compromising, firm compromising, problem-solving, yielding, withdrawing, smoothing, conceding, and contending. In other cases, the party may be dealing with the other only for a short period.

Alternatively, a good relationship may be impossible to maintain, and the party may decide that the best that can be done is to keep a protective guard up by maintaining a more formal relationship with the other. The relationship between lawyers negotiating a divorce is an example of this. Both lawyers often try to maximize their clients' gains; there is little place for trust. Instead, they work on the basis of legal codes and professional practices that maintain decorum, foster progress on issues, and afford protection against cheating. In such cases, building or maintaining a relationship is not of concern and styles that do not show concern for the other may be adopted; that is, forcing and protecting.

4. *How much time pressure is there?* In cases wherein time pressure is great, the best course is to adopt styles that are not time-consuming; that is, forcing, contending, flexible compromising, protecting, withdrawing, or yielding. When there is little time pressure, more time-consuming strategies may be better because they can promote deeper exploration of issues; these include smoothing, conceding, firm compromising, and problem-solving.

5. *To what extent does one party trust the other?* Trust determines the degree to which one party is willing to let the other control the situation. When trust is high, styles that empower the other can be used, including problem-solving, flexible compromising, firm compromising, conceding, and yielding. When trust is low, styles that protect one's own power are safer; that is, forcing, contending, protecting, smoothing, and withdrawing.

Answering the five questions leads the party through the diagram to recommended strategies. It is important to note that these are the optimal strategies for each case under the assumptions reflected in the choice rules. Although the rules represent some of the best evidence available on conflict styles, they do not exhaust all factors one might consider. As the decision tree diagram shows, in some cases not all questions are applicable. For example, time pressure is not relevant in distinguishing some styles. Also, there are a few "twists" to the general rules, as when firm compromising is a "low" trust strategy compared to problem-solving in the very top branch of the tree. Although firm compromising is generally a trusting style, it protects the party relative to problem-solving and is recommended when trust is low and problem-solving is the other alternative.

To illustrate how the decision tree works, consider the following example:

> Jack is a foreman for an industrial cleaning company. He really enjoys his work and has been with the same company, Acme Cleanzit, for twelve years. Recently his boss was replaced by a younger woman, fresh out of business school. Jack's new manager, Ms. Jorgensen, graduated at the top of her class, and while in school worked for the branch of Acme Cleanzit in her college town. Jorgensen has lots of new ideas and is quite impatient to have them tried out. She tends to lean toward using her authority to force issues. She has hinted that she expects Jack to help her implement her ideas and that she might have to replace any problem employees. Jorgensen has the complete faith of top management at Acme, and Jack believes she will have management's backing in whatever she does.
>
> Jack sees a conflict on the horizon. Jorgensen wants to try new water-pressure cleaning equipment to replace the air-pressure equipment Acme Cleanzit has always employed. Jack has used water-pressure equipment in the past and does not like it. Although it cleans faster than air-pressure equipment, it breaks down easily and is somewhat dangerous to repair. He is afraid the rate of absenteeism and resignations will go up because the workers won't like the tedious process of repairing the new equipment. Still, when the water-pressure equipment works, it does increase productivity, so he must concede Jorgensen has a point. When he received her memo asking his input on water-pressure equipment, he wrote her a memo clearly outlining his objections. After Jorgensen received it, she brushed past him on her way out of the plant, saying, "We'll talk about this in the morning." It was clear to Jack that she was angry, and as he had a couple of beers with fellow workers Wilma and Joe, he found himself rehearsing what he would say to the manager the next day.

What Style Should Jack Choose?

In this case, the issues are important to Jack, so he should take the High branch of the tree. The issues are also important to Jorgensen, so again take the High branch. Unless Jack wants to lose his job, his relationship with Jorgensen should be highly important to him, so again, take the High branch. There is little time pressure, so the Low branch is most appropriate. Finally, it is not clear that Jack can trust Jorgensen, so the Low branch regarding degree of trust in the other is most appropriate, leading to the firm compromising style. This style encourages Jack to enter the discussion with clear and well-stated positions, and to demonstrate a willingness to move on views if he is truly convinced by Jorgensen; however, he should remain committed to having some of his important needs met, whatever the outcome of the discussions. This style takes the concerns outlined in the questions into account. Of course, other styles might also work, but they would not meet the criteria in the tree as well as firm compromising.

Consider a second example:

> Cindy and John have been married for three years. As with many married couples, some of their worst fights stem from seemingly simple issues, such as how to decorate their house. They are in the process of redoing their recreation room, and John really wants to put in wallpaper with a hunting motif. Cindy does not like the idea of looking at ducks and pointers while she plays cards and would rather have wallpaper with a modern design of some sort. However, she has found that with the right furniture any kind of wallpaper can look good, and she thinks she could probably live with ducks and dogs if it is really important

(continued)

Continued

to John. What is important to Cindy is that their relationship and their faith in each other not be undermined by incessant arguments over "little things." As they sit together at breakfast, John once again raises the issue of the hunting paper, this time a bit testily.

What Style Should Cindy Adopt?

The best answer in this case is conceding; it takes into account the importance of the issue to John, that it is not as important to Cindy, that their relationship is a high priority to Cindy, and that Cindy trusts John.

Some observations about the decision tree need to be considered. First, it is ambiguous in cases when some issues are important to the party, while others are not. The model confronts us with a dichotomous choice: It assumes issues are either important or they are not. In the common case where there are a number of issues, some important and some not, parties may try to switch styles when different issues are discussed, hoping to set up trade-offs. For example, if John adopts a firm compromising style when discussing his wallpaper and a conceding style when discussing furniture, Cindy may respond positively to his demands about wallpaper because she senses she can pick out furniture that will make even ducks and dogs look good. The combination of styles results in terms acceptable to both.

In applying the decision tree, it is also important to bear in mind that the answers to the questions may change over the course of the conflict. As emphasized throughout this book, conflict is an interactive process. As a result, earlier interactions can influence later ones. A party may begin a conflict episode with a firm conviction that her relationship with the other should be preserved, but as the conflict unfolds, she may find that she no longer wants a relationship with the other. If this happens, styles that were suitable at the outset of the conflict are no longer appropriate. It is important to monitor changing conditions to determine if conflict styles should change. It is also possible that a combination of two styles may be effective. Putnam (1990) summarizes considerable evidence that a mixture of competing and problem-solving styles is effective in inducing cooperation.

Finally, the decision tree procedure is useful because it is quite general and can apply to a wide range of conflicts. However, this also means the tree may be less useful in particular situations. Savage and associates (1989) and Ebert and Wall (1983) lay out decision trees for negotiation tactics specifically adapted to organizational negotiations. Musser (1982) describes a choice tree for subordinate responses to conflicts with superiors. These procedures are tailored to specific contexts and can be highly useful in their intended settings.

---

problem-solving (about half the incidents in which forcing was used had bad results, whereas all instances of problem-solving yielded "good" results). Phillips and Cheston concluded that both methods were effective, but under different circumstances.

Forcing was more successful when:

- There was one best solution to the problem.
- There was a value conflict between the manager and a subordinate.

■ The manager was fair and could give an objective explanation of his or her reasons for forcing a solution.
■ The ultimate outcome benefited the organization rather than one person or a small group.

Problem-solving was more successful when:

■ The parties were highly interdependent and had to work together in the future.
■ There was mutual awareness of the potential for conflict.
■ Those involved were open-minded.
■ There was a willingness to ignore power issues.
■ Formal procedures for problem-solving were available.
■ One or both people detected the conflict early and initiated problem-solving before things got bad.
■ People's attention was focused on solving a common problem rather than defeating or adopting one person's preferred solution.

In a pathbreaking study of organizational effectiveness, Lawrence and Lorsch (1967) found that problem-solving was endorsed as the most effective method of conflict resolution by managers in six different types of organizations. Competing was regarded as a useful backup behavior when problem-solving was not feasible or effective.

Burke (1970) found that engineering managers also chose problem-solving as the most effective method of conflict management, but they believed "smoothing" was a useful style too. Burke argues that it is a backup behavior to problem-solving. Forcing was rated as a poor way to manage conflict, as was withdrawing. Burke replicated the results for problem-solving and forcing with a mixed sample of about seventy managers from various companies.

There is considerable evidence that the outcomes of conflicts depend on the conflict styles employed by individuals and teams. Wall, Galanes, and Love (1987) found that open recognition and expression of conflict—as would occur in competing, compromising, and problem-solving—tended to increase the quality of solutions student groups arrived at. Jehn's (1995) study of work groups indicated that openness to conflict was associated with positive conflict outcomes. An experiment by Sambamurthy and Poole (1992) showed that open confrontation or conflict increased the ability of groups to achieve consensus. In a study of new product development teams in organizations, Lovelace, Shapiro, and Weingart (2001) report evidence that collaborative communication—as would occur in compromising and problem-solving—was associated with a team's innovativeness as rated by their managers. Several studies of negotiations provide evidence that collaborative approaches led to more mutually beneficial outcomes (Brett, Shapiro, and Lytle 1998; deDreu, Weingart, and Kwon 2000; Weingart, Hyder, and Prietula 1996).

In addition, there is evidence that conflict styles influence how people see themselves and others. Canary and Spitzberg (1990) found that a subject's perceptions of his or her competence and effectiveness in recalled conflicts were positively related to his or her use of integrative strategies and negatively related to competitive strategies. Moreover the other party's perceptions of the subject's competence and effectiveness were also positively related to the use of integrative strategies and negatively related to the use of competitive strategies.

Putnam and Poole (1987) summarize evidence that the earlier a conflict is brought out into the open, the more positive its outcome. Lovelace, Shapiro, and Weingart (2001) found that the ability of new product development teams to adhere to budgets and timelines depended on the ability of workers to express doubts and raise problems. However, Wall and Nolan (1987) found that the quality of the outcomes was not associated with whether a group surfaced a conflict or not.

However, styles that surface and openly acknowledge conflicts—problem-solving, competing, compromising—are not uniformly advantageous. One exception to the findings cited here is conflict in marriages and intimate relationships. Although many satisfied couples employ problem-solving, other satisfied couples opt for an avoiding style, consisting of "topic shifts, jokes, denial of conflict, [and] abstract, ambivalent, or irrelevant comments" (Sillars and Weisberg 1987, p. 147). The satisfied problem-solving couples endorse personal values of interdependence, openness, and sharing, whereas the avoiding couples value autonomy and discretion more highly.

An interesting twist to the results on avoidance is that avoiding also seems to be an effective response when the conflict is unimportant. Baxter (1982) found that students playing a classroom game often resorted to avoiding. This may well have been because they were not very involved in the issues behind the conflict.

Cultural and Gender Influences on Conflict Styles

The preceding points on stylistic effectiveness are limited to cultures that favor the confrontational model of conflict management. Indeed the subjects in most of the studies cited in the previous section were from American or British cultures. Research in other cultures, however, suggests that different styles would be effective for the harmony and regulative models discussed in Chapter 1. The harmony model emphasizes avoiding, accommodating, and compromising over other styles (Kozan 1997). Although problem-solving would be valued for its emphasis on the other and cooperativeness, the need to confront the conflict when solving problems would make members of harmony cultures less comfortable with problem-solving than with the three styles just mentioned. Research on conflict styles in different cultures is in its infancy, but evidence from studies of cultures with associative cognitive styles provides some support for this conjecture. Japanese subjects have been found to prefer avoiding or accommodating (Krauss, Rohlen, and Steinhoff 1984). Studies of Arab (Elsayed-Ekhouly and Buda 1996), Turkish (Kozan 1997), and Jordanian (Kozan 1991) subjects indicate that they prefer styles high in cooperativeness and concern for others over competition. Kim and Leung (2000) make a convincing case that the avoiding style has a fundamentally different, much more positive, meaning for people in harmony cultures than for people in confrontational cultures where most studies of avoidance have been conducted.

Parties using a regulative model would be predisposed either to avoiding or to competing in initial stages of the conflict and then to refer the conflict to some authority who resolves the conflict (Kozan 1997). As noted in Chapter 1, relevant authorities would include a superior in the organizational hierarchy, a ranking family member, or a judge using a set of rules or laws. Depending on how the authority proceeded, resolution could occur through compromise or problem-solving or through a flat decision by the authority. In cases when the authority determined that one party was right and one wrong, the losing party would accommodate.

Appropriate styles thus differ depending on whether a culture employs a confrontational, harmony, or regulative model of conflict management. However, it would also be a mistake to assume that cultures are uniform. Local conditions and particular situations can override the general tendencies of a culture. Fry and Fry (1997) found that two adjacent Zapotec communities in Mexico had very different styles of managing conflict. In San Andreas (a pseudonym), there were high levels of aggressive behavior, homicide, wife-beating, and use of physical punishment on children. In contrast, La Paz (also a pseudonym) emphasized tranquility, respectful behavior toward others, reasoning with children, and harmonious relations in the family. The two communities also had very different images of themselves: "The people of La Paz perceived themselves as tranquil and respectful, whereas the citizens of San Andreas more ambiguously complain about jealous, aggressive, troublemakers in their basically good community" (Fry and Fry 1997, p. 16). This study demonstrates that it is important to take local patterns and preferences into consideration, in addition to the more general culture.

The two genders have sometimes been likened to different cultures (Tannen 1990). However, research shows that—at least for conflict styles—there is less difference than we would presume. A number of studies have shown that males and females do not differ in terms of the tactics and styles they use in conflicts (Korabik, Baril, and Watson 1993; Kluwer, deDreu, and Buunk 1998; Watson 1994), though some have shown differences (Mackey and O'Brien 1998; Rubin and Brown 1975). So in practice, females are not necessarily more cooperative than males. However, the genders do differ in what is expected of them in conflicts. Twenty-five years ago, Rubin and Brown (1975) proposed that women use a different standard to interpret interaction than men. They proposed that men primarily focus on the task at hand, whereas women focus on the relationship between the parties. This explained the differences in women's and men's reactions to various types of experimental games noted in Chapter 3, especially with regard to competitiveness. As we noted there, because women are oriented more to interpersonal relationships, they tend to behave more cooperatively than men when first encountering another in an experimental game. However, once the other competes, women often begin competing more forcefully and consistently in reaction to what they perceive as a betrayal (Walters, Stuhlmacher, and Meyer 1998). Men, on the other hand, tend to be more experimental in the face of competition, trying cooperative bids in the hope of getting better task outcomes and resort to competition if these do not yield the expected benefits.

This difference in interpersonal orientation also may explain why women have been found to use styles that surface conflict more than men do. To maintain a good relationship, it is important to confront problems and work them out. Hence, women would focus more on problem-solving and (as a prelude to problem-solving) competing styles in interpersonal relationships than would men. As noted in Chapter 3, this also accounts for the finding that women and men tend to get bound up in the demand–withdraw cycle.

Although the differences in male and female conflict behavior are rather subtle, the expectations of men and women in U.S. society are clearly different, which may influence the effectiveness of styles. Whereas women may undertake competing styles during conflicts, they are evaluated more negatively than are men who compete (Korabik, Baril, and Watson 1993). This is in line with a more general finding that because women are expected to be "nice and supportive," when they behave assertively they violate social expectations and are perceived negatively by other men and women (Ivy and Backlund, 1994). Men who behave assertively are not devalued because this is consistent with what is socially expected of them.

In closing, let us register an important qualification on the impact of culture on conflict interaction. In a thorough review of cultural effects on communication and negotiation, Cai and Drake (1998) document many studies that showed intercultural differences in negotiation behavior. When different cultures were directly compared in experiments, however, results indicated that factors other than culture had a greater influence on negotiation behavior. In one study on negotiation between U.S. and Taiwanese citizens, expected differences in face work behavior did not occur; instead, parties matched each other's face behaviors and the strongest influence on behavior was negotiator role (buyer or seller). Other factors that influenced negotiations more than culture in other studies include authority, hierarchical position of the negotiator, age, and acquaintance level of the parties. Although these results are from controlled experimental settings rather than ordinary situations of intercultural contact, they suggest that we should be careful in assuming that people of different cultures will always act in ways consistent with their cultural upbringing.

Conflict Styles and Organizational Context

As noted in Chapter 1, conflict interaction is shaped by the context in which it occurs. When conflicts occur in organizational contexts, conflict style is not always a matter of individual choice. The structure and culture of organizations or social units also affect which conflict styles are preferred and the effectiveness of them. A conflict in an organization with procedures that emphasize strong management control will be quite different than one with looser, more participative management. In the former organization, a supervisor is likely to be involved in managing the conflict, while in the latter, parties may be left to themselves.

Ury, Brett, and Goldberg (1988) argue that the structure and culture of organizations influence the development of their dispute resolution systems, their preferred ways of managing conflicts. Some organizations have formally established dispute resolution systems, such as a grievance procedure or a mediation office, and others rely on ad hoc systems, such as making it part of the manager's job to handle conflicts that disrupt the work process. Some conflict resolution systems are formally provided by the larger community—for example, the courts or community mediation services.

Three types of dispute management systems common in U.S. organizations have been identified by Ury, Brett, and Goldberg (1988): Interest-based, rights-based, and power-based. *Interest-based* systems attempt to find a resolution that satisfies the parties' underlying interests or needs. One example of a formal interest-based system is the dispute mediation services that are increasingly being adopted by large organizations. For example, one large university has an Office of Dispute Mediation where parties can file formal cases that go through a multistep conflict management procedure. Other organizations, such as the one in Case 5.4 (The Productivity and Performance Report), have cultures that encourage people to adopt interest-based approaches on an informal basis. Interest-based systems tend to favor the problem-solving and compromising styles.

Rights-based dispute resolution systems attempt to establish which party is right based on independent standards accepted as legitimate and fair by the parties. Some standards, such as the legal code, are formally established, while others are socially accepted norms, such as seniority or equity. The most familiar rights-based system is the courts of law, as when an employee sues her employer for discrimination on the basis of gender. Participating in this system requires the assistance of an attorney because its procedures are so technical and complex. However, a parent who cuts a piece of cake in half to stop an argument between two children is also using a rights-based system.

Managers are also called on to use rights-based dispute resolution. Jameson (2001) reports that supervisors were the most commonly relied on third party for disputes among workers. Rights-based dispute resolution systems tend to promote the contending form of the competing style and the protecting form of the avoiding style. Parties make their best cases to the adjudicator—whether judge, parent, or manager—and rely on him or her to make the call.

In *power-based* dispute resolution systems, parties attempt to coerce others into doing what they want. Examples of power-based systems are strikes by workers and lockouts by employers, a manager ordering an employee to do a task the employee finds unpleasant, and fistfights among teenagers. Power-based dispute resolution tends to occur in the absence of interest- and rights-based systems; it is the "default" mode of conflict resolution in most organizations. The Undergraduate Publications Board in Case 4.1, A Raid on the Student Activity Fees Fund, provides an example of a system in which power is the primary means of managing conflict. In power-based systems the competing, avoiding, and accommodating styles are most common.

How do we determine what type of dispute resolution system holds in a given case? Ury et al. recommend asking the following questions:

- What do people do if they have a complaint?
- With whom, if anyone, do they bring up an issue?

- What happens when disputes are negotiated? Do the parties search for solutions that meet the needs of all sides? Do they go to authorities? Do they openly compete or use threats, intimidation, or other power tactics?
- How frequently do negotiations break down? What do parties do when facing a breakdown?
- Is there a formal program or set of rules or procedures parties can use when a dispute occurs?

It is important to note that a resolution system can differ for different types of conflict and for different parties. Union members, for example, may make heavy use of grievance procedures, whereas managers may prefer to use power-based systems when dealing with employees.

The three dispute resolution systems are not entirely independent of one another. Rights-based systems often evolve to correct for the problems and abuses of power-based systems; for example, the labor mediation system may evolve because of the harms caused by strikes and labor–management conflict. Rights-based systems also require the use of power to enforce decisions. A court's verdict or ruling has the force it does precisely because it is backed up by police and/or other government agencies who will compel parties to honor the court's decision. Interest-based dispute resolution systems are often established as alternatives or supplements to rights-based systems. Mediation, for instance, is commonly offered as an alternative to a trial in divorce on the grounds that it offers both parties a chance to satisfy their interests; a decision by a judge or jury often favors the interests of one side over the other.

Ury, Brett, and Goldberg (1988) estimate that in most organizations the use of the three dispute systems resembles a pyramid, with a majority of conflicts handled through power-based approaches, a significant portion through rights-based approaches, and a smaller portion through interest-based approaches. In organizations that do not have formal interest-based systems or organizational cultures that encourage interest-based approaches, power-based and rights-based conflict management is prevalent. Even in organizations with formal dispute resolution systems, power-based approaches are common.

To use formal dispute resolution systems, parties must request or apply; however, there are barriers to bringing a conflict out into the open. Parties may fear being labeled as troublemakers if they formally complain or as incompetent for not being able to manage their own affairs. Those with power may avoid formal systems because they believe they can get their way in any case and that the formal system may not decide in their favor

Ury et al. recommend that organizations try to "invert" this pyramid so that most conflicts are resolved according to interests, a significant portion according to rights, and only a small portion through the use of power. This may require establishing not only a formal dispute resolution system based on problem-solving, but also changing the organization's culture and employees' attitudes. Organizational dispute resolution practices generally develop gradually over the years and are grounded in deep-seated thought and action habits.

In addition, Ury et al. report the case of Bryant High School, which implemented a mediation program to help students manage conflicts more constructively. Bryant had experienced building tensions and violence, some between students and some between students and teachers. A major barrier to the success of the mediation program was students' lack of communication, negotiation, and problem-solving skills. One girl put it this way: "All I ever wanted to do was fight. If someone said something to me I didn't like, I didn't think about talking, I just thought about fighting" (Ury et al., 1988, p. 34). A climate of confrontation and violence was deeply embedded in Bryant's culture, and students and teachers there had learned that competing was the primary mode of conflict management. To remedy the situation, the school undertook a major training effort, providing workshops and classes in problem-solving and nonviolence techniques to more than 3,000 students and staff. The idea was to develop attitudes favoring nonviolent dispute resolution and motivation among students, teachers, and administrators to use the mediation system. After several years of training at Bryant, the mediation program was used for a significant number of conflicts, and violence was reduced. Bryant's program worked because school officials were willing to undertake a prolonged program to change the school's culture, climate, and attitudes.

The dispute resolution systems in an organization can favor certain conflict styles, and it is important to bear this in mind when selecting a style. In a power-based system, competing is the preferred mode, and parties who want to adopt problem-solving or compromising styles will find the going tougher than they might in an organization where interest-based systems are more common. Parties who adopt problem-solving or compromising styles may be seen as weak or vacillators in power-based systems, and others may seek to take advantage by forcing their own solution on the conflict.

Rights-based systems tend to favor competing styles too, but of a different sort. In rights-based systems parties take their arguments to an authority who makes the decision. The competition in this case does not depend on marshaling resources, such as the support of others or even physical strength, but rather it depends on who can make the best argument that appeals to the rules of the system. Employees in a rights-based system often have little incentive to work out conflicts themselves; instead, they polarize and make the best case they can to their superior, a judge, or other authority. Problem-solving, with its emphasis on open communication and consideration of others' interests, can place people at a disadvantage in a rights-based system because it gives important information to the other parties.

This does not mean that parties have to go along with the prevalent approach to resolving a dispute. They can try to "change the venue" of the conflict by moving it into a different dispute resolution system. An employee who is being browbeaten by co-workers can shift from a power-based to a rights-based system by taking the problem to a supervisor or filing a grievance. Conflicts can be taken from power- and rights-based systems into an interest-based system by applying for mediation when this is an option. People also can make styles that are not favored by a system work, but this requires determination and some skill. For example, an employee may need to adopt a competing style initially in order to resist a co-worker's attempts to force her to go along with his preferred work schedule. Once the co-worker realizes that forcing is not going to work, he may seek a compromise or problem solve, even in a workplace where power-based approaches are commonly used.

Conflict Tactics

Tactics are the specific moves and countermoves used to enact the various conflict styles. Several researchers have developed lists or typologies of conflict tactics (Sharp 1973; Roloff 1976; Wilmot and Wilmot 1978). Typologies of influence or compliance-gaining messages also map tactical choices because influence and persuasion are important aspects of certain conflict styles (Marwell and Schmitt 1967; Miller, Boster, Reloff, and Seibold 1976; Kipnis et al. 1980).

It would be impossible to discuss the more than 100 tactics that have been distinguished. Instead, the tactics are defined briefly in Table 7.2 (page 256), indicating their characteristics in terms of the six dimensions that describe conflict styles. Also shown in Table 7.2 are the power modes involved in carrying out each tactic. Tactics are, essentially, the vehicles of the power processes discussed in previous chapters; they constitute "power-in-action." How appropriate and skillful a party's moves are determines his or her effective power. The table groups tactics based on common ratings on the six dimensions and common principles of operation. These groupings expand on those developed by Kipnis et al. (1980) and Miller et al. (1976).

As noted at the beginning of this chapter, the same tactic can be used to carry out several different styles. To match tactics to styles, use the values of the tactics on the six style dimensions. A careful reading of this table also shows numerous tactics that match a given style on all but one or two dimensions. These tactics can be used to create variations on the style. For example, a competing style can be pursued by threatening the other (tactic 4c) or by invoking formal authority, if the authority will side with the party (tactic 7a). The two tactics give a very different "flavor" to the competing style.

As indicated in Chapter 1's discussion of episodes, the same tactic can have different meanings and effects depending on the context and the nature of ongoing conflict interaction. In a discussion marked by verbal aggression and hostile jokes, offering a quid pro quo might invoke suspicion, whereas the same offer would be taken as an attempt to compromise during a discussion full of integrative tactics (15a–g). Although it is useful to consider tactics in isolation, it is important to remember that they form part of more complex interactions.

As noted, although it is impossible to discuss all the tactics listed in Table 7.2, several have been studied extensively and others deserve additional explanation—threats and promises, toughness, tit for tat, coalition formation, issue definition, metacommunication, and integrative. Not included on the list are many formal procedures for managing conflict; these are discussed subsequently.

Threats and Promises

In one form or another, threats and promises appear in almost every conflict described in this book. A *threat* is defined as an individual's expressed intention to behave in a way that appears detrimental to the interests of another if that other does not comply with the individual's request or terms. A *promise* is an individual's expressed intention to behave in a way that appears beneficial to another if the other complies with the individual's request or terms. Threats and promises, then, are two sides of the same coin—one negative and the other positive (Kelley 1965; Deutsch 1973; Bowers 1974). Research suggests that the effectiveness of threats and promises depends on at least five factors—their specificity, the party's credibility, their immediacy, their equitability, and the climate in which they are presented.

If threats and promises operate by constraining another's behavior, then the more *specific* the behavior requested, the more effective the threat or promise is likely to be. Because threats and promises involve the virtual use of power, they constrain the other's behavior only by the instructions they give, and the more specific the instructions, the tighter the constraint (Tedeschi 1970). This line of reasoning is also supported by the finding from bargaining studies that threats generally elicit more compliance than promises because threats are usually more specific than promises (Rubin and Brown 1975; Pruitt and Rubin 1986). Consider the case where one party wants to get another to choose one of four possible behaviors. A promise of the form "If you do X, I will reward you," gives the other a constraint; namely, a reward if he or she does X. A threat, "If you do not do X, I will punish you," carries more constraints because it threatens punishment for three of four choices. In general, the more specific the constraints, the more likely the threat or promise is to prove effective.

The *credibility* of the person making a threat or promise is strongly related to its effectiveness, although the dynamics of credibility differ for the two tactics (Rubin and Brown 1975). In the case of threats, credibility is established by demonstrating the ability and willingness to carry out the threat—in other words, by a show of determination. Accounts of the Cuban Missile Crisis, for example, detail a number of specific "tough" moves the Kennedy Administration made, such as mobilizing armed forces, mounting air patrols, and stirring up public opinion, to demonstrate to the Soviets that it meant business (Allison 1969). Promises, on the other hand, depend much more on a person being perceived as trustworthy and having good intentions toward the other, as well as being able to "deliver the goods." Indeed, the very act of making a promise tends to make others feel friendlier and more trusting toward the promiser and so may set up a cycle reinforcing the person's credibility as long as promises can be delivered (Evans 1964; Heilman 1974; Rubin and Brown 1975).

Burgess (1973) argues that violent threats are effective because they "collapse time"; that is, they require the other to make an immediate choice and therefore heighten the impression of constraint still further. Faced with an urgent choice, the man with a gun at his head complies because there seems to be no safe alternative (although, given time to reflect, he may find several). To the extent that threats or promises can be made *immediate* (for example, by imposing time limits, exhibiting a sample of the reward or punishment to come, or giving a "hard sell") they are more likely to be effective.

A fourth consideration influencing the effectiveness of threats or promises is the degree to which the threat or promise is perceived as *equitable* by those being influenced. In an excellent study on compliance to threats, Kaplowitz (1973) showed that a subject's compliance depended on whether he or she perceived the threatener's request to be equitable or not. This result suggests that threats are more likely to be rejected (with an accompanying decrease in endorsement) if they are perceived as inequitable, and that effective use of threats depends on the threatener's ability to make the required behavior seem fair, reasonable, justifiable, or beneficial to the other. Given the positive value generally placed on equality and fairness in our culture (Walster, Berscheid, and Walster 1973), it seems safe to predict that equity will also enhance the effectiveness of promises: A promise that does not cost the promiser unfairly should elicit more compliance than one that does.

Finally, the effectiveness of threats or promises depends on the *climate* surrounding the conflict. Friedland (1976) found that threats were viewed differently by subjects in a bargaining experiment, depending on whether they were cooperatively or competitively interdependent. In a cooperative climate, threats were seen as attempts by the person to influence the other for the other's own good. In a competitive situation, threats were seen as attempts to coerce. Given these different perceptions, the effectiveness of the threat depends on differences in the two climates. In the cooperative climate, compliance with the threat depended on the other's belief that the person really does know what is best for both of them. In the competitive climate, compliance depended on the other's belief in the person's willingness and ability to punish him or her. It is quite likely that other climate themes, especially supportiveness, may influence how threats are perceived. In the same vein, a promise given in a competitive climate is likely to be perceived quite different from one in a cooperative climate. In general, different climates will influence what makes a threat or promise effective.

Promises and threats have another function in addition to influencing others. They also convey information about the person's preferences and determination and can be used strategically to communicate toughness or the willingness to compromise. If a small child defies her father at bedtime, and he threatens her with no television after school, he conveys that her going to bed is important to him and that he is unwilling to compromise. If he promises to read her a story if she'll go to bed, he is still conveying the importance of the issue, although more "softly," but he is offering a deal: She can stay up for the story if she'll go to sleep afterward.

Threats and promises also convey important information about the person's perceptions of the other. In our father–daughter example, a threat implies that the father thinks his daughter can be intimidated, or that nothing less than the threat of punishment will get her into bed. A promise implies a more easygoing relationship in which both are working for the same ends. Interestingly, making too small a threat can imply that the other can be easily intimidated, while making a large threat can be seen as a sign of respect for the opponent (Raven and Kruglanski 1970).

By carefully observing another's threats and promises (especially those that are implicit or indirect), and how they are carried out, parties can learn about others' values, intentions, and determination (Gibbons, Bradac, and Busch 1992). Conversely, of course, parties may use promises and threats to mislead. A common labor negotiation tactic is to make threatening gestures about a minor issue—say, the number of paid vacation days given employees—to get the employees to focus on that issue and draw their attention away from more important issues such as retirement benefits. Skillful threats and promises can misdirect attention and are often as strategically important for what they do not say as for what they communicate.

In closing, it is important to note some problems with threats. The use of threats tends to beget threats or competition from the other party (Pruitt, Rubin, and Kim 1994). The cycle of threat and counterthreat can easily develop into uncontrolled escalation. Moreover, the successful use of threats often entraps a party into using them again and again (Tedeschi 1983; Zagare and Kilgour 1978). This is because threats earn the hostility and distrust of the other and those who witness the action. As a result of this suspicion, more benign modes of influence, such as promises and reasoning, fail to induce compliance. Therefore the party must continue to rely on threats.

Toughness

Toughness has been studied extensively in experimental gaming research. A *tough* bargainer makes extreme opening demands, relatively few concessions, and small concessions when he or she does move (Bartos 1970). Generally, the negotiator attempts to convey strength and determination and to discourage others sufficiently so that they will yield first. The toughness tactic (4b) is designed to maximize the person's gains at the expense of the other, if need be. It is consistent with the competing, compromising, and collaborative styles discussed earlier: All three orientations imply that the party asserts his or her needs, a necessary prerequisite of toughness.

Research on toughness indicates that a party can obtain a more favorable final agreement by being tough (Chertkoff and Esser 1976). Indeed, Bartos (1970) has shown that if both bargainers are tough, other things being equal, they will achieve the optimal solution. However, there are limitations on this result. If tough bargainers are too uncompromising, their partners may respond with counterattacks or equal intransigence. When there is little pressure on the bargainers to come to an agreement or when time is short, excessive toughness can lead to impasses. In general, it seems best to convey an impression of "tough but fair" and to give on less important points. Toughness encourages the other to take one seriously, but excessive toughness may seem foolish and bullheaded.

Tit for Tat

A good example of an exchange tactic is *tit for tat,* or *matching* (tactic 8e). In this tactic one person matches the moves made by the other. If one party makes a competitive or hostile move, so does the other; if one party makes a cooperative or conciliatory move, so does the other. This strategy can be effective in persuading the other to cooperate, but it can also backfire, trapping both parties in an escalating spiral. Two explanations of this result can be offered. The first is based on Leary's (1957) conception of matching, which was discussed in Chapter 1. Leary argues that partners in a relationship tend to reciprocate similar levels of hostility or friendliness almost unconsciously. This interpersonal reflex leads to perpetuation of hostile or friendly tendencies in relationships. Hence, by matching cooperativeness, one partner may induce the other to unconsciously continue cooperative moves. The second explanation assumes a more conscious process of inference. By matching, the partner is demonstrating to him that she is responsive and therefore could be persuaded to cooperate. This encourages the other to exercise any impulses she may have to cooperate, to see if the partner can be induced to respond (Apfelbaum 1974). This interpretation is strengthened by the finding that if the first person is slow to reciprocate matching behavior, giving the impression that he is deliberating whether to reciprocate or not, the other is more likely to remain cooperative. Apparently, reluctant cooperation suggests conscious or deliberate intention and thereby implies a stronger commitment to cooperation.

Axelrod (1984) demonstrates that matching can generate cooperative behavior under a wide range of circumstances. Most striking, Axelrod's studies show that matching can induce even extremely competitive parties to cooperate. Axelrod cites four properties of matching tactics that tend to make the technique successful in inducing cooperation (1984, p. 20):

> avoidance of unnecessary conflict by cooperating as long as the other player does, provocability in the face of an uncalled for defection by the other, forgiveness after responding to a provocation, and clarity of behavior so that the other player can adapt to your pattern of action.

In his studies, Axelrod shows that tit for tat can create cooperation in large groups, even entire societies, provided that small clusters of individuals base their cooperation on matching and that they interact regularly. Once established on this basis, cooperation based on matching forms a very powerful pattern that persists even if others adopt competing tactics.

Coalition Formation

Consider the following example: Ed and Janet are members of the Affirmative Action Committee of a large corporation. In the two years they have served on the committee, both have grown to dislike Brandon, the committee's chairperson. Brandon is an assistant administrator from the president's office and tends to be very careful in his recommendations on grievance cases because he is afraid to offend his superiors. Janet and Ed have seen Brandon's caution result in the dismissal of several good cases, and they are determined to try to counteract his slowdown of the committee. What should they do?

Although either Ed or Janet could try to control the group singly, it is more likely that they will form an alliance or *coalition* (tactic 9). Because both have less power than Brandon does, they will have a greater probability of success if they team up. There are also costs involved because both Ed and Janet have to give up a certain amount of freedom when they form a coalition. Because their effectiveness depends on joint action, each must trust the other and each is vulnerable if the other decides to betray the coalition. In this case, however, the benefits are likely to outweigh the costs because a coalition will greatly enhance Ed and Janet's chances of influencing their group.

These considerations suggest that the principles of game and social exchange theories would be very useful to explain coalition behavior. Game and exchange researchers have conducted numerous coalition choice studies, which give us some clues as to how coalitions form.

The earliest theory of coalition formation was advanced by Caplow (1956), who argued that coalitions are formed on the basis of the *minimum power necessary to defeat the opponent*. Caplow assumed that parties are guided by a motivation to maximize the number of others they control, and therefore their ability to control the rewards they obtain. If this motivation holds, then relatively strong members will seek to form a coalition with the weakest member who still has enough power to defeat the opponent. For example, for three members—A, B, and C—whose ratio of power is 4 (A) to 3 (B) to 2 (C), the principle of minimum power would predict that coalitions between A and C, or B and C, would be more likely to form than between A and B. Caplow's theory suggests that "weakness is strength"; the weakest member of the triad is the only one who will always be included in a coalition. Evidence from several studies supports this prediction and the minimum power theory.

Gamson (1961) advanced a different theory based on the rewards received from coalitions. He theorized that rewards depend on the *resources a person could contribute to the coalition*: the greater someone's contribution, the greater the share of rewards to which the person would be entitled. On the assumption that each person in the coalition desires to maximize his or her rewards, Gamson predicted that coalitions would form on the basis of minimum resources. This principle predicts that the most likely coalition would be the one capable of controlling the group that involves minimum resources contributed by the two members. In this case, members would attempt to maximize their own rewards by preferring those coalitions where their contribution is as great as possible relative to other members. In the case of A, B, and C, the most likely coalition would be the B–C alliance. Both A and B will seek to ally with C, but C will prefer B because this alliance will maximize C's contributions relative to the others and therefore entitle C to a greater share of rewards.

The two theories make somewhat different predictions about coalition formation: Minimum power theory argues that coalitions A–C and B–C are equally likely, while minimum resource theory predicts that B–C is much more probable than A–C. This difference permits comparison of the principles. Generally, evidence has favored Gamson's minimum resource theory. For example, one way of studying coalition formation is to create a political game simulating a political convention. Subjects are assigned different amounts of power by varying the number of votes they control; in other words, A might control forty votes, B thirty votes, and C twenty votes. In these studies, all three possible coalitions form, but A–C and B–C form much more often than A–B, and B–C is much more likely than A–C (Gamson 1961; Komorita and Chertkoff 1973; Murnigham 1978; Baker 1981). Hence minimum resource theory seems a more plausible explanation than minimum power theory.

Minimum resource theory assumes members of coalitions divide rewards in proportion to their contributions. If B contributes thirty votes and C only fifteen, then B is entitled to twice as much benefit as C. However, Komorita and Chertkoff (1973) studied the division of rewards in coalitions. They found that members bargain over the division of rewards prior to joining coalitions. This bargaining is not always open: It may be done "under the surface" without people's admission that it is occurring. The bargaining process determines which coalitions form, and it may result in distributions of rewards that differ considerably from the proportion of resources contributed. Minimum resources still seem to influence what coalitions form, but it does not necessarily determine the division of rewards.

Going back to Ed, Janet, and Brandon, these findings would suggest that the Ed–Janet coalition was more likely to form than Ed–Brandon or Janet–Brandon alliances. As Ed and Janet talk about working against Brandon, we would also expect them to refer to their contributions as a way of setting the division of rewards. For example, Ed might refer to his verbal skill by saying, "I'll try to point out the flaws in his case, and you back me up." In saying this, Ed implicitly assigns Janet the supporting role and, hence, a weaker contribution. If Janet accepts this, she may be granting Ed a greater claim to any benefits that result, such as the gratitude of other members for stopping Brandon. Of course, Ed and Janet may address the issue of division of rewards directly. Many coalitions depend on members' openly agreeing to do X in exchange for Y. However, there does not have to be an explicit agreement for minimum resource theory to apply. Unspoken agreements may hold just as well as spoken ones.

Minimum resource theory is not sufficient to explain all coalition behavior. There are cases in which Janet or Ed would join forces with Brandon rather than with each other. In every coalition experiment, there are at least some A–B coalitions, a fact that runs counter to both Caplow's and Gamson's predictions. What accounts for this? Research by political scientists reveals that *similarities of attitudes and beliefs can also motivate coalition formation* (Gamson 1961; Axelrod 1970). These political theories assume that people join coalitions not only for rewards, but also because they are interested in getting certain policies or measures enacted. For example, they assume Ed and Janet form a coalition not only to obtain rewards but also because they desire to change the committee, independent of rewards. From this assumption it follows that parties prefer coalitions with others with similar preferences: If both favor similar goals from the beginning, they have a common ground for cooperation, and they are less likely to be sidetracked from their original ends.

The similarity principle implies a considerably different explanation for coalition formation than the minimum resource principle, an explanation not directly tied to rewards. Lawler and Youngs (1975) compared the two explanations with an experimental game simulating a political convention. They found that both rewards and attitude similarity determined coalition choice, but attitude similarity was "by far, the most important determinant." This finding may not hold for other situations where specific platforms are not so important, but it does show that similarity must be taken into account as well as reward.

The study of coalition formation is important because coalitions are a primary path to power for weaker members of a social unit (Janeway 1980). Because of this fact, stronger members often move to head off coalitions among weaker parties, either by forming coalitions themselves or by confusing issues and sowing seeds of discontent among their weaker counterparts. The findings discussed here underscore the importance of communicative processes in coalition formation. Members must convince others of rewards to be won and of their similarities in order to promote coalitions. In addition, they must downplay or make plans to counter any costs or problems they might face. These strategies cut both ways however; just as weaker members can use them to band together, so can stronger members use them to win over weaker ones or prevent their alliances. Conflict interaction is an arena for the struggle over allies.

Issue Definition

There is a tendency to assume that the issues in a conflict are the needs and interests that the parties have at the outset. This view is too static. Issues may be defined and redefined throughout the conflict. The next paragraphs describe several issue definition tactics from Table 7.2.

Umbrellas are issues one party introduces to legitimize grievances when the original issue is one that others would not normally accept as valid (tactic 11b). For example, David may be angry at Jim because Jim received a promotion to a position David wanted. For David to express anger toward Jim because of Jim's promotion would seem petty. However, if Jim persistently comes to meetings late, David can legitimately chide him for that. David can then transfer his anger related to the promotion into an attack on Jim for always being late. The lateness issue serves as an umbrella for the anger generated by the real issue. People often do this in everyday conflicts: They are angry at someone and use the first legitimate issue that arises as an excuse to vent anger.

Bundling boards get their name from an early Midwestern custom (Walton 1969). It was thought that courting couples could get to know each other best by sleeping in the same bed; the bundling board was put between them to ensure that nothing improper occurred. By analogy, bundling boards in conflict are extra issues used to enhance the apparent distance between people's positions (also known as issue expansion, tactic 11g). As more and more issues are added, people see their interests as more and more incompatible. For example, assume David has lashed out at Jim for Jim's lateness. Jim could respond with a remark, such as "Well, you're not perfect yourself—your reports are always late!" David might then comment on Jim's sloppiness and Jim on David's jealousy, and so on, as the conflict develops into a real "everything but the kitchen sink" fight.

Bundling boards are useful in some ways because they allow parties to save face by shifting attention to others' shortcomings, and are a way for members to point out that others share the responsibility for the conflict. However, issue expansion also can contribute to a tangle of issues and can accelerate the conflict.

The tactics of negative inquiry (tactic 11c) and fogging (tactic 11e) redefine issues in ways that narrow and refocus the conflict. *Negative inquiry* involves asking someone what he or she means by ambiguous statements in order to pin down the issues. The simple process of questioning can often encourage people to think through vague and judgmental statements and to reduce them to more objective terms that specify their needs. For example, under questioning, the statement "You are sloppy" may change to "I want you to stop leaving the car such a mess."

Fogging also focuses issues but is more manipulative than negative inquiry. On hearing another's complaint, the party acknowledges only part of it, thus narrowing the "live" issues to those one party is ready or willing to address. For example, A might say to B, "This car is a mess. You are so sloppy!" B then fogs by replying, "It is a mess. I'm so sorry," shunting the sloppiness issue aside. Fogging focuses the issues, which may be useful for problem-solving and compromising. It can also be used in an avoiding style.

Fractionation (Fisher 1964) and the two-column method are two methods of issue definition that can be used to promote integration. *Fractionation* (tactic 11a) involves breaking a complex conflict into component issues that can be dealt with singly or in sequence. It involves setting an agenda for the conflict. In the *two-column method* (tactic 11f), the two parties' interests or needs are listed side-by-side and commonalities are identified.

A good way to follow the progress of a conflict is to pay attention to the shifting patterns of issues. The redefinition, expansion, and narrowing of issues determine what people work on and how the conflict ultimately turns out.

Metacommunication

Metacommunication, explicit discussion about how the parties are handling the conflict, can open up channels of communication (tactic 12a). Handled properly, metacommunication enables the correction of misunderstanding and the negotiation of norms that encourage helpful communication practices and discourage harmful ones. For example, Keith may habitually raise his voice when excited; Marla, however, may interpret Keith's loudness as an attempt to intimidate her. When Marla metacommunicates, she tells Keith how she interprets his loudness and how it affects her, and he has the opportunity to explain that it is just a habit. As a result, Marla may be able to disregard Keith's loudness or Keith may try to keep his voice down more. Metacommunication not only involves immediate problems but can build parties' relationship. Successful metacommunication increases parties' awareness of and trust for each other and fosters open communication.

Sillars and Weisberg (1987) register two warnings about metacommunication in relational conflicts. First, verbal metacommunication is not always effective because people tend to trust nonverbal, analogic messages more in relationships. Keith may tell Marla that his loudness is just a bad habit and not meant to intimidate her, but if he raises his voice as he says this, she may disregard his explanation, reasoning that he is trying to intimidate her into accepting it. There is more to metacommunication than words, especially when the parties know each other well. However, this highlights a second problem with nonverbal metacommunication according to Sillars and Weisberg (1987, p. 151):

> Analogic forms of metacommunication are mostly imprecise. A particular tone of voice, for example, often admits many interpretations of the speaker's intent. Consequently, the same utterance may be variously seen as a compliment, verbal "jab," or good-natured joke.

Metacommunication must be handled carefully; when managed well it is a useful tool for moving conflicts in productive directions.

Integrative Tactics

One of the most effective integrative tactics is to find a common goal that both parties value, commonly called a *superordinate goal* (tactic 15b). The Robber's Cave experiment of Sherif and associates was one of the first studies of this technique (Sherif, Harvey, White, Hood, and Sherif 1961). They created two opposing groups of summer campers, the Bulldogs and the Red Devils. When the two groups had to work together on the common goal of solving several emergencies, between-group conflict was reduced. Numerous subsequent studies have supported the utility of superordinate goals (Hunger and Stern 1976; Pruitt and Rubin 1986). To be effective, the goal must have high appeal for both parties and accomplishing it must be beyond the capabilities of any single party. In addition, competition and conflict among parties over other issues must be set aside. So a couple who often argues about how much to spend on redecorating their house may pull together when threatened by a financial crisis. The common goal of weathering the storm overcomes their perceived differences. As this example illustrates, a superordinate goal need not be something both parties want; it can also be something they want to avoid or a common enemy. Political leaders have used the perception of threats from without to unite factionalized nations from time immemorial.

The superordinate goal tactic is one of the most reliable integrative tactics, but it does not work under all circumstances. If the parties fail to attain the super-ordinate goal, the goal may lose its attractiveness and competition will ensue (Hunger and Stern 1976; Worchel, Anderoli, and Folger 1977). Given their previous conflict, the parties are likely to blame each other for the failure. Then too, finding a superordinate goal does not resolve a preexisting conflict, as the example of our redecorating couple shows. Once the couple is in the clear again, or if they fail to get out of their financial crisis, bickering over redecorating could easily resurface.

The tactic will also fail if each party does not have a clear and distinct role in attaining the superordinate goal (Deschamps and Brown 1983). They must have a clear idea of how their efforts fit together or they may lose their sense of identity. If this happens, he or she is less likely to be attracted to cooperating with the other. It is also worth noting that parties may have trouble discovering or recognizing superordinate goals when hostilities run high. A "cooling off" period is often necessary before the superordinate goal can be used to promote cooperation.

Experimental integration is a tactic designed to overcome lack of trust between parties (tactic 15e). As seen in Chapter 1, moving a conflict in an integrative direction is often difficult because of self-reinforcing cycles of behavior and interpretation, which create and perpetuate distrust, tension, and hostility. This can result in the paradoxical situation wherein neither party wants to compete, but both adopt competing styles because they believe the other is competing. This cycle can create uncontrolled escalation, making it hard to break out of competing orientations. This is the "stuff" of which arms races are made.

The key to experimental integration is to make a conciliatory or cooperative move, yet not let one's guard down so that the other can take advantage. If the other party responds in a positive fashion, then we can answer with more integra-tive moves and eventually move into full-fledged integration. The approach is experimental in that the conciliatory or cooperative move is an experiment—it tests how the other will respond. If it really is a false conflict, the other should respond cooperatively, and the party can then signal back with another coopera-tive move, and so on, to gradually bring about integration.

The best-known method for experimental integration is Osgood's GRIT—graduated and reciprocated initiatives in tension reduction—strategy (Osgood 1959, 1962, 1966; Lindskold 1979). The specific points in the GRIT strategy are as follows (after Lindskold 1979):

1. The climate for conciliatory initiatives needs to be set by making a general statement of intention to reduce tension through subsequent acts, indicating the advantages to the other of reciprocating.
2. Every unilateral move should be announced publicly prior to making it, indi-cating that it is part of a general strategy.
3. Each announcement should invite reciprocation from the other. Reciproca-tion need not come in the form of the same move but should be a conciliatory step of some sort.

4. Each initiative must be carried out as announced without any requirement of reciprocation by the other.
5. Initiatives should be continued for some time even if the other does not reciprocate. This gives one a chance to test the party's sincerity and also puts pressure on the other.
6. Initiatives must be unambiguous and permit verification.
7. Initiatives must be risky and vulnerable to exploitation, but they also must not expose the party to a serious and/or damaging attack.
8. Moves should be graded in degree of risk to match the reciprocation of the other. Once the other begins to reciprocate, the initiator should reciprocate with at least as risky or slightly more risky moves.

The first three points make the initiative clear and may enlist other parties to put pressure on the other to comply with the conciliatory gesture. Points 4 through 6 make it clear to the other that he or she has the freedom to respond or not, that this is not a trick or maneuver. Point 7 is crucial because it gives the party the security to attempt the experiment. The party stands to lose if the other takes advantage of the move but does not expose his or her position so that the other can totally win the day. Finally, point 8 represents an attempt to gradually increase cooperation.

Etzioni (1967) shows how Kennedy and Khrushchev followed a pattern similar to GRIT to bring about the thaw in East–West relations that followed the Cuban Missile Crisis. Improvement in international relations is often launched by small "confidence-building measures" set in motion during negotiations. Lindskold (1979) summarizes evidence from numerous game studies supporting the effectiveness of GRIT. This evidence suggests that what works in the international arena also works in interpersonal conflicts. There is always some risk in embarking on integration. However, experimental integration tactics can ease parties' fears of disaster and encourage them to try to move the first few steps along the problem-solving road.

Another tactic related to experimental integration is *reformed sinner* (tactic 15d). Unlike toughness, which simply aims to maximize the individual's outcomes, the reformed sinner attempts to induce an uncooperative partner to cooperate and thereby enhance outcomes (Pruitt and Kimmel 1977). In this strategy, the person initially competes for a period of time and then shifts over to cooperation. The method demonstrates that the individual could compete if he or she wanted to, but that the person chooses instead to cooperate and reward the other. In most studies this strategy, or a similar one in which the individual is initially tough and then relaxes his or her demands, is unusually effective in inducing the other's cooperation. Of course, for the strategy to work, there must be an incentive for the person responding to the reformed sinner to cooperate rather than exploit the weakness. Thus the reformed sinner must maintain a "stick" and be prepared to resort to it again if the "carrot" does not work.

Why does the reformed sinner strategy work? One explanation points to the respect that such a strategy creates for the person using it. By initially competing, the person demonstrates an ability to punish the other. Voluntarily giving up the punishment possibility and exposing oneself to the other generates respect and also a sense that the person must be sincere in his or her offer of cooperation. This explanation is illustrated in the strategy used by many elementary school teachers who want to have an "open classroom" atmosphere, yet do not want students to abuse this openness. The teachers often try to be somewhat stern at the beginning of the year in an effort to show the students that they can punish them if need be. Only after respect for the teacher's authority is established does the teacher gradually relax and attempt to promote a more open atmosphere. The second explanation is simpler than the first and goes hand-in-hand with it: It posits that once the other has experienced the negative consequences of competition, sudden cooperation will be attractive and motivate the other to cooperate. If this explanation is valid, it implies that the person employing the strategy should take care to make the other recognize the disadvantages of competition and the advantages of cooperation.

Styles and Tactics in Practice

The preceding discussion may create the somewhat misleading impression that people can simply select and use whatever styles and tactics they think will work. When we consider styles and tactics in the rough-and-tumble world of "real conflict," however, things are often more complicated than this. It is one thing to sit and calmly deliberate about the choice of a style or tactic. It is quite another to have to deal with the reactions that styles and tactics provoke in others.

Case 7.2 illustrates how styles interact in a conflict episode. This conflict was not resolved because there was no successful differentiation phase to set the stage for integration. The issues and concerns each party had were never clearly defined. Mary tried to bring the issue out in the open, but Joan persisted in smoothing and withdrawing. In effect, Mary's contending style was neutralized by Joan's successful avoidance. Mary tried several times to shift her style toward compromising or problem-solving, but she was blocked when Joan persisted in avoiding the conflict. Mary could not involve both of them in a discussion unless Joan cooperated, and Joan did not. And if Joan had wanted to discuss the issues openly, she was deterred by Mary's active persistence. Joan feared that she would not be able to hold her own in any discussion, so it probably seemed easier just to avoid. Her only forceful venture was the brief foray into competing when she set the insurance date. In anticipation of Mary's pressure, Joan quickly reverted to an avoiding style. The two were trapped in their respective styles; each style reinforced the other in a destructive self-reinforcing cycle.

The effectiveness of styles and tactics is dependent on others' actions. It is not simply a matter of selecting a tactic on one's own; another's reaction may reinforce or neutralize a tactic, or even cause it to "backfire." A party's ability to

CASE **7.2**

The Would-Be Borrower

Imagine yourself as Mary: What tactics are you using as you respond to these issues?

A roommate conflict developed between Joan and Mary over the use of Joan's new car. When Joan talked to Mary about her anticipated purchase, Joan often said things such as, "It will be wonderful when we have a car." Mary interpreted Joan's use of the word "we" to mean that she might be allowed to borrow the car on certain occasions. When Mary's sister came to visit, Joan drove Mary's sister's car, and Mary figured this was a case of "share and share alike."

Joan began to shop seriously for a car during the two weeks before Thanksgiving. When Joan was about to make her purchase, Mary saw a new opportunity open up for her. Due to scheduling problems on her job, Mary was not able to go home for Thanksgiving. This would be the first Thanksgiving Mary had not been home. Mary asked Joan if she could use her new car to visit her parents, who lived about 120 miles away. Mary knew Joan would not need her car that weekend because Joan was going out of town with her parents for the holiday.

At first, Joan refused, but Mary persisted in raising the subject. Joan reported that she was "appalled that Mary had even asked." For Joan it was an issue of "invasion of personal property." As the tension over this question built, Joan began to use a withdrawing style: She gave Mary ambiguous, noncommittal replies and often simply did not reply at all. Mary had a more forceful, dominating communication style than Joan, and Joan saw avoidance as a way of sparing herself a direct confrontation with Mary. Joan assumed that a direct denial of Mary's request would provoke an emotional outburst, which she wanted to avoid at all costs.

In response to Joan's nonresponsiveness, Mary began to apply pressure indirectly, using a contending style. She pressed Joan to loan her car. Mary also had phone conversations with her parents within earshot of Joan in which she talked about the things they could do if she could get a car from Joan. Joan interpreted this as an attempt to make her feel guilty, and it worked. Joan felt a great deal of stress and turned to her family for support, which they readily gave. The interaction of the two styles set up a competitive climate and an impasse developed: Mary saw the issue as a question of a favor one would willingly do for a friend. Joan saw it as a question of whether Mary could infringe on her personal property.

Joan bought her car on the weekend before Thanksgiving and stored it in her parents' garage until it was insured. Mary mentioned her holiday plans with the car several times during the weekend and interpreted Joan's silence as acquiescence. The blowup occurred when an insurance salesman called on Joan. Mary had been giving Joan advice on insurance and was also present at the meeting. After discussing rates, the salesman asked Joan when she wanted her coverage to begin. Joan replied, "Thursday night at midnight"; therefore, the car would be uninsured on Thanksgiving Day and Mary could not drive it. Joan reported that this move was not premeditated: "I saw an escape hatch and I took it." The significance of Joan's shift to contending was not lost on Mary. She was shocked at "the devious way Joan had gone about it."

Mary reported that after the salesman left, Joan "just started babbling and babbling about nothing at all and getting really nervous." Joan shifted back to withdrawing after her one "trump." In the "twenty-minute scream-fest" that followed, styles shifted several times more. Mary asked Joan if she purposely started the insurance later to keep her from borrowing the car. Joan replied "Yes" and shifted back to other topics. After listening

(continued)

CASE 7.2   Continued

with half an ear for a while, Mary told Joan that she was "really ticked" with her. Joan replied, "I know you are. I knew you'd be like this. I knew you'd do this." Mary said that it would have been better if Joan had just told her "straight out." Joan replied that her mother had said that Mary should not be allowed to use her car. Mary was upset that Joan had told her mother: "Now I suppose you're going to tell your whole family what a rotten, miserable roommate you have!" Joan did not reply to this. Mary kept up her challenges, charging Joan with being selfish. Joan did not respond. Mary tried a normative justification, arguing that Thanksgiving is a special occasion. Joan did not respond. Mary asked Joan if the issue was that Joan thought she was a lousy driver. Joan replied that it was just too soon for someone to borrow her car. "Oh, so you don't want me to soil it before you can use it!" Mary flashed back.

When the shouting match ended, Joan did her laundry and remained in the laundry room for an hour, crying. Mary remained in their apartment, crying. When Joan returned to the apartment, the two did not speak until Joan approached Mary to show her a maga-

zine article Mary had been looking for. This softened the mood somewhat but did not initiate conversation. Eventually, as they prepared for bed, Mary approached Joan: "Look, we've got to end this. I'm sorry I asked for your car. It's too soon for me to be asking. I should have realized this from other things you said." Joan replied that she was sorry she didn't give Mary a straight answer at first. Mary was disappointed at Joan's answer because she expected an apology from Joan for not letting her use her car. Both women went to bed.

The two did not have much contact over the next few days. Mary reported feeling alienated from Joan: "It was a pretty terrible couple of weeks after that." The conflict was never really resolved, but it gradually faded into the background, and the two women resumed their friendship.

Discussion Questions

- *To what extent do your options for approaching a conflict depend on the other person's behavior?*
- *Think of a situation in which you have wanted to use a cooperating style and found that the responses you received made it difficult or impossible.*

choose or change styles and tactics is also limited by what others do. In some cases, things get so out of hand that the parties are trapped, as Joan and Mary were. Only after a concerted effort can the direction of such conflicts be changed. The Would-Be Borrower case clearly illustrates the interactive nature of styles and tactics and underscores an important point: Conflict interaction often acquires a momentum of its own.

This does not mean that selection of styles and tactics is a hopeless undertaking. People always have degrees of freedom that allow them to act in their own interests and to change situations for the better. However, there are limitations on what parties can control, and it is well to bear these in mind. The principles of conflict interaction discussed in earlier chapters offer useful resources for understanding the dynamics of styles and tactics.

Reciprocity Theory: Explaining Conflict Responses

Conversations unfold as each person takes a turn talking. With each turn the person makes a "move"—performs a behavior that has strategic significance. Any particular interaction is created through a particular sequence of moves as each participant takes a turn in response to the other's turn. Each move influences the next move, which in turn influences the following move, and so on. Within the interactional view, this is known as *mutual influence.*

Perhaps the strongest feature of mutual influence is the norm of reciprocity. According to several theorists, reciprocity is a social norm that undergirds all social exchange processes (Roloff and Campion 1985). Gouldner (1960) suggests that the norm prescribes two things: "people should help those who have helped them, and people should not injure those who have helped them." As Roloff (1987b, p. 12) puts it, "a recipient of a benefit is morally obligated to return a benefit in kind."

Reciprocity is defined as the process of behavioral adaptation in which one party responds in a similar direction to another party's behaviors with behaviors of comparable functional value (Street and Cappella 1985; Burgoon, Dillman, and Stern 1991). The key to reciprocity is function. Because the same behavior may serve different purposes, reciprocity is often more complex than matching. For example, a joke may serve to reduce anxiety, establish rapport, or point out an imperfection in a nonthreatening way. If party A tells a joke to defuse tensions, party B is said to have reciprocated if she engages in a behavior that also serves that function, such as laughing at the joke; party B need not tell a joke to reciprocate.

Compensation is the corresponding process of behavioral adaptation in which one responds to a partner's behaviors with opposite behaviors of comparable functional value. For example, suppose party A initially uses dominant gestures and remarks in a conflict situation, while party B uses more conventional messages. If A then reduces dominance in response to B, reciprocity is said to have occurred. The same would be true if B increases dominance in response to A. Reciprocity also occurs in the example of mutual convergence where party A decreases dominance while at the same time party B increases it. But when one or both parties change in opposite directions, then they have compensated rather than reciprocated. This would be the case if B became submissive in response to the dominance of A.

Reciprocity and compensation are highly evident in the use of conflict styles. Research clearly shows that threats are often followed by counterthreats (Deutsch and Krauss 1960), while concessions offered in bargaining situations are frequently followed in kind (Putnam and Jones 1982a, 1982b). In an analysis of oppositional interchanges in fifty-two different families during routine family dinners, Vuchinich (1984, 1990) found strong evidence of a symmetrical matching of conversational behaviors. His analysis showed that the best determinant of any given move was the immediately preceding turn.

Reciprocity theory maintains that escalation and deescalation patterns in conflict interaction are often a result of reciprocity and compensation. Any move is likely to establish a new and powerful sequence in a conflict encounter. In fact, the intensity of a particular episode might even increase reciprocity between the parties (Markey, Funder, and Ozer 2003). Initial moves and patterns set the tone in brief episodes, such as confrontations, whereas more protracted conflicts move through stages of reciprocal patterns. For example, Gottman (1979) observed that in distressed relationships wives often match their husbands' initial moves and engage in one-upmanship, creating a highly charged and bitter interaction. Putnam and Jones (1982a, 1982b) found that bargainers generally engage in an attack–defend style of conflict but uphold the norm of positive reciprocity when cooperative gestures are offered.

TABLE 7.2 Seventeen Conflict Tactics Rated on Seven Dimensions

Tactic	Definition	Assertive	Cooperative	Disclosive	Empowerment Self	Other	Active	Flexibility	Power Mode
1. Avoidance									
a. Topic shift	Change topic from conflict issue (Sillars et al. 1982)	Low	Varies	Varies	Yes	No	Low	Low	Indirect, hidden
b. Leave field	Remove self from contact with other party	Low	Low	Low	Yes	No	Low	Low	Indirect, hidden
c. Refuse to recognize conflict		Low	Low	Low	Yes	No	Low	Low	Indirect, hidden
d. Postponement	Postpone dealing with the conflict until a future time	Low	Low	Varies	Varies	Varies	Low	Varies	Indirect
2. Accommodation	Accede (give concession) to other's demand	Low	High	Varies	No	Yes	Low	High	Indirect
3. Subordination									
a. Appeal, plead		Low	Low	Moderate to high	No	Yes	Moderate	Varies	Indirect
b. Supplication	Act helpless or incompetent as a way of gaining pity or support	Low	Low	Low	No	Yes	Low	Varies	Indirect
4. Assertiveness									
a. Demand concessions		High	Low	Moderate	Yes	No	High	Low	Direct, virtual
b. Toughness	Adopt extreme initial demand and move away from it slowly and reluctantly; justify position logically (Bartos 1970)	High	Low	Moderate	Yes	No	High	Moderate	Direct, virtual

TABLE 7.2 Continued

Tactic	Definition	Assertive	Cooperative	Disclosive	Empowerment Self	Empowerment Other	Active	Flexibility	Power Mode
c. Threat	A statement that if the other does not meet party's demand, negative consequences will result	High	Low	Moderate	Yes	No	High	Low	Direct, virtual
d. Irrevocable commitment	Party makes a commitment to a course of action so that he or she cannot back down from it; others must go along (Pruitt and Rubin 1986)	High	Low	Moderate	Yes	No	High	Low	Direct, virtual
5. Aggressiveness									
a. Verbal aggression	Shouting, blaming, browbeating, etc.	High	Low	Low	Yes	No	Varies	Low	Direct
b. Hostile joke	A joke that insults or derides the other party or his or her behavior (Sillars et al. 1982)	High	Low	Low	Yes	No	Varies	Low	Indirect
c. Physical aggression		High	Low	Low	Yes	No	Varies	Low	Direct
d. Gunnysacking	Attacking the other by addressing a number of accusations or complaints to him or her at once; sometimes a group gangs up on one person (Wilmot and Wilmot 1978)	High	Low	Low	Yes	No	Varies	Low	Direct

(continued)

TABLE 7.2 Continued

Tactic	Definition	Assertive	Cooperative	Disclosive	Empowerment Self	Other	Active	Flexibility	Power Mode
6. Manipulation									
a. Self-abuse	Verbal or physical abuse to self intended to make another comply	Varies	Low	Varies	Yes	No	Varies	Varies	Indirect
b. Guilt	Attempts to make other feel guilty so that he or she will comply	High	Low	Varies	Yes	No	Varies	Low	Indirect
c. Misrepresentation	Misleading other concerning one's true position	High	Low	Low	Yes	No	Low	Varies	Indirect
d. Gamesmanship	Party does things to create a "muddled fluster" in the other; to throw the other off balance and render him or her more likely to concede (Pruitt and Rubin 1986)	High	Low	Varies	Yes	No	Low	Varies	Indirect
7. Authority									
a. Invoke formal authority	Use authority of position to influence another	High	Varies	Low to moderate	Yes	No	High	Varies	Direct
b. Expertise	Use special knowledge or experience to influence others	High	Varies	Moderate to high	Yes	Varies	High	Varies	Indirect
c. Invoke higher authority	Ask superior to resolve conflict	High	Low	Varies	Yes	Varies	Varies	Low	Direct, virtual, or indirect

TABLE 7.2 Continued

Tactic	Definition	Assertive	Cooperative	Disclosive	Empowerment Self	Empowerment Other	Active	Flexibility	Power Mode
8. Exchange									
a. Promise	A statement that if the other meets party's demand, a positive consequence will result (see text)	High	Varies	Moderate	Yes	Yes	High	Low	Direct, virtual
b. Pregiving	Reward other prior to requesting compliance (Marwell and Schmitt 1967)	High	Varies	Low	Yes	Yes	Moderate to high	Varies	Direct
c. Call in debt	Ask other to comply because of a previous favor or concession given by party	High	Varies	Low	Yes	Yes	Moderate to high	Varies	Indirect
d. Quid pro quo	Giving "something for something"—each party gives the other something in exchange for granting something; for example, A agrees not to shout at B, if B will listen better	High	High	Varies	Yes	Yes	Varies	Moderate to high	Indirect
e. Tit for tat	Party responds to each of other's moves with a move from same style; for example, if A adopts a competing style, B answers with competing moves	High	Varies	Moderate	Yes	Yes	Varies	High	Direct

(continued)

TABLE 7.2 Continued

Tactic	Definition	Assertive	Cooperative	Disclosive	Empowerment Self	Empowerment Other	Active	Flexibility	Power Mode
f. Logrolling	Propose solution that involves both parties giving something up to get something (Pruitt and Rubin 1986)	High	High	Moderate to high	Yes	Yes	High	High	Direct
9. Coalition formation	Two or more parties form an alliance against another	High	Low	Varies	Yes	No	High	Low	Direct
10. Ingratiation									
a. Liking	Use other's liking for party to influence other	High	Varies	Varies	Yes	Yes	Varies	Varies	Indirect
b. Flattery	Exaggerate other's admirable qualities and soft-pedal weaknesses to influence other (Pruitt and Rubin 1986)	High	Varies	Low	Yes	Yes	Varies	Varies	Indirect
c. Opinion conformity	Express agreement with other's opinions and values to create impression of similarity and increase other's liking (Pruitt and Rubin 1986)	High	Varies	Low	Yes	Yes	Varies	Varies	Indirect
d. Give favors	Do nice things for other to increase his or her liking of party (Pruitt and Rubin 1986)	High	Varies	Varies	Yes	Yes	Varies	Varies	Indirect
e. Self-promotion	Present self as deserving, virtuous,	High	Varies	Moderate	Yes	Yes	High	Varies	Indirect

TABLE 7.2 Continued

Tactic	Definition	Assertive	Cooperative	Disclosive	Empowerment		Active	Flexibility	Power Mode
					Self	*Other*			
	self-sacrificing to build liking (Pruitt and Rubin 1986)								
f. Entitlement	Claim responsibility for a favorable event to gain other's esteem (Cialdini 1984)	High	Low	Varies	Yes	Yes	Varies	Low	Indirect
g. Basking in reflected glory	Associate oneself with other successful party to gain esteem (Cialdini 1984)	High	Low	Varies	Yes	Yes	Low	Low	Indirect
h. Blasting the opposition	Criticize or derogate unsuccessful or despised other to gain approval (Cialdini 1984)	High	Low	Varies	Yes	Yes	Low	Low	Indirect
11. Issue definition									
a. Fraction-ation	Break conflict down into individual issues that can then be handled separately (Fisher 1969)	High	Varies	High	Yes	Varies	High	High	Varies
b. Umbrellas	Issues introduced to legitimize anger or grievance resulting from another less legitimate issue: For example, A may resent B because of a	High	Low	Low	Yes	No	Low	Low	Indirect

(continued)

TABLE 7.2 Continued

Tactic	Definition	Assertive	Cooperative	Disclosive	Empowerment Self	Other	Active	Flexibility	Power Mode
b. Umbrellas (*continued*)	legitimate excuse to argue; however, if B is unfair to A in some small way, A may use this as an umbrella to take out anger on B (Walton 1969)								
c. Negative inquiry	When B raises an issue, A responds by asking for more information: For example, B charges A with "sloppy work"; A engages in negative inquiry by asking exactly what B means, what A could do differently, and so on. This often clarifies issues and, by so doing, reduces conflict (Wilmot and Wilmot 1978)	High	Varies	Varies	Yes	Varies	High	Varies	Indirect
d. Issue control	Directly or indirectly indicate that an issue is off-limits (see Chapter 4 for explanation)	High	Low	Low	Yes	No	Low	Low	Hidden
e. Fogging	Turn aside a criticism or attack by acknow-ledging only part of it. If B criticizes A—"You	High	Varies	Varies	Yes	Varies	Varies	Moderate	Indirect

TABLE 7.2 Continued

Tactic	Definition	Assertive	Cooperative	Disclosive	Empowerment		Active	Flexibility	Power Mode
					Self	*Other*			
	have ruined this report. You are always so late!"—A may respond, "Yes, the report wasn't as good as it could have been." A fogs by not acknowledging the lateness issue (Wilmot and Wilmot 1978)								
f. Two-column method	List party's needs in column one and other's needs in column two and compare, searching for commonalities	High	High	High	Yes	Yes	High	Varies	Varies
g. Issue expansion	Party purposely adds issues to strengthen case; also called "bundling boards" (Walton 1969)	High	Low	Moderate	Yes	No	Moderate	Low	Direct, virtual
12. Conflict process reflection									
a. Meta-communication	Discussing and commenting on communication patterns, particularly with the goal of improving communication processes	Varies	Varies	High	Yes	Yes	High	High	Varies

(continued)

TABLE 7.2 Continued

Tactic	Definition	Assertive	Cooperative	Disclosive	Empowerment		Active	Flexibility	Power Mode
					Self	*Other*			
b. Labeling	Attaching a name, often unfavorable, indirectly to another's behavior; for example, A says to B: "You don't have to be so hostile!"	High	Varies	Varies	Yes	No	Varies	Low	Direct, virtual
13. Indirect communication									
a. Precueing	Giving information about party's reaction prior to openly dealing with conflict; for example, when A nonverbally indicates disgust at B's mention of an issue	High	Low	Moderate	Yes	No	Varies	Low	Direct, virtual
b. Tacit coordination	Choosing a position the other is likely to accept without discussing it with him or her. Often, this depends on norms or social conventions; for example, A, anticipating B's objections, offers to "split the difference," taking advantage of the equality norm	High	High	Moderate	Yes	Yes	High	High	Indirect
c. Use intermediaries	Party asks an outsider to convey messages or	High	Varies	Varies	Yes	Varies	Moderate	Varies	Varies

264

TABLE 7.2 Continued

Tactic	Definition	Assertive	Cooperative	Disclosive	Empowerment Self	Other	Active	Flexibility	Power Mode
	offers to other (Pruitt and Rubin 1986)								
14. Normative									
a. Moral appeal		High	Varies	Varies	Yes	Varies	Varies	Low	Indirect
b. Altercasting	A tells B to comply with a request because "a good" person would comply; or, alternatively, say "only a bad" person would not comply (Marwell and Schmitt 1967)	High	Low	Low	Yes	No	Varies	Low	Indirect
15. Integrative									
a. Propose novel solution		High	Varies	Moderate to high	Yes	Yes	Varies	Varies	Indirect
b. Invoke superordinate goal	Identify a common goal or end toward which parties can work together; goal should be one both value	High	High	High	Yes	Yes	High	Varies	Indirect
c. Acknowledge legitimacy of position	Party does not agree with other's position but acknowledges that he or she has legitimate interests that should be taken into account	Varies	High	Moderate	Yes	Yes	High	High	Indirect
d. Reformed sinner	Switch to cooperating after a period of competing	High	Low	Moderate	Yes	Yes	Varies	High	Varies

(continued)

265

TABLE 7.2 Continued

Tactic	Definition	Assertive	Cooperative	Disclosive	Empowerment		Active	Flexibility	Power Mode
					Self	*Other*			
e. Experimental integration	Party makes integrative move as an experiment to see if other will reciprocate; if other does, party makes another integrative move and awaits reciprocation	High	Varies	Moderate	Yes	Yes	Varies	High	Varies
f. Joint fact-finding	Parties investigate issues together in an attempt to establish a factual basis for agreement	High	High	Varies	Yes	Yes	High	High	Varies
g. Single text method	Parties work on a written draft of an agreement, passing it back and forth with revisions until consensus is reached (Fisher and Ury 1981)	High	High	Varies	Yes	Yes	High	High	Varies
16. Joking	Party jokes with other in a tangent from the issue	High	High	Low	Yes	Yes	Low	Low	Varies
17. Change conflict forum									
a. Move into formal adjudication	Party takes conflict into formal procedure for judging the merits of two points, such as in a	High	Varies	Varies	Yes	Varies	Varies	Varies	Varies

TABLE 7.2 Continued

Tactic	Definition	Assertive	Cooperative	Disclosive	Empowerment		Active	Flexibility	Power Mode
					Self	*Other*			
	grievance committee or a court of law								
b. Use the media	Party takes issues to the media to either pressure the other or get redress; for example, party uses television "action-line" or "blows the whistle" on illegal practices	High	Low	Varies	Yes	No	Varies	Low	Direct, virtual
c. Call in a third party	Parties agree to have a third party, such as a mediator or counselor, help them work out the conflict	High	High	Moderate	Yes	Yes	High	Varies	Varies

High: The tactic exhibits a high degree of this characteristic.
Moderate: The tactic exhibits some, but not a high degree, of this characteristic.
Low: The tactic exhibits a low degree of this characteristic.
Varies: The amount of this characteristic exhibited by the tactic varies, depending on how the party carries out the tactic.

Summary and Review

How do conflict strategies, styles, and tactics differ?

Strategies refer to a party's general plans for a conflict, whereas tactics refer to the specific moves the party undertakes in carrying out the strategy. Planning ahead can be quite useful in conflict situations, but the fact that interaction generally escapes the control of any single actor also points to the limitations of detailed strategies. Conflict styles refer to the general orientation that a party takes in a conflict. A party adopting a competing style, for example, approaches the situation as a competition and chooses competitive tactics, focusing on attaining his or her goals and showing little regard for the other's goals. Styles are more flexible than strategies in that they do not require the party to plan out a definite set of tactics. Strategies always involve the choice of one or more styles, but someone can enact a style without consciously planning a strategy.

Is a person's style an unchanging characteristic?

Evidence suggests that people can and do change styles during conflicts. However, studies that measure conflict styles also suggest that people develop habitual styles that they tend to employ as their first tendency in conflicts. If we become aware of our conflict styles, it is possible to change them and even to choose them strategically. The main prerequisite for doing this is knowing how to enact different styles. That is why it is important to try styles and tactics that we do not ordinarily use.

What types of conflict styles are there?

Chapter 3 described the five classic conflict styles: competing, accommodating, avoiding, compromising, and problem-solving (also called collaborating). There are also variations within several styles, which represent different ways of carrying out the style; for example, forcing and contending are variations on competing.

Can conflict styles (and conflict behaviors) be described in terms of more basic dimensions?

Styles vary along a number of dimensions. Styles differ in terms of:
- Assertiveness: degree of focus on own goals
- Cooperativeness: degree of focus on other's goals
- Disclosiveness: degree to which information about the party's position or preference is disclosed to the other
- Empowerment: degree to which one grants the other some control or power
- Activeness: degree of one's involvement with one's conflict issues
- Flexibility: degree of movement the party is willing to make to work with the conflict

These dimensions are useful because they give insights into the nature of the style or tactic. They also allow us to compare styles and tactics.

Is problem-solving the best conflict style?

No style is always a good one; it depends on the situation. In the discussion of problem-solving, a number of conditions for effectively using this style were listed. When these hold, problem-solving is the preferred style because it is most likely to result in productive conflict management. But the problem-solving style takes substantial time and energy on the part of all parties. Unless they are willing to commit to this, a less satisfactory outcome will result.

Studies suggest that other conflict styles may be more appropriate in particular situations. For example, forcing will be successful when time is short and when the organization's priorities must take precedent over individual preferences. Avoiding is likely to yield benefits if the other is much more powerful and not inclined to compromise or problem solve. Moreover, effectiveness of styles varies across cultures. Different styles are likely to be effective for the harmony and regulative models of conflict than for the confrontational style emphasized in this book.

How do I select an appropriate conflict style?

Several factors should be considered, including: How effective is the style likely to be in the situation? What responses will this style provoke? What will the consequences of the style be for long-term relationships among parties? Is the style ethical under the current conditions? The decision tree is available to help in choosing an appropriate style. It incorporates several questions that bear on the effectiveness of conflict styles.

Do men and women differ in conflict behavior?

Although it is sometimes assumed that men's and women's conflict behavior are quite different, research suggests differences are not this clear-cut. A number of studies show no differences in conflict behavior, whereas others do show differences. What does seem to differ is that women generally focus on relationships, whereas men more often focus on the task at hand during a conflict. This difference leads to differing interpretations of the others' behavior, which sometimes produces different behavior.

How do tactics relate to styles?

Tactics represent the specific moves parties take during conflicts. Tactics are used to enact styles. However, there is no one-to-one correspondence between tactics and styles: The same tactic may be used in more than one style. There are a wide range of tactics, many of which are displayed in Table 7.2.

What makes threats and promises effective?

Five factors influence the effectiveness of threats and promises: They are more effective when they are specific, when the party making them is credible, when consequences can be made to seem immediate, when they are seen as equitable by the other, and when the climate is cooperative. In addition to being tactics, threats and promises can also be considered to be sources of information about the party's resolve and what he or she values.

What is toughness?

A tough bargainer resists making concessions until absolutely necessary and holds his or her ground in negotiations. Toughness has been shown to lead to favorable outcomes in many negotiation situations.

Is there value in the tit-for-tat tactic?

Earlier in this book we noted that conflicts often move in negative directions because of parties' tendencies to match each other. Tit for tat is a conscious use of matching in a conflict. This tactic indicates to others that the party is responsive—will respond to cooperation with cooperation. As a result, it is often useful to induce cooperation in others.

How do we explain coalition formation?

A number of theories have been advanced to explain coalition formation. Coalitions form on the basis of advantage to the parties, so one explanation for who joins with whom is that parties will select partners who can contribute just enough to give the alliance the power it needs to succeed. This minimum resource principle functions on the assumption that people want to partner with others who have as small an advantage over them as possible, because rewards will be divided within the coalition on the basis of contributions to it. It turns out, however, that in addition to minimum resources, similarities of attitudes and beliefs also explain with whom alliances will be formed.

Why is issue definition an important tactic?

Through issue definition, the grounds of the conflict are set. Also, as noted in Chapter 4, being able to control the definition of issues is one way in which hidden power is enacted. Several issue definition tactics—umbrellas, bundling boards, negative inquiry, and fogging—contribute a negative direction to the conflict. However, other issue definition tactics, such as fractionation and the two-column method, can contribute to integration.

What is metacommunication?

Metacommunication is explicit discussion about the nature and quality of communication. Talking about how we communicate can help us understand one another better and can contribute to productive conflict management. However, metacommunication must be handled carefully because such discussions are always touchy.

Which tactics specifically contribute to integration?

One classic integrative tactic is to find a superordinate goal that both parties value. If managing the conflict can be connected to this goal, parties often work together to achieve an integrative resolution. A second integrative tactic, experimental integration, involves offering someone safe concessions that are meaningful to him or her without putting the party in danger. The other's response to this concession can then be observed for signs that the other is interested in moving in a productive direction. Experimental integration is premised on the assumption that parties often incorrectly assume that the other is competitive, when both want to collaborate. It is therefore one way of overcoming attribution problems in conflict situations. A third integrative tactic is reformed sinner—an elaboration on tit for tat—in which the party demonstrates that he or she could compete, but chooses not to as long as the other cooperates as well.

Conclusion

This chapter has focused on the basic moves in many conflict episodes. The tactics described are used by parties to enact styles of conflict. Styles are general orientations toward conflict and represent the overall approaches that give tactics their meaning. As the discussion of variants on styles indicates, the five styles can be carried out in different ways, each giving something of a different flavor to interactions.

Styles alone are not sufficient to understand conflict, however. The other's style influences how effective one's style can be and whether the party can even stick with the original style. So, at a minimum, the interaction of people's styles and how these reinforce or cancel each other must be studied. Beyond this, we must recognize that descriptions of styles are not sufficient to fully capture what happens when parties enact a conflict. The communication processes discussed in previous chapters create a field of forces driving conflicts, and styles are used to attempt to navigate this field. Styles operate in a context set by other processes. For example, when face-saving is important, a competing style will be received differently than when parties are not attending to face. If people are caught in a spiral of escalation, a competing style may simply increase the escalation. But during periods of integration, brief use of the same style can contribute to constructive movement by increasing pressure for conflict resolution.

The selection of a style does not tell the whole story. Style choice has a major influence on conflict processes, but conflicts are also driven by the larger interaction context and by cycles of action and response, which are beyond any individual's control. It is important not to underestimate the difference judicious style choices can make, but also not to overestimate it.

8 Changing Conflict Dynamics

This chapter, building on the insights of Chapters 1 through 7, discusses how parties can regulate their own conflicts. Self-regulation is the optimal method of managing conflict. People are more likely to accept necessary measures if they personally choose them, and the measures they select are often more appropriate and effective than outsiders' suggestions. The next chapter considers how third-parties can facilitate conflict management. They can do many of the same things those in conflict would, but because of their special role, third-parties' actions often have quite different impacts.

This chapter discusses the role of people's working habits and how these habits can lead to difficulties in addressing conflicts constructively. An awareness of how working habits lead to blindspots—trained incapacities—can help people in conflict see the source of difficult patterns of conflict interaction and, as a result, find better ways to manage persistent unresolved issues.

This chapter also presents two techniques that have great promise for conflict management, procedures for structuring discussion, and methods for reframing conflicts. We do not mean to present these as pat, surefire solutions because conflicts simply have too many variables. It is a mistake to apply any formula strictly and without careful consideration; however, the techniques and procedures here do provide some general guidelines that can prove useful in conflict management.

Working Habits and Trained Incapacities in Conflicts

> But, Wally, don't you see that comfort can be dangerous? I mean, you like to be comfortable, and I like to be comfortable, too, but don't you see that comfort can lull you into a dangerous tranquillity? I mean, my mother knew a woman, Lady Hatfield, who was one of the richest women in the world, but she died of starvation because all she would eat was chicken. I mean, she just liked chicken, Wally, and that was all she would eat, and actually her body was starving, but she didn't know it, because she was quite happy eating her chicken, and so she finally died. . . .

Roc used to practice certain exercises, like, for instance, if he were right-handed, all today he would do everything with his left hand. All day—writing, eating, everything—opening doors—in order to break the habits of living, because the great danger for him, he felt, was to fall into a trance, out of habit.

Wallace Shawn and André Gregory, *My Dinner with André*

Working Habits

Working habits are the habitual interaction strategies people use to accomplish tasks or solve problems. For example, decision procedures such as voting, leadership styles normally employed in a group, or the practice of frequently joking during meetings to vent the frustrations of work are all examples of working habits. Sometimes they are formally and consciously adopted, but more often people are not conscious of their habits or the effects of them; people use them without thinking. Habits are a critical force in conflicts because they establish a framework for interpersonal and group interaction. As habits, they encourage interaction cycles to continue once they start despite changing events or circumstances that may call for new approaches. They establish expectations about how people will obtain ideas for consideration and how alternatives will be evaluated as the conflict is addressed. Working habits can be beneficial or harmful depending on the situation. The most troublesome are habits that normally yield benefits but backfire when the conflict situation changes and people fail to take the changes into account.

Understanding the role of habits in individual and team behavior helps to explain why conflicts get out of hand, why in many cases people cannot see that their behavior is becoming destructive and change it. It is true that people sometimes choose to use force to defeat their opponent, and in these cases a destructive conflict can be stemmed only by altering the motives or power of the participants. However, in many cases, conflicts move in negative directions because people are incapable of diagnosing the conflict and altering their behavior. Once in a conflict cycle, people may be trapped by their own interaction patterns.

When confronted with conflict, parties often fall back on behaviors that proved effective in other contexts. However, behaviors effective in some circumstances may actually worsen conflicts. For example, the common practice of openly evaluating ideas or proposals in an attempt to reach a decision can deepen parties' feelings of anger or competition in conflicts, resulting in escalating hostilities. These behaviors hold a "catch"—because they seem ordinary and have proved useful so often, people may be blinded to the problems they create. The social critic Kenneth Burke (1935) terms this catch a *trained incapacity*. He argues that individuals become so well-trained in their strategies that they begin to serve as blinders. People think they know what to expect, so they ignore signs that something is wrong. The incapacities are particularly pernicious because people may assume they are doing the right thing when actually they are worsening the situation.

Burke offers two simple and somewhat outlandish examples as illustrations of this concept: A chicken can be taught to repeatedly come to a specific place to receive food when it hears a certain pitch of a bell. On one occasion, however, the chicken responds to the bell as it always has by coming to the same place in search of food. This time the chicken finds not food, but the threatening axe of its owner. In Burke's second example, a trout that has had a near miss with a fishhook on its way upstream avoids all food sources that even remotely resemble the color of the bait that nearly caught it. In both cases the animals' past training causes them to misjudge their present situation; their training has incapacitated them.

Certain working habits are adaptive and beneficial in the contexts in which they are learned; however, as conditions change and as conflicts deepen, they become maladaptive, harmful, and irrational. The behaviors are injurious because they shape thinking and perception and, therefore, can prevent recognition of changed circumstances. When this happens, people continue to do "what has always worked," resulting either in no change or in an actual deterioration of the situation.

Trained Incapacities

Trained incapacities play a crucial role in conflict sequences. Confronted with a real or imagined conflict, parties tend toward habitual responses. As previously noted, the stress of differentiation can decrease individuals' ability to think clearly. Several researchers (Beier 1951; Holsti 1971; Dill 1965; Janis and Mann 1977; Smart and Vertinsky 1977; Zillman 1990) provide evidence that people under stress screen out essential environmental cues, distort incoming information, and become less flexible and creative problem solvers. Habitual, preprogrammed responses provide excellent ways to cope under such circumstances; indeed, they are often all a person can think of in the heat of a crisis.

Because of cultural tendencies to repress and avoid conflict if possible, many people have not had much experience with conflict situations; fewer still have reflected at length on how to deal with conflicts. As a result, conflicts are novel, uncertain, and often threatening situations for most people. Faced with such situations, individuals cling to habitual responses.

Some habitual patterns facilitate conflict management; others may immediately seem to improve the situation, but actually cause it to deteriorate over the long run. Patterns can blind people to the negative consequences of their behaviors and prevent them from altering the direction of the conflict when harmful escalation or avoidance cycles begin. Because people cannot recognize that behaviors that were once beneficial are now counterproductive, they become locked in destructive cycles.

Conflicts are, in effect, problems that people must attempt to solve. Therefore, the trained incapacities most likely to worsen conflicts are those arising from work habits that facilitate decision making and problem solving. Work habits become second nature; people come to rely on them as shortcuts to guide work efficiently and solve problems.

Because the major task in resolving conflict is to construct an acceptable and workable decision, working habits usually come into play as people confront conflict issues. These working habits may be adaptive and beneficial because they tend to facilitate decision making. However, they can also have corrosive effects on the ability to manage and contain conflict if parties come to rely on habits in situations where they should be disregarded. Ironically, the benefits of working habits enhance their potential for harm precisely because it is so difficult to determine when the negative consequences will begin to overwhelm the positive ones. By the time participants recognize they are in trouble, their interaction may have become so tangled that it is difficult for them to detect or to correct the destructive tendencies; working habits have become their trained incapacities.

As illustrations of these destructive and often unseen tendencies, the next sections describe two trained incapacities: goal-emphasis and use of procedures.

Goal-Emphasis.   A good deal of our everyday behavior leads toward achieving some goal or plan. As Miller, Galanter, and Pribram (1960) argue in *Plans and the Structure of Behavior,* activities are frequently organized in a sequence of moves that have some desired end point. Plans generate and control the sequence of behaviors we carry out. In everyday life, these goals range in type and in the number of behaviors required for their execution. Obviously, having plans or goals serves people well in various ways. Most important, a plan allows for the completion of critical activities and makes it possible to direct and evaluate our actions, because each action can be assessed by determining whether it contributes to successful plan completion.

In conflict and decision-making situations, one set of goals is the solutions or outcomes parties would like to see adopted. They are individuals' estimates of the best decision or course of action. Entering a discussion with a solution to a problem or conflict in mind is natural and in some respects useful. It is natural because people often have explicit needs, which they believe can only be met by the adoption of a particular solution. Having a solution in mind can also be useful because it provides clear guidance about the type of communicative behavior parties should engage in during conflict interaction. The goal or solution can dictate the type of information each should contribute and the arguments that should be made in support of a position. Each person can build a case for the solution he or she wants adopted. If parties start the discussion of an issue by arguing for alternative solutions, the information and arguments in favor of each solution will be aired and points of difference can be clarified. People need to hear the pros and cons of suggested solutions to evaluate and choose among them.

Goal-emphasis is harmful when it prevents team members from seeing a problem clearly. The experience of a twelve-person food distribution cooperative illustrates this. The members were in conflict over whether to continue publishing the cooperative's newsletter. The conflict was rapidly defined in terms of solutions: either publish the newsletter or discontinue it. The group quickly reached an impasse between these two opposing solutions, and a third-party facilitator was called in. The facilitator turned their attention to the issues behind the conflict; two in particular surfaced. First, a newcomer to the organization was going to succeed to the editorship of the newsletter, and several members doubted that this person could adequately represent the Coop. A second issue was the need for the Coop to keep in touch with other cooperatives. In the ensuing discussion, members realized that the cooperative could substitute e-mail for the newsletter to keep up with the other cooperatives, and that they could also send out newsbriefs, which any member could submit via an online listserve. So the printed newsletter was discontinued, but its functions were maintained, and all Coop members became "writers" of its news, with the new editor coordinating the stories.

Goal-emphasis becomes an incapacity when (1) it prevents parties from conducting an adequate assessment of the problem underlying the conflict (in other words, when it undercuts the group's attempt to orient itself to the problem), or (2) it becomes a way to quickly make a decision without a complete analysis of the chosen solution (in other words, when it prevents the group from establishing criteria for solutions or examining a solution in light of established criteria). In the case of the newsletter, solutions were debated before the group adequately assessed what functions the newsletter served, what needs prompted its publication, or what the possible consequences of not publishing it were. An examination of these issues gave the members a clearer understanding of the problem they were trying to solve. Once the issues were clarified, criteria for what a good solution might look like emerged.

The tendency to be goal-centered may encourage people to begin discussion of an issue with an evaluation of alternative solutions. There is, however, persuasive evidence to suggest that the group's attempt to define the problem—asking "What is wrong here?"—should be separated from the search for solutions—asking "What should be done to alleviate the problem?" (Maier 1967). Time should be divided between analysis of the problem and evaluation of solutions. Thorough analysis of the symptoms and causes of a problem is likely to yield the best solution—the one that comes closest to meeting all parties' needs or all causes of the problem. However, if people make statements about solutions they would like to see adopted at the outset, conflict cannot unfold in a "problem analysis–solution evaluation" sequence. Of course, all solutions are founded on some conception of the problem, but this may never be articulated if the solution is proposed first.

Use of Procedures.   One of the primary characteristics of organizations and teams is their tendency to use structured procedures to help complete tasks (Hall 1972). Although rules are often adopted formally, many procedures evolve without being explicitly acknowledged. A procedure that works becomes institutionalized through repetitive use. For example, when a group often spends the first fifteen minutes of its meetings socializing, members eventually may expect to do so at every session. Procedures become traditions. Members come to assume things should be done in a certain way, and the organization's identity often becomes tied to its procedures; for example, "This is a democratic group—we vote on all major decisions."

Standardized procedures hold several advantages (Poole 1991). If procedures are set before a decision is made, members have sufficient knowledge about the process to participate and contribute. They know, for example, when votes will be taken, how long they have to suggest alternative proposals, and who will end discussion of a topic. Chaotic or ill-defined decision-making procedures discourage participation and can result in an inferior decision because some members feel lost during the meeting. Knowledge of set procedures, such as a parliamentary one, reduces uncertainty about how to behave in the group and may therefore reduce stress for some members.

Procedural rules can also serve as standards for deciding disputes in the group. For example, a disagreement over whether a decision was made fairly might be settled by checking the rules on voting procedures. Because procedural rules are used and accepted by the group before the dispute, they may have a degree of legitimacy in the eyes of all, which allows the disagreement to be settled without arousing personal antipathies.

Finally, set procedures can often equalize power among group members. In the nominal group technique, a structured decision-making method developed by Delbecq, Van de Ven, and Gustafsen (1975), preliminary ideas are elicited by going around the group in order and having each member give one idea. This process is repeated until all members' ideas have been contributed. The nominal group technique ensures that everyone contributes; it gives those who are usually quiet or hesitant a formal opportunity to participate without being interrupted by more talkative or powerful members.

Procedures can become incapacities, however, when (1) they structure interaction so that confrontation and escalation are inevitable, or (2) they are used to suppress or avoid conflict. Procedures that institutionalize controversy and opposition, such as the use of Robert's Rules of Order in meetings, serve a useful function for a group because they ensure that all sides of an issue are heard and they force members to make a definite choice among alternatives. The orderly, sharp debate of a well-run meeting under Robert's Rules often illustrates the benefits of parliamentary-type methods. However, because the discussion of a motion begins with the expectation that a vote is inevitable if a serious conflict develops, parliamentary procedure may polarize opposing factions and cause competition and rifts.

In one labor union that used Robert's Rules, a major conflict erupted over whether to call a work stoppage in response to a grievance against plant administration. As debate proceeded, it became clear that more than two-thirds of the membership did not favor the stoppage, although a large minority remained very much in favor of the move. The minority, however, was able to advocate its position long after it was evident that the union would vote down the work stoppage by using parliamentary rules as tactics. Some members, for example, attempted to add the work stoppage as an amendment to an unrelated proposal generally favored by the union. The tactics resulted in a polarization of union members: Many of those opposed to the work stoppage were outraged at the minority's persistence. The longer members of the minority argued for the stoppage, the more convinced they became of their positions. The end result was a major rift in the union. The minority—voted down— felt cut off from the rest of the membership, left the union, and attempted to form their own organization. In this case, the easily manipulated rules of parliamentary procedure contributed to the problem. Just as important was the general climate that parliamentary methods can create in groups: an adversarial atmosphere that encourages stubborn adherence to one's own position in the face of opposition. Such a climate can be more conducive to factionalism than to common ownership of the problem and a united pursuit of a workable solution.

Procedures can also stifle differentiation by discouraging a direct assault on issues. Voting on proposals is often used to avoid difficult situations (Hall and Watson 1970; Avery, Auvine, Streibel, and Weiss 1981). If two sides appear to be forming, the chairperson calls for a vote and assumes that once the vote is taken the issue is decided and the problem solved. This reasoning is flawed in this case, however, because only the winning side gets what it wants. The members who lose the vote may be dissatisfied and withdraw from the group or be much less committed to the decision. Disagreement can also be stifled by informal or implicit rules, such as "Let's get through our agenda as fast as possible." This kind of attitude can make members feel they are imposing on the group by raising or complicating issues. As Janis (1972) notes, decision-making groups often do not realize that they have suppressed contributions or criticism and may even think they are doing an excellent job of decision making.

There are many other trained incapacities besides the two examined here. Even the most constructive behaviors can undermine interaction if members blindly cling to them. Because they are deeply ingrained habits, trained incapacities mold members' perceptions of the situation so that their negative consequences are not easily discovered. As a result, trained incapacities promote interaction patterns that head toward escalation or avoidance of conflicts.

Recognizing and Counteracting Trained Incapacities

Trained incapacities are work habits inflexibly applied in response to conflict. One way to diagnose the effect of trained incapacities is, therefore, to examine "standard operating procedures" for traps which can provide a set of starting points for a search. Parties can monitor discussions for problems due to goal centeredness, such as insufficient analysis of problems underlying the conflict, or reliance on procedural rules. This monitoring process must go on continuously because people can slip into harmful patterns without recognizing it. Because trained incapacities are "second nature," they are subtle and hard to detect: Parties know something is wrong, but they cannot put their finger on the source.

The chair of an administrative committee at one Midwest social service agency keeps a checklist of possible problems to help her overcome potential blind spots. It includes questions such as: "Is there too little dissent to have a balanced discussion?" "Are votes being used to suppress minority views?" "Are differences discussed in win–lose terms?" The chair goes over this list (or parts of it) during and after every meeting, carefully monitoring the group's process. Although the answers are negative for most meetings, the list has turned up several unexpected problems.

One symptom of the operation of trained incapacities is a high level of tension in the group. Recall from Chapter 1 that differentiation of positions in the early stages of a conflict creates tension that can lead to inflexible behavior and promote trained incapacities. Although there is not a perfect cause–effect relationship between tension level and trained incapacities, tension does increase their likelihood. Situations that create tension—a serious threat from outside, a rapidly approaching time limit, or a severe and important disagreement—make a group ripe for the dangers of differentiation.

Some Useful Conflict Management Procedures

The most straightforward way to counteract the various problems and negative dynamics that can arise in conflicts is for the parties to adopt procedures that correct for them (Poole 1991). The widely used *Reflective Thinking Procedure* for decision making is one such procedure (Scheidel and Crowell 1979; Gouran 1982). Basically, the Reflective Thinking Procedure is designed to avoid errors that can result from trained incapacities such as emphasizing solutions prior to analyzing problems or premature evaluation of ideas.

Reflective thinking avoids these problems by positing a five-step problem-solving procedure and requiring parties to go through the steps in order, keeping deliberations on each step separate:

1. *Definition of the problem or task*—The parties assess the nature of it before them and determine if it is significant enough to act on.
2. *Analysis of the problem*—Once the problem is defined, the parties analyze its causes; only after these are understood do the parties move on to step 3.
3. *Suggestion of possible solutions*—The parties research and develop a wide array of possible solutions. No serious evaluation or elimination of solutions occurs at this stage.
4. *Solution selection*—The parties evaluate and select the best solution.
5. *Implementation*—The parties plan how to put the solution into effect and determine how effectiveness will be evaluated.

This procedure closely parallels logical thought processes and is the basis for most group decision-making methods (see also Etzioni 1968) and conflict management sequences (see also Filley 1975). Requiring parties to analyze the problem prior to developing solutions and to develop a long list of solutions prior to evaluating them, counteracts a tendency to focus on and evaluate solutions prematurely. Focusing attention on a well-defined pattern for thinking about a common problem also helps avoid destructive redefinition.

Filley (1975) proposes one useful addition to this sequence. He notes that many problem-solving sequences are overly rational in that they place most of their emphasis on cognitive operations, such as analysis and generation, ignoring the role of emotion in human behavior. Following Filley's suggestions, which are more appropriate for third-party interventions and so are discussed in Chapter 9, we would suggest dividing the Reflective Thinking Procedure's step 1, Definition of the problem or task, into a three-step procedure:

1a. *Clarification of issues*—Parties share their perceptions of the key issues in the conflict and their own positions. They also should share their perceptions of how others see the key issues; this often helps parties clarify misunderstandings.

1b. *Clarification of feelings*—Parties share their feelings about the conflict and their reactions to others' behavior. In this step it is important that both sides validate others' feelings because feelings cannot be right or wrong—they must simply be accepted. Parties cannot be forced to change their feelings; they must change them of their own accord.

1c. *Problem definition*—Parties develop a shared definition of the problem.

The addition of step 1b is useful because it gets feelings on the table from the outset. However, this is often threatening to one or more parties. If this has the potential to interfere with work on the conflict, it may be best to go back to the original Reflective Thinking Procedure.

A key problem with the reflective thinking steps is that parties may not be able to agree on a problem definition. One option is to use a complex definition that includes all issues and then try to come up with a solution or a package of solutions that resolves most or all of them. Another option is to try to reframe the conflict to develop a shared definition, as we will discuss in the next section.

Hall and Watson (1970) present another useful format. Rather than focusing on *what* the parties talk about at particular decision-making stages, they attempt to develop a set of ground rules for *how* parties should work on a problem. *Consensus-seeking rules* are designed to help parties work through differences and disagreements in a constructive fashion, as follows:

1. Avoid arguing for your own position. Present your position as clearly and logically as possible, but consider seriously the reactions of the group in any subsequent presentation of the same point.

2. Avoid win–lose stalemates in the discussion of positions. Discard the notion that someone must win and someone must lose; when impasses occur, look for the next most acceptable alternative for both parties.

3. Avoid changing your mind *only to avoid* the conflict and to reach agreement. Withstand pressures to yield that have no objective or logically sound foundation. Strive for enlightened flexibility; avoid outright capitulation.

4. Avoid suppressing conflicts by resorting to voting, averaging, coin flipping, and the like. Treat differences of opinion as indicative of an incomplete sharing of information and viewpoints and press for additional exploration and investigation.

5. View differences of opinion as both natural and helpful rather than as a hindrance to decision making. Generally, the more ideas expressed, the greater

the likelihood of conflict will be, but the richer the array of resources will be as well.

6. View initial agreement as suspect. Explore the reasons underlying apparent agreements; make sure that people have arrived at similar solutions for either the same basic reasons or for complementary reasons before incorporating such solutions into an agreement or decision.

These rules encourage parties to air and to address differences rather than to come to agreement quickly. They counteract the tendency to come to premature convergence on a single solution and reliance on objective standards where none exist. Hall and Watson tested these procedures and found that groups trained in the rules produced better answers on a problem-solving task than did untrained groups. They attributed this to a "synergy bonus" from the procedure: It allowed groups to make use of all their members' skills and knowledge. Untrained groups fell prey to difficulties that precluded effective involvement of all members.

There are literally dozens of procedures that can facilitate creativity, decision making, and planning (Scheidel and Crowell 1979; Nutt 1984). Often it is best to tailor and adapt them to a particular situation rather than simply following them by rote.

Although these and other formats are quite valuable, it is important to remember that they, too, can become trained incapacities as described in the previous section. Neither of the two procedures we have just mentioned is appropriate under all conditions. For example, the Reflective Thinking Procedure does not work well when people have fundamental disagreements over values, because it presumes agreement on the criteria used to evaluate solutions. The consensus-seeking rules would not be appropriate for intense disputes wherein parties have long-standing grievances. In such cases, sticking to either procedure would only compound the conflict. Although they protect against some possible problems, the procedures can unintentionally introduce others.

The effectiveness of procedures is limited by the fact that they can only counteract those problems that they are explicitly designed to address. Reflective thinking, for example, does nothing to eliminate attribution biases because its rules do not take this problem into account; however, the addition of the three substeps to step 1 may counteract the biases by encouraging parties to explore misunderstandings.

Framing and Reframing Issues and Interactions in Conflicts

One approach to understanding patterns of thinking and their impact on interaction is to consider ways in which parties frame and reframe issues and episodes. In its broadest sense, the concept of *framing* refers to people's ability to construct interpretations of events or actions and thus define the situations they are in

(Bateson 1972; Goffman 1974). Just as a frame changes one's perception of the painting it surrounds, the perceptual frames people impose on events alter their understanding and reaction to those events. The idea of framing or *reframing*—changing or substituting frames—has been used to examine important aspects of many social phenomena. In some forms of therapy, for example, reframing is used as an approach that enables people to create change in response to difficult problems (Watzlawick, Weakland, and Fisch 1974; Bandler and Grinder 1982). In conflict, reframing is important in two senses: conflict interaction can be redirected in constructive directions (1) when parties reframe substantive issues and (2) when parties reframe the interaction episode itself.

Reframing Issues

There is substantial research suggesting that the way people define problems influences the choices they make in attempting to solve them (Kahneman and Tversky 1979; Tversky and Kahneman 1981). This finding has led conflict and negotiation researchers to examine its implications for the way parties frame and reframe issues during conflict. One line of research in bargaining and negotiations has studied how differential framing of bargaining proposals can influence the evaluations and choices made about those proposals (Bazerman 1983; Bazerman and Neale 1983). Bargaining proposals can be worded to suggest what might be gained by adopting or accepting the proposal. Or the same proposal can be worded to suggest what will be lost by adopting or accepting the proposal.

As an illustration of these *gain* or *loss* frames, consider the following example that has been used as a basis for research on negotiations (Bazerman and Neale 1983, pp. 54–55):

> A large manufacturer has recently been hit with a number of economic difficulties, and it appears as if three plants need to be closed and 6,000 employees laid off. The vice president of production has been exploring alternative ways to avoid this crisis. She has adopted two plans:
>
> > Plan A: This plan will save one of the three plants and 2,000 jobs.
> > Plan B: This plan has a 1/3 probability of saving three plants and all 6,000 jobs, but has a 2/3 probability of saving no plants and no jobs.
>
> Which plan would you select?
> > Both of the proposed plans (A and B) are cast in terms of gain (saving plants).
>
> Now reconsider the same problem but with the following alternative choices:
>
> > Plan C: This plan will result in the loss of two of the three plants and 4,000 jobs.
> > Plan D: This plan has a 2/3 probability of resulting in the loss of all three plants and all 6,000 jobs but has a 1/3 probability of losing no plants and no jobs.
>
> Which plan would you select?

Both of these plans (C and D) are cast in terms of what people can possibly lose if they are adopted. However, these two options are objectively identical to those worded in terms of gains. That is, Plan A is the same as Plan C and Plan B is the same as Plan D. The difference is in the way in which the proposals are framed—as potential gains or losses.

The way options are framed has an important effect on people's preferences. Given the choice between Plans A and B, about 80 percent of people choose Plan A. But given the choice between Plans C and D, the choice is overwhelmingly for Plan D. The difference in framing as potential for gain versus potential for loss is enough to shift the choices that people make. When people choose among options cast in terms of gains, they are more likely to choose the sure thing. In this instance, Plan A is chosen over Plan B because the choice is among plans that offer gain and Plan A is a sure thing, while Plan B is the riskier choice. In contrast, when people choose among options that are cast in terms of losses, they are more likely to choose the riskier option. In this instance, Plan D is chosen over Plan C because the choice is among plans that offer losses and Plan D is the riskier choice.

The difference between wording proposals as gains or losses is a difference in how the proposals are framed. The reactions to this difference have important implications for how formal negotiations unfold. When labor and management frame their proposals in terms of the losses likely to result from various options, parties may be more likely to make riskier choices, including agreeing to let an outside arbitrator decide the outcome rather than settling. On the other hand, if parties frame issues in terms of gains, they may be more likely to choose the less risky choice; they may settle for what is on the table rather than risking a stalemate and turning the choice over to an arbitrator (a riskier option) (Bazerman and Neale 1983). Negotiators who view possible outcomes in terms of gains rather than losses are, in some cases, more likely to attain better overall outcomes (Bazerman, Magliozzi, and Neale 1985; Neale and Northcroft 1986).

Other studies of labor–management negotiations suggest more ways that issues can be framed in negotiations (Putnam and Holmer 1992). Negotiators can differ in how they develop an argument about an issue on the table (Putnam et al. 1986; Putnam 1990). One side in the negotiations might approach an issue by arguing about the harms of a current situation and how a particular proposal will address those harms. The other side might approach the same issue by attacking the possible benefits of a proposal. When parties start with different argument frames, the negotiations may be more likely to head toward problem-solving rather than compromising or trade-offs. It appears that when issues are argued differently at first, the parties develop their cases more fully and tend to search for more alternatives. It is not, then, that one frame wins out in the negotiations, but that frames are altered and new frames are constructed by parties conjointly; frames on the issues emerge and develop in the interaction (Putnam and Holmer 1992).

One side in negotiations can reframe an issue and thereby influence the negotiation process as well (Brown 1983). The decision to support a strike as a tactic in a labor–management dispute is often a troublesome and potentially divisive issue for workers. How striking is framed by the workers—what it means to them to strike—can have a powerful influence on whether the tactic is supported. Striking can be seen as "getting revenge" or striking can be seen as "principled behavior" (Donnellon, Gray, and Bougon 1986). Reframing the meaning of striking during the process can influence the degree of support for adopting the tactic.

Parties in conflicts are known to reframe issues in contexts other than formal negotiation as well. In legal arenas, disputes are sometimes broadened or narrowed to suit the forums available for addressing them (Mather and Yngvesson 1980–1981; Menkel-Meadow 1985). Disputes are narrowed when the issues are reframed in such a way that they can more easily be addressed in available forums such as courts or mediation centers. A complex, interpersonal fight that involves relationship issues, threats, and assault, for example, may be addressed solely in monetary terms by a judge in court. Such treatment narrows the dispute: Many issues go unaddressed because they are not easily handled.

Disputes can also be broadened through reframing. For example, a dispute between a doctor and patient may be broadened into a complaint of discrimination against an entire group of people. In such instances, a single conflict is used as a test case for addressing a much broader social injustice or for protecting a group's rights.

Reframing of issues and problems is unavoidable as the parties discuss them. In many instances, people frame and reframe issues without fully realizing it. Reframing can redirect conflict interaction in either constructive or destructive directions. If parties want to control conflict interaction and direct it constructively, they need to be able to reframe issues and problems so that a wide array of alternative solutions can be considered.

In response to this need, Volkema (1981, 1983) developed the *Problem–Purpose Expansion (PPE) Technique* to help members recognize and transcend narrow thinking. Volkema argues that the effectiveness of any conflict management strategy depends on how people formulate the problems they face. Problem formulation has at least two effects on conflict. First, it channels parties' thinking and can severely limit the range of solutions considered. In the Creativity Development Committee (Case 4.3), the major problem was expressed as "selection of the best possible procedure for making decisions in the research meetings." This formulation of the problem constrained members to search for a single procedure to be used by all project teams, which eventually worsened the conflict. How this problem was formulated implicitly ruled out several solutions that would have allowed members to work on common grounds, such as adopting two procedures and testing each in half of the project teams or adopting several procedures and allowing the project directors to choose whichever they liked best. As we have seen, people tend to converge on solutions prematurely, and an overly narrow problem formulation encourages this.

Second, problem formulation also affects parties' motivations when a conflict emerges. How the research committee formulated its problem set up a win–lose situation once members became divided over the two candidate programs. Because only one program could be adopted in this approach, a win–lose fight became inevitable, with the manager ultimately forcing his preferred solution.

Volkema shows that problem formulations vary along a narrow to broad continuum. For the Creativity Development Committee, the formulation, "Selection of Tom's procedure for the project teams," would be the narrowest scope possible because it focuses on a single solution and specifies what must be done. The alternative problem formulation, "Selection of the best possible procedure for making decisions in the research meetings," is broader than the first. Note that the second formulation admits a greater number of possible solutions than the first because it does not specify which procedure should be chosen and opens up a range of possibilities. The second formulation also focuses attention on a different set of actions than does the first. With the first formulation, parties are likely to focus on how they can get project teams to like Tom's procedure. With the second, they are likely to concentrate on searching for alternative procedures and choosing one. A still broader problem formulation than the second would be: "Selection of the best possible procedures that can be used by the teams." Broader still is: "To make the best possible decisions in the project teams." Both of these formulations open up a wider range of possibilities and imply different actions than do the first two (indeed, the fourth opens up the possibility of chucking the procedures altogether, if members agree it is impossible to find a good one).

Volkema argues that some levels of formulation promote better and more acceptable solutions than others. Exactly which formulations are best varies depending on the parties, the nature of the conflict, the surrounding environment, and other factors. In general, it is difficult to identify the best formulations. However, this chapter's earlier discussion of trained incapacities suggests one way to identify which formulations are not desirable—namely, those that promote trained incapacities.

Identification of the problem formulations being used in a conflict is a complex process. For one thing, problems are not always explicitly stated. Sometimes, in fact, people consciously avoid clear problem statements in an attempt to keep conflicts suppressed. In such cases, problem definitions can be inferred by listening to discussions. Figuring out the definition is fairly easy once one is familiar with some examples of problem formulations. An additional complication is introduced by the fact that problem formulations may change as the group works on an issue. In the Creativity Development Committee (Case 4.3), the problem was initially "selection of the best possible decision-making procedure for the project teams," but over time it shifted to "should we adopt the manager's preference?" which implied confrontation. Clearly, these shifts reflect significant occurrences in the conflict and changes in the relationships among members. Indeed, several researchers have proposed that decision making is nothing more than a series of redefinitions and reconceptualizations of problems leading gradually toward narrow solution statements (Lyles and Mitroff 1980; Poole 1983). It is important to be sensitive to these shifts and their implications for the direction conflict takes.

The PPE Technique has two basic parts. The first is a format for stating the problem: an infinitive + an object + a qualifier. For example, if the problem is presently thought to be "how to convince the residents of a neighborhood that a sidewalk should be installed along their block," the problem might be stated as:

to convince neighbors that a sidewalk is needed
Infinitive + Object + Qualifier

This statement of the problem then serves as the basis for brainstorming a set of possible solutions (see Table 8.1 for possible solutions associated with this formulation of the problem).

The second part of PPE expands the first problem statement by reformulating it, which allows for a second round of brainstorming—one that generates a set of different solutions. Reformulation is done by asking: What are we trying to accomplish by this?

- *We want* (most recent formulation) . . . to convince neighbors that a sidewalk is needed.
- *In order to* (reformulation) . . . get neighbors to pay for the sidewalk installation.

The group might decide it wants to convince neighbors that a sidewalk *is needed* in order to get neighbors *to pay* for sidewalk installation. This process is then repeated to generate a whole set of formulations and solutions (see Table 8.1). Comparison of the levels can enable parties to recognize the narrowness in their thinking and the trained incapacities that may be operating. By making parties aware of different formulations, PPE can disclose the values and assumptions underlying a current way of looking at a problem and suggest innovative viewpoints.

TABLE 8.1   A Hierarchy of Expanded Problem Statements

Problem Statements	Possible Solutions
To convince neighbors that a sidewalk is needed (What are we trying to accomplish by this?)	Gather data; hold public hearings; go door to door
To get neighbors to pay for sidewalk installation (What are we trying to accomplish by this?)	Go to the Transportation Department; sue neighbors; introduce a resolution at City or Town Hall
To get a sidewalk installed (What are we trying to accomplish by this?)	Pay for sidewalk yourself; install sidewalk yourself
To make the area where a sidewalk would go passable (What are we trying to accomplish by this?)	Level off area; build walkway
To make pedestrian traffic safe	Reroute auto traffic; partition off part of street; stop auto traffic for pedestrians; put up caution signs for autos

The PPE technique can also be used when the problem in question is "about" a relationship or group itself rather than about something people might do. For example, in the Riverdale Halfway House (Case 6.1), the problem was formulated as how "to resolve the animosities between George and Carole." PPE might lead to other formulations conducive to constructive dialogue, such as how "to clarify lines of authority at Riverdale" or how "to create a more supportive climate at Riverdale." In both cases these broader reformulations change the focus of the problem from Carole and George to the group as a whole and provide a common problem that the entire group can work on.

PPE tries to jolt people out of their well-worn, unreflective channels and encourages them to consider new ideas. As Chapter 6 noted, a surprising or startling move can also do this. A former chair of the board of General Motors is reputed to have said during a particularly docile meeting, "Well, it appears as if we're all in agreement. Why don't we all try to work up some conflicts over the weekend so when we come back on Monday we'll be able to think this proposal through thoroughly?" The chair's statement was designed to surprise the other members and jolt them out of their premature agreement. When members return to their task they may well do so with greater concentration and renewed vigor.

Reframing Interaction

We have seen that conflict interaction unfolds in phases and episodes and that parties see themselves doing certain episodes at various points during a conflict. What parties see themselves doing is often crucial in shaping conflict interaction (Bartunek and Reid 1992). When people change their perception of what they are doing, it can have a powerful influence over conflict interaction. When done strategically, this can promote constructive approaches. Through reframing interaction, parties can move conflict in new and more productive directions.

At times, the momentum and force of conflict interaction itself cause parties to reframe interaction. At the outset, people may attempt to launch certain types of episodes that they feel will help them reach their goals. However, once an interaction has started to unfold, the individual's goals are not the only—or even the primary—influence on how the conflict develops. The series of actions, reactions, and responses create a force of their own, which shapes perceptions of what is being done and, in turn, changes parties' goals (Putnam 1990). In other words, the types of interaction episodes the parties perceive themselves engaged in are influenced by the emerging interaction itself. Interaction often gets reframed based on what people find themselves doing, rather than on what they may have planned to do.

Axelrod's (1984) research on concession-making (discussed in Chapter 7) illustrates how interaction is reframed by the moves and responses of the parties. The tit-for-tat interaction sequences engaged in—exchanging small concessions over a series of moves—led to further cooperative action as parties reassessed possible outcomes and revised goals. What parties interpreted as being in their interests was influenced by the experiences they had in the tit-for-tat sequences. The

How Can We Manage Extreme Conflict?

The terrorist attacks on September 11, 2001, forever changed America's view of its own vulnerability and the nature of conflict in a world of global differences. For those interested in the study of conflict, one fundamental question rose from the ashes of that dreadful day: What moves individuals and groups toward extreme remedies such as violence and acts of terrorism? Of the many approaches to that question, one stands out for its commonsense value.

Eidelson and Eidelson (2003) suggest that individuals and groups can hold dysfunctional beliefs that are both self-perpetuating and destructive. Five beliefs stand out for their potential to lead to horrific violence, such as terrorism: superiority, injustice, vulnerability, distrust, and helplessness. When these belief domains are present in individuals or groups, the capacity for extreme remedies against others exists.

Superiority is the belief that a person or group is better than others in special ways. When holding this belief, people feel as if they deserve or are entitled to special treatment. Societal rules and laws are often thought not to apply fully in light of the status these people hold. *Injustice* is the belief that the individual or group has been mistreated by specific others or by the world at large. The sense of unfairness from this "treatment" becomes the center of sense-making and a debilitating or immobilizing preoccupation. *Distrust* is the belief that others are truly out to get an individual or group and intend to do harm; hostility and malevolent action lurks around corners and can be interpreted as such by the simplest of acts. Those who distrust expect to be humiliated or abused at any moment. *Vulnerability* is the belief that the welfare or position of person or group is in the hands of powerful others, that dangers exist virtually everywhere. An exaggerated sense of defenselessness is a sign that fear of vulnerability is in play. *Helplessness* is the conviction that even carefully crafted plans will result in dismal failure. Individuals believe nothing they do will make a difference, while groups feel powerless or at a distinct disadvantage compared to other groups.

In a world of varying socioeconomic means and cultural and religious differences, one or more of these belief domains is not uncommon, especially toward those outside the culture we ascribe to. When each of the domains is present in a person or a social unit, savage acts of violence toward others can occur in conflict situations. When social realities clash, tactics that usually work to alleviate conflict, such as compromising or collaborating, can actually make matters worse (Pearce and Littlejohn 1997). So what can be done to manage conflicts that arise from such beliefs? The answer seems to be to confront the foundations of expected violence before it begins. Of course, this is not an easy proposition. How can we dramatically challenge the core beliefs of individuals and groups around the world?

There is no simple answer to this complex dilemma; however, in addition to reframing, two ideas appear to be more promising than others. First, these belief domains are steeped in rational thought, albeit dysfunctional in bias. Keeping "real" data in front of people goes a long way toward diluting the five critical beliefs. What facts, evidence, and information can we muster to show and prove that people are not vulnerable, helpless, or superior? What actions can we take to reduce the feelings of distrust or injustice that others feel? Whether at a national, local, or individual level, when faced with these beliefs in people or in groups, we can use rational thought to disarm the strength of such distorted reality.

Second, it is important to do the unexpected (McRae 1998). The very nature of these five beliefs is to assume the worst, to see a pessimistic reality at odds with their worldviews. Sometimes we need to engage in the least expected, positive actions as a contrast to the deeply held convictions that people are out to harm or humiliate. As the ancient lesson of holding sand in one's hand implies, the harder you squeeze, the more sand you lose. By doing the opposite of what's expected, a new way of seeing a problem may emerge. We are told that athletes learn this same lesson under wet conditions—one has to hold a football or baseball loosely, not firmly, when it is raining or snowing in order to control it. Doing the unexpected can produce surprising results.

---

experience of the sequences produced a framing of the interaction as a cooperative endeavor and induced additional cooperative moves.

Analyses of labor–management contract negotiations also illustrate how interaction is reframed by the actions and reactions of unfolding negotiations. Putnam (1990) describes a pivotal interaction sequence in a contract negotiation between teachers and school administrators wherein the framing of interaction was key in determining how the bargaining developed. After considerable negotiating, the bargaining representatives for the teachers made several comments about an offer on the table that were somewhat ambiguous. Some administrators in the negotiations felt that the comments meant the teachers might renege on an earlier concession. Interpreting the comments as reneging was one possible frame for how the interaction was about to unfold. If the teachers' signals were framed as reneging, the interaction might produce face threats, accusations, and destructive escalation. However, some of the administrators framed the teachers' comments differently; they heard the same comments but thought they were an inadvertent error or oversight on the teachers' part. Ultimately, the spokesperson for the administrators cast the moves as an error rather than strategic reneging. This allowed the teachers to correct the problem gracefully. (From all indications, the teachers had made an inadvertent error.) The teachers' move was framed in such a way that it encouraged the negotiations to proceed in a sequence of cooperative rather than competitive, escalating moves.

It is also possible to reframe how parties *think* about conflict interaction. Burrell and Buzzanell conducted studies on the mental schemas people held concerning what would typically occur during conflicts (Burrell, Buzzanell, and McMillan 1992; Buzzanell and Burrell 1997). To identify these schemas, they analyzed the metaphors workers and students used to describe conflicts in their families and at workplaces. Three distinct metaphorical schemas were found.

The *conflict is war* schema identifies conflict as a battle that involves great cost to the participants. Examples of metaphors reflecting this schema include "clash of the Titans," "fighting like cats and dogs," and "guerilla warfare." The war schema assumes that conflict is a win–lose proposition and that competing and forcing would determine the outcome. The ultimate conclusion of a conflict involving this metaphor is victory for one side and defeat for the other.

The *conflict is impotence* schema depicts conflict as a "victimizing process in which participants were powerless to influence or alter unpredictable events" (Buzzanell and Burrell 1997, p. 125). The parties see themselves as trapped in a conflict not of their making, often trying vainly to protect themselves or to change a situation that is beyond their control. All this effort is felt to be wasted because they have little control. Metaphors reflecting this theme include "a bear preying on a defenseless infant," "running up a steep hill with lead weights in my pockets," "whatever I say isn't heard," and "I am a ghost."

The third schema, *conflict is a rational process,* portrays conflict in collaborative terms and emphasizes its potentially positive outcomes. This view of conflict is quite similar to integrative problem solving and emphasizes discussion, debate, and exploring issues. Examples of metaphors in this schema include "a discussion handled responsibly," "the comedy cabaret; we end up laughing most of the time," and "Mother Theresa (my boss never shows anger or reacts in a hostile way; everything is handled in a very cool and collected manner)."

The three metaphorical schemas signal very different expectations about how conflicts unfold. A party who uses the *war* metaphor is likely to act competitively and will tend to provoke competition in another. The *impotence* metaphor is likely to encourage the party to use the avoiding or accommodating style. The *rational process* metaphor is likely to promote problem solving or compromising.

This suggests that a useful way to reframe conflicts is to induce parties to change the metaphors they use to describe them. If someone who views a conflict as a war can shift his or her view to the rational process schema, then his or her behavior is likely to change as well. For example, in Case 6.4, The Consulting Agency, it is likely that Joe and Juanita viewed conflict as a war, which encouraged them to hide issues and not bring out the conflict. Karen's behavior in bringing out the conflict in a constructive way reframed the conflict as a rational process. Once they had a constructive conflict experience with Karen, Joe, and Juanita would be more likely to think back on this as a rational process and approach their next conflict with Karen in these terms.

Reflections

These days an overused phrase asks people to try to think "out of the box." Reframing ultimately relies on the ability of parties to see past their preconceived ideas and rethink issues. This is a difficult—and sometimes humbling—undertaking. One of the authors recalls a time when he chaired a program to bring speakers to his college. He was certain that a co-worker was arguing against his proposals because she wanted to control how the program was run. He confronted her with this and found to his surprise that her resistance was due to her fear of losing her job as a result of a reorganization of the speaker series (in fact, no such possibility existed). This immediately reframed the conflict, and the author was able to reassure her that her job was not in jeopardy and to establish a good working relationship. Afterward, the author wondered why he had jumped to the conclusion that his co-worker was a "stubborn control freak." Did he unintentionally adopt a competitive orientation at the outset and send signals that made her fear her job was at stake? Was he that uncharitable toward others? Reframing not only helps to move conflicts along, but offers an opportunity to learn about ourselves, to reflect, and to change.

Summary and Review

What are trained incapacities?

People often develop habitual approaches to decision making and problem solving based on what has worked for them in the past. The better these habits work, the more likely people are to stick to them. During conflicts, however, habits that work well in nonconflictive situations can have destructive consequences. The habits become trained incapacities—abilities that blind people to negative consequences—because they assume that their behavior will be beneficial. It is important to be aware of the possibility of trained incapacities and to guard against them.

How does the Reflective Thinking Procedure help in managing conflict?

Reflective thinking is designed to help parties avoid potential problems by tightly structuring discussion so that they do not consider solutions until they understand the problem. The procedure attempts to keep parties' minds open to the problem rather than focused on particular resolutions. Premature focus on solutions often blinds us to important aspects of the conflict and may lead to less effective resolutions. The Reflective Thinking Procedure also encourages parties to explore a range of options when considering resolutions to the conflict and to evaluate each option thoroughly. During this process of generating and evaluating options, parties often accidentally stumble onto integrative solutions they would not otherwise have considered. This process may also produce a different view of the conflict, leading parties to recycle to earlier steps to redefine or reanalyze their problem.

Why is it important to consider feelings when working with conflicts?

There is a tendency in U.S. culture to assume that emotions get in the way of clear, rational thinking. In fact, acknowledging and coming to terms with feelings about the conflict is often essential in moving forward toward a workable resolution. This is why Filley suggests that the initial steps of conflict management must surface and help parties understand one anothers' emotional reactions to the conflict.

What are the consensus-seeking rules and how do they differ from reflective thinking?

There is a set of rules designed to promote openness and creativity in reaching consensus. The rules encourage parties to surface conflicts, confront them directly, and not to fall for easy solutions to ensure a secure, meaningful agreement. They take a different approach from the Reflective Thinking Procedure by giving people a general set of guidelines, rather than a specific set of steps to follow.

What is framing and what are its effects on conflict interaction?

Framing is how parties construct interpretations of events or actions that define the situations they are in. For example, parties might interpret others' actions as threatening to them, defining the situation as a competitive one. Because people's actions are based on their definition of the situations, framing influences how they act and react to others.

What is reframing?

Reframing occurs when parties reinterpret the situation in a new light. This reframing alters how they orient to the conflict and their actions and reactions toward others. Two kinds of reframing can be distinguished. First, parties may reframe the issues when they redefine what the conflict is about or how the conflict issues are expressed. Second, parties may reframe their interpretations of the conflict interaction itself.

What are gain and loss frames?

Gain framing states the issues in terms of the possible gains that a party might make, while loss framing states the issues in terms of possible losses or harms parties might suffer. Whether issues are framed as gains or losses influences behavior. Parties who frame issues in terms of losses are likely to take more risks than those who frame issues in terms of gains.

What are some other ways to frame conflict issues?

Issues can be framed differently depending on how parties develop arguments for their positions. For example, one party might develop a case that focuses on the harms that the other has done and the remedies that should be applied to eliminate those harms. The other party might reply by refuting the remedies, showing that they are too expensive or will not solve the problem. Research suggests that if parties start with a different definition of the issues and pursue different arguments, better outcomes can be achieved because they look closely at all aspects of the conflict.

Issues can also be reframed by labeling the conflict or tactics that are employed. For example, calling a statement an insult introduces a new issue into the conflict—that one party wants an apology from the other.

The Problem–Purpose Expansion Technique is designed to help parties find different ways to frame conflicts. It asks them to consider their goals and how a goal at one level relates to goals at higher or lower levels. Higher-level goals indicate *why* we are trying to do something, whereas lower-level goals indicate *what* we have to do to achieve our immediate goal. By moving up and down this goal ladder, we often see the conflict differently. These insights can help us reframe the conflict in a productive way.

What does it mean to reframe conflict interaction?

How parties label and interpret episodes influences how they act during them. If parties interpret an interaction as a "fight," they are likely to act very differently than if they interpret the same episode as "giving someone a hard time" (teasing). Reframing conflict interactions refers to relabeling them so that parties look at them different to be able to break out of their current interaction patterns.

Conclusion

In one sense, people involved in a conflict are always intervening in their own interactions. Each move or response directs interaction, at least for the moment. Not all moves are self-regulating, however; self-regulation requires parties to consciously work with the conflict. To do this they must diagnose the forces that are pushing the conflict in a destructive direction and develop the ability to act in a way that mitigates those forces. Self-regulation is difficult because parties may not see that the destructive turn interaction has taken until repetitive patterns are firmly in place. Moreover, when someone who is involved in a conflict attempts to alter interaction with the interests of all in mind, motives can be questioned and moves misinterpreted.

Despite formidable obstacles, there are a number of ways that parties can diagnose their conflicts and act to redirect them. Previous chapters discussed how people can change a group's climate, assess power differentials and develop ways to deal with power imbalances, facilitate face-saving, and select styles that are appropriate for the situation and move the conflict in productive directions. This chapter has focused on working habits and trained incapacities and two additional ways to productively work with conflict: the use of procedures and reframing issues in conflicts.

CHAPTER

9   Third-Party Intervention

Chapter 1 noted that conflict interaction tends to be self-perpetuating. This characteristic of conflict has important implications for understanding how patterns of interaction develop, how escalation cycles gain momentum, and how constructive or destructive climates are sustained. This property is also important in understanding why people who are not parties in a conflict have—since time immemorial—intervened in ongoing disputes. The self-perpetuating nature of moves and countermoves, actions and reactions, can stifle attempts at self-regulation, even when we try assiduously to track or alter these patterns. Moreover, trained incapacities can prevent parties from recognizing the problems in their interaction patterns. An outsider has some distance and can often see persistent cycles and ways of altering them. By necessity, the mere entry of a third-party alters conflict interaction, if for no other reason than that the intervenor's moves become part of the sequence.

The term *third-party intervention* connotes a wide range of activities that span diverse conflict contexts, from the spontaneous attempts of parents to settle conflicts between siblings, to the carefully planned attempts to mediate the release of hostages across international borders. Third-party intervenors may be fact-finders, process consultants, go-betweens, ombudspersons, clergy, managers, conciliators, mediators, group facilitators, attorneys, friends of the court, or arbitrators. As this list suggests, third-parties enact different roles and have different responsibilities in different conflict settings.

Over the past twenty years, there has been increasing interest in using a variety of third-party roles in diverse conflict settings. For example, more than 400 community dispute–resolution programs have been established in the United States in recent years. These programs often use trained volunteers to intervene in neighborhood, student-to-student, small claims, or landlord–tenant disputes. In the past, if these cases were severe enough, they might end up in court. In many cases, conflicts simply festered because the parties had no recourse outside the courts to help resolve them (Merry 1979; Marks, Johnson, and Szonton 1984; Folger 1991). In divorce cases, mediators are now used in many states to try to settle issues related to child custody or property rather than having a judge impose a decision about such matters (Riskin 1985).

In business environments, a market has developed for dispute-resolution services that can provide out-of-court settlements for a wide range of conflicts (Singer

1990). In addition, changes in employer–employee relationships have brought changes in third-party roles within organizations. Businesses, medical facilities, and educational institutions have developed intervention roles, such as hearing officers, ombudspersons, and client representatives, to address conflicts "in-house." Middle managers have increasingly been viewed as dispute resolvers who intervene in conflicts among subordinates or between department members.

This chapter examines how third-parties influence the course of conflict interaction. No matter what intervention third-parties perform, the moves they make can be examined in light of their impact on conflict interaction. This chapter provides a framework for thinking about and analyzing conflict interaction as influenced by third-party intervenors.

This analysis of third-party intervention is organized around the four conflict interaction properties introduced in Chapter 1. Although conflict interaction is often quite different when a third-party is involved, it is still shaped by these properties—by moves and countermoves, exertion of power, self-perpetuating momentum, episodic structure, predictable themes, and relational influences. Each of the properties points to important and unique features of third-party intervention and its impact on communication. This chapter examines how these four properties help describe and explain the effects of third-party involvement on conflict interaction.

Property 1: Conflict Interaction Is Constituted and Sustained by Moves and Countermoves During Interaction

When third-parties intervene in conflicts, they become active participants in the interaction sequences. Third-parties make *moves*—initiatives that spark reactions and launch sequences of interaction. They also respond with *countermoves*—reactions to disputants' moves. In this sense, the third-party is as vulnerable to the moment-to-moment influences of action and reaction as the disputing parties themselves. Although the conflict issues may be of more (or different) consequence for the parties than the intervenor, the conflict interaction has consequences for both: The interaction emerges as the product of the third-party's and disputants' actions, it has moment-to-moment effects on the third-party's moves, it shapes the third-party's interpretations of unfolding events, and it has relational consequences for the intervenor.

The moves a third-party makes clearly influence the conflict interaction. What gives third-parties the ability to shape conflict? What powers are available to any particular intervenor? Given a third-party's available power, what influences the moves he or she actually makes? To understand how third-party influence occurs on a move-by-move basis, it is important to understand that the potential for third-party moves stems from two primary sources: the third-party's *mandate*—the ascribed source of power the intervenor holds—and the third-party's moment-to-moment *responsiveness* to the emergent characteristics of the unfolding conflict interaction. Each of these influences on third-party moves are considered next.

Third-Party Mandate

Any move a third-party makes is rooted in the power he or she is able or willing to exert. In this sense, the basis of third-party moves is identical to that of the disputing parties. However, the sources of third-party power are often quite different from those held by the disputants. This is because the type of interdependence between third-parties and disputants is very different from what defines the conflicting parties' relationships. Disputants are dependent on intervenors for such functions as structuring the interaction, reducing hostilities, and providing expertise on specific substantive or legal issues. These sources of dependency stem from the authority or *mandate* given to the third-party by the disputants (Delbecq et al. 1975; Auvine et al. 1977; Shubert and Folger 1986; Kaufman and Duncan 1989). Like the forms of power discussed in Chapter 4, the third-party's mandate is fundamentally relational: It is power endorsed by the disputing parties and thereby gives the intervenor certain resources that can be drawn from on a move-by-move basis to control the interaction and substantive issues. If endorsement of the mandate is withdrawn or questioned, the ability of the third-party to act is altered or curtailed (Merry and Silbey 1984). Of course, some third-party mandates, such as those given to judges, stem from broadly based endorsements that societies or large groups of people provide. Disputing parties are under strong pressures to endorse third-party mandates when they are so widely accepted.

A third-party's mandate—as an endorsed basis of power—can stem from formal or informal sources (Kaufman and Duncan 1989). Many third-party roles carry formal endorsements, which authorize certain types of interventions in specific conflict arenas. Such roles are typically established by law, societal traditions, or rules of an organization. The adjudicative role that judges play in legal contexts and the ombudsperson role employed to settle disputes within organizations are examples of formally defined third-party mandates (Kolb 1987, 1989; Rowe 1987).

Other third-party mandates are granted informally, usually via the implicit expectations people have about who can appropriately intervene in conflicts. These informal mandates are often the result of resources the third-party holds, such as specialized knowledge or skill in intervening, or of the third-party's relationship to the disputants. Informal mandates are given to a wide range of individuals, including managers in organizations, parents or older siblings in families, group members who are skillful at framing problems and facilitating productive interaction, community leaders, and clergy. When third-party mandates are informal and hence less clearly specified, questions may arise about the appropriateness of or limits on intervention. In such cases, the nature of the third-party's mandate may require explicit negotiation in order for the intervention to proceed.

Third-party mandates can carry a range of possible powers to conflict interaction. Specifically, three forms of third-party control can be distinguished: process control, content control, and motivational control (Sheppard 1984).

Process Control.   This refers to the third-party's ability to organize or structure the procedures that disputants follow during interaction. *Process control* includes such diverse activities as arranging when and where the parties should meet, setting time limits on speaking turns or intervention sessions, establishing how decisions will be made, and setting rules for decorum. Third-parties whose mandates are formally established often impose clearly specified forms of process control, which can be stated explicitly to the parties at the outset. Process control is often less clearly specified when a third-party's mandate emerges informally. Frequently, less forethought is given to the procedural rules, which are more likely to emerge during intervention than be stated initially. For example, a group member who is trying to intervene in a conflict among other members may ask that each person speak in turn rather than allowing a free-for-all to escalate.

Content Control.   Third-parties also vary in the amount of control they have over the content of the dispute. *Content control* refers to the third-party's influence over the arguments and substantive positions taken by the parties or over the terms parties accept as a final agreement. Third-parties differ in their ability or willingness to refute or attack specific points made by the parties; interpret, frame, or add issues; present additional information relevant to the topics under discussion; or suggest or impose the terms that the parties adopt as an agreement or solution.

For some third-party mandates, the last item in this list, the amount of control over outcomes, is the most important defining feature of the intervention. The following list contains descriptions of the three forms of intervention, which differ in numerous ways but whose character stems primarily from the degree of control a third-party has over outcomes.

1. Arbitrators have clear control over the terms of a final agreement. An *arbitrator* is given authority to hear all sides of a case, discuss it with each party, and then make a final decision on how the dispute will be settled, much like the judge in a legal case. In most cases, the parties are compelled by law or prior agreement to enact the terms an arbitrator imposes. One less widely used form of arbitration is called *nonbinding arbitration.* In this form of arbitration, the third-party follows the same general process, but the arbitrator's decision is not one the parties are bound by law or prior agreement to accept. Rather, the arbitrator's decision is a neutral opinion that the parties can consider.

An arbitrator often has special background knowledge that enables him or her to grapple with the specific issues underlying the conflict. For example, arbitrators generally are used for highly technical disputes, such as labor contracts, which require knowledge of both economics and labor law. Arbitrators can also be used for "hopeless" cases for which a decision must be made but repeated attempts to settle have proved impossible.

2. Less authority over settlement terms is given to mediators. *Mediators* are third-parties who facilitate negotiations. They may or may not have special knowledge about the issues. The key characteristic of mediation is that final resolution rests with the parties themselves. The process of reaching a settlement is essential to winning the parties' commitment to reaching a solution. Mediators intervene mostly by allowing the parties to clarify their choices, resources, and decision points and by recognizing each other's perspectives (Bush and Folger 1994).

For example, mediators frequently intervene in environmental disputes (Wehr 1979; Lake 1980; Mernitz 1980; Riesel 1985; Singer 1990; Crowfoot and Wondolleck 1990). In these types of disputes, a number of parties are involved, such as government representatives, citizens, and industry spokespeople. The objective is to help diverse parties negotiate an acceptable resolution to issues such as land use, watershed preservation, or highway construction.

Although mediators have traditionally been used in environmental and labor disputes, over the last three decades they have been employed in a wider array of contexts. Volunteer or professionally trained mediators now attempt to assist parties in reaching agreements in community and neighborhood disputes, student conflicts, landlord–tenant conflicts, small claims issues, consumer and business disputes, divorce and child custody cases, and international peacemaking efforts (Haynes 1981; Folberg and Taylor 1984; Beer 1986; Stulberg 1987; Haynes and Haynes 1989; Singer 1990; Duffy, Grosch, and Olezak 1991; Jones and Brinkman 1994; Garcia 2000; Bercovitch and Kadayifci 2002).

Although there are a range of mediator styles and differences in how willing mediators are to risk influencing outcomes, the important point to note here is that mediators have no explicit mandate to make or implement choices for the parties. They do, however, have a mandate to inform the choices the parties consider and discuss during an intervention (Kaufman and Duncan 1989). It is not uncommon, for example, for divorce mediators to offer suggestions or solutions that the parties have not thought of, based on solutions the mediator has seen work for other couples (Lemmon 1985).

Occasionally, mediators consciously or inadvertently promote certain choices (Folger and Bernard 1985; Greatbatch and Dingwall 1989; Shailor 1994; Schwerin 1995). For example, a divorce mediator may push for an agreement that gives one spouse greater financial autonomy once the marriage is dissolved. Such a move is often controversial because it may overstep the bounds of a mediator's mandate or be seen as a potential breach of neutrality (Bernard, Folger, Weingarten, and Zumeta 1984). Pushing for financial autonomy for one spouse may cause the other spouse to view the mediator as biased. The mediator, on the other hand, may believe the spouse's autonomy will contribute to a more workable settlement.

3. Even less involvement with settlement terms is enacted by third-party facilitators or conciliators. Facilitators and conciliators are process experts who have neither extensive expertise related to the issues under discussion nor the power to make a final decision (Auvine et al. 1977; Schwarz 2002). They are often brought in when the parties believe they can reach a resolution through direct negotiations but need help managing the process.

Although the two roles are quite similar, the labels "facilitator" and "conciliator" are used to describe third-parties who intervene in somewhat different settings. The *facilitator* label is used most often to describe a third party who intervenes in ongoing decision-making groups such as management teams, boards of directors, or department staff. The *conciliator* label is used to describe third-parties who intervene in multiparty disputes among recognizable adversaries such as those involved in public policy disputes, environmental conflicts, or race-related issues.

Facilitators or conciliators offer process expertise but are not at the "center" of the interaction. They can, nonetheless, be an active force directing the conflict. However, all the impetus for substantive movement—proposals, compromises, changes in position—arises from the parties themselves. Facilitation and conciliation differ from arbitration or mediation not because they are more passive forms of intervention, but because they carry a narrower range of possible involvement with substantive issues. The third-party called into the Riverdale Halfway House (Case 6.1) was a facilitator. He chaired several meetings at which members tried to talk out their problems and offered assistance in clarifying needs and proposals, but he did not try to direct the discussion in any forceful or intrusive way.

An important consideration in determining the degree of process and content control to exert is how fair parties perceive the intervention to be. Thibaut and Walker (1975) argue that perceived fairness of intervention styles varies according to the nature of the dispute. In disputes involving highly intense conflict, and high degrees of interdependence among parties, arbitration (high process and content control) is perceived as the fairest approach (Sheppard, Saunders, and Minton 1988). On the other hand, for conflicts that are less intense, mediation, with its lower degree of control, is perceived as more fair. Arbitration was also found to be preferred in disputes for which a settlement seemed very difficult to attain, whereas mediation was preferred for cases where a settlement seemed possible (Heuer and Penrod 1986). Finally, other things being equal, participants who have some say in the selection of the third-party role generally seem to perceive the intervention to be fairer than those who do not (Sheppard et al. 1988).

Motivational Control.   Besides process and content control, third-party mandates also differ in the motivational control they grant to the intervenor. *Motivational control* refers to the degree to which the third-party can induce parties to perform desired actions. Some informal third-party intervenors, such as parents or managers, control incentives that can influence the parties and ultimately the outcomes of a dispute. Managers, for example, can indicate that they might reallocate or demote a recalcitrant employee if he or she does not address an ongoing dispute with a co-worker. In an attempt to encourage movement, a labor mediator may indicate that he or she is going to tell the press that one side in a dispute is making unreasonable demands (Sheppard 1984). Many third-parties, including parents, clergy, and teachers, have a significant motivational influence over disputants. Other intervenors may have very little direct motivational power. Of course, the arguments all third-parties make—to continue negotiating, to move from a position, to accept a compromise, and so on—are another source of potential motivational influence.

Responsiveness to Emerging Interaction

The third-party's mandate provides the broad framework of endorsed powers, the possible bases third-parties can draw on in making moves. Like all characterizations of behavior in terms of roles, however, a third-party mandate only delimits the range of possible moves perceived to be appropriate or expected. It does not entirely account for the moves a third-party actually makes in the interaction or the timing of those moves. Even though a third-party is involved, the conflict interaction still unfolds turn-by-turn and is subject to all the momentary forces—such as defensiveness cycles, episodic structure, immediate face threats—at play in any emergent interaction. Third-party moves can start from some formally or informally defined sense of what the nature of the intervention will be and what role the third-party will adopt, but on a move-by-move basis, any given act is inevitably responsive: It is part of the stream of interaction and is, in a fundamental sense, a product of it.

In many discussions of third-party intervention and dispute processing, there has been an increasing recognition of the emergent nature of conflict intervention processes (Felstiner, Abel, and Sarat 1980–1981; Mather and Yngvesson 1980–1981; Sarat 1988). Theorists and critics have attempted to debunk what they see as a static image of disputes, dispute processing, and third-party intervention. This static image depicts disputes as fixed entities that are brought to third-parties and are then acted on by intervenors to achieve some goal, such as reaching a settlement or handing down a decision. The conflict that the parties bring to the table is seen as relatively unchanged as the dispute moves through the intervention process. This image also implies that third-parties and the intervention process remain unaffected by the dispute being addressed.

The critics of this image say that it is misleading and fails to capture all the dynamics—the elements of change and influence—in third-party interventions. They would replace this image with a less static conception—one that casts disputes and third-party processes as much more fluid and malleable activities. It has been argued, for example, that "disputes, even after they emerge and are articulated, are indeterminate. They do not exist in fixed form prior to the application of particular dispute processing techniques; they are instead constituted and transformed as they are processed" (Sarat 1988, p. 708). In this view, the very act of presenting a dispute to a third-party can reframe the conflict.

Several researchers have demonstrated how disputes are presented to intervenors in ways that "fit" the third-parties' modes of intervention (Mather and Yngvesson 1980–1981; Merry and Silbey 1984; Conley and O'Barr 1990). Courtroom disputants might, for instance, narrow the issues in a conflict, simplifying a complex history of events, injuries, and relationship struggles so that a judge can impose or suggest readily available settlement terms, such as monetary awards. In the organizational context, employees sometimes select issues and define disputes in ways that will increase the likelihood that they will be addressed by their managers (Kolb 1986). Other research suggests that mediators in several conflict contexts influence the parties' views of the issues and may even take a strong hand in shaping attitudes toward possible settlement terms (Folger and Bernard 1985; Greatbatch and Dingwall 1989; Lam, Rifkin, and Townley 1989; Bush and Folger 1994). In such cases, key dispute elements—how parties view the issues, what they think is reasonable or worth fighting for, what they are willing to agree to—are transformed as the intervention occurs.

Just as disputes are influenced by a third-party and the intervention process, so too are third-parties influenced by the disputes, the parties, and the context of intervention. In this more dynamic view of intervention, third-parties are not unresponsive either. Because they are part and parcel of interaction, they are constantly adapting to contingencies that arise as interventions unfold.

To understand how third-parties and intervention forums adapt to cases and disputing parties, third-party mandates must be seen as dynamic. For many third-party roles, even those for which the mandate is relatively clear, there is considerable leeway in the amount of process, content, or motivational control exerted in any given intervention. In practice, third-parties acting as arbitrators, mediators, facilitators, or ombudsperson engage in a wide range of moves that often blur their mandates and can erode any hard-and-fast distinctions among the forms of intervention. Parties who have clear arbitrative powers, such as judges or labor arbitrators, sometimes act in mediative capacities (Wall and Rude 1989; Phillips 1990). Judges in divorce and custody cases, for example, often attempt to construct settlements rather than impose them. They may try to assess what terms are acceptable for both parties, encourage compromise, and involve parties in creating viable options. There are also forms of arbitration that build in a certain degree of disputant control over the outcome. In "last-offer–best-offer" arbitration, the arbitrator decides a settlement for a dispute by having each party submit their last best offer and then chooses from among these options (Feuille 1979). The decision of the arbitrator is limited to one of the settlement terms suggested by the parties. In this form of arbitration, the parties have somewhat more control over the substantive outcome of a final settlement than they would in "stricter" forms of arbitration because the options for settlement are determined by what they put forth.

In the same vein, mediators' actual behaviors during interventions have been found to vary considerably. Several different studies of mediators in diverse contexts paint a diverse picture of what mediators actually do in practice; at times, this picture blurs the line between mediators and arbitrators. Descriptive studies of labor mediation suggest that mediators adopt quite different styles of intervention (Kolb 1983; Shapiro, Drieghe, and Brett 1985). Some labor mediators have been characterized as *deal-makers* because they take an active role in shaping the substantive issues, put pressures on parties to move, and spend considerable time caucusing with each side in an active attempt to forge a deal (Kolb 1983). *Orchestrators* take a different approach to mediation. This is a less impositional style in which mediators orchestrate the negotiations among the parties, setting up processes that allow them to keep talking and leaving substantive issues more directly under the disputants' control.

Differences have been found in intervention styles in other arenas of mediation as well. Studies of those who intervene in community, neighborhood, and small claims disputes suggest that mediators adopt bargaining and therapeutic styles of intervention (Silbey and Merry 1986). In the *bargaining* style, mediators place great emphasis on reaching settlements through control over the interaction and encouraging less direct discussion among the disputants. Caucuses—private discussions between the mediator and one of the parties—are more frequent in this style, as are explicit attempts to narrow issues, to push for compromise, and to synthesize arguments and positions. In the *therapeutic* style, mediators emphasize increasing understanding among the disputants and overcoming relationship problems. Face-to-face contact between the parties is maximized during the intervention, as are attempts to uncover underlying issues and veiled interests. The goal is not simply to reach agreements but to use the intervention as an opportunity to improve communication and to develop a foundation for addressing problems in general.

As might be expected in informally mandated third-party roles, there is as much or more leeway in how the third-party intervenes. Studies of managers in organizations suggest, for example, that they also take on a range of roles (Kolb 1986). In some instances, they adopt an *advisory* role, consulting with one or more of the parties in the dispute and suggesting moves parties might make to help direct a conflict. At other times, the same manager may become more of an *investigator*, collecting facts and assessing the source and nature of the problem. In other conflicts, the manager may become a *restructurer*, dealing with the conflict by moving personnel or reorganizing subunits or chains of command. In still other situations, the manager steps into a *mediative* role, guiding communication among the disputing parties and attempting creative problem-solving.

Given the range of third-party options in both formally and informally mandated third-party interventions, what influences the intervention style and thus the specific moves that third-parties make? This is a difficult question to answer because of the range of factors that can influence the third-party's moves—from habits individual third-parties fall into to specific characteristics and demands of the case and disputing parties.

Third-parties adapt to the conflict cases at hand in important ways. Consider Cases 9.1 and 9.2, which illustrate how third-parties with informal mandates developed styles that they felt were appropriate for the circumstances and conflict as it unfolded.

These cases suggest that contingencies influence the general approach and specific intervening moves third-parties make. Although all possible contingencies have not been systematically studied, some attempts have been made to examine third-party adaptation.

In one line of research, four general approaches to intervention have been studied (Carnevale and Pegnetter 1985; Carnevale 1986; Carnevale, Conlon, Honisch, and Harris 1989; Carnevale, Putnam, Conlon, and O'Connor 1991). In

CASE **9.1**

The Food Distribution Company

Imagine yourself as the third-party, Richard: What would you need to find out to develop the strategy you chose in this interaction?

A third-party was called in to mediate a conflict between two managers of a food distribution company. The conflict began as a quarrel over bookkeeping procedures and soon developed into a fight over lines of authority between two managers. In the midst of a stalemate wherein neither manager would talk to the other, the other managers decided to call in a third-party. The third-party, Richard, was a distinguished-looking man in his late forties. He held a Ph.D. in economics, had written several books, and had a local reputation as a knowledgeable and impartial intervenor. Richard first interviewed each party separately. From these interviews he discovered that the roots of the conflict lay in one manager's emotional needs. The more blustery combatant, Thad, had a great need for warmth and support from his co-workers, a need he traced to bad experiences with his family and his first wife. Thad was not getting the support he needed and believed the others were purposely freezing him out (although Richard found no evidence that this was the case). Thad's anger was channeled toward Marlena, the other manager and second party. The jurisdictional dispute had rapidly escalated into a bitter, brutal fight that fed on itself. Thad and Marlena could not even work in the same room without harassing each other.

In determining his strategy, Richard took the following facts into account: (1) A serious emotional problem, which might take years to untangle, underlay the conflict. Other members probably were not aware of this problem, and it was uncertain whether they would be sympathetic if they knew of it.

(2) The conflict was long-standing and sides were clearly drawn. It was going to be difficult for parties to move from their entrenched positions. (3) The conflict was very damaging for the company. It had been going on for four months and was beginning to hurt the business financially. Something definitely had to be done. (4) The managers of the company were all young. They tended to look to Richard for help and accorded him considerable respect.

These considerations led Richard to adopt what he termed a "paternalistic style." He took on a role very close to that of arbitrator and in a caring, yet somewhat domineering, way told the managers what they should do. He took the managers aside and said, "Thad is in pain; he needs support." The managers tended to scoff at this initially, but Richard did notice that they were more supportive in later meetings. Richard also wrote a formal report with definite recommendations and urged the company to adopt and enforce them "from the top down." By taking this tack, Richard hoped to break the conflict by catching the participants "off balance" and pushing them to change before they could draw back into their well-worn positions. Quick action would mean a quick remedy for the company's problems. The paternalistic approach also protected Richard's position as a third-party; the paternal role is characteristically slightly distant, which kept Richard one step removed from the "action" of the conflict.

Discussion Questions

- *What are the risks of the approach that Richard took?*
- *What other approaches could have been taken?*

CASE **9.2**

The Radio Station

Imagine yourself as the consultants, Louis and Sue: How would you know that your basic disposition is one that suits the needs of this group?

In another intervention, two private consultants, Louis and Sue, were called in by a radio station with administrative problems. Lines of authority among the programming, advertising, and engineering departments were unclear. As a result, conflicts often arose over the scheduling of commercials and the purchase of air time. Workers at the station concluded that a reorganization was needed to clarify which departments were responsible for decisions and to establish procedures for making decisions in an orderly fashion. One of the managers in the advertising department knew Louis and Sue and obtained permission to invite them to a meeting.

Through observation of the meeting and interviews with several members, Louis and Sue discovered that the station was operating effectively and was in no immediate financial trouble. Workers felt a strong need to do something about their problems because the constant friction over decisions was beginning to create personal animosities. Their decision to act had been crystallized by a shouting match between the director of advertising and two disc jockeys. This incident had disturbed several workers, who brought the problem out during a stationwide staff meeting. After kicking it around for a while, the staff had then decided to try a reorganization. They held a goal-setting meeting during which workers raised problems and then drew up a list of possible changes. Because the changes were rather complex and members were not sure they could manage the change process themselves, they called in the third-parties.

Faced with this situation, Louis and Sue decided to adopt a facilitative style. The group obviously recognized a need for change and had a sense of direction. Members were able to talk out their differences and saw the importance of good working relationships. Even during tense discussions, workers attempted to offer emotional support to each other. It was clear that the staff had the skills and sensitivity needed for constructive work. The consultant's role was to help the staff channel its own efforts and initiatives. Moreover, there was ample time for the staff to work through the conflict at its own pace. The station was in no immediate danger; a relatively slow, measured process of discussion and consensus-building was feasible. The third-parties recognized the value of facilitating the group's efforts to develop its own unique solution "from the inside" because it would greatly increase members' commitment to the reorganization plan.

The facilitative style also had three additional advantages. As facilitators, Louis and Sue took a neutral stand toward any particular proposal for restructuring; they managed the negotiations and let the members work out proposals on their own. This enabled them to avoid being perceived as favoring the member who invited them in; as "process managers" they were able to distance themselves from partisan proposals and to help the workers come to mutually acceptable conclusions. Louis and Sue also found facilitation a more comfortable style than those requiring a higher degree of control, such as arbitration. Both Sue and Louis believed strongly in participatory management. As facilitators, they were in a position to maximize member participation. Because the facilitative style was consistent with their values, Sue and Louis were able to fit into the restructuring process in a way that felt natural and appropriate to them. This allowed them to relax, and they believe it contributed greatly to the ultimate effectiveness of the intervention.

Finally, the facilitative role was more in line with the staff's expectations than a more authoritative style would have been. The staff had actively worked with its problems and had considerable knowledge about communication and group process. Members had a definite idea of the part they wanted the third-party to play: They wanted someone to guide their decision-making processes, but they wanted control over the form and content of the solutions. An outsider—even an expert—who tried to take over the restructuring process would likely have been perceived as overly controlling and condescending. By adopting a facilitative style, Louis and Sue achieved legitimacy almost immediately, because they filled the staff's needs. Moreover, having demonstrated that they were in tune with the staff, the third-parties were later able to criticize the group's ideas without creating resentment. They took advantage of what Hollander and Julian (1969) have termed "idiosyncrasy credit." By conforming in their early relations with the group, the intervenors established "credits" that gave them greater leeway as the intervention progressed.

Discussion Questions

- *What skills do Louis and Sue seem to have that enable them to facilitate this conflict successfully?*
- *What specific communication skills would you need in this situation?*

establishing a general orientation to intervention, third-parties can (1) *integrate:* attempt to solve a conflict through encouraging negotiations and reaching a mutually acceptable agreement (a problem-solving approach); (2) *compensate:* persuade one or more of the parties to move or reach settlement by some reward or incentive offered by the third-party (such as a manager acting as intervenor offering a "perk" in exchange for accepting some outcome in a conflict with a co-worker); (3) *be inactive:* allow the disputants to handle the conflict themselves; and (4) *press:* pressure disputants to change their goals or willingness to settle (for example, persuading a party to move from a currently held position, giving information that shapes perceptions of fairness). These four approaches were originally developed to apply to mediators, but they apply more broadly to any third-party with some leeway in his or her general intervention mandate.

Research suggests that third-party selection of approaches depends on two primary factors (Carnevale et al. 1989). First, the choice seems to be contingent on how much value the third-party attaches to the achievement of disputants' goals. The importance the intervenor places on this outcome may stem from a concern about the parties' welfare or it may come from some vested interest of the intervenor (such as a manager whose unit's performance is being influenced by the conflict). Second, the choice can also hinge on the third-party's perception of whether there is sufficient common ground to reach a mutually acceptable solution. This factor suggests that third-parties' approaches are influenced by an assessment of how likely it is that the disputants can reach an agreement.

Figure 9.1 summarizes the choices third-parties are likely to make among the four approaches, given their concern for parties' aspirations and their perceptions of common ground. Third-parties attempt integration when concern for the goals of the parties is great and the intervenor feels there is sufficient chance that the parties can reach an agreement. The third-party is most likely to be inactive when

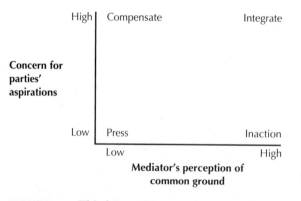

FIGURE 9.1   Third-Party Intervention Approaches

there is a good chance of reaching agreement and is concerned about a positive result. In this situation, he or she may believe that parties will reach an agreement on their own and thus third-party involvement is unnecessary. Third-parties are likely to compensate when they are highly concerned about the parties' reaching an agreement but the chances for one appear slight. In this case, the third-party has significant motivation to use available resources as incentives to promote agreements. Finally, the third-party is most likely to press when the intervenor is not highly concerned about having the parties reach settlement and there appears to be little common ground on which to build the intervention. In this case the third-party may feel there is nothing to lose in pressuring parties because the outcome is not seen as greatly significant. It has also been found that third-parties may be more likely to use pressing tactics at later stages of the intervention because intervenors may become increasingly pessimistic about the amount of common ground as the intervention proceeds.

Of the four intervention approaches in this model, the *press* stance has received the most attention in other studies of third-party adaptation. Several other factors appear to influence whether third-parties adopt a pressing strategy (Kressel, Pruitt, et al. 1989). There is a tendency for intervenors to become more directive when the intervenors' own values or interests clash with the parties'. One study of labor arbitrators found, for example, that arbitrators often settled labor grievances in ways consistent with the interests and rights of management rather than workers (Gross and Greenfield 1986). Pressure tactics also appear to be more likely when the disputing parties are very hostile toward each other. For instance, mediators have been found to press for concessions, mention costs of failing to settle, and attempt to change bargaining expectations when parties are hostile (Kochan and Jick 1978; Hiltrop 1985, 1989). Similarly, divorce and family mediators have been found to impose more procedural structure and control when parties became defensive (Donohue 1991). Third-parties may also be more directive under the pressures of a deadline or when they have well-defined formal mandates (Kressel, Pruitt, et al. 1989).

In addition to studies that bear on the general approaches to intervention, such as those discussed in the Carnevale and associates model, other more specific moves that third-parties make are contingent on emerging factors as well. When bargainers bring too many issues to the table during negotiations, mediators often attempt to reduce the agenda, develop an overarching framework, or prioritize issues (Carnevale and Pegnetter 1985). When bargainers lack experience, mediators also simplify agendas and try to educate parties in impasse processes. When issues have a potential impact on absent parties (such as children in a custody mediation) and absent parties' interests are not well represented by the disputants, third-parties are more likely to reject parties' suggestions and terms for settlement (Folger and Bernard 1985).

It is clear from this discussion that intervenors are, in a real sense, interactors in the ongoing conflict. Their moves shape and define interaction in ways similar to the disputing parties' moves: Moves by third-parties are possible because of endorsed power, they are adaptive to moment-to-moment influences in the unfolding conflict, and they are influential in shaping conflict as it emerges during an intervention. When a third-party is involved in conflict, conflict interaction is, in important ways, constituted by his or her moves and countermoves as well as those of the disputants. The following section examines the second property of conflict interaction and how it helps to describe and explain third-party involvement in conflict interaction.

Property 2: Patterns of Behavior in Conflict Tend to Perpetuate Themselves

Third-Parties and Conflict Cycles

The self-perpetuating nature of conflict interaction is often a rationale for bringing a third-party into a conflict. If interaction is self-perpetuating, if momentum becomes difficult for disputing parties to control or direct, or if cycles of interaction are difficult to recognize because parties contribute to them, then a third-party may have the best chance to alter the self-sustaining tendencies. But the discussion of how the first property of conflict interaction applies to intervention showed that third-parties do not stand apart from the conflict interaction—they are interactors themselves. Does this mean that third-parties' moves are vulnerable to the self-perpetuating tendencies of conflict interaction? Or that interaction involving third-parties is itself self-perpetuating? The discussion of this second property shows that certain forms of third-party intervention are capable of controlling or redirecting patterns, that third-parties can alter cycles and patterns of conflict interaction. But we also show how conflict interaction involving third-parties is itself susceptible to self-perpetuation.

Although there are a wide range of third-party mandates, most intervention roles put third-parties in a position to alter repetitive patterns in conflict interaction. Many intervention moves are aimed specifically at the interaction itself and

hence can counteract self-perpetuating tendencies. Restructuring of conflict interaction occurs in diverse and often subtle ways. It occurs any time the third-party
sets time limits; organizes the agenda; controls when parties talk; focuses interaction on the problem before considering solutions; encourages parties to make
statements in a clearer, less hostile, or more productive way; fosters an exchange of
small concessions; or sets a climate that allows the parties to provide previously
unstated information. These are just a few examples of the type of third-party
moves that direct the process and thereby influence conflict interaction.

Parties are immersed in the conflict and often cannot easily monitor or control aspects of the interaction that third-party moves influence. As a result, disputing parties rarely address these issues themselves. In the midst of an unfolding
conflict, people typically have all they can do to track issues, deal with emotions,
and plan responses. It is difficult for parties to channel or control the interaction as
a whole. Partly because disputants cannot easily make moves, these interventions
are central to a third-party's ability to alter well-grooved patterns and cycles of
interaction.

There are some forms of intervention, such as arbitration or court hearings, in
which the process is highly structured and the parties are prohibited from carrying
on the interaction patterns that characterized the conflict before the intervention.
The third-party takes almost total control of the process and thereby ensures a radically different sequence of moves and countermoves, actions and reactions. Under
some process rules, the parties may not even speak for themselves; for example, in
a courtroom an attorney may speak for them. In these interventions, cycles of interaction are often broken. There are potential downsides to these interventions as
well, however. Because existing patterns are altered by the strong hand of an intervenor, the process does little to foster new patterns that could be sustained by the
parties themselves after the intervention ends. The parties have not initiated new,
sustainable interaction among themselves due to the intervention. Moreover, these
forms of intervention can, in some instances, exacerbate destructive cycles. Arbitration or other adjudicative procedures can encourage blaming or can dwell heavily on the history of the conflict, thereby reinforcing destructive tendencies.

Other forms of intervention attempt to strike a balance between controlling
the process and allowing the parties to control their interaction. In these cases,
third-parties try to structure the interaction by setting ground rules and intervening in ways that redirect parties' moves. At the same time, the intervenor wants to
encourage the parties to interact freely with each other so that they have a strong
hand in shaping the outcome and new patterns of interaction are initiated. Most
forms of mediation and facilitation are premised on this attempt to balance process
control with free-form interaction. Particular mediators or facilitators may give
more emphasis to either objective, but the intervention as a whole attempts to
achieve a balance.

In interventions that attempt to balance control of the process and spontaneous interaction, there is variation in the success third-parties have in altering the
self-perpetuating cycles of interaction. If the intervenor leaves too much room for
uncontrolled interaction, the parties' patterns of interaction can prevail. Surpris-

ingly, third-parties themselves can contribute to and become part of these patterns. The kinds of intervention that mediators rely on to achieve a balance include summarizing; pointing to common ground; redirecting the substantive focus of the interaction; and, in general, placing a high premium on controlling the process.

Becoming trapped in the disputants' destructive cycles is not the only problem the self-perpetuating nature of conflict interaction can cause in third-party interventions. The intervention itself is vulnerable to repetitive tendencies, much like other forms of conflict interaction. Two brief examples will show how self-perpetuating tendencies establish themselves in third-party interventions.

Studies of mediation in labor and business contexts suggest that third-parties set up similar patterns of intervention across different cases (Shapiro et al. 1985; Kolb 1986). Early in a case, mediators tend to assess and classify the dispute before them. In essence, they ask themselves: "What is possible in this case? How can this case develop? What outcomes are possible?" After answering these questions, they tend to draw from a small repertoire of favored approaches and choose one based on previous cases they have handled (Shapiro et al. 1985). The interaction following from this approach then becomes quite predictable and similar across cases. The third-party may, for instance, pressure one of the parties to make concessions; or the intervenor may encourage negotiation; or the approach could be to separate the parties and shuttle back and forth between them in individual caucuses. The type of approach the mediator thinks will work for the dispute at hand shapes the mode of intervention and consequent interaction among the parties.

This work suggests that, just like disputing parties, intervenors find it useful to "know what to expect." Predictability is helpful in anticipating the way the parties may react and in planning future moves. In attempting to attain the security that comes with predictability, third-party approaches to intervention thus become self-perpetuating. A limited number of solutions or intervention moves are applied across a wide range of cases. The danger is, of course, that the "canned" solutions favored by the intervenor may not work in new and different circumstances and that intervenors' well-defined scenarios may blind them to the need for different approaches.

Third-party interventions can become vulnerable to self-perpetuation in a second sense as well. The form of intervention applied in a case can shape future interventions. This tendency has been found in analyses of informal third-party–ship, wherein the third-party's mandate is an informal one such as those typically held by parents, managers, or even friends. In these settings, the same third-party often becomes involved in a series of conflicts with the same parties over some length of time. Once a style of intervention is adopted with disputants, it may be reapplied in future conflicts. Although there is only anecdotal evidence to support this claim, several reasons to expect such repetition have been advanced (Sheppard, Blumenfeld-Jones, and Roth 1989).

First, the type of resolution produced by an initial intervention is likely to shape the future direction of what may develop into an ongoing conflict. For example, a manager may intervene in a dispute between two employees over how vacation time will be scheduled. The manager may decide to talk to each worker separately and then assign the vacation time in a way that he or she feels is fair. When the same issue comes up a year later, the workers may have learned little about how to interact with each other. Seeing that the employees are unable to deal with the second conflict, the manager may believe that he or she has no choice but to take the same approach—hand down a decision on how the issue should be settled.

Moreover, in interacting with an intervenor, the parties learn something about how the third-party is likely to deal with the conflict. As a result, future conflicts with the same party may be shaped in ways that the intervenor is likely to address. For example, a parent might intervene in a sibling conflict by having each child state his or her case and then judging who was in the right. In future conflicts, the children are likely to get better at stating a defensible case because they know that is how the parent will decide things. So whereas they may have directly fought in the past, the children may instead turn to the parent with a prepared complaint.

Finally, the third-party may be likely to approach future conflicts with the same parties similarly because the approach may be salient in memory or may be seen as "the" most effective way to respond to the parties. Interventions can be influenced by force of habit.

Third-Parties and the Overall Shape of Conflict Behavior

Like other forms of conflict interaction, third-party interventions can be viewed as a series of episodes and phases unfolding over time and "shaping" parties' understandings of what is going on at any point along the way. To the extent that third-parties take a hand in establishing the unfolding interaction, they can significantly influence how people view their own conflict activity during the intervention. This principle of conflict interaction points to important ways in which third-parties (1) steer broad phases of interaction by structuring the process and (2) shape specific conflict episodes by framing issues.

Considerable effort has been spent describing the way interaction develops over time during third-party interventions. This work suggests that third-party interventions are characterized by broad, but recognizable, *phases* of interaction. Table 9.1 summarizes two different phase models of third-party interventions.

It is important to note that not all mediations actually pass through phases like those in the table (Jones 1988). At best these are the phases of interaction that are likely to occur if the parties actually reach agreement. They are derived from recommendations about the course mediations should take (Donohue 1991; Domenici, 1996). In this sense, the four categories in the phases are based more on prescriptions about what interaction should look like than on documented descriptions of what does occur. Nonetheless, the phases capture a widely held sense of how mediation develops, especially when the intervention moves toward a positive outcome.

This last point suggests an important difference between phasic development in third-party interventions and other self-regulated forms of conflict. In

TABLE 9.1   Two Phase Models for Third-Party Interventions

Phase Model 1 (Sheppard 1984)

- *Definition*—parties select a procedure; get a sense of each other and the intervenor; and determine issues in dispute, relevant information, and settlement alternatives
- *Discussion*—parties present relevant information and argue for alternatives
- *Alternative selection*—parties and/or intervenor assesses validity of information, weighs arguments, and selects an alternative
- *Reconciliation*—parties accept and enact an agreement

Phase Model 2 (Donohue 1991)

- *Orientation*—parties gain an understanding of the process; set ground rules for the intervention, and the role of the third-party
- *Background information*—parties tell their stories, share information about the dispute, and state objectives or desired outcomes
- *Issue processing*—parties address points of difference, clarify preferences, and raise underlying issues that may not have been raised initially
- *Proposal development*—parties attempt to reach agreements by negotiating, compromising, accommodating, or dropping issues

---

interventions, third-parties often make a conscious attempt to move interaction through a set of preconceived phases such as those described by either Sheppard or Donohue. Intervenors are often taught a prescribed series of phases as part of their training (Haynes 1981; Folberg and Taylor 1984; Moore 1986; Stulberg 1987); they use process rules that promote the emergence of the phases in sequence. Third-parties also make specific moves, such as summaries, questions, or paraphrases, that help keep the interaction within a phase or move it from one phase to another. Moreover, intervenors may track the progress of the interaction through the phases as the intervention occurs and make the parties aware of the need to remain in, or move into, a particular phase. Without third-party involvement, there is rarely such a conscious attempt to envision and enact a sequence of phases.

In using phases to steer interaction, intervenors frame interactions for the disputing parties. Through the explicit *labeling and control of stages* that third-parties exert, disputants come to have a clear sense of what they are doing as the intervention process unfolds. Not only does this establish boundaries for what moves seem appropriate or inappropriate, but it also creates a redefining force much like that covered in the discussion of reframing interaction in Chapter 8. Part of the power of third-party intervention is its ability to transform disputants' goals. As parties enter various phases of intervention, their involvement in that interaction shapes their goals; it influences what they think can or should be done. The type of interaction the parties see themselves engaged in is influenced by the emerging interaction itself. Interaction is framed by what they see themselves doing rather than by what they planned to do. This effect reveals how the process itself holds the potential for creating significant change. The conscious use of phases in intervention—structuring interaction around sets of broad interactive goals that change over time—plays a key role in reframing conflicts.

In adjudicative forms of intervention wherein third-parties impose final agreements, the interaction is very likely to flow through phases such as those Sheppard summarized. Even if a judge, hearing panel, or manager (acting adjudicatively) downplays discussion of issues, he or she must know enough about the issues to make a decision; thus the process progresses toward an imposed agreement. However, in intervention formats wherein third-parties do not have the power to impose settlements, disputants may or may not progress through the phases. Some interventions only reach a discussion of issues and then head "back" toward more information exchange, or even further orientation (Jones 1988).

What propels movement through the phases in nonadjudicative forms of intervention? How is it that some interventions lead to settlement or proposal development and others do not? There is no single, easy answer to these questions. How interventions develop depends on a broad range of factors, including the issues in dispute, the extent of common ground among the parties, the third-party's talent, and the conditions under which the disputants enter the intervention, to name just a few. What is clear is that all forms of nonadjudicative intervention attempt to move parties through the two broadest phases of conflict examined in detail in Chapter 1—differentiation and integration. Moving from definition and discussion to alternative selection and reconciliation in the Sheppard model, or moving from orientation and background information to issue processing and proposal development in the Donohue model, is essentially a move from differentiation to integration. Thus movement through the intervention phases hinges critically on the third-party's ability to lead disputants through successful differentiation and effective integration (Walton 1969).

A third-party's skill in performing certain functions is crucial in propelling movement through the various phases of interaction just described. Some of these functions are linked to differentiation in that they help sharpen conflicts without fostering spiraling escalation. Other functions are linked to integration in that they help induce consensus and support for mutual agreements. These functions are related to several tactics discussed in Chapter 7, but they take on a different cast in third-party applications.

Thus far, in examining the second property of conflict interaction, it has been shown that third-party interventions can be viewed as developmental sequences and that intervenors play an active role in defining and controlling the unfolding conflict interaction. In addition to influencing broad phasic development by conceiving of and enacting interventions in stages, third-parties can also influence sequences of conflict interaction by the way in which they frame conflict issues. In discussing self-regulation, Chapter 8 noted that the way in which issues are framed by parties influences perceptions of the conflict and in turn may direct or redirect the interaction. Third-parties can have as great an influence on the framing of issues as the disputants themselves. As in self-regulation, the framing of issues directs the interaction. The way issues are framed may encourage initiation of episodes parties believe they need to engage in to address the problem.

Third Parties, Differentiation, and Integration

Sharpening Conflicts

In many nonadjudicative contexts, an intervenor's most important and difficult task is to "sharpen" the conflict (Van de Vliert 1985). A sharpened conflict results from a successful differentiation phase: When a conflict is sharpened, parties have an accurate, and often painful, understanding of the issues; see the consequences of not resolving the problem; and have some understanding of what a solution must do to reach the needs of all involved. The success or failure of an intervention ultimately rests on whether the third-party can guide parties through differentiation without developing inflexible avoidance or spiraling escalation.

An effective third-party will structure interaction in differentiation so that the concerns can emerge clearly without locking parties into solutions that stifle creative thinking, produce inflexibility, or promote escalation. Although the specific techniques that the third-party must use to achieve this general goal depend on the specific conflict, the following three intervention functions can facilitate the sharpening of conflicts.

Unearthing the Historical Roots of the Problem. By the time a third-party is called in to help work through a conflict, the parties may have lost sight of important facts or events that played a significant role in shaping the problem. As they argue for preferred solutions and "fight things out" at this level, some dimensions of the problem itself may be lost. Having parties review the conflict chronologically may seem pointless at first but it often provides important breakthroughs. It encourages parties to write a more careful definition of their own problems.

Encouraging a Statement of Needs Rather Than a Fight over Solutions. Successful differentiation depends on a clarification of parties' needs. Any solution a party advocates meets some set of needs that he or she has. A problem exists not because people are pressing for different solutions or positions but because none of the solutions being considered or advocated meet all parties' needs (Fisher and Ury 1981). Conflicts, in other words, stem from the apparent inability of the parties' to meet diverse needs on some issue. The continual fight over solutions is a symptom that all parties' needs will not be met if any of the solutions being considered is adopted.

Third-parties can take an active role in confronting parties with the incompatibility of needs. This often requires that the intervenor (1) make people clarify what their needs are, (2) discourage individuals from regarding each other as the cause of the problem, and (3) prevent people from suggesting solutions before all members' needs are clarified. The process of clarifying needs in a conflict can be straightforward and explicit. The third-party can turn to each person and ask: "What needs of yours must any solution fulfill?" or "You have suggested that X be done. Why do you want to see this solution adopted? What needs of yours would it meet?" Third-parties often find it beneficial to put people's "need" statements on paper or a board in front of the whole group. This method can allow for greater depersonalization of the conflict because specific needs become less associated with the parties who state them. People begin to "see," almost in a literal sense, that the problem they need to address lies above the needs of any one individual and rests in the incompatibility of positions. There is a problem "out there" that the parties as a whole can attack.

(continued)

Continued

Cutting through Multiple Issues. For the differentiation phase of conflict to be successful, issues must be clarified. Often parties are unable to work through their conflicts because the issues seem overwhelmingly complex. Multiple layers of problems may never be discussed separately. Issues may appear confused or ambiguous because parties' aggression is displaced and frustrations and anxiety from other unaddressed problems drive the interaction.

A third-party is sometimes in a better position to see the multiple layers of problems than the parties themselves. An outsider can break the problem down into smaller, more manageable parts and separate areas on which parties already agree from areas that still remain unsettled (Guetzkow and Gyr 1954; Avery et al. 1981; Folberg and Taylor 1984). To cut through multiple issues, the third-party must watch for cues indicating that aggression or frustration is displaced. Heated discussions that seem to go nowhere or comments that imply a relational or face-saving problem (such as, "I'm sorry I can't answer that question because I feel like you're talking to me like a three-year-old") may be cues that aggression is displaced. The third-party can talk to people individually to determine whether problems that have not surfaced are influencing the interaction. If the problems are critical to a successful resolution of the conflict, the third-party can raise them and explain why the parties were hesitant to address them. Careful introduction of a problem enables discussion to start cautiously. The third-party can place constraints on the interaction to help control issues that may be volatile or to enable people to vent frustrations and emotions in a safe climate.

Inducing Integration

When a conflict has been successfully sharpened, the parties move through a productive differentiation phase. People have a clear understanding of the differences among them, the needs of each person, and the likely consequences of not attaining a resolution. Moving the parties from this phase to integration and acceptance of a solution that meets all parties' needs is often a difficult task for a third-party. The three approaches that third-parties employ to induce integration are: suggesting common goals, defining the integration process, and inducing cooperation.

Suggesting Common Goals. In many conflict situations, there is often more agreement than parties realize because they become heavily focused on points of disagreement and lose sight of the commonalities. A third-party can stay attuned to points of agreement and remind parties of these points at crucial times (Avery et al. 1981). People often share a common goal but differ over the means to achieve this goal. If the third-party focuses attention on shared goals when conflicts escalate, the tension of the moment can be relieved and members may reexamine their commitments to specific solutions. Comments that point to shared goals allow parties to discover commonalities and may offer significant encouragement to those who feel discouraged, exhausted, or frustrated.

Defining the Integration Process. In suggesting common goals, the third-party attempts to integrate the two sides around a shared issue. This second approach assumes that the parties must define issues and move toward integrative solutions themselves by attempts to control the process by which they do so. In essence, the third-party sets up an agenda for the areas the parties will discuss and ground rules for discussion. By controlling the process, the third-party tries to get the sides to talk without letting the conflict escalate or deescalate.

There are a number of procedures for integrative conflict management. Probably the best known is Filley's (1975) Integrative Decision-Making (IDM) Technique, which is premised on several assumptions. First, it assumes people must untangle the substantive and emotional issues surrounding a conflict before they can develop a solution. Second, the technique assumes that people must have certain attitudes to successfully manage conflicts—including a belief in the possibility of a mutually acceptable solution, a belief that the other's position is legitimate (if not acceptable), trust of the other, and a commitment to work for an integrative outcome. Finally, in line with earlier discussions, the IDM model assumes that problem definition should be separated from solution generation.

Based on these assumptions, Filley (1975) outlines a six-step technique for finding integrative solutions:

1. *Review and adjustment of relational conditions.* In this step conditions conducive to a cooperative climate are set up; such conditions are discussed in Chapter 6.
2. *Review and adjustment of perceptions.* Here the parties use procedures outlined by Filley to clarify the factual basis of the conflict to establish the beliefs held by each member.
3. *Review and adjustment of attitudes.* Parties clarify their feelings and attitudes. Here parties state and clarify emotional issues in the conflict and how they feel about each other.
4. *Problem definition.* The mutual determination of the depersonalized problem. Techniques discussed earlier, such as Volkema's Problem–Purpose Expansion, could be used at this point.
5. *Search for solution.* This step is for the nonjudgmental generation of possible solutions to the problem.
6. *Consensus decision.* Evaluation of alternative solutions and agreement on a single solution.

The first steps of IDM are designed to untangle conflict issues. Attitudes consistent with IDM are fostered throughout, but especially by steps 1 through 3. Finally, problem definition is separated from solution generation in steps 4 through 6.

Third-parties impose ground rules, such as the IDM technique, to regulate interaction between the parties. Regulation is useful for several reasons. First, it makes parties discuss areas that must be clarified to attain an integrative solution. Often parties are simply unaware of the issues that have to be worked out to resolve a conflict; this agenda lets them know what they have to cover. Second, the agenda constrains parties to limited areas of discussion at any one time. This eliminates chaotic, "kitchen-sink" fights in which both sides toss in any comments or issues they think are to their advantage. Finally, ground rules offer tangible evidence of the third-party's activity and willingness to intervene in the conflict. This can reassure the parties that they are not at each other's mercy and that there is an impartial person regulating the interaction.

Inducing Cooperation. In the third approach, the third-party enlists one side as an ally in moves designed to get both sides to cooperate. A lack of trust and willingness to cooperate often prevents people from endorsing some solution that "on paper" seems to meet everyone's needs. Solutions may not be endorsed because parties do not trust that everyone will

(continued)

Continued

carry through on the commitments the solution requires. There is no assurance, in other words, that people are willing to cooperate even if they give their assent to a proposed solution or agreement. This lack of trust may prevent parties from moving past differentiation and toward integration; moreover, it often is a catalyst for competitive escalation.

Osgood's GRIT proposal (discussed in Chapter 7) can be used by a third-party when disputants are "locked in a bond of mutual distrust" and "any innocent-seeming action is perceived as manipulative and threatening" (Lindskold 1978, p. 777). The steps in the GRIT proposal may be most useful in cases where one of the conflicting parties wants to initiate concessions but is afraid to do so or is not being clear about his or her willingness to make concessions without a promise of reciprocity. In this instance, the third-party can make sure that others recognize that a promise of concessions is being made, and that the concession is not linked to a demand for similar moves by others. The third-party can also note when the promised concessions have been carried out and thereby point to the willingness of some parties to make a sincere effort to settle the conflict.

The third-party's active involvement in clarifying the implicit steps in a GRIT-like offer can help establish a climate of mutual trust. He or she is a witness to the disputants' willingness to respond appropriately once a sincere conciliatory move has been made. If others fail to respond with reciprocal concessions or moves, it can be read by the third-party as a sign of poor faith. There is some pressure on the responding parties to make reciprocal concessions or risk losing the third-party's involvement in the process.

When third-parties first become involved with a conflict, their knowledge of the issues, events, and parties' relationships can be quite limited because the information is not always easily attainable. Conflicts are not isolated events that can be removed, unchanged, from the stream of interaction in which they have unfolded (Beer 1986; Kolb 1986). As we have seen in the discussion of third-party responsiveness to the conflict interaction, disputes are not fixed entities. The very act of presenting a case to a third-party can alter the issues and mask or mute dimensions of the conflict that previously were pressing or important. How a third-party comes to understand and represent the issues in a conflict may or may not reflect the way the conflict was understood or represented by the parties before the intervention process began.

How a third-party eventually frames conflict issues depends on a number of factors, including how the parties present the issues to the intervenor, the third-party's own interpretive assumptions about what the issues are or which issues need to be addressed, the third-party's repertoire of intervention strategies (for example, which issues the intervenor feels capable of addressing), and the third-party's willingness to cast issues in ways that promote agreements consistent with their values or interests. These factors suggest that, as a third-party becomes involved, issues are likely to be reframed: The way the parties view the conflict can be changed dramatically or subtly (Lam et al. 1989). Moreover, the ensuing conflict interaction follows from the third-party's casting of the issues. Unfolding episodes of interaction are, in direct ways, linked to the third-party's framing of the issues (Putnam and Holmer 1992).

As an illustration of the link between framing and interaction in third-party interventions, consider the options available in informal settings, such as when a parent intervenes in a dispute among siblings, or when a supervisor intervenes in a conflict among office workers. In these contexts, third-parties try to get a sense of what the conflict is about; as they make sense of the situation, the problem is framed. Some research on framing suggests that third-parties in informal settings draw from four broad framing strategies (Sheppard et al. 1989).

First, the third-party can cast the conflict within a *right–wrong frame;* in this frame, the conflict issue is seen as one that stems from a violation of some rule or expectation. The problem requires identifying one party as right and the other as wrong. Second, the conflict can be cast within a *negotiation frame;* here the problem is seen as one that requires compromise. It necessitates asking both parties to consider their interests and the interests of other parties simultaneously. Third, the problem can be cast within an *underlying conflict frame;* in this case, the third-party views the stated issue as a symptom of other issues not explicitly discussed. The conflict is complicated because issues are not all above board. Parties may be avoiding issues because they are riven with a history of painful or frightening experiences or because the status quo protects someone's interests. Once an issue is framed as an underlying conflict, the third-party tends to believe that no satisfactory solution can be found until the buried concerns are unearthed. Finally, a problem can be viewed as *stop frame;* from this standpoint, the third-party views the conflict as one that must be made to stop at almost any cost. When a conflict is cast in this frame, the issues themselves are downplayed. The third-party has less concern for resolving issues than for making the conflict interaction cease. This occurs, for example, when a parent simply insists that two siblings stop fighting and makes no attempt to assess what problem instigated the ruckus.

Whatever framing a third-party chooses, it is enacted through the sequence of moves as the intervention develops. The third-party's framing of an issue is thus integrally tied to the way the conflict interaction is likely to unfold. For example, if a third-party adopts a right–wrong frame, the interaction is likely to unfold as a series of question and response episodes regarding what the facts are, who actually did what, and what the understanding of the rule or expectation was. If the issue is perceived as one that requires negotiation, the third-party is more likely to engage the parties in interaction sequences that seek possible compromises. Tit-for-tat exchanges and other forms of concession exchanges are likely. If the issue is cast within an underlying conflict frame, the third-party is more likely to encourage a series of interaction episodes to foster diagnosis of deeper issues. The intervenor might, for example, prompt a series of self-disclosing exchanges followed by attempts at clarification and confirmation from the parties on what he or she thinks may be the real issues. In these interactions, intervenors often paraphrase a comment that a party has just made and, in the paraphrase, suggest an unspoken concern (Lemmon 1985; Donohue 1991).

In sum, understanding the framing of issues by third-parties is important in understanding the influence they have on conflict interaction. Framing is sometimes done strategically by a third-party to move interaction in a particular direction. In formal contexts, such as mediation, framing allows only certain forms of interaction to occur. Framing can also be inadvertent or unconscious, perhaps occurring with almost every substantive comment an intervenor makes. In these less strategic framings, third-parties may exert influence over settlement terms by shaping values or preferences and by pursuing or dropping subissues. Here again, influence is exerted through interaction. The questions the intervenor asks and the reactions the intervenor gives to parties' comments create episodes of interaction that ultimately determine which issues get pursued, which values are supported, or which preferences are challenged.

Property 3: Conflict Interaction Is Shaped by the Culture and Climate of the Situation

This property of conflict interaction indicates the way in which culture and climate set expectations for behavior and, as a result, guides interaction and intervention.

Third-Party Roles and Culture

As has been the case throughout this book, the discussion of third-party roles was oriented toward the confrontational pattern of conflict management. Third-party mandates and interventions are likely to be somewhat different in cultures that employ harmony and regulative models of conflict management. Whereas most of the concepts and processes described in this chapter remain valid in these cultures, the emphasis on third-parties and expectations about what they will do changes.

Third parties are a much more "natural" part of conflict management in harmony and regulative cultures than they are in confrontational cultures. In harmony cultures, third-parties are important for several reasons, as Kozan (1997, p. 347) explains:

> First, disputes are seen as a problem of the collectivity, i.e., the group, organization, or community, rather than a problem concerning the two parties alone. . . . Second, face-giving concerns lead to indirect face-negotiation strategies in this culture (Ting-Toomey, Gao et al. 1991). This is because a direct communication approach in a conflictual situation may create embarrassing results for the other party and disrupt harmony. On the other hand, parties may communicate negative feelings more easily through intermediaries whose function is sometimes to soften those feelings and present them in more acceptable terms or within the context of underlying concerns and difficulties. Finally, in associative cultures, conflicts get defined in their broader context, and it is difficult to abstract specific issues. Third-parties' role is to delineate particular issues and concession points in conflict.

In harmony cultures third-parties are often quite intrusive in their activity. It is expected that they will exert considerable process and content control, and they may have considerable motivational control as well by virtue of their position in the community (Le Resche 1992). They are more likely to play the role of arbitrators or strong mediators than facilitator. For example, Wall and Blum (1991) report that mediators have a good deal of prestige in Chinese workplaces, which enables them to be quite forceful in dealing with conflicts. Peers may also play third-party roles in harmony cultures by representing parties to others. With their distance from the conflict and greater impartiality, they are able to represent the issues to others without fear of face and without challenging the stability of the collective.

In regulative cultures, third-parties are typically representatives of the bureaucracy that parties rely on for conflict management. They may be hierarchical superiors, mediators working within a grievance system, or judges applying laws and rules to handle disputes. Studies in France and Spain, for example, show that disputes are typically referred to arbitrators, judges, or superiors. These third-parties typically employ a good deal of process and content control and also have a high degree of motivational control. In general, third-parties in regulative cultures have much more power over the parties than would be comfortable for confrontational cultures.

The contrast in third-party roles highlights an interesting dilemma facing people in North America and Britain: One of the key barriers to effective conflict management in confrontational cultures is to induce parties to seek out a third-party when one is needed. The emphasis on direct contact between parties in confrontational cultures sometimes creates a tendency for them to feel that they have failed if either party has to bring in a third-party. Hence, there are some disincentives to use third-parties in confrontational cultures. The rise of the mediation movement and increased emphasis on therapy in the United States has counteracted this tendency to some extent, but it is still often difficult to get parties to introduce outsiders into a conflict.

Third-Party Roles and Climate

Conflict interaction usually develops around, and is bounded by, recognizable themes. These themes suggest how conflict is likely to be handled. When third-parties intervene in conflicts, shifts in climate are likely for several reasons. At the most basic level, third-parties are "new" interactors in the conflict. They contribute to establishing a climate that reflects at least one additional interactor's moves and responses (Table 9.2).

Next, intervenors are more than just additional interactors in the conflict; they are interactors with mandates to control process or outcomes to a lesser or greater extent. The third-party's mandate carries, in this sense, the power to enforce new expectations for behavior—to establish a new climate. Many of the process controls that third-parties impose are aimed at managing parties' interaction. These controls may limit when and how long parties talk, stifle personal attacks, and/or arrange

TABLE 9.2   Why Third-Party Involvement Can Shift the Conflict Climate

- Third-parties enter the stream of conflict interaction.
- Third-parties control process and set new expectations for communication.
- Disputants may want to look "good" for the third-party.
- Third-parties create a sense of optimism.
- Interventions are often conducted in places that are conducive to changes in climate.

agenda items so that more explosive issues are surrounded by innocuous or mundane topics. As seen in the earlier discussions of climate, conflicts may not be well defined because parties feel it is not safe to state their positions or to express their emotions. The parties may believe that if they are honest, "things will get out of hand" or irreconcilable personal animosities will develop. Third-party controls over interaction can establish a safe climate wherein conflicts can be sharpened without risk of spiraling escalation.

Third, because intervenors are initially "outsiders" to the dispute, the mere presence of a third-party can change conditions considerably. When he or she first becomes involved, there is often a sense that parties need to "perform well"—to be on their best behavior—for the intervenor. Although this performance may seem inauthentic at first and can fade fast once the parties start interacting, it often encourages people to be more careful about word choices and style of presentation. Parties may be more descriptive than evaluative and less likely to blame others as they define the issues. Disputants begin to recognize that more care is being taken in how others are stating their positions and making evaluations. This becomes a sign that people are trying to work on the problem without destructive escalation. Even though parties may suspect that others are on their best behavior because the third party is present, this period can allow for a greater clarification of issues than has ever been achieved previously. Moreover, climates change as interaction patterns change. Stepping through constructive exchanges, even under the guiding hand of a third-party, creates the realization that such exchanges are possible.

Fourth, third-parties acting in mediative or other nonadjudicative capacities often bring a sense of optimism that the parties may have lost in failed attempts to resolve the conflict on their own (Walton 1969). When interventions start, there can often be a sense that something new is being tried and that the intervenor may have approaches, insights, techniques (even mirrors or legerdemain) that will ease tensions and settle issues. Third-parties often begin an intervention by explicitly stating that they believe a constructive outcome is possible or that they have seen parties in more fractious disputes come to mutually satisfying agreements.

Finally, third-party interventions are often conducted in places conducive to changes in climate (Walton 1969; Folberg and Taylor 1984; Stulberg 1987). Intervenors often choose sites where threatening behavior is less likely because it seems inappropriate, such as a church or library. Any change in physical location may influence expectations about what behaviors are appropriate during the intervention.

Although all these factors contribute to third-party influence on climate, there is no guarantee that new climates will be sustained during an intervention. As discussed earlier, the self-perpetuating tendencies in conflict interaction can overwhelm attempts at intervention. The parties' well-worn interaction patterns can recreate previous climates.

There is another way in which this third property of conflict interaction helps to understand third-party interventions. Our discussion of third-party mandates suggests that there is usually considerable leeway within any mandate for third-parties to select a variety of roles. In part, the approach a third-party adopts may be explainable if the overarching climate is taken into account. The climate carries expectations for third-party behavior that influence his or her choice of style or approach.

For example, we have described how managers in organizations can adopt a range of roles in handling conflict among subordinates. These approaches vary from advisory, adjudicative, or restructurer roles, on the one hand, to less interventionist roles such as investigator, mediator, and problem solver. Although quite a range of intervention roles is available, managers tend to prefer the more controlling advisory and adjudicative styles (Sheppard et al. 1989), which tend to impose outcomes rather than guide parties to construct their own solution. The explanation for this tendency is tied to established expectations for how managers act in their working environment (Kolb and Sheppard 1985; Kolb 1986; Karambayya and Brett 1989, 1994).

Unlike third-parties who intervene in legal settings, managers often have no prescribed guidelines for acting as an intervenor. As a result, managers tend to fall back on the authoritative stance they take in everyday supervisory activities such as planning, delegating work, conducting performance appraisals, and the like. Subordinates come to expect managers to take an authoritative stance when they act as third-parties, and they sometimes misinterpret less authoritative intervention moves a manager may try to make. For instance, when managers offer mild suggestions in an attempt to encourage parties to settle their own dispute, subordinates may take these suggestions as binding directives (Kolb 1986).

Besides the influence of their generally authoritative role, managers' adjudicative stance in intervention can be explained by a second reason. Managers are often "insiders" who hold vested interest in the outcomes of conflicts in which they intervene. The productivity or morale of their entire unit may ride on how an internal dispute turns out. Their concern for outcomes may predispose them to take a stronger adjudicative role when conflicts arise in managers' work units.

In sum, it is the general set of expectations established for managerial behavior in the workplace—how managers see themselves acting and how subordinates expect them to act—that fosters the tendency to rely on more adjudicative styles of intervention. Managers' third-party moves are understandable given the climates typically already established in the workplace.

Intervenors in other settings may choose certain intervention roles because of established climates as well. In some divorce or community mediation programs, climates that place a heavy emphasis on reaching high rates of agreement are established. At base, this emphasis may stem from financial concerns. Funding for mediation programs may be contingent on rates of reaching agreements in cases. But, like all climates, these expectations are established and embedded in inter-action. Mediators in the programs talk to each other about their agreement rates, obstacles they have to overcome in attaining settlements, and/or intervention techniques that work for them. Mediators who work in climates in which there is pressure to reach agreements may be more likely to adopt "strong arm" styles, shaping agreements in ways that other mediators might view as inconsistent with the goals of mediation (Pearson and Thoennes 1989; Bush 2002).

In other mediation programs, the climate may emphasize that mediators reserve judgment about substantive issues and not press for settlements (Harring-ton and Merry 1988; DellaNoce, Folger, and Antes 2002). In these programs, an expectation is set through interaction among mediators and program directors that the disputants should be allowed to construct their own solutions, even if it means that agreements are not reached. In this climate, intervenors are more likely to adopt a nonimpositional style of mediation, one in which mediators allow parties to exchange information and remain focused on the issues. These mediators are unlikely to promote settlement terms.

Property 4: Conflict Interaction Is Influenced by and in Turn Affects Relationships

Throughout this book it has been shown that the negotiation of relationships is an integral and inevitable part of conflict interaction. Relationships are defined and altered during any exchange of messages. In an attempt to be strategic, people often try to manage their own images, to define the image of the other, and to establish particular types of relationships. Sometimes these attempts at controlling relational issues are in parties' self-interest and sometimes they are in the mutual interests of all sides. Regardless of strategic intent, the way in which relationships are defined and managed is as much a part of the "settlement" or "solution" as the substantive decisions. When people work through conflicts, they work through relationships as well.

When third-parties intervene in a conflict, they establish relationships with the disputants through the messages they send. Third-parties make conscious attempts to present certain images of themselves. These images differ depending on the third-party's intervention role, but there are important commonalities as well. Foremost is the need for third-parties to establish a credible image in the eyes of the disputants (Walton 1969; Folberg and Taylor 1984).

For adjudicators, credibility may rest on establishing that they have substan-tive expertise related to the issues; for example, labor arbitrators may try to show that they understand contract law, pension funds, fair labor practices, and so on. For mediators, facilitators, adjudicators, and many informal third-party inter-venors, credibility rests on parties' perception that the intervenor is neutral (has no personal preference about the outcome of the dispute) and impartial (treats all parties in substantively and procedurally comparable ways) (Stulberg 1987). For many third-party roles, credibility may also rest on a sense that the third-party is objective—that the intervenor has sufficient detachment to keep a clear head about the issues and unfolding interaction. Objectivity is linked to disputants' perceptions that third-parties can maintain process control and establish safe climates while simultaneously tracking and fostering substantive movement on issues.

Like all images, those fostered by third-parties are under continuous negotiation during interactions. Third-parties make bids for an image. These bids can be accepted or rejected by the disputants. If the expertise, neutrality, impartiality, or objectivity of the third-party is challenged, there can be significant consequences for the intervention (Bernard et al. 1984). In such cases, the relationships between the third-party and the disputants shift: Disputants may gain greater control over the interaction process and revert to patterns of interaction that existed prior to the intervention. Studies of mediation, for example, suggest that disputants are more likely to deadlock in sessions in which a mediator loses objectivity and becomes emotionally involved in the process (Donohue 1989). Alternatively, if impartiality or neutrality is lost, one party may think the intervention is slanted against him or her and withdraw from the process.

Third-parties not only establish relationships with disputants during the intervention, they alter relationships between the parties themselves. In particular, third-parties have a significant impact on face-saving concerns between the parties. As discussed in Chapter 5, disputants are frequently concerned about appearing weak. They can suffer "image loss" if others in the dispute think they will make concessions or crumble easily under pressure (Pruitt 1971). People may act tough and refuse to move from positions they are actually willing to concede for fear that giving an inch will mean conceding a mile. Third-parties alter this dynamic in an interesting way; they allow movement without altering the relational image the disputants want to preserve.

When they move from an intransigent position, disputants can claim that it was the third-party who suggested the idea or persuaded them to make the concession (Shapiro et al. 1985). As a result, parties can move without suffering damage to their images: They are not weak, they are simply acting under the guidance or pressure of the third-party. Significant strides in breaking impasses can occur when third-parties shoulder the responsibility for concessions or unpopular options (Carnevale 1986; Hiltrop 1989). Without the third-party's presence, options that the parties are actually willing to accept may not even be explored.

Third-parties alter relational dynamics in a second sense as well. Third-parties alter the emotional tenor of the dispute and thereby change how parties see each other (Jones and Bodtker 2001). We have noted that the presence of an intervenor may put parties, at least for a time, on their best behavior. This has important consequences. The presence of third-parties has been found, for example, to dampen parties' desire for retribution (Peachey 1989). It may be that simply having an outsider hear the issues makes parties feel as if they have already "gotten even" in some sense. Also, once parties know that someone else has heard about the mistreatment or grievance, it may be less important to take a tough stand on substantive issues. Similarly, third-parties reduce defensiveness by encouraging disputants to talk about themselves, rather than defending the other party and by opening the possibility of apology (Jones 1989; Schneider 2000).

Third-parties also alter the emotional tenor of a conflict by controlling how and when hostility is expressed. In the caucus—a separate and confidential meeting between each party and the intervenor—third-parties have a powerful tool for channeling the expression of hostility. Disputants can release a great deal of hostility toward others in caucuses. Much of this hostility is often personalized attacks in the form of character assassination and venting (Pruitt, McGillicuddy, Welton, and Fry 1989; McGillicuddy, Pruitt, Welton, Zubek, and Peirce 1991); however, movement and creative solutions seem to come on the heels of releasing hostility. Third-parties can use caucuses to facilitate private hostility release, fostering creative movement on issues without further damaging relationships (Beer 1986).

Finally, intervenors can influence relationships by controlling or altering the distribution of power between disputants (Lemmon 1985; Welton 1991). In many intervention settings, third-parties influence power by controlling process. Parties who have difficulty getting the floor or expressing their arguments, and thus are in a less powerful position vis-à-vis the interaction, may have a "level playing field" during an intervention. The redistribution of power comes as a result of interaction ground rules established by the intervenor.

Third-parties also influence the power balance by controlling the exchange or provision of information. It is common in many types of disputes for some parties to have more information than others about the issues, legal options, or long-term consequences of possible settlement terms. In divorce, for example, one spouse may have more information about employment pensions, real estate laws, or financial investment programs. It has become general practice in private-sector divorce mediation for mediators to require each spouse to obtain legal and financial counseling before negotiating on these issues during the intervention. Mediators are reluctant to provide such information themselves because it may undermine their impartial stance. However, by encouraging parties to each have comparable information, the power distribution is altered during negotiations.

Third-parties also equalize power by not allowing either party to lose ground when concessions are exchanged. As the rationale for the GRIT proposal suggests, parties are often reluctant to make the first move because, if no concession is returned, the initiator may not be able to easily back away from the offer. The party "loses" because he or she moved first. When third-parties act as go-betweens and caucus with each side, they often "test the waters," propose hypothetical concession exchanges, and arrange for simultaneous moves. This prevents either side from suffering what Pruitt (1971) calls "position loss"—the loss of bargaining ground during negotiations. Many third-parties maintain equality of power by counterbalancing concessions and movement as negotiations unfold.

All of the preceding examples illustrate how third-parties influence power during the intervention itself. There is good reason to believe that most third-party influence over power is limited to the time the intervenor is interacting with the parties. More long-term and fundamental influence over relationships is less likely to occur (Kressel, Pruitt, et al. 1989). There is a tendency for intervenors not to probe too deeply into underlying issues, or to have the parties rethink or change how they are dependent on each other (Kolb and Sheppard 1985; Donohue 1991). Given most intervenors' concerns of neutrality, impartiality, and objectivity, this restraint is not surprising. Most nonadjudicative forms of intervention are not aimed at producing the type of social change that necessitates shifts in power among disputing parties.

A Different View of Third-Party Interventions

Theory and practice of third-party intervention, particularly mediation, has blossomed over the past twenty-five years. Most perspectives on mediation focus on problem solving—finding a solution that represents a satisfactory outcome for all parties. Such a solution, the thinking goes, is most likely to be accepted by the parties and most likely to result in a long-term settlement. However, Bush and Folger (1994) have criticized the problem-solving perspective on the grounds that it neglects an even more important outcome of conflict—building the capacities, self-confidence, and insight of the parties so that they can manage this and future conflicts themselves.

When third-parties focus on solving problems, Bush and Folger argue, they tend to overemphasize the issues and outcomes with a relative neglect of the parties themselves. This is a conscious strategy of the third-party approaches described in this chapter: They attempt to focus attention on the issues and not on the people in order to reduce defensiveness and increase the energy devoted to working out integrative solutions. This focus on problem-solving, however, creates pressure on the third-party to come up with a resolution. One result of this is that third-parties may reframe the conflict in a way that they believe is most likely to lead to a productive solution. This may also involve ignoring or dropping issues that are seen as too thorny or explosive on the grounds that some agreement is better than none at all. This is problematic though because mediators reframe and redefine the issues based on their views of what is productive, not on the parties' views. In doing this the mediator takes the process away from the participants, molding it so that an agreement can be obtained. The third-party may also feel a need to directly influence the solutions that are considered, for example, by suggesting certain options and discouraging others. Again, the problem is that the solutions are the ones that the third-party views as good ones, and may not be what the parties themselves would have chosen. Several studies have documented that such practices lead to solutions that are not particularly beneficial or that omit important interests (Bush and Folger 1994). In particular, parties low in power may be disadvantaged because they depend more on the mediator for support.

Instead of problem-solving mediation, Bush and Folger advocate *transformative mediation* (Bush & Folger 1994; Folger and Bush 2001; DellaNoce, Bush & Folger 2002). In transformative mediation, the third-party's goal is not to solve the problem for the parties, but to transform the parties' conflict interaction so that they experience personal growth as they work toward their goals. Bush and Folger (1994, p. 82) argue:

> A conflict confronts each party with a challenge, a difficulty or adversity to be grappled with. This challenge presents parties with the opportunity to clarify for themselves their needs and values, what causes them dissatisfaction and satisfaction. It also gives them the chance to discover and strengthen their own resources for addressing both substantive concerns and relational issues. In short, conflict affords people the opportunity to develop and exercise both self-determination and self-reliance.

Each conflict presents people with the potential for change, and the role of the mediator is to help parties determine for themselves how they want to change.

To afford this opportunity, transformative mediation has two goals—empowerment and recognition. *Empowerment* is achieved when parties experience "a strengthened awareness of their own self-worth and their own ability to deal with whatever difficulties they face, regardless of external constraints" (Bush and Folger 1994, p. 84). Empowerment takes many forms. Parties would be empowered, for example: When they reach a clearer understanding of their goals; when they arrive at a better understanding of options open to them; when they increase their skills in conflict management; when they realize that they have something of value to communicate to others.

Recognition is achieved "when, given some degree of empowerment, disputing parties experience an expanded willingness to acknowledge and be responsive to other parties' situations and common human qualities" (Bush and Folger 1994, pp. 84–85). Note that recognition is related to empowerment in that parties who feel low in power are often defensive and unable to open up to another's point of view. Like empowerment, recognition can take a number of forms: When a party realizes that it is valuable to reflect on and consider the other's position from the other's point of view; when a party can see the other's behavior not as an intentionally competitive act, but as a result of the other's attempt to deal with real pressures and problems; when a party apologizes to another out of true sympathy.

Adopting the goals of empowerment and recognition does not mean that the transformative mediator is not concerned with the outcome or with reaching a settlement. However, the settlement is viewed as something that flows from the transformation. Empowered parties come to settlements that they value, and parties who feel recognized understand the importance of taking the other into account in a settlement. As a result, when they are reached, settlements are more likely to get at the heart of the matter and hold over the long run (Antes, Folger, and DellaNoce 2001; Bingham and Nabatchi 2001).

Transformative mediators do not regard interventions in which no settlement is reached as failures, but rather as part of a continuing conversation among the parties. A transformative mediator attempts to ensure that parties develop their positions and arguments and understand each other so that, even if they do not come to an agreement, their positions are sharpened and possible resolutions are considered for further work in the future. They do this by focusing closely on the give-and-take of interaction, intervening as facilitators to help parties elaborate the reasons for their positions and possible solutions they might accept. The mediator leaves control of the interaction in the hands of the parties and does not interject his or her own opinions or solutions. Parties are encouraged to clarify their options and to make their own choices. The transformative mediator supports perspective-taking by reinterpreting, translating, and summarizing statements in order to make the parties' input more intelligible to each other (DellaNoce 2001).

In making a case for this broader view of mediation, Bush and Folger (1994, p. 30) argue that:

> The goal of transformation embodies the premise that it is not only being better off that matters, but being better. Human beings are more than receptacles for satisfaction; we are possessors of moral consciousness. We have within us the potential for positive and negative, good and evil, higher and lower, human and inhuman, and the ability to know the difference. What ultimately makes our existence meaningful is not satisfying our appetites but developing and actualizing our highest potentials. . . . [T]he highest human need is to be fully developed, fully human. A smoothly working world of satisfaction and equity leaves this need untouched. Only a changed world, of changed individuals, fulfills it. In this respect, the goal of transformation is unique because it involves a supreme value that the other goals do not encompass. Not only is the goal of transformation uniquely important, it is also a goal that the mediation process is uniquely capable of achieving.

Although reaching a positive outcome is a worthy goal of third-party interventions, Bush and Folger set the bar higher and ask third-parties to help improve the human condition through transformation of human interaction.

Summary and Review

What is a third-party intervention?

This refers to the case in which an outside party works with the principal parties to the conflict to help them manage and resolve it. There are a wide variety of third-parties, from judges in formal judicial proceedings, to consultants serving facilitator roles, to clergy, therapists, and even friends of the parties.

How do mandates influence third-party interventions?

A third-party's mandate is the degree of authority he or she is given to manage the conflict. Sometimes mandates are formally granted; for example, in many mediations, participants discuss the "ground rules" and the role of the mediator at the outset and come to a formal agreement. In other cases, mandates are set informally.

This is the case, for example, when there is an existing relationship between third- and first-parties—that is, a superior may try to mediate a conflict between two subordinates. Mandates differ in terms of the degree of process control, content control, and motivational control granted to the third-party. Process control is the degree to which the third-party is allowed to structure the procedures parties should follow. Content control is the degree to which the third-party influences the content of the discussion. Motivational control is the degree to which the third-party can influence the parties to come to a particular type of agreement.

Third-party roles differ in the degree of control they exercise, with facilitators being rather loose, mediators in an intermediate place (process control, but little content control), and arbitrators having the highest degree of control (high on process and content control).

How are third-parties influenced as they work with conflicts?

Mandates define the power that the third-party has and therefore depend on the relationship between parties and the third-party. During the intervention, mandates may be redefined and renegotiated. We have emphasized throughout this book that conflicts are beyond the control of any party; so, too, they are greater than the third-party and can attain a life of their own. Third-parties attempt to channel interaction, but as they do so, their reputations and endorsement are influenced by the interaction, sometimes increased, sometimes maintained, and in some cases eroded. Mandates may change as the conflict interaction unfolds.

What are the different styles mediators can adopt?

Research has indicated a number of styles. Key distinctions to differentiate: the dealmakers, who strongly shape the deal; the orchestrators, who help the parties work together; a bargaining style, which restricts contact among parties; a therapeutic style, which emphasizes increased understanding and direct contact among parties; and advisory, investigator, restructurer, and mediative roles.

What factors shape the styles third-parties adopt?

Carnevale advanced one model that suggests that third-party styles depend on two factors: how much value the third-party attaches to achievement of the disputants' goals and the third-party's perception of the degree of common ground. Depending on the values on these two factors, the third-party will attempt to integrate, compensate, press, or be inactive.

How does culture influence third-party roles?

In harmony and regulative cultures, third parties are likely to be used more quickly than they are in confrontational cultures. They are also likely to have higher degrees of control.

How does a third party influence conflict cycles?

Evidence suggests that successful third-parties are able to avoid being pulled into the cycles of behavior that emerge during conflicts. Instead, they help parties break these cycles. Ironically, though, third-parties may themselves set up repetitive patterns in their own interventions that may become trained incapacities.

Are there recognizable phases in third-party interventions?

A general, but not universal, pattern in interventions is composed of four phases: definition, discussion, alternative selection, and reconciliation. There may also be an orientation phase right after definition, in which the process for the intervention is clarified and defined. Interventions are more likely to follow this phase pattern when arbitration or adjudication styles are used.

What can third-parties do to help participants move through differentiation and integration?

Effective third-parties sharpen conflicts to help people move through differentiation. They can facilitate this by unearthing the roots of the problem, encouraging statements of needs rather than solutions, demonstrate the incompatibility of needs, help parties set high aspirations, and help parties sort out and define multiple issues. These actions help parties understand and appreciate the legitimacy of each other and motivate parties to seek a resolution.

Third-parties may also induce integration by suggesting common points of agreement and common goals, defining the integrative process, inducing cooperation, and reframing issues. Filley's Integrative Decision-Making Technique was described as one means of defining the integrative process. Osgood's GRIT procedure was described as one means of inducing cooperation.

How do third-parties influence climate?

Having a third-party adds another interactor, which automatically affects climate. The third-party's control over the process can shift the climate by, for example, increasing parties' feelings of safety. Third-parties may also bring a sense of optimism to the situation, rejuvenating parties' hope that a solution can be found. Third-party interventions can also be conducted in an unusual location, which may change the climate as well.

Do third-party interventions affect relationships?

Third-party interventions shape relationships between the intervenor and the parties. Their credibility, impartiality, and expertise are continuously under negotiation as third-parties work with the conflict. Third-party interventions also alter the relationships among the parties themselves, both during the intervention and through to the final resolution. During the intervention, third-parties may influence participants to move from established positions, affect the emotional tenor of the interactors, and alter the balance of power between parties.

How does transformative mediation differ from most approaches to third-party intervention?

Transformative mediation focuses on developing parties' ability for self-determination and insight into themselves and others. Whereas most third-party approaches regard achieving a satisfactory settlement as the primary goal, transformative mediation believes that achieving empowerment and recognition are prior conditions for a satisfactory settlement. When parties are empowered and recognize others' views, they have the best chance of creating outcomes that are truly their own.

Conclusion

Any intervention in conflict is difficult and risky. Third-parties always walk a slippery slope. The principles of conflict interaction examined in this chapter suggest why. An intervention is never completely under the third-party's control. Although intervenors may have mandates to control aspects of the process or influence the outcome, the spontaneous nature of conflict interaction can lead third-parties down a variety of intervention paths. As interactors themselves, third-parties respond contingently to the issues on the table and the unfolding sequence of actions and reactions.

Although intervenors can break parties' destructive, repetitive cycles, they can just as easily contribute to existing cycles or become part of new ones. The momentum of parties' destructive patterns can overtake third-parties' attempts to direct or redirect the interaction or to create collaborative, less hostile climates. If intervenors take unwarranted measures to control interactions or issues, they run the risk of losing credibility and, ultimately, their effectiveness.

Although the issues in a conflict may appear straightforward, they are often complex and malleable. They change as the parties present them to an intervenor and as the intervenor represents them to the parties during the intervention. The way third-parties frame issues can influence the approach they take to intervention. If intervenors frame issues in ways that the parties themselves cannot understand or fully accept, any agreement will be difficult for the parties to enact. In this case, the third-party runs the risk of addressing his or her own version of the dispute, rather than the parties'.

Although third-parties have useful techniques for altering the way parties relate to each other during an intervention, it is often more difficult to create long-term, stable changes in ongoing relationships. Intervention is difficult when it seeks more than short-term gains.

The Technological Future

Computers play an increasing role in everyday interactions. E-mail, faxes, computer conferencing, and electronic systems to manage group meetings are all creating new possibilities for human interaction. The influence of computers also extends to conflict management, as Case P.1 shows.

Computerized systems, such as the Negotiation Support System (NSS), that support conflict management are being developed and adopted. They cannot replace third-parties, but they will be an important tool in supporting third-party interventions.

A careful reading of the case will show that Michelle used many strategies that contribute to third-party effectiveness; however, the NSS also contributed. Research suggests that computerized systems to support communication and conflict management have several beneficial effects on interactions (Poole, Shannon, and DeSanctis 1992). First, entering positions and solutions into a computer and displaying them objectifies parties' stances, helping to depersonalize issues and focuses attention on issues, not people. Second, computer support systems provide procedures to structure negotiations. Evidence suggests that groups perform better when they use systematic procedures, but many people resist them because the procedures require preparation and are often difficult to carry out (Poole 1991). Computerizing a procedure makes it much easier to use and reduces preparation time because a system is already set up.

Moreover, procedures can be made available with no cost in efficiency; indeed, there is evidence that computer-assisted conflict management systems make discussions much more efficient (Dennis, George, et al. 1988). Members can enter lists of ideas much faster than they can list them verbally, and with word processing capabilities permit quick manipulation of information, including editing and rewriting of issues, positions, and solutions. The end result is that parties are free to concentrate on the content of the negotiations and spend less time and energy on clerical and recording functions. In addition, computerized systems act as the "memory" of the parties. The system stores all lists and entries and can call information up if the parties want to go back to review, or choose to adjourn and meet again later.

Studies suggest that groups using computer-assisted support systems address conflicts more often than do those without access to computers (Poole, Holmes, and DeSanctis 1991) for at least two reasons. First, the system often calls on parties to rate, rank, or vote on items, as Caitlin and Tony did. This is particularly useful in multiparty negotiations. A display of ratings or votes clarifies where

CASE P.1

The Negotiation Support System

Imagine yourself as Tony or Caitlin: What benefits do you derive from using the NSS? What possible concerns might you have in using the system?

Tony and Caitlin are two project managers from an international food distribution company, FoodCo. They have become embroiled in a conflict over personnel assignments. Each project manager at FoodCo has to build his or her own team by having qualified persons assigned to him or her; project managers become "internal recruiters" and try to find talented individuals so that their projects will succeed. Caitlin and Tony both have their eyes on the same two employees and cannot agree on who should have them. After several discussions that led nowhere, Caitlin and Tony had an extended argument during their division's "staffing" meeting, a monthly session to determine personnel assignments. The argument ended in a stalemate, and their supervisor rec-

ommended that Caitlin and Tony participate in a computer-assisted negotiation session.

Caitlin and Tony contacted Michelle, a staff member in charge of the Negotiation Support Room. Michelle set up a meeting and explained to them how their session would go. She also met with Caitlin and Tony separately prior to the session to help them clarify their needs and positions.

Tony and Caitlin then met at the room. They walked into a comfortable setting dominated by a U-shaped table with computer stations at each of the eight seats, as shown in Figure P.1. These were the input devices for the Negotiation Support System (NSS) they would use to help them work on their conflict. At the front of the U was a large screen for the display of information. Michelle had Tony and Caitlin sit at stations at the two lower corners of the U and took a seat between them. She then instructed them to work silently at their comput-

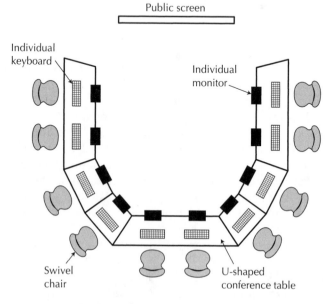

FIGURE P.1   Layout of Negotiation Support Room

ers for an hour, responding to the prompts on the screens. They worked through a series of questions asked by the system, including:

- "What are the main issues in this conflict?"
- "What does the other party think the main issues are?"
- "What are your needs or requirements for a successful resolution of this conflict?"
- "What are the other party's needs and requirements for a successful resolution of this conflict?"
- "What are some possible solutions that would meet your needs?"
- "What solutions would meet both of your needs?"
- "How do you feel about this conflict?"

Michelle assured Tony and Caitlin that the system would keep their information confidential. They could choose what to divulge later on. Caitlin was struck by how much better she understood what she wanted as a result of this exercise. She had not really thought through the issues in the conflict. Tony had never reflected on how this conflict was making him feel or how his feelings might have contributed to the problem. He had some sobering insights during the silent work period.

After about an hour, Michelle had Tony and Caitlin turn their attention to each other. Michelle started the discussion: "Tony and Caitlin, we are going to try to find a solution to this conflict that will meet or exceed your expectations. I know you have been locked into this situation for a while, but experience has shown that the Negotiation Support System can help break through a deadlock. It is designed to focus discussion on defining your needs and finding creative solutions to this conflict. The various procedures you will use today have been shown to be effective in resolving conflicts countless times. You have spent the past hour reflecting on your own point of view and analyzing your position. Hopefully this has led to some insights for

you. Now we will work together for a couple of hours to try to find a solution to this conflict.

"During the first stage of our work, we will compare positions to look for common ground. Following this, we will generate some solutions that meet both your needs. Remember several important things as we work through this conflict. Make sure the solutions we come up with meet your needs. But also, don't become wedded to a particular solution. There are usually several different solutions to any problem and at least one will meet everyone's needs. A mistake people commonly make is to cling to a single solution when a different one would really be better. Don't be afraid to experiment. Do you have any questions? If not, then let's begin."

Michelle directed Tony and Caitlin to enter their own lists of important issues into the NSS. If they wished, they could simply copy the lists they had generated during the silent period. However, they could also omit items from their private lists that they did not wish to divulge. After they finished, Michelle displayed the two lists of ideas side-by-side on the public screen. The lists were somewhat different. Caitlin's list was:

1. Tony has tried to prevent me from obtaining the services of employees I need for my project.
2. Tony has gone behind my back and talked to our supervisor.
3. My project cannot succeed without the right personnel.
4. Tony insulted me at our last meeting.

Tony's list was:

1. Caitlin is stubborn and demands what she needs, even if it hurts my project. We should pull together.
2. Caitlin wants the same employees I need for my project.
3. Caitlin embarrassed me at the staffing session by claiming her project was more important.

(continued)

CASE **P.1**   **Continued**

First, Michelle had Tony and Caitlin compare their "definitions" of the conflict. She pointed out that several of the points on the lists were not really issues. She also pointed out that there were clearly some bad feelings between them. Tony apologized to Caitlin for insulting her, stating that he did not know he had done so. She accepted his apology and reassured him that she did want them to all pull together to make FoodCo successful.

Tony and Caitlin also found several common issues on their lists, and a few differences. Tony found that Caitlin regarded his project as less important than hers. He explained to Caitlin how the success of her project depended on the success of his. She was skeptical at first, but began to see connections. After some discussion, Tony and Caitlin began to think of their projects as interdependent. Caitlin commented, "Our two projects depend so much on each other that we should coordinate our efforts better." This caused Tony to suggest a new issue: "How to coordinate our efforts given the shortage of personnel." Michelle entered this new issue into the display. The NSS allowed almost instantaneous editing of comments, so Tony and Caitlin could see the list of common issues emerging. After about an hour of discussion, a common list of issues was displayed on the screen:

1. Shortage of qualified personnel for projects A and B, and desire to assign the same people to both projects.
2. How to coordinate our efforts, given the shortage of personnel.
3. History of attempts by Tony and Caitlin to block each other's efforts.

Michelle commented that the common list of issues was much more "team-oriented" than the original lists. Then she said: "OK, let's find out if we really agree with this list. I want each of you to enter your degree of agreement with the list on the screen on a five-point scale with five indicating 'Strongly Agree' and one

indicating 'Strongly Disagree.' Make your ratings according to how you really feel about this issue. I also want you to enter your degree of agreement on the same scale with the following statement: 'We should go on to consider some solutions now.'"

Tony and Caitlin entered their ratings. The display on the screen showed ratings of 5 and 4 for the list, indicating strong agreement. Both also agreed that they should go on to the next step.

Michelle then led them into the next phase, solution generation. "First, we are going to brainstorm solutions to this conflict. I want you to enter ideas for how this conflict could be resolved into the NSS. Enter as many as possible, and don't worry about how good they are right now. We will evaluate them later. Right now we just want to think creatively. You never know what idea will turn out to be a winner, no matter how weird it seems at first."

Caitlin and Tony silently entered their ideas and then displayed the list on the public screen. A list of 13 solutions appeared. Michelle, Caitlin, and Tony discussed each item on the list, eliminating duplicates and combining similar ideas. This reduced the list to 6.

The next step was to have Caitlin and Tony rate the solutions on two scales—desirability and feasibility. They used a 10-point scale for each dimension, with a higher value corresponding to greater desirability and feasibility. After Caitlin and Tony had entered their ratings, the 6 solutions were displayed on a two-dimensional diagram on the public screen, as shown in Figure P.2. (In the interest of simplifying this figure we simply labeled them as S1 to S6.)

Michelle commented: "It looks like S3 and S4 won't work at all. S6 is desirable but not feasible, and S2 is feasible but not so desirable. I'd suggest we focus on solutions S1, 'Meet to coordinate the two projects,' and S5, 'Share the two employees.' Do you agree?"

Caitlin and Tony agreed and began to discuss the two solutions. They agreed to have

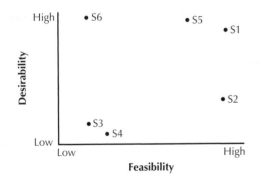

FIGURE P.2   Display of Solutions Evaluations

regular coordinating meetings and to work together to get resources for their projects. They also agreed to do a study to determine the proportion of time the two employees would need to spend on each project for them to be successful. An additional advantage of sharing the two employees, they concluded, was that the employees would be aware of the two projects and therefore able to make sure they coordinated well. Caitlin and Tony also agreed that they would look into combining their two projects to take advantage of synergies. Michelle asked if they wanted to use the NSS to rate their agreement with the solution, but both said that they knew they were in agreement.

The last step was to write a contract detailing the solution and their respective rights and obligations. The NSS provided a form for this purpose and Michelle helped Tony and Caitlin fill it out. At the end of the meeting, Michelle printed out records of their issue definition, solutions, and the contract, giving a copy to each. She told Tony and Caitlin that they should feel free to use the Negotiation Support Room at any time. She also set up a follow-up meeting for one month later to evaluate how well the solution was working out.

Caitlin and Tony were very pleased with this session. Both admitted they had been skeptical at first but were very satisfied with the resolution. Tony said: "Being able to see things on the screen gave them an objective quality. We had some distance from our ideas and were not as stubborn as a result." Caitlin commented: "I'll tell others about this system."

Discussion Questions

- *How might this conflict have been different if Tony and Caitlin had not been face to face or if Michelle had not been present?*
- *Would the NSS be helpful in: a divorce mediation? a neighbor or student dispute? an employee greivance? an international dispute?*

differences lie. Once disagreement is out in the open, people are more likely to pursue a conflict solution. Nonsupported groups, on the other hand, generally deal with issues verbally and do not have readily available mechanisms for clarifying differences or summarizing them precisely, resulting in avoidance or smoothing over of conflicts.

Second, parties' entries into computerized support systems can be kept anonymous; the system asks people to enter ideas and then displays them without revealing who made particular contributions. This has been shown to encourage frankness, even from parties with little power. As a result, conflict issues are more likely to be stated outright. The larger the team using the system, the stronger this effect; anonymity offers greater protection in larger groups than in small ones where people may be able to guess who entered something.

There are also some possible drawbacks to computerized conflict management support. For instance, the system may depersonalize some conflicts too much, causing parties to act without regard for others' feelings, which may result in uncontrolled escalation. As noted in the discussion of styles in Chapter 7, addressing conflict can be beneficial under some conditions and harmful under others. This should be taken into account when using computerized negotiation support. The various positive and negative impacts of computer use to improve conflict interventions are just beginning to be studied. Future research will clarify how to design computer-assisted support systems so that they can facilitate constructive conflict management.

REFERENCES

Adler, A. 1927. *The practice and theory of individual psychology.* New York: Harcourt, Brace and World.

Alberts, J. 1990. The use of humor in managing couples' conflict interactions. In *Intimates in conflict: A communication perspective,* edited by D. Cahn. Hillsdale, NJ: Lawrence Erlbaum.

Albrecht, T. L. 1979. The role of communication in perceptions of organizational climate. In *Communication yearbook 3,* edited by D. Nimmo. New Brunswick, NJ: Transaction Press.

Allison, G. T. 1969. Conceptual models and the Cuban Missile Crisis. *American Political Science Review 63:* 689–718.

Allport, G. W. 1954. *The nature of prejudice.* New York: Anchor.

Antes, J., J. Folger, and D. DellaNoce. 2001. Transforming conflict interaction in the workplace: Documented effects of the USPS REDRESS program. *Hofstra Labor and Employment Law Journal 18(2):* 385–398.

Apfelbaum, E. 1974. On conflicts and bargaining. In *Advances in experimental social psychology, vol. 7,* edited by L. Berkowitz. New York: Academic Press.

Apfelbaum, E. 1979. Relations of dominance and movements for liberation: An analysis of power between groups. In *The social psychology of intergroup relations,* edited by W. G. Austin and S. Worchel. Monterey, CA: Brooks/Cole.

Applegate, J. L, and J. G. Delia. 1980. Person-centered speech, psychological development, and contexts of language use. In *The social and psychological contexts of language,* edited by R. N. St. Clair and H. Giles. Hillsdale, NJ: Lawrence Erlbaum.

Arendt, H. 1969. *On violence.* New York: Harcourt Brace Jovanovich.

Auvine, B., B. Densmore, M. Extrom, S. Poole, and M. Shanklin. 1977. *A manual for group facilitators.* Madison, WI: The Center for Conflict Resolution.

Avery, M., B. Auvine, B. Streibel, and L. Weiss. 1981. *Building united judgment.* Madison, WI: The Center for Conflict Resolution.

Axelrod, R. 1970. *Conflict of interest: A theory of divergent goals with applications to politics.* Chicago: Markham.

Axelrod, R. 1984. *The evolution of cooperation.* New York: Basic Books.

Babcock, J. C., J. Waltz, N. S. Johnson, and J. M. Gottman. 1993. Power and violence: The relationship between communication patterns, power discrepancies, and domestic violence. *Journal of Consulting and Clinical Psychology 61:* 40–50.

Bachrach, P., and M. S. Baratz. 1962. Two faces of power. *American Political Science Review 56:* 947–952.

Bachrach, P., and M. S. Baratz. 1970. *Power and poverty.* New York: Oxford University Press.

Baker, P. 1981. Social coalitions. *American Behavioral Scientist 24:* 633–647.

Bales, R. F., and S. Cohen. 1979. *SYMLOG: A system for multiple level observation of groups.* New York: Free Press.

Bandler, R., and J. Grinder. 1982. *Reframing.* Moab, UT: Real People Press.

Bartos, O. J. 1970. Determinants and consequences of toughness. In *The structure of conflict,* edited by P. Swingle. New York: Academic Press.

Bartunek, J. M., and R. D. Reid. 1992. The role of conflict in a second order change attempt. In *Hidden conflict in organizations,* edited by D. M. Kolb and J. M. Bartunek. Newbury Park, CA: Sage.

Bateson, G. 1958. *Naven,* 2d ed. Stanford: Stanford University Press.

Bateson, G. 1972. *Steps to an ecology of mind.* New York: Ballentine Books.

Baxter, L. A. 1982. Conflict management: An episodic approach. *Small Group Behavior 13:* 23–42.

Baxter, L. A., W. W. Wilmot, C. A. Simmons, and A. Swartz. 1993. Ways of doing conflict: A folk taxonomy of conflict events in personal relationships. In *Interpersonal communication: Evolving interpersonal relationships,* edited by P. J. Kalbfleisch (pp. 89–107). Hillside, NJ: Lawrence Erlbaum.

Baxter, L., and T. Shepard. 1978. Sex-role identity, sex of other, and affective relationship as determinants of interpersonal conflict management styles. *Sex Roles 4:* 813–824.

Bazerman, M. H. 1983. A critical look at the rationality of negotiator judgement. *American Behavioral Scientist 27:* 211–228.

Bazerman, M. H., T. Magliozzi, and M. A. Neale. 1985. Integrative bargaining in a competitive market. *Organizational Behavior and Human Decision Processes 35:* 294–313.

Bazerman, M. H., and M. A. Neale. 1983. Heuristics in negotiation: Limitations to dispute resolution effectiveness. In *Negotiating in organizations,* edited by M. H. Bazerman and R. Lewicki. Beverly Hills, CA: Sage.

Beckman, L. J. 1970. Effects of students' performance on teachers' and observers' attributions of causality. *Journal of Educational Psychology 61:* 76–82.

Beer, J. E. 1986. *Peacemaking in your neighborhood.* Philadelphia: New Society Publishers.

Beier, E. G. 1951. The effect of induced anxiety on flexibility of intellectual functioning. *Psychological Monographs 65:* 3–26.

Bercovitch, J., and A. Kadayifci. 2002. Exploring the relevance and contribution of mediation to peace-building. *Peace and Conflict Studies 9(2):* 21–40.

Berger, C. R. 1994. Power, dominance, and social interaction. In *The handbook of interpersonal communication,* edited by M. L. Knapp and G. R. Miller. Newbury Park, CA: Sage.

Berk, M. S., and S. M. Anderson. 2000. The impact of past relationships on interpersonal behaviors: Behavioral confirmation in the socio-cognitive process of transference. *Journal of Personality and Social Psychology 79(4):* 546–562.

Bernard, S., J. P. Folger, H. R. Weingarten, and Z. Zumeta. 1984. The neutral mediator: Value dilemmas in divorce mediation. *Mediation Quarterly 4:* 61–74.

Berryman-Fink, C., and C. C. Brunner. 1987. The effects of sex of source and target on interpersonal conflict management styles. *Southern Speech Communication Journal 53:* 38–48.

Bies, R. J., D. L. Shapiro, and L. L. Cummings. 1988. Casual accounts and the management of organizational conflict. *Communication Research 15:* 381–399.

Billig, M. 1976. *The social psychology of intergroup relations.* New York: Academic Press.

Bingham, L., and T. Nabatchi. 2001. Transformative mediation in the USPS REDRESS program: Observations of the ADR specialists. *Hofstra Labor and Employment Law Journal 18(2):* 399–428.

Blake, R. R., and J. S. Mouton. 1964. *The managerial grid.* Houston: Gulf Publishing.

Blake, R. R., H. Shepard, and J. S. Mouton. 1964. *Managing intergroup conflict in industry.* Houston: Gulf Publishing.

Blau, P. 1964. *Exchange and power in social life.* New York: Wiley.

Bono, J. E., T. L. Boles, T. A. Judge, and K. J. Lauver. 2002. The role of personality in task and relationship conflict. *Journal of Personality 70(3):* 311–344.

Bormann, E. G. 1972. Fantasy and rhetorical vision: The rhetorical criticism of social reality. *Quarterly Journal of Speech 58:* 396–407.

Bormann, E. G. 1986. Symbolic convergence theory and communication in group decision-making. In *Communication and group decision-making,* edited by R. Y. Hirokawa and M. S. Poole. Beverly Hills, CA: Sage.

Boulding, K. 1990. *The three faces of power.* Newbury Park, CA: Sage.

Bowers, J. W. 1974. Beyond threats and promises. *Communication Monographs 41:* ix–xi.

Bradley, G. W. 1978. Self-serving biases in the attribution process: A reexamination of the fact or fiction question. *Journal of Personality and Social Psychology 36:* 56–71.

Brett, J. M., D. L. Shapiro, and A. L. Lytle. 1998. Breaking the bonds of reciprocity in negotiations. *Academy of Management Journal 41:* 410–424.

Brown, B. R. 1977. Face-saving and face-restoration in negotiation. In *Negotiations,* edited by D. Druckman. Beverly Hills, CA: Sage.

Brown, L. D. 1983. *Managing conflict at organizational interfaces.* Reading, MA: Addison-Wesley.

Brown, P., and S. Levinson. 1978. Universals in language usage: Politeness phenomena. In *Questions and politeness: Strategies in social interaction,* edited by E. N. Goody. Cambridge: Cambridge University Press.

Brown, P., and S. Levinson. 1987. *Universals in language usage: Politeness phenomena.* Cambridge: Cambridge University Press.

Burgess, P. G. 1973. Crisis rhetoric: Coercion vs. force. *Quarterican Political Science Review 56:* 947–952.

Burgoon, J. K., L. Dillman, and L. A. Stern. 1991. Reciprocity and compensation patterns in dyadic interaction: I. Definitions, operationalizations, and statistical analysis. Paper presented at the International Communication Association Convention, Chicago.

Burgoon, J. K., and T. J. Saine. 1978. *The unspoken dialogue: An introduction to nonverbal communication.* Boston: Houghton Mifflin.

Burke, K. 1935. *Permanence and change.* Berkeley: University of California Press.

Burke, R. J. 1970. Methods of resolving superior–subordinate conflict: The constructive use of subordinate difference and disagreements. *Organizational Behavior and Human Performance 5:* 939–411.

Burrell, N. A., P. M. Buzzanell, and J. J. McMillan. 1992. Feminine tensions in conflict management as revealed by metaphoric analysis. *Management Communication Quarterly 6:* 115–149.

Bush, R. B. 2002. Substituting mediation for arbitration: The growing market for evaluative mediation, and what it means for the ADR field. *Pepperdine Dispute Resolution Law Journal 3(1):* 111–131.

Bush, R. B., and J. P. Folger. 1994. *The promise of mediation: Responding to conflict through empowerment and recognition.* San Francisco: Jossey-Bass.

Buzzanell, P. M., and N. A. Burrell. 1997. Family and workplace conflict: Examining metaphorical conflict schemas and expressions across conflict and sex. *Human Communication Research 24:* 109–146.

Cahn, D. 1990a. *Intimates in conflict: A communication perspective.* Hillsdale, NJ: Lawrence Erlbaum Assoc.

Cahn, D. 1990b. Confrontation behaviors, perceived understanding and relationship growth. In *Intimates in conflict: A communication perspective,* edited by D. Cahn. Hillsdale, NJ: Lawrence Erlbaum Assoc.

Cai, D. I., and L. E. Drake. 1998. The business of business negotiation: Intercultural perspectives. In *Communication yearbook 21,* edited by M. Roloff (pp. 153–189). Thousand Oaks, CA: Sage.

Canary, D. J., and B. H. Spitzberg. 1989. A model of the perceived competence of conflict strategies. *Human Communication Research 15:* 630–649.

Canary, D. J., and B. H. Spitzberg. 1990. Attribution biases and associations between conflict strategies and competence outcomes. *Communication Monographs 57:* 139–151.

Caplow, T. 1956. A theory of coalitions in the triad. *American Sociological Review 21:* 489–493.

Carnevale, P., and T. Probst. 1997. Good news about competitive people. In *Using conflict in organizations*, edited by C. DeDreu and E. Van DeViest. London: Sage.

Carnevale, P. J. 1986. Strategic choice in mediation. *Negotiation Journal 2:* 41–56.

Carnevale, P. J., C. E. Conlon, K. A. Hanisch, and K. L. Harris. 1989. Experimental research on the strategic-choice model of mediation. In *Mediation research: The process and effectiveness of third party intervention*, edited by K. Kressel, D. G. Pruitt, and Associates. San Francisco: Jossey-Bass.

Carnevale, P. J., and R. Pegnetter. 1985. The selection of mediation tactics in public sector disputes: A contingency analysis. *Journal of Social Issues 41(5):* 65–81.

Carnevale, P. J., L. Putnam, D. E. Conlon, and K. M. O'Connor. 1991. Mediator behavior and effectiveness in community mediation. In *Community mediation: A handbook for practitioners and researchers*, edited by K. Grover Duffy, J. W. Grosch, and P. V. Olczak. New York: Guilford Press.

Chetkoff, J. M., and J. K. Esser. 1976. A review of experiments in explicit bargaining. *Journal of Experimental Social Psychology 12:* 464–486.

Christiansen, A., and C. Heavey. 1990. Gender and social structure in the demand/withdraw pattern of marital conflict. *Journal of Personality and Social Psychology 59:* 73–81.

Christiansen, A., and L. Pasch. 1993. The sequence of marital conflict: An analysis of seven phases of marital conflict in distressed and nondistressed couples. *Clinical Psychology Review 13:* 3–14.

Chusmir, L., and J. Mills. 1989. Gender differences in conflict resolution styles of managers: At work and at home. *Sex Roles 20:* 149–163.

Cialdini, R. B. 1984. *Influence: How and why people agree to things.* New York: William Morrow and Co.

Colquitt, J. A. 2001. On the dimensionality of organizational justice: A construct validation of a measure. *Journal of Applied Psychology 8:* 386–400.

Conley, J. M., and W. M. O'Barr. 1990. Rules versus relationships in small claims disputes. In *Conflict talk*, edited by A. D. Grimshaw. Cambridge: Cambridge University Press.

Conrad, C. 1991. Communication in conflict: Style-strategy relationships. *Communication Monographs 58:* 135–155.

Conrad, C., and M. S. Poole. 2004. *Strategic organizational communication*, 5th ed. Belmont, CA: Wadsworth.

Conrad, C., and M. Ryan. 1985. Power, praxis, and self in organizational communication theory. In *Organizational communication: Traditional themes and new directions*, edited by P. K. Tompkins, and R. McPhee. Newbury Park, CA: Sage.

Cooper, J., and R. Fazio. 1979. The formation and persistence of attitudes that support intergroup conflict. In *The social psychology of intergroup relations*, edited by W. G. Autin and S. Worchel. Monterey, CA: Brooks/Cole.

Coser, L. 1956. *The functions of social conflict.* New York: Free Press.

Cosier, R. A., and T. L. Ruble. 1981. Research on conflict handling behavior: An experimental approach. *Academy of Management Journal 24:* 816–831.

Cragan, J. F., and D. C. Shields. 1981. *Applied communication research: A dramatistic approach.* Prospect Heights, IL: Waveland.

Craig, R. T., K. Tracy, and F. Spisak. 1986. The discourse of requests: Assessment of a politeness approach. *Human Communication Research 12:* 437–468.

Crenson, M. A. 1971. *The un-politics of air pollution: A study of nondecision making in the cities.* Baltimore: Johns Hopkins Press.

Cronen, V., B. Pearce, and L. Snavely. 1980. A theory of rule-structure and types of episodes and a study of perceived enmeshment in undesired repetitive patterns URPs. In *Communication yearbook 3*, edited by D. Nimmo. New Brunswick, NJ: Transaction Books.

Crowfoot, J., and J. M. Wondolleck. 1990. *Environmental disputes: Community involvement in conflict resolution.* Washington, DC: Island Press.

Cupach, W. R., and S. Metts. 1994. *Facework.* Newbury Park, CA: Sage.

Dalton, M. 1959. *Men who manage.* New York: Wiley.

DeDreu, C. W., W. Harnnick, and A. M. Van Vianen. 1999. Conflict and performance in groups and organizations. In *International review of industrial and organizational psychology, vol. 14,* edited by C. L. Cooper and I. T. Roberston (pp. 369–414). Chichester UK: Wiley.

DeDreu, C. W., L. Weingart, and S. Kwon. 2000. Influence of social motives on integrative negotiations: A meta-analytic review and test of two theories. *Journal of Personality and Social Psychology 78:* 889–905.

DeDreu, C. W., and A. M. Van Vianen. 2001. Managing relationship conflict and the effectiveness of organizational teams. *Journal of Organizational Behavior 22(3):* 309–328.

Deetz, S., and D. Mumby. 1985. Metaphors, information and power. In *Information and behavior, vol. 1,* edited by B. Ruben. New Brunswick, NJ: Transaction Books.

Delbecq, A., A. Van de Ven, and D. Gustafsen. 1975. *Group techniques for program planning.* Glenview, IL: Scott, Foresman.

DellaNoce, D. 2001. Recognition in theory, practice, and training. In *Designing mediation: Approaches to training and practice in a transformative framework,* edited by J. Folger and R. B. Bush. New York: Institute for the Study of Conflict Transformation.

DellaNoce, D., R. B. Bush, and J. Folger. 2002. Clarifying the theoretical underpinnings of mediation: Implications for practice and policy. *Pepperdine Dispute Resolution Law Journal 3(1):* 39–66.

DellaNoce, D., J. Folger, and J. Antes. 2002. Assimilative, autonomous or synergistic visions: How mediation programs in Florida address the dilemma of court connection. *Pepperdine Dispute Resolution Law Journal 3(1):* 11–38.

Dennis, A. R., J. George, L. Jessup, J. F. Nunamaker Jr., and D. Vogel. 1988. Information technology to support electronic meetings. *MIS Quarterly 12:* 591–624.

Deschamps, J. C., and R. Brown. 1983. Superordinate goals and intergroup conflict. *British Journal of Social Psychology 22:* 189–195.

Deutsch, M. 1973. *The resolution of conflict.* New Haven: Yale University Press.

Deutsch, M., and R. M. Krauss. 1960. The effect of threat upon interpersonal bargaining. *Journal of Abnormal and Social Psychology 61:* 181–189.

Deutsch, M., and R. M. Krauss. 1962. Studies of interpersonal bargaining. *Journal of Conflict Resolution 6:* 52–76.

Deutsch, M., and R. M. Krauss. 1965. *Theories in social psychology.* New York: Basic Books.

Dill, W. R. 1965. Business organizations. In *Handbook of organizations,* edited by J. G. March. Chicago: Rand McNally.

Dirks, K. T., and D. L. Ferrin. 2002. Trust in leadership: Meta-analytic findings and implications for research and practice. *Journal of Applied Psychology 87:* 611–628.

Doise, W. 1978. *Groups and individuals.* Cambridge: Cambridge University Press.

Domenici, K. 1996. *Mediation: Empowerment in conflict management.* Prospect Heights IL: Waveland Press.

Donnellon, A., B. Gray, and M. G. Bougon. 1986. Communication, meaning and organized action. *Administrative Science Quarterly 31:* 43–55.

Donohue, W. A. 1981. Development of a model of rule use in negotiation interaction. *Communication Monographs 48:* 106–120.

Donohue, W. A. 1989. Criteria for developing communication theory in mediation. In *Managing conflict: An interdisciplinary approach,* edited by M. Rahim. New York: Praeger.

Donohue, W. A. 1991. *Communication, marital dispute and divorce mediation.* Hillsdale, NJ: Lawrence Erlbaum.

Donohue, W. A., M. E. Diez, and M. Hamilton. 1984. Coding naturalistic negotiation interaction. *Human Communication Research 10:* 403–425.

Donohue, W. A., M. E. Diez, and R. B. Stahle. 1983. New directions in negotiation research. In *Communication yearbook 7,* edited by R. W. Bostrom. Beverly Hills, CA: Sage.

Donohue, W. A. and R. Kolt. 1992. *Managing interpersonal conflict.* Newbury Park, CA: Sage.

Douglas, A. 1962. *Industrial peacemaking.* New York: Columbia University Press.

Downs, C. W., G. P. Smeyak, and E. Martin. 1980. *Professional interviewing.* New York: Harper and Row.

Duane, M. J. 1989. Sex differences in styles of conflict management. *Psychological Reports 65:* 1033–1034.

Duffy, K., J. W. Grosch, and P. V. Olczak, eds. 1991. *Community mediation: A handbook for practitioners and researchers.* New York: Guilford Press.

Eagly, A. H., and V. J. Steffen. 1986. Gender and aggressive behavior: A meta-analytic review of the social psychological literature. *Psychological Bulletin 100:* 309–330.

Ebert, R. J., and J. A. Wall. 1983. Voluntary adoption of negotiation processes. In *Negotiating in organizations,* edited by M. Bazerman and R. Lewicki. Beverly Hills, CA: Sage.

Eidelson, R. J., and J. I. Eidelson. 2003. Dangerous ideas: Five beliefs that propel people toward conflict. *American Psychologist 58(3):* 182–192.

Eisenberg, A. R., and C. Garvey. 1981. Children's use of verbal strategies in resolving conflicts. *Discourse Processes 4:* 149–170.

Eisenhardt, K., J. Kahwajy, and L. Bourgeois. 1998. In *Navigating change,* edited by D. Hambrick, D. Nadler, and M. Tushman. Boston: Harvard Business School Press.

Ellis, D., and B. A. Fisher. 1975. Phases of conflict in small group development. *Human Communication Research 1:* 195–212.

Ellis, D., and I. Maoz. 2002. Cross-cultural argument interactions between Israeli-Jews and Palestinians. *Journal of Applied Communication Research 30(3):* 181–194.

Elsayed-Ekhouly, S. M., and R. Buda. 1996. Organizational conflict: A comparative analysis of conflict across cultures. *The International Journal of Conflict Management 7:* 71–81.

Emerson, R. M. 1962. Power-dependence relations. *American Sociological Review 24:* 31–41.

Endler, N. S., and D. Magnusson. 1976. Toward an interactional psychology of personality. *Psychological Bulletin 83:* 956–974.

Epstein, S. 1962. The measurement of drive and conflict in humans: Theory and experiment. In *Nebraska Symposium on motivation,* edited by M. R. Jones. Lincoln: University of Nebraska Press.

Etzioni, A. 1967. The Kennedy experiment. *Western Political Quarterly 20:* 361–380.

Etzioni, A. 1968. *The active society.* New York: Macmillan.

Evans, G. 1964. Effect of unilateral promise and value of rewards upon cooperation and trust. *Journal of Abnormal and Social Psychology 69:* 587–590.

Felstiner, W. L., R. L. Abel, and A. Sarat. 1980–1981. The emergence and transformation of disputes: Naming, blaming, claiming. *Law and Society Review 15(3–4):* 631–654.

Feuille, P. 1979. Selected benefits and costs of compulsory arbitration. *Industrial and Labor Relations Review 33(1):* 64–76.

Filley, A. 1975. *Interpersonal conflict resolution.* Glenview, IL: Scott, Foresman.

Fink, E. L., and S. Chen. 1995. A Galileo analysis of organizational climate. *Human Communication Research 21(4):* 494–522.

Finkelstein, S. 2003. *Why smart executives fail.* New York: Portfolio.

Fisher, R. 1964. Fractionating conflict. In *International conflict and behavioral science: The Craigville papers,* edited by R. Fisher. New York: Basic Books.

Fisher, R. 1969. *International conflict resolution for beginners.* New York: Harper and Row.

Fisher, R., and W. Ury. 1981. *Getting to yes: Negotiating agreement without giving in.* Boston: Houghton Mifflin.

Fletcher, J. 1999. *Disappearing acts: Gender, power, and relational practice at work.* Cambridge, MA: MIT Press.

Folberg, J., and A. Taylor. 1984. *Mediation: A comprehensive guide to resolving conflicts without litigation.* San Francisco: Jossey-Bass.

Folger, J. P. 1980. The effects of vocal participant questioning behavior on perceptions of dominance. *Social Behavior and Personality 8:* 203–207.

Folger, J. P. 1991. Assessing community dispute resolution needs. In *Community mediation: A handbook for practitioners and researchers,* edited by K. Grover Duffy, J. W. Grosch, and P. V. Olczak. New York: Guilford Press.

Folger, J. P., and S. E. Bernard. 1985. Divorce mediation: When mediators challenge the divorcing parties. *Mediation Quarterly 10:* 5–23.

Folger, J. P., and R. B. Bush. 2001. *Designing mediation: Approaches to training and practice within a transformative framework.* New York: Institute for the Study of Conflict Transformation.

Folger, J. P., and A. Sillars. 1980. Relational coding and perceptions of dominance. In *Interpersonal communication: A relational perspective,* edited by B. Morse and L. Phelps. Minneapolis: Burgess.

Folger, R., and R. Cropanzano. 2001. Fairness theory: Justice as accountability. In *Advances in organizational justice,* edited by J. Greenberg and R. Cropanzano (pp. 1–55). Palo Alto, CA: Stanford University Press.

Fraser, B. 1981. On apologizing. In *Conversational routine,* edited by F. Coulmas. New York: Moulton Publishers.

French, R. P., and B. Raven. 1959. The bases of social power. In *Studies in social power,* edited by D. Cartwright. Ann Arbor: University of Michigan Press.

Freud, S. 1925. *The unconscious.* Translated by J. Riviere. London: Hogarth Press.

Freud, S. 1947. *The ego and the id.* Translated by J. Strackey. London: Hogarth Press. (Original work published in 1923.)

Freud, S. 1949. *An outline of psychoanalysis.* Translated by J. Strackey. New York: Norton.

Freud, S. 1953. *The interpretation of dreams.* Translated by J. Strackey. London: Hogarth Press. (Original work published in 1900.)

Friedland, N. 1976. Social influence via threats. *Journal of Social Psychology 88:* 552–563.

Frost, J., and W. Wilmot. 1978. *Interpersonal conflict.* Dubuque, IA: Wm. C. Brown.

Fry, D. P., and C. B. Fry. 1997. Culture and conflict-resolution models: Exploring alternatives to violence. In *Cultural variation in conflict resolution: Alternative to violence,* edited by D. P. Fry and K. Bjorkqvist. Mahwah, NJ: Lawrence Erlbaum Associates.

Gaelick, L., G. V. Bodenhausen, and R. Wyer. 1985. Emotional communication in close relationships. *Journal of Personality and Social Psychology 49(5):* 1246–1265.

Gamson, W. A. 1961. A theory of coalition formation. *American Sociological Review 26:* 273–282.

Garcia, A. 2000. Negotiating negotiation: The collaborative production of resolution in small claims mediation hearings. *Discourse and Society 11(3):* 315–343.

Gaylin, W. 2003. *Hatred: The psychological descent into violence.* New York: Public Affairs.

Geist, P. 1995. Negotiating who's order? Communicating to negotiate identities and revise organizational structures. In *Conflict and organzations,* edited by A. M. Nicotera. Albany, NY: State University of New York Press.

Gibb, J. 1961. Defensive communication. *Journal of Communication 2:* 141–148.

Gibbard, G. S., J. J. Hartman, and R. D. Mann. 1974. *Analysis of groups.* San Francisco: Jossey-Bass.

Gibbons, P. A., J. J. Bradac, and J. D. Busch. 1992. The role of language in negotiations: Threats and promises. In *Communication and negotiation,* edited by L. Putnam and M. E. Roloff. Newbury Park, CA: Sage.

Giles, H., and P. F. Powesland. 1975. *Speech style and social evaluation.* London: Academic Press.

Giles, D., and J. Wiemann. 1987. *Language, social comparison and power.* In *The handbook of communication science,* edited by C. R. Berger and S. H. Chaffee. Beverly Hills, CA: Sage.

Glen, E. S. 1981. *Man and mankind: Conflict and communication between cultures.* Norwich, NJ: Ablex.

Goffman, E. 1955. On facework: An analysis of ritual elements in social interaction. *Psychiatry 18:* 213–231.

Goffman, E. 1967. *Interaction ritual: Essays on face-to-face behavior.* Garden City, NY: Doubleday.

Goffman, E. 1974. *Frame analysis: An essay on the organization of experience.* New York: Harper and Row.

Goodwin, M. H. 1982. Processes of dispute resolution among urban black children. *American Ethnologist 9:* 76–96.

Gormly, J., A. Gormly, and C. Johnson. 1972. Consistency of sociobehavioral responses to interpersonal disagreement. *Journal of Personality and Social Psychology 24:* 221–224.

Gottman, J. M. 1979. *Marital interaction: Experimental investigation.* New York: Academic Press.

Gouldner, A. 1954. *Wildcat strike.* Yellow Springs, OH: Antioch Press.

Gouldner, A. W. 1960. The norm of reciprocity: A preliminary statement. *American Sociological Review 25:* 161–178.

Gouran, D. S. 1982. *Making decisions in groups.* Glenview, IL: Scott, Foresman.

Greatbatch, D., and R. Dingwall. 1989. Selective facilitation: Some preliminary observations on a strategy used by divorce mediators. *Law and Society Review 23(4):* 613–641.

Grice, H. P. 1975. Logic and conversation. In *Syntax and semantics, vol. 3,* edited by P. Cole and J. L. Morgan. New York: Academic Press.

Grimshaw, A. D., ed. 1990. *Conflict talk: Sociolinguistic investigations of arguments in conversations.* Cambridge: Cambridge University Press.

Gross, J. A., and P. A. Greenfield. 1986. Arbitral value judgements in health and safety disputes: Management rights over worker's rights. *Buffalo Law Review 34:* 645–691.

Guetzkow, H., and J. Gyr. 1954. An analysis of conflict in decision-making groups. *Human Relations 7:* 367–381.

Hall, J. 1969. *Conflict management survey: A survey on one's characteristic reaction to and handling of conflicts between himself and others.* Monroe, TX: Teleometrics International.

Hall, J., and W. H. Watson. 1970. The effects of a normative intervention on group decision-making performance. *Human Relations 23:* 299–317.

Hall, R. H. 1972. *Organizations: Structure and process.* Englewood Cliffs, NJ: Prentice-Hall.

Harre R., and L. van Langenhove. 1999. *Positioning theory.* Oxford, UK: Blackwell.

Harre, H., and P. F. Secord. 1972. *The explanation of social behavior.* Totowa, NJ: Littlefield Adams.

Harrington, C., and S. E. Merry. 1988. Ideological production: The making of community mediation. *Law and Society Review 22:* 709–737.

Hawes, L., and D. H. Smith. 1973. A critique of assumptions underlying the study of communication in conflict. *Quarterly Journal of Speech 59:* 423–435.

Hayes, D. P., and L. Meltzer. 1972. Interpersonal judgments based on talkativeness 1: Fact or artifact? *Sociometry 35:* 538–561.

Haynes, J. M. 1981. *Divorce mediation: A practical guide for therapists and counselors.* New York: Springer.

Haynes, J. M., and G. L. Haynes. 1989. *Mediating divorce*. San Francisco: Jossey-Bass.

Heavey, C., C. Layne, and A. Christensen. 1993. Gender and conflict structure in marital interaction: A replication and extension. *Journal of Consulting and Clinical Psychology 61:* 16–27.

Heider, F. 1958. *The psychology of interpersonal relations*. New York: Wiley.

Heilman, M. E. 1974. Threats and promises: Reputational consequences and the transfer of credibility. *Journal of Experimental Social Psychology 10:* 310–324.

Heuer, L. B., and S. Penrod. 1986. Procedural preferences as a function of conflict intensity. *Journal of Personality and Social Psychology 51:* 700–710.

Hewitt, J. P., and R. Stokes. 1975. Disclaimers. *American Sociological Review 40:* 1–11.

Hilgard, E., and G. Bower. 1966. *Theories of learning*. New York: Appleton-Century-Crofts.

Hill, W. A. 1973. Leadership style: Rigid or flexible? *Organizational Behavior and Human Performance 9:* 35–47.

Hiltrop, J. M. 1985. Mediator behavior and the settlement of collective bargaining disputes in Britain. *Journal of Social Issues 41:* 83–99.

Hiltrop, J. M. 1989. Factors associated with successful labor mediation. In *Mediation research: The process and effectiveness of third-party intervention*, edited by K. Kressel, D. G. Pruitt, and Associates. San Francisco: Jossey-Bass.

Hofstede, G., and M. Bond. 1984. Hofstede's culture dimensions. *Journal of Cross-Cultural Psychology 15:* 417–433.

Hollander, E. P., and J. W. Julian. 1969. Contemporary trends in the analysis of leadership processes. *Psychological Bulletin 71:* 387–397.

Holmes, M. 1992. Phase structures in negotiation. In *Communication perspectives on negotiations*, edited by L. Putnam and M. Roloff. Beverly Hills, CA: Sage.

Holsti, O. R. 1971. Crisis, stress and decision-making. *International Social Science Journal 23:* 53–67.

Homans, G. C. 1961. *Social behavior: Its elementary forms*. New York: Harcourt, Brace and Jovanovich.

Hu, H. C. 1944. The Chinese concept of "face." *American Anthropologist 46:* 45–64.

Hunger, J. D., and L. W. Stern. 1976. An assessment of the functionality of the superordinate goal in reducing conflict. *Academy of Management Journal 19:* 591–605.

Infante, D. A. 1987. Aggressiveness. In *Personality and interpersonal communication*, edited by J. C. McCroskey and J. A. Daly. Beverly Hills, CA: Sage.

Infante, D. A., and W. I. Gorden. 1985. Superiors' argumentativeness and verbal aggressiveness as predictors of subordinates' satisfaction. *Human Communication Research 12:* 117–125.

Infante, D. A., and C. J. Wigley. 1986. Verbal aggressiveness: An interpersonal model and measure. *Communication Monographs 53:* 61–69.

Ivy, D. K., and P. Backlund. 1994. *Exploring genderspeak: Personal effectiveness in gender communication*. New York: McGraw-Hill.

James, L. R., and A. P. Jones. 1974. Organizational climate: A review of theory and research. *Psychological Bulletin 81:* 1086–1112.

Jameson, J. K. 2001. Employee perceptions of the availability and use of interest-based, rights-based, and power-based conflict management strategies. *Conflict Resolution Quarterly 19:* 163–196.

Janeway, E. 1980. *Powers of the weak*. New York: Morrow-Quill.

Janis, I. 1972. *Victims of groupthink*. Boston: Houghton Mifflin.

Janis, I., and L. Mann. 1977. *Decision-making*. New York: Free Press.

Jehn, K. A. 1995. A multimethod examination of the benefits and detriments of intragroup conflict. *Administrative Science Quarterly 40:* 256–282.

Jehn, K. A., and J. A. Chatman. 2000. The influence of proportional and perceptual conflict composition on team performance. *International Journal of Conflict Management 11(1):* 56–73.

Jewell, L. N., and H. J. Reitz. 1981. *Group effectiveness in organizations.* Glenview, IL: Scott, Foresman.

Johnson, D. W., and F. P. Johnson. 1975. *Joining together.* Englewood Cliffs, NJ: Prentice-Hall.

Jones, E. E., K. J. Gergen, and R. G. Jones. 1963. Tactics of ingratiation among leaders and subordinates in a status hierarchy. *Psychological Monographs 77:* 120.

Jones, E. E., and R. E. Nisbett. 1971. The actor and the observer: Divergent perceptions of the causes of behavior. In *Attribution: Perceiving the causes of behavior,* edited by E. E. Jones, E. Kanouse, H. H. Kelley, R. E. Nisbett, S. Valins, and B. Weiner. Morristown, NJ: General Learning Press.

Jones, R. E., and B. H. Melcher. 1982. Personality and preference for modes of conflict resolution. *Human Relations 35:* 649–658.

Jones, R. E., and C. S. White. 1985. Relationships among personality, conflict resolution styles, and task effectiveness. *Group and Organization Studies 10:* 152–167.

Jones, T. S. 1988. An analysis of phase structures in successful and unsuccessful divorce mediation. *Communication Research 15:* 470–495.

Jones, T. S. 1989. Lag sequential analyses of mediator-spouse and husband-wife interaction in successful and unsuccessful divorce mediation. In *Managing conflict: An interdisciplinary approach,* edited by M. Rahim. New York: Praeger.

Jones, T. S., and A. Bodtker. 2001. Mediating with heart in mind: Addressing emotion in mediation practice. *Negotiation Journal 17(3):* 217–244.

Jones, T., and H. Brinkman. 1994. "Teach your children well": Recommendations for peer mediation programs. In *New directions in mediation: Communication research and perspectives,* edited by J. P. Folger and T. Jones. Newbury Park, CA: Sage.

Kahneman, D., and A. Tversky. 1979. Prospect theory: An analysis of decision under risk. *Econometrica 47:* 263–291.

Kanter, R. M. 1977. *Men and women of the corporation.* New York: Basic Books.

Kaplowitz, S. A. 1973. An experimental test of a rationalistic theory of deterrence. *Journal of Conflict Resolution 17:* 535–572.

Karambayya, R., and J. M. Brett. 1989. Managers handling disputes: Third-party roles and perceptions of fairness. *Academy of Management Journal 32(4):* 687–704.

Karambayya, R., and J. M. Brett. 1994. Managerial third parties: Intervention strategies, process, and consequences. In *New directions in mediation: Communication research and perspectives,* edited by J. P. Folger and T. Jones. Newbury Park, CA: Sage.

Kaufman, S., and G. T. Duncan. 1989. Third-party intervention: A theoretical framework. In *Managing conflict: An interdisciplinary approach,* edited by M. A. Rahim. New York: Praeger.

Kelley, H., J. Cunningham, J. Grishman, L. Lefebvre, C. Sink, and G. Yablon. 1978. Sex differences in comments made during conflict within close heterosexual pairs. *Sex Roles 4:* 473–492.

Kelley, H. H. 1965. Experimental studies of threats in interpersonal negotiations. *Journal of Conflict Resolution 9:* 79–105.

Kelley, H. H. 1979. *Personal relationships: Their structure and processes.* Hillsdale, NJ: Lawrence Erlbaum.

Kelley, H. H., and J. Thibaut. 1978. *Interpersonal relations: A theory of interdependence.* New York: Wiley.

Kiesler, C. 1971. *The psychology of commitment.* New York: Academic Press.

Kim, M. S., and T. Leung. 2000. A multicultural view of conflict management styles: Review and critical synthesis. In *Communication yearbook 23,* edited by M. Roloff (pp. 227–269). Thousand Oaks, CA: Sage.

Kipnis, D. 1990. *Technology and power.* New York: Springer-Verlag.

Kipnis, D., S. Schmidt, and I. Wilkerson. 1980. Intraorganizational influence tactics: Explorations in getting one's way. *Journal of Applied Psychology 65:* 440–452.

Kluwer, E. S., C. K. W. deDreu, and B. P. Buunk. 1998. Conflict in intimate vs. nonintimate relationships: When gender role stereotyping overrides biased self-other judgment. *Journal of Social and Personal Relationships 15:* 637–650.

Kochan, T. A., and T. A. Jick. 1978. The public sector mediation process: A theory and empirical examination. *Journal of Conflict Resolution 22:* 209–241.

Kolb, D. 1983. *The mediators.* Cambridge, MA: MIT Press.

Kolb, D. 1986. Who are organizational third parties and what do they do? In *Research on negotiation in organizations,* edited by R. J. Lewicki, B. H. Sheppard, and M. H. Bazerman. Greenwich, CT: JAI Press.

Kolb, D. 1987. Corporate ombudsman and organizational conflict. *Journal of Conflict Resolution 31:* 663–692.

Kolb, D. 1989. Labor mediators, managers and ombudsmen: Roles mediators play in different contexts. In *Mediation research: The process and effectiveness of third-party intervention,* edited by K. Kressel, D. G. Pruitt, et al. San Francisco: Jossey-Bass.

Kolb, D., and J. M. Bartunek, eds. 1992. *Hidden conflict in organizations.* Newbury Park, CA: Sage.

Kolb, D., and B. H. Sheppard. 1985. Do managers mediate or even arbitrate? *Negotiation Journal 1:* 379–388.

Komorita, S. S. 1977. Negotiating from strength and the concept of bargaining strength. *Journal of the Theory of Social Behavior 7(1):* 65–79.

Komorita, S., and J. Chertkoff. 1973. A bargaining theory of coalition formation. *Psychological Review 80:* 149–162.

Korabik, K., G. Baril, and C. Watson. 1993. Managers' conflict management style and leadership effectiveness: The moderating effect of gender. *Sex Roles 29:* 405–420.

Korsgaard, A., S. Brodt, and E. Whitener. 2002. Trust in the face of conflict: The role of managerial trustworthy behavior and organizational context. *Journal of Applied Psychology 87:* 312–319.

Kozan, M. K. 1991. Interpersonal conflict management styles of Jordanian managers. In *Conflict resolution: Cross-cultural perspectives,* edited by K. Avruch, P. W. Black, and J. A. Scimecia. Westport, CT: Greenwood Press.

Kozan, M. K. 1997. Culture and conflict management: A theoretical framework. *The International Journal of Conflict Management 8:* 338–360.

Krauss, E. S., T. P. Rohlen, and P. G. Steinhoff, eds. 1984. *Conflict in Japan.* Honolulu: University of Hawaii Press.

Kressel, K., D. G. Pruitt, et al., eds. 1989. *Mediation research: The process and effectiveness of third-party intervention.* San Francisco: Jossey-Bass.

Kriesberg, L. 1973. *The sociology of social conflicts.* Englewood Cliffs, NJ: Prentice-Hall.

Kritek, P. B. 1994. *Negotiating at an uneven table.* San Francisco: Jossey-Bass.

LaFasto, F., and C. Larson. 2001. *When teams work best.* Thousand Oaks, CA: Sage.

Lake, L. 1980. *Environmental mediation: The search for consensus.* Boulder, CO: Westview Press.

Lam, J. A., J. Rifkin, and A. Townley. 1989. Reframing conflict: Implications for fairness in parent–adolescent mediation. *Mediation Quarterly 7(1):* 15–31.

Larson, C. E., and F. M. LaFasto. 1989. *Teamwork.* Newbury Park, CA: Sage.

Lawler, E. J., and G. A. Youngs. 1975. Coalition formation: An integrative model. *Sociometry 38:* 1–17.

Lawrence, P. R., and J. W. Lorsch. 1967. *Organization and environment.* Boston: Division of Research, Harvard Business School.

Leary, T. 1957. *Interpersonal diagnosis of personality.* New York: Ronald Press.

Lederach, J. P. 1991: Of nets, nails, and problems: The folk language of conflict resolution in a Central American setting. In *Conflict resolution: Cross cultural perspectives,* edited by K. Avruch, P. W. Black, and J. A. Scimecia. Westport, CT: Greenwood Press.

Lemmon, J. A. 1985. *Family mediation practice.* New York: Free Press.

LeResche, D. 1992. Comparison of the American mediation process with a Korean-American harmony restoration process. *Mediation Quarterly 9(4):* 323–339.

Leveque, C., and M. S., Poole, 1998. Systems thinking in organizational communication. In *Organizational communication and change,* edited by P. Salem. Creskill, NJ: Hampton.

Levinger, G. 1979. A social psychological perspective on marital dissolution. In *Divorce and separation,* edited by G. Levinger and O. Moles. New York: Basic Books.

Lewin, K. 1951. *Field theory in social science.* New York: Harper Brothers.

Lim, T., and J. W. Bowers. 1991. Face-work: Solidarity, approbation, and tact. *Human Communication Research 17:* 415–450.

Lindskold, S. 1978. Trust development, the GRIT proposal, and the effects of conciliatory acts on conflict and cooperation. *Psychological Bulletin 85:* 772–793.

Lindskold, S. 1979. Managing conflict through announced conciliatory initiative backed by retaliatory capacity. In *The social psychology of intergroup relations,* edited by W. G. Austin and S. Worchel. Belmont, CA: Wadsworth.

Lindskold, S., B. Betz, and P. S. Walters. 1986. Transforming competitive or cooperative climates. *Journal of Conflict Resolution 30:* 99–114.

Lovelace, K., D. L. Shapiro, and L. R. Weingart. 2001. Maximizing cross-functional new product teams' innovativeness and constraint adherence: A conflict communications perspective. *Academy of Management Journal 44:* 779–793.

Luchins, A., and E. Luchins. 1959. *Rigidity of behavior.* Eugene: University of Oregon Books.

Lukes, S. 1974. *Power: A radical view.* London: MacMillan.

Lyles, M. A., and I. I. Mitroff. 1980. Organizational problem formulation: An empirical study. *Administrative Science Quarterly 25:* 102–119.

Mackey, R. A., and B. A. O'Brien. 1998. Marital conflict management: Gender and ethnic differences. *Social Work 43:* 128–141.

Maier, N. 1967. Assets and liabilities in group problem solving: The need for an integrative function. *Psychological Review 74:* 239–249.

Mansbridge, J. 1980. *Beyond adversary democracy.* Chicago: University of Chicago Press.

Mansbridge, J. 1990. *Beyond self-interest.* Chicago: University of Chicago Press.

Markey, P. M., D. C. Funder, and D. J. Ozer. 2003. Complementarity of interpersonal behaviors in dyadic interactions. *Personality and Social Psychology Bulletin 29:* 1082–1090.

Markman, H., L. Silvern, M. Clements, and S. Hanak. 1993. Men and women dealing with conflict in heterosexual relationships. *Journal of Social Issues 49:* 107–125.

Marks, J., E. Johnson, and P. L. Szanton. 1984. *Dispute resolution processes in America: Processes in evolution.* Washington, DC: National Institute for Dispute Resolution.

Marwell, G., and D. R. Schmitt. 1967. Dimensions of compliance-gaining behavior: An empirical analysis. *Sociometry 30:* 350–364.

Mather, L., and B. Yngvesson. 1980–1981. Language, audience and the transformation of disputes. *Law and Society Review 15:* 3–4, 775–821.

Maurer, R. 1994. *Feedback toolkit.* Portland, OR: Productivity Press.

McGillicuddy, N. B., D. G. Pruitt, G. L. Welton, J. M. Zubek, and R. S. Peirce. 1991. Factors affecting the outcome of mediation: Third-party and disputant behavior. In *Community mediation: A handbook for practitioners and researchers,* edited by K. Grover Duffy, J. W. Grosch, and P. V. Olczak. New York: Guilford Press.

McLaughlin, M. L. 1984. Conversation: *How talk is organized.* Beverly Hills, CA: Sage.

McLaughlin, M. L., M. J. Cody, and N. E. Rosenstein. 1983. Account sequences in conversations between strangers. *Communication Monographs 50:* 102–125.

McRae, B. 1998. Negotiating and influencing skills. *The art of creating and claiming value.* Thousand Oaks, CA: Sage.

Menkel-Meadow, C. 1985. The transformation of disputes by lawyers: What the dispute paradigm does and does not tell us. *Journal of Dispute Resolution 2:* 25–44.

Mernitz, S. 1980. *Mediation of environmental disputes.* New York: Praeger.

Merry, S. E. 1979. Going to court: Strategies of dispute resolution in an American urban neighborhood. *Law and Society Review 13:* 891–925.

Merry, S. E., and S. S. Silbey. 1984. What do plaintiffs want? Reexamining the concept of dispute. *Justice System Journal 9(2):* 151–178.

Meyer, J. W. 1983. Organizational factors affecting legalization in education. In *Organizational environments: Ritual and rationality,* edited by J. W. Meyer and W. R. Scott. Beverly Hills, CA: Sage.

Meyer, H. H., E. Kay, and J. R. P. French, Jr. 1965. Split roles in performance appraisal. *Harvard Business Review 43:* 123–129.

Millar, F. E., and L. E. Rogers. 1987. Relational dimensions of interpersonal dynamics. In *Interpersonal process: New directions in communication research,* edited by M. E. Roloff and G. R. Miller. Beverly Hills, CA: Sage.

Miller, A. 1976. Constraint and target effects in the attribution of attitudes. *Journal of Experimental Social Psychology 12:* 325–339.

Miller, G., E. Galanter, and K. Pribram. 1960. *Plans and the structure of behavior.* New York: Holt, Rinehart and Winston.

Miller, G. R., F. Boster, M. Roloff, and D. Seibold. 1976. Compliance-gaining message strategies: A typology and some findings concerning effects of situational differences. *Communication Monographs 44:* 37–51.

Mischel, W. 1968. *Personality and assessment.* New York: Wiley.

Moore, C. W. 1986. *The mediation process.* San Francisco: Jossey-Bass.

Moore, J. C. 1968. Status and influence in small group interaction. *Sociometry 31:* 47–63.

Morley, I. E., and G. M. Stephenson. 1977. *The social psychology of bargaining.* London: Allen and Unwin.

Morris, G. H., and R. Hopper. 1980. Remediation and legislation in everyday talk: How communicators achieve consensus. *Quarterly Journal of Speech 66:* 266–274.

Moscovici, S. 1976. *Social influence and social change.* New York: Academic Press.

Mura, S. S. 1983. Licensing violations: Legitimate violations of Grice's conversation principle. In *Conversational coherence: Form, structure and strategy,* edited by R. T. Craig and K. Tracy. Beverly Hills, CA: Sage.

Murnigham, J. K. 1978. Models of coalition behavior: Game theoretic, social psychological, and political perspective. *Psychological Bulletin 85:* 1130–1153.

Musser, S. J. 1982. A model for predicting the choice of conflict management strategies by subordinates in high-stakes conflicts. *Organizational Behavior and Human Performance 29:* 257–269.

Neale, M. A., and G. B. Northcroft. 1986. Experts, amateurs, and refrigerators: Comparing expert and amateur decision making on a novel task. *Organizational Behavior and Human Decision Processes 38:* 305–317.

Neel, A. F. 1977. *Theories of psychology.* New York: Shenkman.

Newell, S. E., and R. K. Stutman. 1988. The social confrontation episode. *Communication Monographs 55:* 266–285.

Newell, S. E., and R. K. Stutman. 1989/1990. Negotiating confrontation: The problematic nature of initiation and response. *Research on Language and Social Interaction 23:* 139–162.

Newell, S. E., and R. K. Stutman. 1991. The episodic nature of social confrontation. In *Communication yearbook 14,* edited by A. Andersen. Beverly Hills, CA: Sage.

North, R. C., R. A. Brody, and O. Holsti. 1963. Some empirical data on the conflict spiral. *Peace Research Society Papers I:* 1–14.

Northrup, T. 1989. The dynamic of identity in personal and social conflict. In *Intractable conflicts and their transformation,* edited by L. Kreisberg, T. Northrup, and S. Thorson. Syracuse, NY: Syracuse University Press.

Nutt, P. C. 1984. *Planning methods for health and related organizations.* New York: Wiley.

Osgood, C. E. 1959. Suggestions for winning the real war with communism. *Journal of Conflict Resolution 3:* 295–325.

Osgood, C. E. 1962. *An alternative to war or surrender.* Urbana: University of Illinois Press.

Osgood, C. E. 1966. *Perspectives on foreign policy,* 2d ed. Palo Alto, CA: Pacific Books.

Papa, M. J., and E. J. Natalle. 1989. Gender, strategy selection, and satisfaction in interpersonal conflict. *Western Journal of Speech Communication 53:* 260–272.

Peachey, D. E. 1989. What people want from mediation. In *Mediation research: The process and effectiveness of third-party intervention,* edited by K. Kressel, D. G. Pruitt, et al. San Francisco: Jossey-Bass.

Pearce, W. B. 1976. The coordinated management of meaning: A rules-based theory of interpersonal communication. In *Explorations in interpersonal communication,* edited by G. R. Miller. Beverly Hills, CA: Sage.

Pearce, W. B., and V. E. Cronen. 1980. *Communication, action and meaning.* New York: Praeger.

Pearce, W. B., and S. W. Littlejohn. 1997. *Moral conflict: When social worlds collide.* Thousand Oaks, CA: Sage.

Pearson, J., and N. Thoennes. 1989. Divorce mediation: Reflections on a decade of research. In *Mediation research: The process and effectiveness of third-party intervention,* edited by K. Kressel, D. G. Pruitt, et al. San Francisco: Jossey-Bass.

Pelz, D. C. 1952. Influence: A key to effective leadership in the first-line supervisor. *Personnel 29:* 209–217.

Penman, R. 1991. Goals, games and moral orders: A paradoxical case in court? In *Understanding face-to-face interaction,* edited by K. Tracy. Hillsdale, NJ: Lawrence Erlbaum.

Perrow, C. 1986. *Complex organizations: A critical essay.* New York: Random House.

Pfeffer, J. 1978. *Organizational design.* Arlington Heights, IL: AHM Publishing.

Phillips, E., and R. Cheston. 1979. Conflict resolution: What works? *California Management Review 21:* 76–83.

Phillips, S. U. 1990. The judge as third party in American trial-court conflict talk. In *Conflict talk,* edited by A. D. Grimshaw. Cambridge: Cambridge University Press.

Pondy, L. R. 1967. Organizational conflict: concepts and models. *Administrative Science Quarterly 12:* 296–320.

Poole, M. S. 1981. Decision development in small groups I: A comparison of two models. *Communication Monographs 48:* 1–25.

Poole, M. S. 1983. Decision development in small groups III: A multiple sequence theory of decision development. *Communication Monographs, 50:* 321–341.

Poole, M. S. 1985. Communication and organizational climates. In *Organizational communication: Traditional themes and new directions,* edited by R. D. McPhee and P. Tompkins. Beverly Hills, CA: Sage.

Poole, M. S. 1991. Procedures for managing meetings: Social and technological innovation. In *Innovative meeting management,* edited by R. S. Swanson and B. O. Knapp. Austin, TX: 3M Meeting Management Institute.

Poole, M. S., M. Holmes, and G. DeSanctis. 1991. Conflict management in a computer-supported meeting environment. *Management Science 37:* 926–953.

Poole, M. S., and R. D. McPhee. 1983. Bring intersubjectivity in: A structurational analysis of climate. In *Communication and organizations: An interpretive approach,* edited by L. Putnam and M. Pacanowsky. Beverly Hills, CA: Sage.

Poole, M. S., D. Shannon, and G. DeSanctis. 1992. Electronic modes of negotiation. In *Communication and negotiation,* edited by L. Putnam and M. Roloff. Beverly Hills, CA: Sage.

Powell, G. N., and D. A. Butterfield. 1978. The case for subsystem climate in organizations. *Academy of Management Review 3:* 151–157.

Powell, G. N., and D. A. Butterfield. 1979. The "good manager": Masculine or androgynous? *Academy of Management Journal 22:* 395–403.

Powell, G. N., and D. A. Butterfield. 1984. If good managers are masculine, what are bad managers? *Sex Roles 10:* 477–484.

Pruitt, D. G. 1971. Indirect communication and the search for agreement in negotiation. *Journal of Applied Social Psychology 1:* 205–239.

Pruitt, D. G. 1981. *Negotiating behavior.* New York: Academic Press.

Pruitt, D. G. 1983. Achieving integrative agreements. In *Negotiating in organizations,* edited by M. Bazerman and R. Lewicki. Beverly Hills, CA: Sage.

Pruitt, D. G., and P. J. Carnevale. 1993. *Negotiation in social conflict.* Pacific Grove, CA: Brooks/Cole.

Pruitt, D. G., and D. F. Johnson. 1970. Mediation as an aid to face saving in negotiation. *Journal of Applied Social Psychology 14:* 239–246.

Pruitt, D. G., and M. J. Kimmel. 1977. Twenty years of experimental gaming: Critique, synthesis, and suggestions for the future. *Annual Review of Psychology 28:* 363–392.

Pruitt, D. G., and S. Lewis. 1977. The psychology of integrative bargaining. In *Negotiations,* edited by D. Druckman. Beverly Hills, CA: Sage.

Pruitt, D. G., N. B. McGillicuddy, G. L. Welton, and W. R. Fry. 1989. Process of mediation in dispute settlement centers. In *Mediation research: The process and effectiveness of third-party intervention,* edited by K. Kressel, D. G. Pruitt, et al. San Francisco: Jossey-Bass.

Pruitt, D. G., and J. Rubin. 1986. *Social conflict: Escalation, stalemate and settlement,* New York: Random House.

Pruitt, D. G., J. Rubin, and S. Kim. 1994. *Social conflict: Escalation, stalemate, and settlement,* 2d ed. New York: McGraw-Hill.

Putnam, L., ed. 1988. Communication and conflict styles in organizations [Special issue]. *Management Communication Quarterly 1(3).*

Putnam, L. 1990. Reframing integrative and distributive bargaining: A process perspective. In *Research on negotiation in organizations, vol. 2,* edited by R. J. Lewicki, B. H. Sheppard and M. H. Bazerman. Greenwich, CT: JAI Press.

Putnam, L., and J. P. Folger. 1988. Communication, conflict and dispute resolution: The study of interaction and the development of conflict theory. *Communication Research 15:* 349–359.

Putnam, L., and M. Holmer. 1992. Framing, reframing and issue development. In *Communication perspectives on negotiations*, edited by L. L. Putnam and M. E. Roloff. Beverly Hills, CA: Sage.

Putnam, L., and T. Jones. 1982a. The role of communication in bargaining. *Human Communication Research 8(3):* 262–280.

Putnam, L., and T. Jones. 1982b. Reciprocity in negotiations: An analysis of bargaining interaction. *Communication Monographs 49:* 171–191.

Putnam, L., and M. S. Poole. 1987. Conflict and negotiation. In *Handbook of organizational communication*, edited by F. Jablin, L. Putnam, K. Roberts, and L. Porter. Beverly Hills, CA: Sage.

Putnam, L., and C. E. Wilson. 1982. Communicative strategies in organizational conflicts: Reliability and validity of a measurement scale. In *Communication yearbook 6*, edited by M. Burgoon. Beverly Hills, CA: Sage.

Putnam, L., S. Wilson, M. S. Waltman, and D. Turner. 1986. The evolution of case arguments in teachers' bargaining. *Journal of the American Forensic Association 23:* 63–81.

Rahim, M. A. 1983. A measure of styles of handling interpersonal conflict. *Academy of Management Journal 26:* 369–376.

Rapaport, A. 1960. *Fights, games and debates.* Ann Arbor: University of Michigan Press.

Rapaport, D. 1951. *Organization and pathology of thought.* New York: Columbia University Press.

Raven, B., and A. Kruglanski. 1970. Conflict and power. In *The structure of conflict*, edited by Paul Swingle. New York: Academic Press.

Renwick, P. A. 1977. The effects of sex differences on the perception and management of superior–subordinate conflict: An exploratory study. *Organizational Behavior and Human Performance 19:* 403–415.

Richardson, L. F. 1960. *Arms and insecurity.* Pittsburgh: The Boxwood Press.

Riesel, D. 1985. Negotiation and mediation of environmental disputes. *Ohio State Journal on Dispute Resolution 1:* 99–111.

Riggs, C. J. 1983. Communication dimensions of conflict tactics in organizational settings: A functional analysis. In *Communication yearbook 7*, edited by R. W. Bostrom. Beverly Hills, CA: Sage.

Riskin, L., Ed. 1985. *Divorce mediation: Readings.* Washington, DC: American Bar Association.

Roloff, M. E. 1976. Communication strategies, relationships, and relational changes. In *Explorations in interpersonal communication*, edited by G. R. Miller. Beverly Hills, CA: Sage.

Roloff, M. E. 1981. *Interpersonal communication: The social exchange approach.* Beverly Hills, CA: Sage.

Roloff, M. E. 1987a. Communication and conflict. In *Handbook of communication science*, edited by C. Berger and S. H. Chaffee. Beverly Hills, CA: Sage.

Roloff, M. E. 1987b. Communication and reciprocity within intimate relationships. In *Interpersonal processes: New directions in communication research*, edited by R. E. Roloff and G. R. Miller. Beverly Hills, CA: Sage.

Roloff, M. E., and D. E. Campion. 1985. Conversational profit-seeking: Interaction as social exchange. In *Sequence and pattern in communicative behavior*, edited by R. L. Street, Jr., and J. N. Cappella. London: Edward Arnold.

Roloff, M., and D. Cloven. 1990. The chilling effect in interpersonal relationships: The reluctance to speak one's mind. In *Intimates in conflict: A communication perspective*, edited by D. D. Cahn. Hillsdale, NJ: Lawrence Erlbaum.

Ross, L. 1977. The intuitive psychologist and his shortcomings: Distortions in the attribution process. In *Advances in experimental social psychology, vol. 10*, edited by L. Berkowitz. New York: Academic Press.

Ross, M. H. 1993. *The culture of conflict: Interests, interpretations and disputing in comparative perspective.* New Haven: Yale University Press.

Ross, R. G., and S. DeWine. 1988. Communication messages in conflict: A message-focused instrument to assess conflict management styles. *Management Communication Quarterly 1:* 389–413.

Roth, S. 1993. Speaking the unspoken: A work-group consultation to reopen dialogue. In *Secrets in families and family therapy,* edited by E. Imber-Balck. New York: Norton.

Rousseau, D. M., S. B. Sitkin, R. S. Burt, and C. Camerer. 1998. Not so different after all: A cross-discipline view of trust. *Academy of Management Review 23:* 393–404.

Rowe, M. 1987. The corporate ombudsman. *Negotiation Journal 3:* 127–141.

Roy, D. F. 1959. "Banana time": Job satisfaction and informal interaction. *Human Organization 18:* 158–168.

Rubin, J. Z., and B. Brown. 1975. *The social psychology of bargaining and negotiation.* New York: Academic Press.

Rubin, L. 1983. *Intimate strangers.* New York: Harper and Row.

Ruble, T. L., and K. W. Thomas. 1976. Support for a two-dimensional model of conflict behavior. *Organizational Behavior and Human Performance 16:* 143–155.

Rummel, R. J. 1976. *Understanding conflict and war, vol. 2.* Beverly Hills, CA: Sage.

Sambamurthy, V., and M. S. Poole. 1992. The effects of variations in capabilities of GDSS designs on management of cognitive conflict in groups. *Information Systems Research 3:* 224–251.

Sarat, A. 1988. The "new formalism" in disputing and dispute processing. *Law and Society Review 21(3):* 695–715.

Savage, G. T., J. D. Blair, and R. L. Sorenson. 1989. Consider both relationships and substance when negotiating strategically. *The Academy of Management Executive III:* 37–48.

Scarf, M. 1987. *Intimate partners: Patterns in love and marriage.* New York: Ballantine Books.

Scheff, T. J. 1967. Toward a sociological model of consensus. *American Sociological Review 32:* 32–46.

Scheidel, T., and L. Crowell. 1979. *Discussing and deciding.* New York: Macmillan.

Schneider, C. D. 2000. What it means to be sorry: The power of apology in mediation. *Mediation Quarterly 17(3):* 265–280.

Schneider, B., and C. J. Bartlett. 1970. Individual differences and organizational climate II: Measurement of organizational climate by the multi-trait, multi-rater matrix. *Personnel Psychology 23:* 493–512.

Schwarz, R. M. 2002. *The skilled facilitator.* San Francisco: Jossey-Bass.

Schwerin, E. 1995. *Mediation, citizen empowerment and transformational politics.* Westport CT: Praeger.

Selznick, P. H. 1969. *Law, society, and industrial justice.* New York: Russell Sage Foundation.

Shailor, J. G. 1994. *Empowerment in dispute mediation.* Westport, CT: Praeger.

Shapiro, D., R. Drieghe, and J. Brett. 1985. Mediator behavior and the outcome of mediation. *Journal of Social Issues 41(2):* 101–114.

Sharkey, W. F. 1988. Embarrassment: A review of literature. Paper presented at the International Communication Association conference, New Orleans.

Sharp, G. 1973. *The politics of nonviolent action.* Boston: Porter-Sargent.

Shaw, J. C., E. Wild, and J. A. Colquitt. 2003. To justify or excuse: A metaanalytic review of the effects of explanations. *Journal of Applied Psychology 88(3):* 444–458.

Shawn, W., and A. Gregory. 1981. *My dinner with André.* New York: Grove Press.

Shenkar, O., and S. Ronen. 1987. The cultural context of negotiations: The implication of Chinese interpersonal norms. *Journal of Applied Behavioral Science 23:* 263–275.

Sheppard, B. H. 1984. Third-party conflict intervention: A procedural framework. In *Research in organizational behavior, vol. 6,* edited by B. Staw and L. L. Cummings. Greenwich, CT: JAI Press.

Sheppard, B. H., R. J. Lewicki, and J. W. Minton. 1992. *Organizational justice: The search for fairness in the workplace.* New York: Lexington Books.

Sheppard, B. H., K. Blumenfeld-Jones, and J. Roth. 1989. Informal third partyship: Studies of everyday conflict intervention. In *Mediation research: The process and effectiveness of third-party intervention,* edited by K. Kressel, D. G. Pruitt, et al. San Francisco: Jossey-Bass.

Sheppard, B. H., D. M. Saunders, and J. W. Minton. 1988. Procedural justice from the third-party perspective. *Journal of Personality and Social Psychology 54:* 629–637.

Sherif, M., O. J. Harvey, B. J. White, W. R. Hood, and C. W. Sherif. 1961. *Intergroup conflict and cooperation: The Robber's Cave experiment.* Norman, OK: University Book Exchange.

Shubert, J., and J. P. Folger. 1986. Learning from higher education. *Negotiation Journal 2:* 395–406.

Shubik, M. 1987. *Game theory in the social sciences: Concepts and solutions.* Cambridge, MA: MIT Press.

Silbey, S. S., and S. E. Merry. 1986. Mediator settlement strategies. *Law and Policy 8:* 7–32.

Sillars, A. L. 1980a. Stranger and spouse as target persons for compliance gaining strategies. *Human Communication Research 6:* 265–279.

Sillars, A. L. 1980b. Attributions and communication in roommate conflicts. *Communication Monographs 47:* 180–200.

Sillars, A. L. 1980c. The sequential and distributional structure of conflict interactions as a function of attributions concerning the locus of responsibility and stability of conflicts. In *Communication yearbook 4,* edited by D. Nimmo. New Brunswick, NJ: Transaction Press.

Sillars, A. L., S. F. Coletti, D. Parry, and M. A. Rogers. 1982. Coding verbal conflict tactics: Nonverbal and perceptual correlates of the "avoidance-distributive-integrative" distinction. *Human Communication Research 9:* 83–95.

Sillars, A. L., and D. Parry. 1982. Stress, cognition and communication in interpersonal conflicts. *Communication Research 9:* 201–226.

Sillars, A. L., and J. Weisberg. 1987. Conflict as a social skill. In *Interpersonal processes: New directions in communication research,* edited by M. E. Roloff and G. R. Miller. Beverly Hills, CA: Sage.

Simmel, C. 1955. *Conflict.* New York: Free Press.

Simon, H. A. 1955. A behavioral model of rational choice. *Quarterly Journal of Economics 69:* 99–118.

Simons, T. L., and R. S. Peterson. 2000. Task conflict and relationship conflict in top management teams: The pivotal role of intragroup trust. *Journal of Applied Psychology 85(1):* 102–111.

Simmons, A. 1998. *Territorial games.* New York: Amacon.

Singer, L. R. 1990. *Settling disputes.* Boulder, CO: Westview Press.

Skidmore, W. 1979. *Theoretical thinking in sociology,* 2d ed. Cambridge: Cambridge University Press.

Smart, C., and I. Vertinsky. 1977. Designs for crisis decision units. *Administrative Science Quarterly 22:* 640–657.

Smith, K. I. 1989. The movement of conflict in organizations: The joint dynamics of splitting and triangulation. *Administrative Science Quarterly 34:* 1–20.

Smith, K., and D. Berg. 1987. *Paradoxes of group life.* San Francisco: Jossey-Bass.

Snead, K. C., and A. A. Ndede-Amadi. 2002. Attributional bias as a source of conflict between users and analysts in an information systems development context. *Systemic Practice and Action Research 15(5):* 353–365.

Snyder, M., and E. E. Jones. 1974. Attitude attribution when behavior is constrained. *Journal of Experimental Social Psychology 10*: 585–600.

Sternberg, R. J., and L. J. Soriano. 1984. Styles of conflict resolution. *Journal of Personality and Social Psychology 47*: 115–126.

Stevens, C. M. 1963. *Strategy and collective bargaining negotiation.* New York: McGraw-Hill.

Stogdill, R. 1974. *Handbook of leadership.* New York: Free Press.

Stokes, R., and J. P. Hewitt. 1976. Aligning actions. *American Sociological Review 41*: 838–849.

Street, R. L. Jr., and J. N. Cappella. 1985. Sequence and pattern in communication behavior: A model and commentary. In *Sequence and pattern in communicative behavior,* edited by R. L. Street and J. N. Cappella. London: Edward Arnold.

Stulberg, J. B. 1987. *Taking charge/managing conflict.* Lexington, MA: Lexington Books.

Stutman, R. K. 1988. Denying persuasive intent: Transparently false disavowals of intention to influence. Paper presented at the Western Speech Communication Association convention, San Diego.

Stutman, R. K., and L. L. Putnam. 1994. The consequences of language: A metaphorical look at the legalization of organizations. In *The legalistic organization,* edited by S. Sitkin and R. Bies. Thousand Oaks, CA: Sage.

Sullivan, H. S. 1953. *The interpersonal theory of psychiatry.* New York: Norton.

Swensen, C. 1973. *Introduction to interpersonal relations.* Glenview, IL: Scott, Foresman.

Tagiuri, R. 1968. The concept of organizational climate. In *Organizational climate: Explorations of a concept,* edited by R. Tagiuri and G. Litwin. Boston: Harvard University Press.

Tajfel, H. 1978. *Differentiation between social groups: Studies in the social psychology of intergroup relations.* London: Academic Press.

Tajfel, H., and J. Turner. 1979. An integrative theory of intergroup conflict. In *The social psychology of intergroup relations,* edited by W. G. Austin and S. Worchel. Monterey, CA: Brooks/Cole.

Tannen, D. 1986. *That's not what I meant.* New York: William Morrow.

Tannen, D. 1990. *You just don't understand: Men and women in conversation.* New York: William Morrow.

Tedeschi, J. T. 1970. Threats and promises. In *The structure of conflict,* edited by P. Swingle. New York: Academic Press.

Tedeschi, J. T. 1983. Social influence theory and aggression. In *Aggression: Theoretical and empirical reviews,* edited by R. G. Geen and E. I. Donnerstein. New York: Academic Press.

Tedeschi, J. T., and M. Riess. 1981. Identities, the phenomenal self, and laboratory research. In *Impression management theory and social psychological research,* edited by J. T. Tedeschi. New York: Academic Press.

Tedeschi, J. T., B. Schlenker, and T. F. Bonoma. 1973. *Conflict, power, and games.* Chicago: Aldine.

Tedeschi, J. T., R. B. Smith III, and R. C. Brown, Jr. 1974. A reinterpretation of research on aggression. *Psychological Bulletin 81*: 540–563.

Thibaut, J., and H. H. Kelley. 1959. *The social psychology of groups.* New York: Wiley.

Thibaut, J., and L. Walker. 1975. *Procedural justice: A psychological analysis.* Hillsdale, NJ: Lawrence Erlbaum.

Thomas, K. W. 1975. Conflict and conflict management. In *Handbook of industrial psychology,* edited by M. Dunnette. Chicago: Rand McNally.

Thomas, K. W., and R. H. Kilmann. 1974. *Thomas-Kilmann conflict MODE instrument.* Tuxedo, NY: Xicom.

Thomas, K. W., and L. R. Pondy. 1977. Toward an "intent" model of conflict management among principle parties. *Human Relations 30*: 1089–1102.

Thompson, L. 1998. *The mind and heart of the negotiator*. Englewood Cliffs, NJ: Prentice Hall.

Tingley, J. 2001. *The power of indirect influence*. New York: Amacon Books.

Ting-Toomey, S. 1983. An analysis of verbal communication patterns in high and low marital adjustment groups. *Human Communication Research 9(4):* 306–319.

Ting-Toomey, S., and A. Kurogi. 1998. Facework competence in intercultural conflict: An updated face-negotiation theory. *International Journal of Intercultural Relations 22(2):* 187–225.

Ting-Toomey, S., G. Gao, P. Trubisky, Z. Yang, H. S. Kim, S. Liu, and T. Nishida. 1991. Culture, face maintenance, and styles of handling interpersonal conflict: A study of five cultures. The *International Journal of Conflict Management 2:* 275–296.

Ting-Toomey, S. 1999. *Communicating across cultures*. New York: Guilford.

Tjosvold, D., and T. L. Huston. 1978. Social face and resistance to compromise in bargaining. *Journal of Social Psychology 104:* 57–68.

Tracy, K. 1991. The many faces of facework. In *The handbook of language and social psychology*, edited by H. Giles and R. Robinson. Chichester: Wiley.

Tucker, J. 1993. Everyday forms of employee resistance. *Sociological Forum 8:* 25–45.

Turner, L., and S. Henzel. 1987. Influence attempts in organizational communication: The effects of biological sex, psychological gender and power position. *Management Communication Quarterly 1:* 32–57.

Tversky, A., and D. Kahneman. 1981. The framing of decisions and the psychology of choice. *Science 211:* 453–458.

Ury, W. L., J. M. Brett, and S. B. Goldberg. 1988. *Getting disputes resolved: Designing systems to cut the costs of conflict*. San Francisco: Jossey-Bass.

Van de Vliert, E. 1985. Escalation intervention in small group conflicts. *Journal of Applied Behavioral Science 21:* 19–36.

Van Maanan, J. 1992. Drinking our troubles away: Managing conflict in a British police agency. In *Hidden conflict in organizations*, edited by D. M. Kolb and J. M. Bartunek. Newbury Park, CA: Sage.

Volkan, V. D. 1994. *The need to have enemies and allies*. Northvale, NJ: Jason Aronson.

Volkema, R. J. 1981. *An empirical investigation of problem formulation and problem-purpose expansion*. Unpublished Ph.D. Thesis, University of Wisconsin, Madison.

Volkema, R. J. 1983. Problem formulation in planning and design. *Management Science 29:* 639–652.

Von Neumann, J., and O. Morgenstern. 1947. *Theory of games and economic behavior*. Princeton, NJ: Princeton University Press.

Vuchinich, S. 1984. Sequencing and social structure in family conflict. *Social Psychology Quarterly 47:* 217–234.

Vuchinich, S. 1986. On attenuation in verbal family conflict. *Social Psychology Quarterly 49:* 281–293.

Vuchinich, S. 1990. The sequential organization of closing in verbal family conflict. In *Conflict talk*, edited by A. D. Grimshaw. Cambridge: Cambridge University Press.

Wall, J. A., and M. Blum. 1991. Community mediation in The People's Republic of China. *Journal of Conflict Resolution 35:* 3–20.

Wall, J. A., and D. E. Rude. 1989. Judicial mediation of settlement negotiations. In *Mediation research: The process and effectiveness of third-party intervention*, edited by K. Kressel, D. G. Pruitt, et al. San Francisco: Jossey-Bass.

Wall, V. D., G. J. Galanes, and S. B. Love. 1987. Small, task-oriented groups, conflict, conflict management, satisfaction, and decision quality. *Small Group Behavior 18:* 31–55.

Wall, V. D., and L. L. Nolan. 1987. Small group conflict: A look at equity, satisfaction, and styles of conflict management. *Small Group Behavior 18:* 188–211.

Walster, E., E. Berscheid, and G. W. Walster. 1973. New directions in equity research. *Journal of Personality and Social Psychology 25:* 151–176.

Walster, E., G. W. Walster, and E. Berscheid. 1978. *Equity theory and research.* Boston: Allyn and Bacon.

Walters, A. E., A. F. Stuhlmacher, and L. L. Meyer. 1998. Gender and negotiator competitiveness: A meta-analysis. *Organizational Behavior and Human Decision Processes 76:* 1–29.

Walton, R. 1969. *Interpersonal peacemaking: Confrontations and third-party consultation.* Reading, MA: Addison-Wesley.

Wanberg, C. R., L. W. Bruce, and M. B. Gavin. 1999. Perceived fairness of layoffs among individuals who have been laid off: A longitudinal study. *Personnel Psychology 52:* 59–84.

Watson, C. 1994. Gender versus power as a predictor of negotiation behavior and outcomes. *Negotiation Journal 10:* 117–127.

Watzlawick, P., J. Beavin, and D. Jackson. 1967. *The pragmatics of human communication.* New York: Norton.

Watzlawick, P., J. H. Weakland, and R. Fisch. 1974. *Change.* New York: Norton.

Wehr, P. 1979. *Conflict regulation.* Boulder, CO: Westview Press.

Weingart, L. R., E. B. Hyder, and M. J. Prietula. 1996. Knowledge matters: The effect of tactical descriptions on negotiation behavior and outcome. *Journal of Personality and Social Psychology 70:* 1205–1217.

Weisinger, J. Y., and P. F. Salipante. 1995. Toward a method of exposing hidden assumptions in multicultural conflict. *The International Journal of Conflict Management 6:* 147–170.

Welton, G. L. 1991. Parties in conflict: Their characteristics and perceptions. In *Community mediation: A handbook for practitioners and researchers,* edited by K. G. Duffy, J. W. Grosch, and P. V. Olczak. New York: Guilford Press.

Wheeless, L. R., and L. S. Reichel. 1988. *A reinforcement model of the relationships of supervisors' general communication styles and conflict management styles to task attraction.* Paper presented at International Communication Association meeting, New Orleans.

White, R., and R. Lippitt. 1968. Leader behavior and member reaction in three "social climates." In *Group dynamics,* 3d ed, edited by D. Cartwright and A. Zander. New York: Harper and Row.

Wilmot, J. H., and W. W. Wilmot. 1978. *Interpersonal conflict.* Dubuque, IA: Wm. C. Brown.

Wilson, S. 1978. *Informal groups.* Englewood Cliffs, NJ: Prentice-Hall.

Wilson, S. 1992. Face and facework in negotiation. In *Communication and negotiation,* edited by L. Putnam and M. E. Roloff. Newbury Park, CA: Sage.

Wish, M., and S. Kaplan. 1977. Toward an implicit theory of interpersonal communication. *Sociometry 40:* 234–246.

Worchel, S., V. A. Anderoli, and R. Folger. 1977. Intergroup cooperation and intergroup attraction: The effect of previous interaction and outcome of combined effort. *Journal of Experimental Social Psychology 13:* 131–140.

Yelsma, P., and C. Brown. 1985. Gender roles: Biological sex and predisposition to conflict management. *Sex Roles 12:* 731–747.

Yudof, M. G. 1981. Law, policy, and the public schools. *Michigan Law Review 79:* 774–790.

Zand, D. E. 1972. Trust and managerial problem-solving. *Administrative Science Quarterly 17:* 229–239.

Zagare, F. C., and D. M. Kilgour. 1998. Deterrence theory and the spiral model revisited. *Journal of Theoretical Politics 10(1):* 59–87.

Zillman, D. 1990. The interplay of cognition and excitation in aggravated conflict among intimates. In *Intimates in conflict: A communication perspective,* edited by D. D. Cahn. Hillsdale, NJ: Lawrence Erlbaum.

Zuckerman, M. 1979. Attribution success and failure revisited, or: The motivational bias is alive and well in attribution theory. *Journal of Personality 47:* 245–287.

Zupnik, Y. K. 2000. Conversational interruptions in Israeli–Palenstinian "dialogue" events. *Discourse Studies 2:* 85–110.

INDEX